No Place to Run

No Place to Run

*The Canadian Corps and Gas Warfare
in the First World War*

TIM COOK

UBC Press · Vancouver · Toronto

I would like to dedicate this book to my family:
Sharon, Terry, Graham, Parkin, and Tracey.

Printed in Canada on acid-free paper
ISBN 0-7748-0739-3 (hardcover)
ISBN 0-7748-0740-7 (paperback)

Canadian Cataloguing in Publication Data

Cook, Tim, 1971-
    No place to run

    Includes bibliographical references and index.
    ISBN 0-7748-0739-3 (bound) ISBN 0-7748-0740-7 (pbk.)

    1. Gases, Asphyxiating and poisonous – War use.   2. World War, 1914-1918 – Chemical warfare.   3. World War, 1914-1918 – Personal narratives, Canadian.   4. Canada, Canadian Army – History – World War, 1914-1918.   I. Title.

UG447.C66   1999   358´.34´09409041   C99-911019-5

This book has been published with the help of a grant from the Humanities and Social Sciences Federation of Canada, using funds provided by the Social Sciences and Humanities Research Council of Canada.

UBC Press gratefully acknowledges the ongoing support to its publishing program from the Canada Council for the Arts and the British Columbia Arts Council. We also wish to acknowledge the financial support of the Government of Canada through the Book Publishing Industry Development Program (BPIDP) for our publishing activities.
Canadä

Printed and bound in Canada by Friesens
Set in Minion by Brenda and Neil West, BN Typographics West
Copy editor: Barbara Tessman
Proofreader: Valerie Adams

UBC Press
University of British Columbia
6344 Memorial Road
Vancouver, BC V6T 1Z2
(604) 822-5959
Fax: 1-800-668-0821
E-mail: info@ubcpress.ubc.ca
www.ubcpress.ubc.ca

Contents

Illustrations

Acknowledgments

Being immersed in poison gas for years now, I would like to acknowledge the individuals along the way who have helped to guide me through the sometimes murky vapours.

Four happy years were spent at Trent University in Peterborough, Ontario, and in between rugby matches, two important classes on the World Wars with Professor Stuart Robson introduced me to studying the "new military history." A gifted teacher and kind soul, Stuart Robson exemplifies the best of Trent University. Professor Jack English, then at Queen's University, also gave helpful advice on gas warfare and strengthened my understanding of the many nuances of Canadian military history. Special thanks must also be extended to Professor Ronald Haycock, whose guidance as my thesis supervisor at the Royal Military College of Canada was just one more burden added to his heavy load as Dean of Graduate Studies. It goes without saying that he deserves special credit and a place in academic royalty when, after he asked for an introductory chapter to gauge my progress, he received two hundred and fifty pages instead. He simply murmured that this was a good start.

Interspersed between the academic school year was summer employment at the National Archives of Canada. Managers such as Jim Burant, Carol White, and Gabrielle Blais ensured that I had interesting and educational work. More specific to this project, I had the pleasure to work with both Dr. Bob McIntosh and Paul Marsden in the Military Archives section of the Government Archives Division. Not only was it an intellectually stimulating and challenging environment, but their good nature, friendly advice, and collective wisdom added immeasurably to this manuscript. Tim Dube, military archivist for the Manuscript Division, must also be thanked for keeping me apprised of any incoming collections relating to gas warfare. Owen Cooke, Bill Rawling, Dennis Julian, and Lieutenant-Colonel Ian McCullough also took time out from their busy schedules to help strengthen various aspects of this work. The sometimes massive borrowing of books leaves me indebted to the understanding library staff at the National Library of Canada, the Royal Military College of Canada, and the National Archives Library.

Upon completion of the initial thesis, there was the always disconcerting process of an oral defence. Not only was this normally nerve-wracking experience made pleasant by the kind words of Dr. Steve Harris, senior historian of the Directorate of History and Heritage, but his ongoing enthusiasm for my work stimulated and energized me to further research and rework the original manuscript. With these significant additions, Steve Harris read through the manuscript again, thoroughly editing and imparting valued academic skills. At UBC Press I wish to thank Emily Andrew and Camilla Jenkins, who helped to guide this work to publication.

The highest praise, however, must be reserved for my father, an editor of the highest quality, Dr. Terry Cook. Throughout my life he has taught me the mysteries of writing while sharing with me his love for history. This guidance has played no small part in my passion for history. An international scholar, he has always made the time to be genuinely interested in my work. And that has made working with gas all the more enjoyable.

Despite the fact that it sometimes felt like all work and no play, I was buoyed by my friends in Ottawa, Kingston, and Peterborough, who were kind enough to remind me that there were other things in life than poison gas. Trips home always bolstered my spirit, especially reuniting with my brother Graham, who has always played a important role in my life with his sly wit and piercing observations. Additional praise and recognition must be given to my parents, Sharon and Terry, whose patience, support, and love over the years have produced a fairly well-rounded kid. No series of acknowledgments, however, can make up for the years of 6:00 a.m. hockey practices.

As anyone who has written a book knows, a unfair burden falls to the significant other. My then girlfriend, later fiancée, and now wife, Tracey, who survived the gas cloud and paper explosion that loomed constant in our one-bedroom Kingston apartment, has been a continual inspiration to me. Not only did she have the unenviable task of reading through the first draft, but she has always supported me in this lengthy endeavour. And although she probably knows more about gas warfare than she ever expected or wanted to, I credit her with my ability to bring this to fruition. As my best friend, to her must go my deep-felt thanks and love.

Despite the encouragement and guidance of many, the mistakes are the author's alone.

An honest attempt has been made to secure permission for all material used, and if there are errors or omissions, these are wholly unintentional and the publisher and author will be grateful to learn of them.

of the war. By 1918, all soldiers on the Western Front lived in an environment where gas was a daily fact of life, and where their survival depended on reliable anti-gas equipment and protective doctrines involving common and accepted actions. It should be noted, however, that the gas war affected all soldiers differently. One who was invalided out of the war by May 1915 would have a vastly different perception of poison gas than an infantryman who had to advance through the gas environment of the Last Hundred Days. Despite the fluctuating nature of gas, it remained a dangerous weapon that hounded soldiers at the front.

Even though poison gases caused over a million casualties, were used in coherent offensive and defensive tactical doctrines, and were powerful psychological weapons, the gas war has been relegated to the periphery of First World War history. In most comprehensive works, only a few concerted pages deal with gas – generally focusing on the gas cloud attacks at 2nd Ypres and the British retaliation at Loos – with sporadic additional references. In no general history has there ever been an attempt to integrate poison gas into the larger perspective of the war. As a result, when reading the history of the Great War, one is left with the perception that gas was barely used after its initial battlefield experiments. Yet by the last half of the war, gas was used in every engagement – from company-sized raids to planned advances involving corps – and was delivered in intricate artillery fireplans to accomplish a variety of tactical purposes. When gas was stigmatized as an immoral weapon during and after the war, the official historians, writing in the anti-war climate of the 1920s and 1930s, conveniently relegated gas to an unimportant role. The nuanced role of gas as a psychologically and physically debilitating agent was ignored in favour of the uncomplicated but commonly held view that chemical agents were contained and beaten by issuing respirators. The numerous causes for this historical neglect will be examined later in the text, but one of the most compelling observations was given by Brigadier General Harold Hartley, who held numerous high-ranking appointments in the British Gas Services during the war. While speaking at the Royal Artillery Institution in 1919, he remarked that "gas has very few friends, people are only too ready to forget it."[2]

Many soldiers and civilians during the war, moreover, believed that gas was an unfair and unsoldierly method of fighting, amounting to the reduction of warfare to suffocation by chemical agents. Of course, vast artillery bombardments and the machine gun had already reduced battles to mass murder, as anyone who survived the first months of the war could attest. But gas was viewed as the more villainous weapon system, because it denied soldiers the chance to stay alive by using their battlecraft skills and pitting themselves against the enemy. With gas there was no bravery, and there were no heroics; men fell to their knees clutching their throats as they slowly asphyxiated. It was a torturous death, and there was no escape.

Introduction

THE GAS WAR UNEARTHED

More than eighty years after the end of the First World War, specially trained French demolition experts still pull over nine hundred tons of shells from old battlefields every year. The French *demineurs* (de-miners) estimate that there are still twelve million unexploded shells in the soil around Verdun alone. As they do this work, the demineurs from time to time will find a mouldy, corroded shell that "swishes." The "swishing" noise is the sound of poison liquid, which, on exposure to air, turns to deadly gas. With shell cases dangerously corroded after decades in the ground, these poison gas shells provoke the most fear among the *demineurs*. Merely handling them can result in terrible burns, blindness, or a slow painful death brought on by having one's lungs burned out. Although only thirty tons of gas shells are unearthed each year, they cause a fear entirely out of proportion to their numbers.[1]

And so it was with the men in the trenches in 1914-8. To the trench soldier, poison gas also provoked extraordinary fear and hardship. This book examines the nature of gas warfare, the creation of the Canadian Corps Gas Services and its mandate to develop an anti-gas doctrine for the Canadian Corps, the tactical considerations of gas in attack and defensive fireplans, an analysis of the role of gas in selected Canadian battles, and its psychological impact on the soldiers.

The gas war, which effectively began in April 1915 at the 2nd Battle of Ypres, continued to evolve in scope, intensity, and deadliness right up to the last days

No Place to Run

Or at least so it seemed. For as we shall see, the reality of the gas war could be, and sometimes was, different from this starkest of all images: the helpless soldier retching away his life. Yet although counter-measures were eventually developed – some more effective than others – the stigma attached to the gas war survived long into the postwar years, and even into the Second World War, when gas was manufactured and carried on campaign by all the major belligerents, but – for many reasons – was never used.

Given that chemical warfare was not used at the tactical level in the Second World War, this work focuses on the Great War. The initial shock of poison gas had soldiers, civilians, and politicians immediately labelling it as a barbarous method of waging war. During the history of warfare there have been relatively few occasions when one side has been able to introduce a weapon to which the other had no reply.[3] This was the case, however, at 2nd Ypres, where the Germans unleashed chlorine gas for the first time and routed two French Territorial Divisions. While the French ran, the Canadian Division, whose position albeit was not in the direct path of the gas cloud, did not break. This heroic stand has been mythologized through time and history: how the 1st Canadian Division grimly held off the German advance until British reinforcements could be rushed to fill the gaping hole in their line. Accordingly, it was the initial use of gas that became ingrained in Canadian history, overshadowing all other aspects of the gas war.[4] In fact, one would be hard pressed to find poison gas mentioned again in most standard Canadian texts. Despite holding the line against overwhelming odds and a sickening new weapon, the full story of the Canadian Corps and the gas war was one of constant adaption and training.

The 2nd battle of Ypres.

The employment of gas was not a question of changing an existing tactical doctrine and adapting it to the realities of the war; rather, it involved, for most soldiers, working with a weapon altogether different from anything previously conceived. After the surprising success of chlorine gas at 2nd Ypres, all belligerents believed they had found a method to break the "riddle of the trenches." But, as quickly as it was viewed as a potential war-winning weapon, gas was almost completely rejected due to its unstable nature and the evolution of more effective gas masks. With the introduction of deadlier gases and superior delivery systems in 1916, however, gas was reborn, this time as an effective harassing weapon, and eventually integrated into coherent offensive and defensive tactical doctrines. As a result, Canadian soldiers were confronted by phosgene and later mustard gas, delivered in artillery shells and projector drums; the question remained as to how new methods and doctrines were going to be implemented to protect Canadians from the increasingly lethal nature of the gas war. Filling that void was the Canadian Corps Gas Services.

The de facto creation of the Canadian Corps Gas Services in May 1916 mirrored the development of the Canadian Corps in many ways. Although the Canadian Corps developed into one of the finest fighting formations on the Western Front – and by 1918 was known, along with the Australian Corps, as the "shock troops" of the British Expeditionary Force (BEF) – its professionalization did not occur overnight. Indeed, one British officer, on seeing the 1st Canadian Division arrive in England in 1914, had frankly remarked that the Canadians would make excellent soldiers if all their officers were shot. The eventual success of the Canadian Corps, especially as a result of its attack doctrine of combining infantry and artillery, was developed and refined throughout the war. The Gas Services followed a similar evolution.[5]

Surviving the gas war was very similar to surviving the regular hardships of the trenches; it required learning through mistakes (one's own, but preferably those of others) and the constant re-examination of training. Yet even with the development of anti-gas appliances, especially gas respirators, the battle against gas was not over, as some historians have implied through its exclusion in their writing. To be sure, the possession of a gas mask was a step toward protection, but learning how and when to use it, how to identify various poisonous gases and their harmless substitutes, and how as a consequence to adjust one's mask quickly or to take it off, were equally important. It took some time to develop the right technology to protect against poison gas; it took even longer to set a proper doctrine, and longer still to implement it and have it accepted by the soldiers. All this, however, was taught by the Gas Services. Without the Gas Services, then, attempting to protect the soldiers of the corps against gas through "trial and error" would have resulted in a vast increase in the number of Canadian gas casualties. Moreover, the creation of a central agency meant that individual units did not have to find solutions on their own; instead, once one unit of the Canadian Corps or even the whole BEF encountered a new gas or new delivery system, the Gas Services quickly and (eventually) efficiently implemented a system of training and warning.

From the outset, the Canadian Corps Gas Services knew that it could not stop all gas casualties, and thus its aim was to control and reduce the attrition of the Canadian Corps from gas. In addition, the Gas Services emphasized the defensive aspect of the gas war, largely because of the enemy's initial superiority in offensive battle gases, but also because, until April 1917, the British Army in France reserved the right to control its chemical attack operations.

German trench soldier Rudolf Binding believed that the true nature of the First World War would never fully come across in histories because "Those who could write it will remain silent. Those who write it have not experienced it."[6] Considering this, one of the most interesting aspects of the historiography of the gas war is its almost total silence on the psychological impact on the trench soldier. As a weapon, gas went through many transformations throughout the war, but as illustrated through the writings of the soldiers in the trenches, it was an ever-present factor in their lives. The British poet Wilfred Owen wrote one of the most powerful evocations of the war, while convalescing in hospital in 1917. Titled "Dulce et Decorum Est," it conveys the inhumane horror of the new gas warfare, and how alien it was in contrast to everything previously associated with the allegedly chivalrous conduct of war.

> Bent double, like old beggars under sacks,
> Knock-kneed, coughing like hags, we cursed through sludge,
> Til on the haunting flares we turned our backs
> And towards our distant rest began to trudge.
> Men marched asleep. Many had lost their boots
> But limped on, blood-shod. All went lame; all blind;
> Drunk with fatigue; deaf even to the hoots
> Of gas shells dropping softly behind.
>
> Gas! GAS! Quick, boys! – An ecstasy of fumbling.
> Fitting the clumsy helmets just in time,
> But someone still was yelling out and stumbling
> And flound'ring like a man in fire or lime ...
> Dim, through the misty panes and thick green light,
> As under a green sea, I saw him drowning.
>
> In all my dreams, before my helpless sight,
> He plunges at me, guttering, choking, drowning.

> If in some smothering dreams, you too could pace
> Behind the wagon that we flung him in,
> And watch the white eyes writhing in his face,
> His hanging face, like a devil's sick of sin;
> If you could hear, at every jolt, the blood
> Come gargling from the froth-corrupted lungs,
> Obscene as cancer, bitter as the cud
> Of vile, incurable sores on innocent tongues, –
> My friend, you would not tell with such high zest
> The old Lie: Dulce et decorum est
> Pro patria mori.[7]

Terror, revulsion, and grotesque pain are interspersed throughout the poem as they were throughout the gas war. The true face of poison gas was shown starkly by Owen. In addition, however, throughout the hundreds of diaries, letters, and memoirs of Canadian soldiers held in archival repositories, if one takes the time to look, poison gas is depicted, if not as skilfully as Owen, then as passionately. Through these testimonials, and a reinterpretation of archival documents, this "hidden" gas war can be reclaimed.

This work has two decidedly different aspects to its research: the role and development of the Canadian Gas Services and the integration of poison gas into the attack doctrine and, against that context, the evolution of the Canadian Corps as the storm troopers of the BEF within the growing gas environment. Among the areas of examination are: the development of gas as a battlefield weapon; the creation of the Canadian Corps Gas Services and its evolution in developing both an offensive and defensive gas doctrine; the unique aspect of soldiers living and surviving in an ever-increasing gas environment; the effects of gas on the battlefield; innovations in both medical and weapons technology; the importance of artillery and the development and then refinement of a gas shell tactical doctrine; and finally, the hidden factor of fear as told by the soldiers.

The focus of this work is gas; other chemical agent activities, such as flame-throwers and the employment of smoke, have been ignored. The perception of the gas war on the home front in Canada is also beyond the scope of this work. Research remains to be done on the role of gas in wartime propaganda, on the diplomatic and political protests over its use, and on the concerns and fears of society and of family members, who generally could only imagine what their husbands, brothers, and sons were being subjected to by this new terrible weapon.

John Keegan, in his masterful work *The Face of Battle* (1976), wrote that much of military history in the past has been "a highly oversimplified depiction of human behaviour on the battlefield."[8] Following the methodology espoused by

Keegan, and combining it with the one of the most recent and best additions in Canadian military historiography, Desmond Morton's *When Your Number's Up* (1993), this work attempts not only to understand the gas war and its many nuances, but also to delve into the minds of the men who were there: the men who stood their ground as half-mile-wide clouds rolled over their positions or lethal shells spewed their deadly cargo into the trenches.

All information on the Gas Services has had to be gathered and reconstructed, based on archival research in the voluminous records of the Departments of Militia and Defence and of National Defence, in the custody of the Government Archives Division at the National Archives of Canada (NAC). Numerous private papers have been examined in the Manuscript Division at the NAC and in published memoirs in order to depict the individual Canadian soldier's perspective on the gas war. In addition, the transcribed notes of the 1964 Canadian Broadcasting Company radio show, "In Flanders Fields," in the Government Archives Division of the NAC, helped to flesh out the gas war as experienced by Canadians. In keeping with the old military truism, "on the actual day of battle naked truths may be picked up for the asking; by the following morning they have already begun to get into their uniforms," oral history can be a tricky form of documentation.[9] That is understood, especially with memoirs written or interviews occurring years after the original experience. Yet such sources are still useful and, indeed, are essential to reflect the feelings and emotions of what occurred at the time, rather than the hard facts of names, dates, or specific places that can blur in the memory in a way that searing emotions do not.

Although it is only through the personal reflections of soldiers who were there that the true psychological role of gas can be fully comprehended, archival sources abound on the complicated role of gas on the battlefield. What is more, the development of the Canadian gas doctrines can be viewed as a microcosm of how attack and defensive doctrines evolve in times of war, when lives are at stake. There are also comparisons to be made. The American Expeditionary Force, for example, fared very poorly with gas (and almost crippled their fighting efficiency in the process), while the Canadian Expeditionary Force was able to survive and fight through the chemical battlefield. Nevertheless, throughout the war poison gas was an agent that caused over a million casualties, inflicted immeasurable psychological stress, and forced commanders to be aware of the tactical and strategic limitations imposed on their men by gas, which by 1918 was used in every offensive and defensive operation on the Western Front.

The lethal effects of gas were initially (and reasonably effectively) contained with the introduction of efficient gas masks in early 1916. But following the introduction of gas shells and disabling agents like Blue Cross and mustard, the gas war entered a new era in which its major effect was to reduce fighting efficiency, cause a steady stream of physical and psychological injuries, and kill the careless. As a result, the psychological aspect of gas was never truly quelled. There remained, in every trench soldier, intense fear as the gas alarms clanged. Will my respirator work? Is there a rip in it? What happens if my mask is knocked from my head? Can I still perform my duties? Such fears played in every soldier's mind, and it is this aspect of the gas war, previously unexamined, that will rise to the surface in this work.

Despite the importance of understanding the human nature of war, military historians have tended to analyze the operational performance of armies, corps, and divisions in attempts to understand broad themes and patterns. This work examines what has been neglected – the training and discipline that was needed before great battles could be won. The common image of the First World War soldier, lurching zombie-like from one disaster to the next, simply waiting for a bullet or shell to put him out of his misery, is inaccurate. For as Bill Rawling has illuminated, the *frontsoldaten* on all sides attempted to find methods of survival within their environment, and it is in that light that we must see the development of an anti-gas doctrine and its acceptance by the common soldier. Though unschooled in chemistry, he quickly realized that constant learning, re-examination, and drill would allow him to adapt to and, eventually, overcome most aspects of the gas war.

This work is essentially chronological, but there are instances where chronology must defer to the examination of such themes as gas tactics and technology, the development of new battlefield gases, training in England, and the evolution of the medical services. Of course, the analysis of the Canadian Corps and the battles in which it took part is critical in judging the use and role of gas on the battlefield, but the intervals between the great battles must also be examined in order to appreciate the full difficulty of surviving on the chemical battlefield.

Just as gas shells continue to be pushed to the top of European soil by winter frost, so too will the role of the Canadian Corps and its gas war come to the surface in this work. The part of the Canadian Corps and its place in the gas war has been buried and forgotten in Canadian historiography. Now it too is unearthed.

CHAPTER ONE

Trial by Gas

2ND BATTLE OF YPRES

THE COMEDIAN CONTINGENT

The ultimate success of the Canadian Corps as one of the finest fighting formations on the Western Front was the product of a difficult and bloody evolution. When Great Britain declared war on 4 August 1914, resulting in war for Canada as one of its dominions, there was no Canadian Corps ready to fight; in fact, there was almost no army at all.[1] If Great Britain were to be defended, the task would fall to the volunteers.

The myth of the militia has been a strong one in Canadian history, dating back to the supposed defence of Canada by a few British regulars and resilient Canadian militia on several occasions in the early and mid-nineteenth century. Strengthened by the growth of their volunteer movement, and reinforced by the Canadians who served in the Boer War, by 1914 the image of citizen-soldiers ready and willing to put down the plough and pick up the gun to defend king and country was powerful indeed. It was only augmented by the minister of militia, Sam Hughes, who described regular force officers as "bar-room loafers" and argued that most ordinary Canadians could do just as good a job, if not better.[2]

Legendary for his fierce convictions and pugilistic manner, Sam Hughes on 6 August 1914 chose to disregard the pre-planned mobilization orders of 1911 and took it upon himself to send out 226 letters to colonels throughout the country ordering them to recruit volunteers for overseas battalions.[3] As a result of this patriotic call, young men, keen for adventure and travel, scrambled to join the colours and head off to France to "teach the Hun a lesson or two." Few expected the war to last past Christmas, but the volunteers expected to see action long before then.

After arriving in England, the eager Canadians found they were not to be sent to France, but rather would first be trained in the art of war. This decision would save them from the intense slaughter of the early days of the Western Front – described by one historian as "an automated corpse factory" – where there were over 1.6 million casualties before Christmas 1914. Camped, instead, on England's Salisbury Plain, where it rained for 89 of the 124 days they trained there, the Canadians marched, shot, and dug trenches in ankle-deep mud, unable to find anything dry, and stewing because war was raging on without them. In time, reflecting its reputed poor officers and lack of discipline, other troops, and some Canadians, were calling the fledgling Canadian Expeditionary Force (CEF) the "Comedian Contingent."[4]

On 14 February 1915 the Canadians finally got their long-awaited wish as they boarded ships and set sail for France. Upon arriving after a stormy channel crossing, the 1st Canadian Division, under command of the British general Edmund Alderson, who had previously commanded Canadian units in the Boer War, was attached to III Corps in General Sir Horace Smith-Dorrien's Second Army. The men were anxious to get into the fighting, but if the carnage on the Western Front in 1914 had illustrated anything, it was that inexperienced troops thrown into battle would suffer needless casualties if they had not first been taught basic survival tips by trench veterans. Accordingly, they were sent in with experienced British troops, who were to show them the skills required to survive at the front.[5]

The Canadians were given a relatively gentle introduction to the Western Front, but for men who had been farmers, bankers, and clerks less than a year before it was a harrowing experience. The intense terror caused by snipers, Jack Johnsons, and whizz bangs (high explosives and shrapnel shells), along with the necessity of learning how to make grenades and other trench warfare tools, left Private R.L. Christopherson of the 5th Battalion remembering that he was "never so scared in [his] life."[6] It was soon evident that any time spent in the trenches would result in "wastage," as the High Command clinically described it. But wastage to trench soldiers meant having their friends and companions killed and wounded by stray shells and sniper bullets as they held the trenches with no chance to retaliate.

Although this first experience in the trenches was a shock to many Canadians who thought war would be more glamorous, it nevertheless gave them confidence that they too could play a role in the struggle. On 3 March, the Canadian Division relieved the 7th British Division and took over a section of the front.

As the Canadians moved into the front line, their British commander, General Alderson, told them: "My old regiment, the Royal West Kent, has been here since the beginning of the war and it has never lost a trench. The Army says, 'the West Kents never budge.' I now belong to you and you belong to me: and before long the Army will say, 'The Canadians never budge,' Lads, it can be left there, and there I leave it."[7] These were encouraging if as yet unearned words for the 1st Division, who would soon be entering a recently quiet area of the front: the Ypres salient in southwest Belgium.

The town of Ypres – familiarly known as Wipers – had been reduced to little more than rubble, its famous medieval Cloth Tower battered yet still overlooking the ruins. The whole salient protruded into the German lines like a rounded tumour, eight miles wide and six miles deep. It was costly acreage to hold, but the sanctity of the ground as a result of the harsh fighting already carried out over it required that it not to be relinquished lightly. The Canadians had been rotated in and out of the line several times since they had first come to France, and it was into this salient that they entered on 14 April, relieving the French 11th Division and taking over a sector of 4,500 yards. The 2nd and 3rd Brigades were in the line (left to right) on the northeast edge, flanked on the left by the 45th Algerian Division and on the right by the 28th British Division. Behind them was Gravenstafel Ridge, but the whole area was surrounded on three sides by the Germans, who had their five-to-one advantage in artillery accurately

Near the Ypres salient, 1916.

registered from superior observation points on Passchendaele Ridge, a few miles to the east. As John Creelman, former lawyer and financier turned Canadian artillery officer, noted in his diary, "Shells came from everywhere except straight behind us."[8]

Upon entering the line, the Canadians were shocked at the state of the trenches they took over from the French. Apprenticed to the British, and having spent so much of their time digging "perfect" trenches at Salisbury, the Canadians were angered to find that the trenches they moved into "weren't really trenches at all." As Private F.C. Bagshaw of the 5th Battalion remembered disgustedly, they were simply muddy "holes in the ground," with parapets easily penetrated by bullets and surrounded by unburied and rotting bodies.[9] In this graveyard, the Canadian infantrymen desperately attempted to put their trenches into good order, all the while evading enemy snipers and trying to forget about the tormenting lice and the stench that assaulted their nostrils.

The Conduct of War

Like love, war has sometimes been described as an act with no rules, where all is fair, but the reality of history has generally been different. A common culture, common weapons, common tactics, and even the intermarriage of ruling families gave fighting in Western Europe a shared code throughout the centuries, with rules of conduct understood and respected by both sides. As a result, war was viewed as a dangerous but clearly structured event.

Some weapons – the bow and crossbow in earlier times – were considered unfair if, for example, they could kill from a distance. These projectile weapons, which advanced warfare from a trained art to simply murder from afar, shocked the accepted codes of the warrior. Indeed, the use of the crossbow against fellow Christians was outlawed by the Roman Catholic Church's Lateran Council of 1139; luckily for God, it was still allowed against heathens. Clearly the crossbow was proscribed not because it was immoral, but because it was considered too dangerous to the warrior elites of the period, who had no effective way to combat its killing power. Later, gunpowder and hand-held guns were similarly viewed as unfair by nobles who, wielding swords and lances, fought encased in bullet-pierceable armour. These modern weapons were great equalizers. They reduced warfare to pulling a string or trigger, and a man's strength or prowess on the battlefield, previously marks of a great fighter, was reduced. Firearms and their users were regarded as cowardly or debased by the same elite class that was in most danger from their evolution. Subsequently, gun-toting soldiers were subjected to contempt from their own side and much worse if caught by the enemy.[10]

Laws of war, therefore, were constraints against certain weapons and certain actions by the ruling elite. The most dangerous weapons were not always the ones that were banned: the initial hand guns were much inferior in killing power to the long bow. Eventually though, most outlawed weapons, from the crossbow to the long bow, from firearms to the submarine, were accepted when their valuable contributions to warfare were acknowledged. Rules of war are necessary on the whole, but once one side gains a decisive advantage, those rules are generally bent or discarded in favour of victory.

The traditional view of warfare as heroic and gallant saw brave warriors going off to vanquish the enemy. This idea, which had been a virtual constant in the history of warfare, was strengthened with each generation of myth-making and subsequent literature and art that depicted cavalry charges and heroic last stands. British, French, German, and even Canadian youth had been brought up with tales of glorious warriors and their deeds – accounts that invariably contained images of good and evil, fair play, and gentlemanly conduct. The Great War was thus first perceived to be a quick adventure, over by Christmas, where young men would come of age and inherit their destinies.[11]

In the summer of 1914, the High Commands (with the possible exception of Lord Horatio Kitchener, British Secretary of State for War) not only expected a quick victory by Christmas but also a war of rapid movement. But with the "riddle of the trenches"[12] confounding the generals and serving up horrendous casualties on both sides, there was a desperate need to break the deadlock – a need to break the self-imposed subterranean sieges of the trenches.

When it was introduced into the First World War, chemical warfare was not a new invention, but its scope, killing power, and tactical uses were all radically different from anything conceived in the past. Throughout history, chemical warfare had often been used to help end sieges and to injure an enemy out of reach of conventional weapons. The Spartans burned wood soaked in pitch and sulphur to hinder the Athenians, "stink pots" were often catapulted into medieval fortresses in attempts to smoke out the enemy, and the mysterious "Greek fire" was used to defend Constantinople with devastating effect.[13] Yet chemical warfare was used only infrequently in modern conflicts due to the failure to develop an efficient delivery system.

Diversifying technologies and the Industrial Revolution in the nineteenth century promised to forever change how warfare would be waged. Lacking both industry and trained manpower, Russia called a series of conferences in order to curtail the use of new weapons – weapons it could not hope to create or develop in the same quantities. The resultant Hague Conventions, in 1899 and 1907, attempted to codify some of the laws of war and abolish weapons that caused "unnecessary suffering." These laws gave some predictability to war by controlling and limiting the war-fighting capabilities of armies and nations. Although the major powers were not about to ban weapons that would reduce their status and their ability to protect and police their country and colonies, the Hague Conventions were attempts at cooperation. During the proceedings, nations that were unable to come to a consensus on banning weapons like the explosive shell or the submarine, agreed that projectile gas shells should be forbidden in war.

The United States remained the only major world power that abstained from signing the accord. Navy Captain Alfred T. Mahan, head of the U.S. delegation, voted against the proposed ban on asphyxiating gas shells and told the delegates that his country opposed stifling "the inventive genius of its citizens in providing the weapons of war."[14] Equally important, he asked what the difference was between a defenceless ship and crew being torpedoed in the dead of night and a soldier suffocating to death by a chemical agent. Another participant recorded that poisonous gases were thought to kill in a more agonizing way than conventional weapons and that "war is destruction, and the more destructive it can be made with the least suffering the sooner will be ended that barbarous method of protecting national rights."[15]

The outlawing of gas remained an awkward issue but was made more palatable because no nation had yet to embark on a chemical weapons production program. Although the letter of the law was initially followed, the spirit was not. Prior to the Great War, the French Army had experimented with tear-gas grenades, and in one celebrated case police had used them to catch a gang of famous bank robbers. If this form of gas had been useful in clearing out an entrenched gang of thieves, it was of little use in war involving millions over hundreds of miles.[16]

Although participants at the conferences in the Hague had discussed powders, explosives, and field guns as weapons that could be limited or banned, it was only poison gas, a weapon of military insignificance, that was ultimately labelled as an immoral and diabolical agent. Sceptics could point out that gunpowder and firearms were also derived from chemicals, but the idea of death from the air, where there was no chance of retaliation or survival, went against the accepted norms of warfare. Poison gas was also associated with poison, which for centuries had been the weapon of the treacherous and weak; it was a dodgy agent to be used against the unsuspecting and innocent.[17] These characteristics were transferred to phantom future chemical agents.

Very early in the war, the development of machine guns, new powders and shells, and improved rifles and artillery guns had altered forever the reality of warfare. It became suicidal to attack over open ground. Yet for a time generals were trapped in their prewar paradigms, which strongly advocated the "cult of the offensive" in overcoming the fixed defences of the enemy.[18] The technology of war had progressed faster than the outdated European battlefield tactics of the nineteenth century. Those generals who did not heed these military evolutions blundered through the initial stages of the First World War, leaving hundreds of thousands of young men rotting in the fields of Europe.

The slaughter of close-order attacking troops in the first months of the war forced soldiers to dig into the ground to escape the destructive firepower. The result was a battlefield that assumed an eerie, empty feeling: tens of thousands of men were within a mile of each other, but not one person was ever seen above ground.[19] To leave the trenches invited almost instant death. As soldiers settled into their imposed defensive lines, they strengthened their positions with sand bags, barbed wire, and interlocking angles of fire. The outcome of any advance against fixed defences was a foregone conclusion; the only unknown was how many men would be able to crawl back into the trenches after their lines were mowed down.

Once the dreadful uniqueness of the Great War stalemate became clear, the Germans had to find a way to end the two-front (western and eastern) crisis in which they found themselves. All the years at staff college, practising encirclements and moving battalions and divisions, meant little on the static fronts. In 1915 alone, the German casualties were over 2,500,000, driving Erich von Falkenhayn, Chief of the General Staff, to remark to the German chancellor Theobald von Bethmann-Hollweg: "This is no longer the kind of war with which we are familiar. In a very real sense it has become a struggle for survival for all the belligerents."[20] Within this context, the first use of chlorine gas by the Germans was an experiment to break the stalemate of the trenches in the titanic conflict.

THE ROAD TO YPRES

The Germans were the first to use chemical shells in the Great War. This occurred against the British, not at the 2nd Battle of Ypres, but on 27 October 1914 in the Neuve-Chapelle area. The German decision to undertake experimentation with gas shells was due to dwindling powder and shell reserves and to complaints from the front that defenders could not be dislodged from their positions with high explosives (HE) or shrapnel shells. The first 3,000 Ni tear-gas shells ("Ni" stood for *Niespulver,* or sneezing powder) fired had no effect, nor were they even noticed by the British – a quality one does not want in one's weapon. Showing his derision toward this new type of warfare, General Erich von Falkenhayn's son was said to have won a case of champagne by remaining in a cloud of the substance for five minutes without displaying any signs of discomfort. The next use of chemical weapons came on 31 January 1915, when the Germans fired their T-shell, a mixture of liquid lachrymator combined with two-thirds HE, from 150 mm howitzers.[21] But once again the shells had little effect: the intense cold prevented the vaporization of the gas.

The failure of the T-shell provoked Dr. Fritz Jacob Haber, the future Nobel prize-winning scientist who efficiently ran the German gas program, to change the focus of gas warfare from tearing to lethal agents with the implementation of chlorine.[22] An ideal weapon, chlorine was a deadly lung irritant, easily compressed into a liquid inside shells for efficient transport, and then readily vaporized into gas when released. Just as important, it was available in large quantities because Germany had the most powerful chemical industry in the world.

All war gases employed in the Great War were closely related to chlorine or its derivatives and were initially products of the dyestuff industry that grew up in Germany during the nineteenth century. Chlorine combined with water, and later slaked lime, was used in the bleaching process. Liquid chlorine in cylinders became a part of the chemical industry in the late 1880s, although it was largely ignored in the United States and Britain until a few years before the war. By 1913, German chemical companies dominated the world market, producing approximately 140,000 tons of dyes out of a world total of around 160,000 tons. Germany's thriving chemical industry had the ability to produce a surplus of chlorine, while Great Britain lagged far behind in any type of chlorine production that could be converted into battlefield use. The German chemical industry provided both the materials and the chemists for wartime gas usage.[23]

Operation "Disinfection"

The Ypres sector had already been the scene of some of the bloodiest fighting in the war and would continue to have that dubious distinction until the Armistice. As early as December 1914, General Falkenhayn (who had replaced Moltke the younger after the failure of the Schlieffen Plan) had announced his desire to cut off the Ypres salient. An attack would serve two purposes for the Germans: testing the new chlorine gas as a weapon and, more important, shielding the transfer of troops from the Western to the Eastern Front for an attack against the Russians in Galicia.[24]

Initially, Falkenhayn had a difficult time finding a commander willing to use gas. Crown Prince Rupprecht of Bavaria, commander of the Sixth Army, and Colonel-General Karl von Einem, commander of the Third Army, believed that the use of gas was immoral, an unchivalrous and cruel method of driving the enemy from their lines. Others argued that gas should not be used because, except for a spell in spring, the prevailing winds blew toward the German lines over a greater part of the front and thus would give the Allies an inherent advantage in gas warfare. Moreover, the use of gas would introduce a completely new type of warfare. Yet both Falkenhayn and Haber, in his new position as "chemico-technical advisor," believed that their troops would be protected from swift retaliation because Germany's chemical industry was so far ahead of those of the Allies. Also, Falkenhayn hoped that this new weapon, although legally questionable under the Hague Convention, would shorten the war and therefore save lives. Of his front-line commanders, only the Duke of Württemberg, commanding the Fourth Army, and facing Ypres, agreed to the use of gas in his sector. The operation would be cryptically code-named "Disinfection."[25]

Sir Algernon West, one of W.E. Gladstone's secretaries, once remarked that "a secret is no secret when it is known to more than three persons." Gas was not a secret. Those in command at Ypres just did not know what to do about it. Although both the French and British had been amply warned by intelligence reports and prisoners that the Germans were planning to employ gas at Ypres, they chose to ignore the fact. Why was nothing done?[26]

No one on the Allied side had any idea of what the appearance or effect of gas would be. The initial failure of the generals to heed the early warnings of an imminent gas attack can partially be explained by the fact that they had no point of reference. The Allied commanders had no concept of what a gas cloud was or how it would be used against their men on the battlefield. Nor, for that matter, did they know what type of gas would be employed. Major Victor Odlum, second-in-command of the 7th Canadian Battalion, was discussing the situation with his commanding officer, Lieutenant-Colonel William Hart-McHarg (who would be dead within days), and later recounted that neither had "the faintest idea" of what gas was. "We couldn't visualize an attack with gas, we could not guess where the gas would come from or how we could recognize it when it did come, and we did not know what were the necessary precautions."[27]

Brigadier Arthur Currie, commander of the 2nd Brigade, recorded in his diary on 15 April that an attack was "expected at night to be preceded by the sending [over] of poisonous gases to our lines." Currie, uncertain of how the gas was to be delivered, ordered the artillery to fire on the German lines in hopes of ascertaining some information. Major Andrew McNaughton, whose career, like Currie's, was to rise meteorically during the war, was given ninety rounds of ammunition to fire on the German line. He described the experience as "one of the best days I had in the war." Unbeknownst to Currie or McNaughton, they had actually stumbled upon one of the ways to locate gas cylinders. Unfortunately, the shots did not crack any of the buried canisters, and thus the German "secret" was not revealed. At the same time, senior British commanders in the area – following the lead of the French, whose command had declared, "All this gas business need not be taken seriously" – ordered their soldiers to be more worried about the German conventional military build-up than some real or imagined gas cloud. If gas were to be used, at least one British General Headquarters report indicated "that the Germans were notoriously preparing something of this kind, but it was believed to be intended for use in trenches captured by us and not for offensive purposes." Perhaps for this reason, the infantry were not told anything. They remained defenceless, not even privy to the fact that some new weapon would be used against them.[28]

By 10 March, 6,000 gas cylinders had been placed along the front of the German XV Corps, on the southeastern side of the Ypres salient, and manned by 1,600 gas soldiers from Pionier Regiments 35 and 36, units made up of regular combat engineers and men with backgrounds in chemistry and commanded by Colonel Otto Peterson. For five weeks the Germans waited for a favourable wind, which not only caused an agonizing delay in the attack but also left the German infantry suspicious of this new weapon. More detrimental still were the stray shells that occasionally burst the steel canisters (code named "F" Batteries) and caused a growing number of gas casualties among German troops. Eventually, on 5 April, many of the gas canisters were moved north, across from the French Territorial Divisions, where the wind was more accommodating. The German offensive was to be a limited operation, carried out by two corps on a four-mile front, with their objective the Pilckem Ridge, in the northern sector of the salient.[29]

It was a beautiful day on 22 April, and many Canadians were relaxing and sunning themselves as they lay in the trenches or in reserve. The systematic shelling of Ypres and the reserve lines behind them stopped in the early part of the day. Major J. Jeffery of the 13th Battalion remembered that an "ominous quiet" settled over the region, but on the whole most Canadians were simply glad to have the shelling reduced, for their "tour" in the front lines was almost up. Shortly after four o'clock in the afternoon, as the day was coming to a close, the Germans opened up with a furious artillery bombardment on the Allied lines, Ypres, and roads in the rear. In reserve at Vlamertinghe (a few miles to the west of Ypres), George Bell of the 1st Battalion was watching a soccer game when he heard the "thunder of the artillery increasing in intensity." He recalled stopping for a few minutes to watch shells bursting in the distance: "'Our 2nd Brigade must be giving Fritzie an extra dose of iron rations,' I said. 'Those aren't our shells,' says the man next to me. 'They're coming our way.'" And along with the shells came an ominous green-grey cloud four miles wide and half a mile deep.[30]

The German gas units, derisively described by their own infantry as "Stink-pioniere," had released 160 tons of chlorine gas from 5,730 canisters. The sight was perplexing to the Canadians, General Alderson describing it as "two clouds of yellowish-green smoke ... which appeared to merge into each other." Indeed, few recognized what was happening, an official British report concluding that "nobody appears to have realised the great danger that was threatening, it being considered that the enemy's attempt would certainly fail and that whatever gas reached our line could be easily fanned away [like smoke]. No-one felt in the slightest degree uneasy, and the terrible effects of the gas came to us as a great surprise." The densest parts of the gas cloud passed through the 45th Algerian (Colonial) Division and the 87th French Territorial Division, both to the left of the Canadian sector.[31]

As the green-yellow tendrils moved toward the French, perplexed Canadians in the front line viewing the cloud thought that a new type of gun powder had been employed. "At first a faint, sour pungency, that dried our mouths and set us coughing," was how Canadian George Gibson, who was resting with a medical officer in the rear, remembered his puzzled reaction to the first vapours of gas. One by one the French guns fell silent only to be replaced by screaming and choking Algerians running into and past the Canadian lines, struggling for breath and grunting "asphyxiate, asphyxiate." As the cloud passed over and obscured position after position, insidiously seeping into the very crevices where the soldiers were protecting themselves from conventional fire, the French defenders were smothered; the Canadians had only minutes to react before the outer edge of the cloud reached them.[32]

The victims of the gas attack writhed on the ground. Their bodies turned a strange grass-green as they struggled to suck oxygen into their corrupted lungs. The chlorine attacked the bronchial tubes, which caused the membranes to swell into a spongy mass and ever-increasing amounts of fluid to enter from the bloodstream. The swiftly congested lungs failed to take in oxygen, and the victims suffocated as they drowned in their own fluids. Major Andrew McNaughton remembered the Algerians streaming past him, "their eyeballs showing white, and coughing their lungs out – they literally were coughing their lungs out; glue was coming out of their mouths. It was a very disturbing, very

"The German Poison Belt," supplement to the *Illustrated London News*. The illustration caption reads, "The on-rolling cloud of gas: the suffocating fumes forcing the Zouaves and Turcos to retire from the trenches. Near Langemarck, from which the enemy had failed to dislodge them by recognised methods of war."

disturbing sight." McNaughton saw the immediate effects of the gas; British sergeant E.W. Cotton, while at a dressing station, witnessed the victims in the later stages of suffering: "their colour was black, green and blue, tongues hanging out and eyes staring – one or two were dead and the others beyond human aid, some were coughing up green froth from their lungs."[33]

The fate of the French was viewed with horror by their allies in the line. James Davidson Pratt, serving with the 4th Battalion of Gordon Highlanders, observed the French lines from Hill 60: "A lot of the fellows ... had sort of started to scoot away from the gas; in fact doing the very thing they shouldn't have because the gas was drifting with them and the result was that you found them dead and lying all over the place."[34] With a mile-long gap in the Allied line from the routed French colonial divisions, 50,000 British and Canadian troops in the southern salient risked being flanked and cut off.

Although the German gas specialists were issued crude gas masks of cotton pads dipped in a solution of sodium thiosulphate and potassium bicarbonate, no protection was offered to the German infantry. As the infantry tentatively advanced, sometimes with their officers pushing them onward with sword or pistol, over the ravaged land and through the greenish-coloured French dying and dead, they were understandably afraid of catching up with their own cloud. But within ten minutes the Germans were on top of Pilckem Ridge, a position they had unsuccessfully attacked for months before the release of gas. The surprise was complete, with very few casualties to attackers, an abnormality in a war that churned up men more quickly than they could be sent over the top. Immediately digging into the hill, the German infantry waited for the expectant counter-attack. But there was no one left. "Its surprise was very great," recalled General Falkenhayn. "Unfortunately we were not in a position to exploit it to the full."[35]

The effects of the rout left the inexperienced Canadian Division as the closest formation and the only hope for the Allies. One Canadian colonel expressed the fear felt by imperial and dominion staff officers that the Germans might get through: "Nothing lay between them and Calais but the Canadian Division, and whether the Canadians could hang on long enough in face of this new terror of poison gas until new troops arrived, no one could even venture to guess. We felt that they would do all that men could do under the circumstances, but without means of combatting the poison it was doubtful what any troops could do. Supposing the Germans just kept on discharging gas?"[36] While the feelings of panic in the headquarters of the rear are understandable, the commonly noted assumption that, because of the routed two divisions, the Germans could have driven on to the channel ports is incorrect. Not only were their strategic objectives limited, but, given the two previous failed gas experiments, Falkenhayn did not predict the tactical success of the gas. Many historians have claimed that this oversight wasted a valuable strategic experiment; although true, that observation is made with a healthy dose of hindsight.

Escaping the worst of the cloud, the Canadian lines were still deluged with tear and chlorine gas vapours. Those on the left could see the French streaming from their trenches, and in the Report of Operation it was indicated that by "8:45 pm there appeared to [be] no formed body [of French troops] east of the canal." The Canadian response was to counter-attack a force that was many times larger than itself in order to buy time for the British to bring up reinforcements.[37]

The Germans continued to blast the Canadian trenches with their artillery, and the Canadians were forced to shift their defences to keep from being enveloped by the German troops occupying the French position on their left. With disaster imminent, the 1st Canadian Brigade in reserve was quickly rushed up to the front. Victor Lewis and his company struggled to move from reserve toward the front amidst the panic-stricken French colonials and retreating residents of Ypres. They passed a British company just as a shell fell near the road. "As soon as they [the British] heard the rattle [of the shell], which we thought was vehicles going over cobblestones, they all hit the ditch. We didn't, pure ignorance, but those Englishmen sure had a great respect for us. 'Blimey, look at them damn fools, they took no notice of that shell.'"[38] Adrenalin, mixed with childhood memories of patriotism and last stands, led many Canadians to view the situation naïvely. The following song, scribbled on a piece of paper, was found on the body of Private Wilfred Bouch, who was killed in his first firefight:

> Submarines beneath the sea and Zeppelins in the air
> Tons of Huns with great big guns, his soldiers everywhere
> Said Bill, "I'll first take Calais then for Dover, Oh Mein Gott!"
> Britain let her bulldog loose and fucked the Goddamn lot.
>
> It's a long way to Calais, it's a long way to go
> It's so damn far to get to Dover, that you'll never stand the blow.
> Goodbye German Empire
> Farewell Kaiser Bill
> If you don't know the way to Hell, God help you
> You Goddamn soon will.[39]

Belligerent as they were, the colonials had almost no battlecraft experience. In the words of one veteran thinking back on that day, they were being sent like "lambs to the slaughter."[40]

At a withering cost the Canadians desperately counter-attacked the Germans' newly won positions and succeeded in forcing them to dig in cautiously from the fury of the onslaught. Although the German orders had been to hold the French lines, some of the infantry had begun to push forward when it appeared that little stood in their path. Isolated pockets of French and Canadian troops put an end to that. Colonel W.S.M. Mactier of the 13th Battalion noted that the counter-attacks were little more than a bluff. "There appeared [to the Germans in the chaos of a night battle] to be far more men than there actually were. That's what held them, because every conceivable man who could walk was thrown into the line somewhere."[41] The Germans, not able to gauge the number of Canadians who seemed to be holding on everywhere, failed to exploit the situation before British reinforcements were moved to stem the advance.

The cost of staving off disaster was high, as Private Bert Goose of the 3rd Canadian Field Ambulance reflected in his diary:

> 1,800 was put through inside 24 hours, many of my chums have been through. The wounded came at such a great pace, it was a great job to attend them all.
>
> … Some awful wounds were attended to, gashes large enough to put your fist in, many came with bullet wounds, many poor boys will have to have their arms or legs taken off. Other poor fellows will never live to tell the tale.[42]

Within the first day, the Canadians had launched savage counter-attacks while trying to form a new flank to protect themselves and the British from the German advance. Major J.W. Warden of the 7th Battalion noted that the Germans heavily shelled the makeshift trenches the reinforcing Canadians had huddled in, and throughout the day the German fire escalated to a frenzy.[43] Yet still the Canadians were dug in and refused to retreat. Although they had been lucky enough to miss the full force of the enemy's gas, they had been victims of the first gas cloud attack; yet they had not broken and run but rather had counter-attacked and prevailed. Their initial luck was, however, about to run out.

Grim Defenders

At 4 a.m. on 24 April 1915, the Germans launched a whirlwind bombardment on the Canadian lines. Ten minutes later the German gas pioneers attached hoses to the gas canisters and released the second poisonous gas attack of the war against the apex of the 8th and 15th Battalions, which still held the original Canadian line. Major Harold Mathews of the 8th Battalion vividly remembered the fifteen-foot-high wall of greenish haze slowly but inexorably moving toward the Canadian trench: "It is impossible for me to give a real idea of the terror and horror spread among us by this filthy loathsome pestilence. It was not, I think, the fear of death or anything supernatural, but the great dread that we could not stand the fearful suffocation sufficiently to be each in our proper places and able to resist to the uttermost the attack which we felt must follow, and so hang on at all costs to the trench that we had been ordered to hold." As Lieutenant R.L. Christopherson ominously noted, when the gas came there was "no place to run."[44]

Some of the Canadians in the trenches noticed the green tarnish to their brass buttons from two days earlier and realized that only chlorine would have that effect. Thus, with the gas rolling directly toward the Canadian line, with "invisible death creeping up on you," as one man described it, officers ordered their men to urinate on a cloth or bandage and cover their mouths with it. As Samuel Johnson once said, there is nothing like a death sentence for concentrating the mind. Those officers and men who had taken chemistry at high school or university realized that the ammonia in the urine would crystallize and partially neutralize the chlorine. As George Bell excitedly remembered, "'Piss on your handkerchiefs and tie them over your faces,' yells our lieutenant. There are some who do not make this precaution. They roll about gasping for breath." Some were just plain lucky in escaping the effects of the gas: Private Boyd, a stretcher bearer for the 8th Battalion, was drinking his rum tot when the cloud was released: "Next thing I knew I fell face downward" into the soil of the trench. When he came to, he realized he had been saved by soil filtering out most of the gas. Even so, his "chest felt stuffy and dry." Major Lester Stevens, commanding a company in the direct path of the cloud, tied a cloth round his mouth, but "two [former] lumberjacks on each side of him, dropped" and later died in hospital. Those who stuffed urine-soaked cloths in their mouths generally survived without permanent lung damage, but those who were too embarrassed or too scared or were unable to urinate for other reasons, or who gave in to the temptation to rip the foul rags from their mouths, were rendered unconscious, maimed, or killed.[45]

As the Canadians in the front line suffered from weeping eyes and wracking coughs, a tiny chemist, Lieutenant Colonel George Nasmith, was busy identifying the chlorine gas used by the Germans. Having been rejected for service in the 1st Division due to his stature (he stood only four feet, six inches), Nasmith subsequently convinced Sam Hughes to allow him to organize a mobile laboratory to test drinking water for troops in the field. In this capacity he was the first to formally diagnose the use of chlorine on 22 April.[46] Understandably nervous, he was brought before General Sir Henry Rawlinson on the afternoon of the 23rd to explain what the gas was and how it was used. The famed British scientist Dr. J.S. Haldane, who arrived at Ypres on 26 April to investigate the effects of the gas on dead and dying soldiers, seconded the diminutive colonial's early diagnosis. While correctly identifying the gas, Nasmith also suggested a compound of hypo-sulphite to combat the chlorine, but the Canadians in the field had already come up with a partial solution born of necessity.

Behind the gas cloud, the German assault waves moved cautiously. With their overwhelming numbers and their unexpected success earlier against the French, the Germans had less fear of the defenders than of their own gas. But to their shock, those Canadians who could still stand began rapid-firing into the massed ranks of the attackers, despite the failure in many cases of their inadequate Ross rifles. The German infantry was thus stopped by half-blinded men, vomiting blood-tinged fluid through constricting throats, desperately firing jamming rifles. The bravery and tenacity of Canadians at 2nd Ypres determined that gas was not to be the war-winning weapon envisioned from its earlier success against the French.[47]

The 8th and 15th Canadian Battalions, which received the full force of the gas with no artillery support of their own, due to the poor positioning of supporting field guns, slowly fell back under the onslaught to Gravenstafel Ridge. In an account of the battle, Lieutenant A.W. Woods wrote that "The chaos of the front was immeasurable, with conflicting orders, German troops behind Canadian lines, intense artillery barrages and the gas attack which knocked out many of the commanding officers." The gas greatly added to the fog of war. The two front-line Canadian brigadiers, Arthur Currie and Richard Turner, suffering from running noses and eyes and crushing headaches from the gas, were without accurate information while their battalions were cut off from each other by the German forces moving through and behind their lines. Although sometimes surrounded, the Canadians did not have the good sense to know that they were in a hopeless situation. Many refused to surrender and continued fighting even as they retreated. Even the German Official History noted the "tenacious determination" of the dominion troops. At the sharp end of the fighting, German officer Rudolf Binding, hating gas but accepting its practical value, was in one of the forward attacking battalions and described the stubborn defence of the Canadians: "a sleeping army lies in front of one of our brigades, they rest in good order, man by man, and will never wake again – Canadian divisions. The enemy's losses are enormous."[48]

The fighting withdrawal of Canadian units, who "were literally blown out of position after position," was a heart-wrenching, weary operation for men who had been shelled and fired on for two days, gassed, plagued with jammed rifles, and deprived of food and water. Major Lester Stevens of the 8th Battalion, when moving his gassed men to a farm, jumped into a trench and stumbled over one of his men sleeping waist-deep in frigid water. "I thought he was dead, but he had merely passed out due to the exhaustion, lack of food and the effects of the gas." Others like H. Ronald Stewart, a gas casualty who barely made it to the rear, later wrote: "I shall never forget it. Hell was let loose and remained loose! Such a noise and such sights I did not think were possible ... The Germans in using gas have put on the last straw. They will never be forgiven." The Canadian infantry's suffering was almost as legendary as their heroic stand.[49]

J.H. Bowyer's company of the 5th Battalion was rushed in to help the 8th and 15th Battalions, and he was horrified at the effects of gas on his fellow Canadians: "Men came staggering up that were gassed. At first we ran into an orchard and I went and helped these fellows to make them comfortable by the side of a barn. I gathered up any old coats that were laying around and covered them up.

That night I got cold ... and went back to see if I could find a coat or something and saw these fellows and they were all dead, great bunch of bubbles at their mouths and nostrils, drowned."[50]

Others were forced to choose between holding their ground against impossible odds or leaving the wounded to be overrun by the Germans. Private W.F. Dodds of the 13th Battalion risked capture or death by carrying two of his poisoned companions back to a safe area near the wreck of a house. He remained haunted for the rest of his life by the half cries, half chokes of those gassed men he left behind, who "begged and prayed that they wouldn't be left to the Germans." There were no cures for gassed victims; severely gassed soldiers who were not carried by companions to the rear risked execution – a not uncommon occurrence by both German and Canadian troops.[51]

As the exhausted troops retreated from the front line, running from crater to crater, many of the gassed simply could not keep up and collapsed into ditches, dying by the side of the road or becoming prisoners. Canadian Lieutenant Scott, who was gassed on the 24th, later remarked that he made it to the rear only because of two friends who "coaxed, dragged and pushed me over the most uncomfortable four miles I had ever gone. I wanted to lie down every twenty yards to get my breath back." Sid Cox of the 10th Battalion remembered running across a friend lying in the sun and already turning black and green. Assuming him dead, he left him there. Only after the war did he find out that his buddy had been gassed, was still alive, and had spent the rest of the war in a prison camp.[52]

Barely staving off annihilation, the average Canadian Tommy had no idea of what to do with his gassed companions. Gas wounds were not like conventional ones; these men were slowly suffocating to death. The insidious nature of gas was that it killed the uninformed and the weak. As the gas, heavier than air, slowly rolled over the Canadian lines, it seeped into and filled every crater and shell hole, killing those who were seeking safety in them. In taking cover from the conventional dangers of battle like bullets and high explosives, soldiers were forced into their infected trenches and slit holes. "The chlorine was heavy," Colonel T.S. Morrissey observed, "and it lay in the trench and the boys were smothered to death." Those Canadians wounded by shell or bullet would have been bound up and placed at the bottom of the trenches or dugouts, awaiting stretcher services to clearing stations in the rear. It was they, the wounded and defenceless, whom gas was most likely to kill. John N. Beaton of the 7th Battalion wrote a letter to his father following the battle: "It was the poisonous gases that killed a lot of our poor fellows. They did not have a chance to fight." Those who were standing and firing, with their rags over their mouths, were generally able to keep above the suffocating vapours of gas once the cloud had moved past them, but the chlorine clung in some dugouts for two hours, dispatching all those who could not get out. The malevolence of poison gas was being learned the hard way.[53]

AIR HUNGER

The chaos inflicted by the gas also affected the doctors and medical officers. As the gassed soldiers moved to the rear in hope of finding help for their affliction, there were lines of soldiers walking back with their arms in the air, gasping desperately for breath in the way long distance runners do after a race. The strain of walking left men stranded along the road, turning blue as they gradually suffocated. "You couldn't get a lungful," remembered one scared Canadian. "You couldn't use any energy because you felt as though your windpipe had been partly shut off."[54]

Private W.F. Dodds of the 13th Battalion stumbled into a converted casualty-clearing station and lay down alongside a man on a stretcher: "The schoolyard was packed, stretcher to stretcher all the way across with men in all cases of asphyxiation." Dunlap Pearce Penhallow, a doctor with the Royal Army Medical Corps, frankly admitted that "it is difficult to convey the mental impression produced when the first batch [of gassed men] was unloaded." "I saw some hundred poor fellows laid out in the open, in the forecourt of a church, to give them all the air they could get, slowly drowning with water in their lungs – a most horrible sight, and the doctors quite powerless," was how British General John Charteris recounted in his diary the scene of one makeshift hospital. The much lower-ranking Canadian private, Harold Baldwin, arriving as a reinforcement, was equally shocked when he stumbled across gassed men: "Row after row of brawny Canadian Highlander lay raving and gaspy with the effects of the horrible gas, and those nearing the end were almost as black as coal. It was too awful – and my nerves went snap!" Having to care for hundreds of men slowly strangling to death was a daunting task for any doctor, especially ones that had to deal with soldiers suffering from horrible conventional wounds as well.[55]

James S. Walker of No. 2 Canadian Stationary Hospital remarked on the Canadian gas casualties: "The deadly gas which had been pressed into use so effectively by the enemy had told the ghastly tale. Staggering, dumbfounded and stupefied they were brought in, after having been conveyed from the ambulance train ... The effect of these gas fumes which wrought such deadly havoc is a noticeably watery running of the eyes. Later the features become discoloured by a sort of green and yellowish hue. Many took the precautions to stuff handkerchiefs in their mouths. However, once too much gas has been inhaled its action has the same effect upon the lungs as a slow process of drowning."[56]

The process of death was ugly, with men flopping around, making gagging, choking sounds, pulling at their clothes, uncontrollably vomiting "greenish slime," propping themselves up to gasp for help and then falling back exhausted from their struggles. In the most advanced cases, where the soldiers' breath could be heard rattling out of their ravaged lungs, they were simply given a wet cloth to place over their mouths in hope of soothing their agony. Some of these patients clung to life for days before they finally died.[57]

Canadian doctors and surgeons of No. 3 Canadian Field Ambulance, who had just spent forty-eight hours binding wounds and amputating limbs, had little idea of how to treat gassed patients. One man pleaded with a doctor: "I don't know what's wrong with me, I can't breathe. I'm jittery as if I were a piece of haywire ... It's just as if someone was tying that tighter. I thought the fresh air would get me over it but I'm getting worse." The doctors did their best to develop a cure, but as Major Lester Stevens remembered, the doctor "looked at my throat and he stuck needles, long steel things, up my nose." Only a trench soldier, in describing such proddings, would add laconically: "I didn't like the idea of it at all." Neither did the doctors, who had few notions about how to cure their suffering men, and could only prescribe rest with fresh air.[58]

A sergeant of the 15th Battalion was one of hundreds of gassed Canadians carried off the battlefield into the medical clearing stations. A Royal Army Medical Corps officer attempted to treat the suffering man, but the Canadian died two days later in a puddle of his own discharged fluid. One of the medical officers who tried to save him labelled his death as being from "air hunger." A post-mortem report indicated: "The Body showed definite discolouration of the face and neck and hands. On opening the chest the two lungs bulged forwards. On removing the lungs there exuded a considerable amount of frothy light yellow fluid, evidently highly albuminous, as light beating was sufficient to solidify it like white of egg. The veins on the surface of the brain were found greatly congested, all the small vessels standing out prominently."[59] The army doctors and surgeons had little idea how to help their suffering men, but the search for a better cure started on that day.

A Reputation Forged

After the bloodbath on 24 April, both sides dug in for the night to recuperate. The Canadians had been pushed back on all fronts, but only a thousand yards at most. The men of the devastated Canadian Division grimly clung to their positions, even though they had endured the terrible confusion induced by two gas clouds, piecemeal counter-attacks, the destruction of their lines of communication, and fighting against overwhelming forces while having their lines incessantly shelled.[60] When British reinforcements eventually stabilized the line, the Canadian battalions were sent into reserves.

Having moved into the rear on the afternoon of 24 April, Sir John French, the commander of the British Expeditionary Force, sent a message to General Alderson expressing "to you and Canadian troops my admiration of the gallant stand and fight they have made. They have performed a most brilliant and valuable service." Equally important to the Canadians was the recognition by the same British troops with whom they had just apprenticed. In some rear areas British troops gave hearty cheers for the ragged Canadians returning from the front, and the Sherwood Foresters' band played "Hold Your Hand Naughty Boy," as the decimated 7th Battalion marched by, leaving Major J.R. Mellree to declare "that he'd never forget that [gesture]" as long as he lived.[61]

Not all infantrymen received marching music, as was the case of one unnamed Canadian gassed on the 24th and placed along with eighteen other poisoned Canadians in a burned-out building near Ypres. Unable to lie down, he spent the whole night gasping for breath and pulling "thick, tenacious, blood-stained secretions from his nose and mouth." Left behind as the Canadians moved past them, the other eighteen men had suffocated to death by morning, and he was forced to drag himself from the shelter toward the rear. On his way he stumbled upon some concentrated beef, which he ate and promptly vomited up, along with spurts of greenish liquid. Feeling better, he continued struggling to the rear, where he was eventually found and carried to a clearing station. Still unable to lie down for fear of suffocating, he was tied in a sitting position to a bed for six nights before he was able to take moderate breaths again.[62] After the gas clouds had passed through, the difference between life and death was narrow: it depended on the length of exposure, concentration of chlorine, and type of protection, no matter how crude; but for some nameless Canadians it came down to a stranglehold on life that they were unwilling to release.

The Canadians stumbled out of the line dirty and exhausted, dehydrated from going without food or water for two days, and, in varying proportions, suffering from the effects of gas. As Colonel W.S.M MacTier remarked, "Everyone in that vicinity got gassed to some degree." Another Canadian wrote that "It would be useless to try to describe the battle in detail. It was simply four days of murder, that's all it was." Others tried to make sense of the chaotic fighting, and in a letter by Canadian engineer William Johnson to his worried wife, he briefly described his experience on the battlefield, which could double for any man who survived the ordeal: "I have had an awful time this last ten days ... I got ... about six hours sleep in a week. I was in the hottest part of it ... and never expected to get out alive. I've missed death by inches." He finished with a statement hoping to reassure his wife: "Don't worry about me, whatever happens keep a stiff upper lip and if I should go under remember its [sic] not hard to die in the heat of battle and when up against it no man regrets his life but I don't expect to fall. I've had a hunch that I'm coming through alright ... The Devil looks after his own and the good only die young so perhaps I'm not in much danger."[63]

The devil may have been watching out for Johnson, but 6,036 good and young Canadian lads were captured, maimed, or found their graves in their brief but vicious battle.[64] In less than three days the 1st Canadian Division had lost over half of its fighting infantry strength.

Just as the Canadians were moving out of the line, three fresh Allied divisions were rushed to the Ypres sector and sent into battle. On 26 April, a French attack was characteristically late, and the Indian Lahore Division, relying on their allies-in-arms but unaware that they were actually attacking alone, was massacred as it attempted to retake Mauser Ridge. The Indians lost almost 2,000 casualties in the assault, with the Germans releasing canistered chlorine gas to send their already tattered units into retreat.[65]

Reflecting the need to counter the overwhelming German weight of fire, the Canadian artillery remained in the line and continued to support British divisions in the salient, and on 2 May it furiously bombarded the German lines. On that day, with proper wind conditions, the Germans released gas against the 4th British Division between St. Julien and Berlin Woods. Canadian gunner Harry Crerar described how the British and Canadian guns dealt with the Germans: "We had a tight half hour of it. The infantry couldn't stick it and had to pull back several hundreds of yards but in the meantime, our artillery had opened up such a rate of fire along their parapet that the Germans were held behind it and as soon as the gas dissipated, our chaps took up the ground again."[66] The shock of poison gas remained strong, but it could be countered by bullet and shell.

Although they had not been overwhelmed, the Canadians who survived these initial gas attacks dreaded the alien nature of such a weapon and believed it to be a diabolical addition to warfare. In a letter home to his mother, Private W.H. Curtis railed against gas and called the Germans "cowards." Some were more emphatic in their beliefs, like Colonel George Nasmith after returning from the front and reaching No. 3 Field Ambulance at Vlamertinge: "Lying on the floors were scores of soldiers with faces blue or ghastly green in colour choking, vomiting and gasping for air, in their struggles with death, while a faint odour of chlorine hung about the place ... These were some of our own Canadians who had been gassed, and I felt, as I stood and watched them, that the nation who had planned in cold blood, the use of such a foul method of warfare, should not be allowed to exist as a nation but should be taken and choked until it, too, cried for mercy." Others were forced to constantly relive that battle as their lungs burned for years afterward. Those who survived realized that a new form of warfare, one more indiscriminate and merciless, had been introduced and the fighting would never be the same. When death was borne on the very air that men breathed, the notion of fighting as valorous and chivalrous was further superseded by a scientific and mechanical method of warfare.[67]

Gas casualties were numbered at over a million for the entire war, but the death rates were very low. With only about 3 percent of victims dying, gas has been labelled a poor weapon. Of course at 2nd Ypres, where the soldiers had no gas masks, the death rate for gassed men was much higher: fatality ratios for gas clouds attacks in 1915 and 1916 suggest that it could have been anywhere between a quarter and a third.

As well, it is unequivocal that during the first gassing there were numerous Canadians who, like Private William Walkinshaw, were immobilized by the gas: "I could hardly breathe, I had no pain. I just couldn't take any interest in anything. I knew there was people around me but I couldn't speak to them, I couldn't do anything, I was more or less paralyzed."[68] How many of these men were left behind and captured by the Germans? Or, more important, how many of the wounded were also gassed and died on the battlefield when they would normally have survived their non-gas wounds? In the chaos of a fighting retreat, there would not have been much attention given to an already dead man. What of the cases like Private J. Carolan of the 1st Battalion, who was shot in the head and woke up three hours later to find that he had been "badly gassed"? Although he managed to crawl to shelter, and the wound caused by the bullet through his brain miraculously healed, by 1917 he had still not recovered from his gassing. How many more men never regained consciousness from their combined conventional and gas wounds? It is not the role of the historian to guess, but by following the methodology of John Keegan, who has tried to understand what happened in battle at the soldier's level, one is better able to understand the real effects of gas. This, coupled with knowledge that the Germans deliberately downplayed the number of gas casualties after the world condemned them for their new barbarous weapon, meant that initial gas casualties shall remain forever skewed.[69]

Although it is impossible to determine how many Canadians were affected and succumbed to the chlorine gas at 2nd Ypres, this is an attempt to draw together and analyze existing information, whether from military records or anecdotal accounts. The recorded figures range anywhere from the 122 admitted to hospital for gas treatment to 1,556 men evacuated for sickness, of whom a very high proportion would have been gassed men. A more detailed postwar study by the Army Historical Section went through every 1st Division War Diary and noted every man listed as gassed. The figures list 3 dead, 248 non-fatal, and an additional 55 gassed men captured as prisoners of war. From anecdotal accounts alone, however, it is clear that the number of dead is incorrect. It must also be kept in mind that the figures account for only those men who were counted and acknowledged as gassed. The British Official Medical History gives some indication of the ambiguous nature of gas casualties at 2nd Ypres:

> A large number of men were killed outright by gas in the field, but deaths due to this cause are included in the casualty lists under the general heading "killed in action," for the severity of the fighting and the fact that the Germans gained ground allowed little opportunity for distinguishing those who died from the direct effects of gas from those killed by shell fire or rifle bullets. Again and again officers and men who went up in support as the infantry fighting developed described how they passed men lying in groups in the trenches and on the roads who had apparently died of asphyxia.[70]

It was even worse in the 1st Canadian Division, which took the full brunt of the gas, and one Canadian senior officer later wrote in his diary that "at that time [at 2nd Ypres], those who were shocked, gassed or concussed were not called 'wounded' as they are now." Although it is a little unclear from his rushed diary entry, Lt. Colonel Creelman was implying that in most cases the battlefield wounded remained unclassified. Thus soldiers who became casualties from shell, bullet, gas, or shell shock at 2nd Ypres might haphazardly be lumped together under the generic heading of "wounded." Moreover, as already indicated, the gas would have accounted for many more dead among those unconscious wounded who were left in the muddy wasteland of the Ypres battlefield.[71]

There is no way to quantify accurately the number of men affected by the gas cloud, or how many finally succumbed, because there was no way to count during the chaos of battle. Some historians have remarked that the gas casualties at 2nd Ypres included 5,000 dead and another 10,000 wounded, but that is a serious exaggeration. On the other hand, the figures must surely be higher than the number given by German doctors, who for propaganda reasons claimed they came across fewer than a dozen gassed men. An analysis of subsequent gas attacks in April and May – for which more exact figures were kept – is instructive in giving some context to the gas casualties. On 1 May at Hill 60, there were 2,413 gas casualties among British soldiers, of which 227 were fatal. Even then, those who compiled the figures acknowledged that many British soldiers who had been gassed and captured went unrecorded. Despite issuing primitive cotton gas masks to the troops, the British suffered another 557 gas casualties, 22 of which were fatal, in the 6 May gas cloud attack. Finally, after a gas cloud attack on 24 May of unusual density and length, the British lost another 3,284 men to gas, with many more of the gassed men taken prisoner or left on the battlefield. Such high figures among the British troops, even after they were issued gas masks, give some indication of the deadly nature of the first gas clouds. Those Canadian battalions who faced the full force of the chlorine suffered harshly, and it is not unreasonable to assume that hundreds perished and many more were permanently maimed due to the immediate and long-term effects of the gas.[72]

Gas struck terror in soldiers as they were not able to defend themselves against such a repugnant weapon. The helplessness of being stuck in a trench, of not being able to evade the wall of poison that steadily crept forward until it enveloped all in its path, left an indelible print on many veterans of the German gas attack. At least the horror of shell fire and machine-gun bullets could be partly defended against, and the use of deep trenches and shell holes helped psychologically as well as physically. Not so for those caught amidst a gas cloud seeping ever closer into their hiding places, threatening their lives with an agonizing death if they stayed hidden and exposing them to sniper and machine-gun fire if they stood up. This was the stuff of mythical fears.

Word of the poison gas spread rapidly through the BEF, and for the Canadians who stood their ground against this chemical pestilence came a newly won respect. Major William Murray, a British officer of the 27th Brigade, Royal Field Artillery, noted in his diary: "22 April … Hear that Germans used gas and wiped out the French – 50 guns lost but Canadians saved the day." It was not only the British who took notice of the battered colonials. While moving up the line, Colonel George Nasmith noticed French civilians heading to the rear: "When the people of the little villages through which we passed saw the name 'Canadian' on our car they nudged each other and repeated the word 'Canadian.' It was the name in everybody's mouth those days, for it was now general knowledge that the Canadian division had thrown itself into the gap and stemmed the German rush to Calais."[73]

Even with the gaping holes in their ranks, many Canadians took pride in standing the test of their trial by fire. To commemorate the Canadians' stand, Corporal Jocko Vinson of the 7th Battalion composed the following poem:

> England as the mother, and Canada as the son,
> And proud of the deeds they have fought and won.
> Yes, it was Ypres, where the battle raged high,
> And we left on the field many heroes to die.
>
> It was not by their shells, but by gas we all know,
> That choked and blinded us wherever we go,
> But they hung to the trench til they dropped down with pain,
> And the shells burst around them, yes time and again.
>
> But move not them, they were game to the core,
> They stood in defiance, and ready for more;
> We are proud, we can say, we fought side by side
> With our brave Highland laddies, to try stem the tide …
>
> A hard struggle at hand, and every man they could find,
> When the cry of a general soon passed through the lines,
> "For God's sake hang on, men, it's the key to the West!"
> And the boys from dear Canada they surely did their best.[74]

The poem filled all the criteria for a heroic epic. It spoke of the Canadians holding out against high odds and a new, diabolical weapon. It evoked images of imperialism and bespoke of sacrifice. What it did not do, though, was to illustrate the new and soon fast-growing feelings of independence that Canadians fighting at the front earned with their battlefield exploits.

Harry Crerar, in a letter home to his fiancée, rightly described the stand of the 1st Division: "The Canadians have made a name – a real name and have done one of the big things of the war."[75] The Canadians had not only begun to forge a reputation, but they showed they were not simply dull colonials. The image of the tough dominion troops may have been partly true, but Canadian success was also due to the speed with which the officers and privates learned to combat the chlorine. The front-line units directly in the path of the gas cloud and the many Canadians rushed in as reinforcements, who would have suffered through the gas in varying degrees, survived by listening to those among them who had knowledge of chemistry and knew how to partially negate the gas. These resourceful initiatives foreshadowed the role of the future Canadian Gas Services. Canadians had been caught unprepared by gas once – they intended to be ready the next time it was used against them.

CHAPTER TWO

Rabbits
in a Warren

APRIL 1915–DECEMBER 1915

REACTION TO THE GAS WAR

Weapons of war are not simply governed by rational thought regarding their function and practical battlefield utility. Rather, their value is a combination of their physical effectiveness and, though this is often neglected, their psychological and cultural impacts.[1] Thus, it is impossible to fully comprehend the nature of gas as a weapon without first understanding how it was perceived by the soldiers it was used against.

After the first gassing there was an immediate outcry, not only by the British, but also by many Germans, who protested that gas was an unethical weapon. Such protests occurred on the home front as well as among soldiers and generals who had experienced war at the sharp end. War Secretary Lord Kitchener, who was outraged by the gas attack, described it as "contrary to the rules and usages of war." One British infantryman remarked on the new role that gas brought to the battlefield: "Clean killing is at least comprehensive but this murder by slow agony absolutely knocks me. The whole civilized world ought to rise up and exterminate those swine across the hill." It certainly did not occur to these outraged citizens and soldiers to wonder if indiscriminate shelling, which ripped huddled soldiers to pieces, was fair or within the "rules of the game." An aspect of this anger on the part of the Allies arose from the feeling

that the Germans had pulled one over on them. The surprise value of gas –
which, unlike artillery shells or bullets, had never seriously been contemplated
for use in war – left many wondering to what new low level the Germans would
stoop. Perhaps many more secretly feared that the Germans were better suited
for this new game of modern warfare. Much of their outrage was a result of
efficient propaganda, but there was also a genuine feeling of revulsion toward
the perception of being killed by something against which you could not defend
yourself.[2]

The British were not sure how to retaliate against the German gas attack.
They were not willing simply to break international law or to move against public opinion, whether in Britain or abroad.[3] The British citizens on the home
front still believed in "playing the game fairly," but they demanded retribution.
The British dilemma was described by Lieutenant-General Charles Ferguson,
commander of II Corps:

> It is a cowardly form of warfare which does not commend itself to me or to other
> English soldiers, but it is clearly impossible to get the enemy to desist from this
> and other contraventions of previously recognised rules of warfare by holding up
> our hands with abhorrence at such unseemly conduct on his part.
>
> We cannot win the war unless we kill or incapacitate more of our enemies than
> they of us, and if this can only be done by copying the enemy in his choice of
> weapons, we must not refuse to do so.[4]

While acknowledging that they may be forced to adopt the enemy's own methods, British leaders were not above using the German poison gas as propaganda.

The evident truth about the use of gas was exploited to confirm more dubious or plainly fabricated atrocity stories.[5] The mass rape of Belgian women,
the skewering of babies on bayonets, and the crucifixion of Allied soldiers were
lumped in with the execution of British nurse Edith Cavell, unrestricted submarine attacks, and now gas warfare. The unleashing of poison gas, which
allegedly broke the laws and codes of war, provided a continuous flow of material to vilify the Germans. One of the better examples was a cartoon by the
Australian war artist Will Dyson, which was published during the war in the
popular magazine *The Great War*. It portrayed a German professor straddling
a doorway talking to the devil. The placard notes that it is the "Academy of War
Kultur – Torment Section – Poison Gases." The caption reads: *"The professor:*
'I am sorry we have no further openings for instructors.' *The Devil:* 'Ah, you
misjudge me – I come as a pupil.'" Another example, this one a letter written by
a British officer and published in the *New York Times* on 22 June 1915, was typical of the attempt to focus on the horrendous nature of the German war
machine: "I am sure the public has yet the slightest idea of this damnable effort
on the part of the Germans to disregard all laws of humanity and civilization."

Referring to a visit to gas casualties in a hospital, he writes, "They are all sitting bolt upright or swaying backward and forward, gasping for breath; their faces, hands, and necks a shiny gray-black color, their eyes glazed, and unable absolutely to speak or eat. It takes two days for these men to die."[6] Primarily, the propaganda focused on the inhuman nature of the slow choking death by chemical agents. Poison gas became another effective tool in demonizing the enemy and was used to illustrate just one more immoral act by the Hun, whose *Kultur* knew no bounds.

This propaganda splurge was eventually nullified by the Allies' own use of poison gas; but the decision to retaliate with chemical agents was overshadowed by the more serious problem of actually producing gas. The weak state of the British chemical industry initially left the military with only one company, Castner-Kellner Alkali, which could expand its output of liquid chlorine to produce enough gas for military operations.[7] Although the Allies wished to respond to the Germans with some form of chemical retaliation, both the British and French munitions industries were busily engaged in producing conventional artillery shells for the troops. When the British shell shortage was leaked to the public in early 1915, there was a general outcry over the failure to support the boys at the front. Much of the munitions effort, as a result, went into producing conventional HE shells rather than experimenting with dubious gas armaments.[8] To divert factories, scientists, and workers to the manufacture of gas was, at the time, counter-productive to the war effort. The same was not true of the production of a gas mask.

Understanding the brutal nature of this unseen death, some British commanders feared for the morale of their troops and wondered how they would hold up against sustained German gas attacks. The initial panic of the Algerians was a worry to everything the British High Command viewed about the superiority of British morale in eventually bringing victory.[9] If the British Tommy had not broken like the black colonials – something most in command attributed to superior racial or patriotic characteristics – the stress of this new weapon was still atrophying the fighting efficiency of the infantry. The need to protect the man in the trench and his ever-important morale was one of the vital factors in devising some sort of defensive gas mask to counter the psychological dread as well as the physical debilitation caused by gas. While many historians have failed to understand the subtleties of the fighting man in the trenches, historian George Cruttwell, who had been in the trenches at Ypres in April 1915, displayed his understanding of the nature of poison gas in his influential history of the Great War:

> In fact there is little to choose in horror and pain between the injuries inflicted by modern war. The extent to which a human body can be mangled by the splinters of a bomb or shell, without being deprived of consciousness, must be seen to be believed. The real explanation of the fury felt by the soldiers, which invested the

war with a more savage character, is to be sought elsewhere. In the face of gas, without protection, individuality was annihilated; the soldier in the trench became a mere passive recipient of torture and death. A final stage seemed to be reached in the whole tendency of modern scientific warfare to depress and make of no effect individual bravery, enterprise, and skill. Again, nearly every soldier is or becomes a fatalist on active service; it quietens his nerves to believe that his chance will be favourable or the reverse. But his fatalism depends upon the belief that he has a chance. If the air which he breathes is poison, his chance is gone: he is merely a destined victim for slaughter.[10]

Although overshadowed by the more pressing need for physical protection, morale was a significant factor in the response to the new chemical war right from the start.

After the first gas attack a plea by Lord Kitchener to the women of Britain to reproduce replicas of captured German masks resulted in 30,000 cotton pads within the first thirty-six hours. Infused with patriotic rhetoric, the women of Britain turned to their sewing needles to defeat the Hun. Crates of pads were moved from England to France and were rushed by rail to troops in the Ypres sector. As early as 3 May, British troops were issued with the cotton masks. Stored in boxes in the rear of the trench, hundreds were issued to each battalion. Officers were instructed to inform their men that they were to dip the pad in a chemical solution and then fold it over the mouth and nose during a gas attack. The uncoordinated task was carried out with varied success and enthusiasm. Even after the orders were issued, there was nothing to hold the mask in place, so the men had to stuff the chemically impregnated rags in their mouths. As one soldier quipped, "These practices were popular for once or twice, but when it began to be realised that the wads were not always used by the same man the novelty waned."[11]

The cotton wool used as a pad for the mouth was almost useless as a protector, for it dried out too quickly or became a soaked mess when saturated with a chemical solution by terrified soldiers who neither had faith that these pads would work nor confidence that the scant training they received would be relevant. On this very point Robert Graves characterized his first gassing in May 1915: "A soldier came rushing in, his eyes blank with horror and excitement. 'Gas, sir, gas! They're using gas!' ... Gas had become a nightmare. Nobody believed in the efficacy of our respirators, though advertised as proof against any gas the enemy could send over. Pink army forms marked 'Urgent' constantly arrived from headquarters to explain how to use these accessories: all contradictory."[12] Clearly, these crude early forms of gas protection left soldiers confused and frightened about what they might encounter during a gas attack.

In attempting to explain the high British gas casualties in May 1915, one after-battle report issued by Lieutenant-General C.F.H. Macready, adjutant-general of the British Expeditionary Force, noted that "very few" troops had been "properly trained in the use of respirators." Generals and senior officers alike had felt that simply issuing masks would keep their men safe. They were partially correct, but without drill and training the chance for mistakes was high. Cases were reported of soldiers putting masks over their mouths and leaving their noses exposed to the poisoned air. Others were said to have applied cotton waste pads to their chests because that was where they felt pain. Such actions might seem absurd, but one must remember that most men had never seen or even imagined what gas could do or how it affected a person. More often, the masks were not put on quickly enough or were taken off too soon. Without proper gas training, the "poor bloody infantry" generally had little idea about how to defend against a gas attack. The concept of gas discipline therefore became important to all combatants and was developed, although crudely at first, from the inception of the first gas mask.[13]

Hearing of the patriotic response of Britain's women in making cotton masks, Charles Aiken of McGill University in Montreal forwarded his version of a new gas mask to the Canadian Minister of Militia, Sam Hughes. This unique protective device was a long metal pole with perforations at the bottom end of the tube and topped with a rubber mask that covered the mouth, nose, and eyes. The metal tube was driven into the ground and the natural oxygen from the soil gave adequate protection against lethal gases, as Aiken proved when he tested it in a tent full of gases on the college grounds on 2 June 1915. Delighted with the idea, Hughes forwarded the drawings and report to Lord Kitchener and the War Office later that month. Theoretically the apparatus worked, at least in dry soil – a justifiable concern for soldiers in the muddy trenches of Flanders – but the wearer was tied to a mask that was stuck in the ground. The idea of soldiers defending their trenches while tethered like horses as they waited for the German infantry to come over the top did not even warrant a response from the War Office.[14] The amateurs continued to lend a hand and plan for the war effort, but success would be won or lost on the battlefield or by scientists who understood the realities of trench warfare.

They would have ample opportunity. The Germans launched four more gas attacks against the British around the Ypres salient between 2 and 24 May, all of them accompanied by artillery and infantry attacks. Casualties were heavy – the gas required the British to take efficient counter-measures, and their actions were still rudimentary – but there was no repeat of the hysteria and mile-deep penetrations of 22 April. Following the gas attack on 24 May, there was not another German canister gas attack on the Western Front until December. This, of course, did not preclude the fear that gas would be used again. As British infantryman Guy Chapman remarked about an aborted attack on 16 June 1915, when all the officers in the front trenches had been killed or wounded, "someone had raised an alarm of gas, and the men had panicked and run."[15] But with the prevailing wind blowing unfavourably for the Germans, the Canadians were given a natural period of grace in which officers attempted to provide some basic gas training.

On 4 May, the 1st Canadian Division moved to a billet area following a gruelling sixteen-mile march that both angered and devastated many of the men who were still suffering from exhaustion and the effects of gas. As 10th Battalion infantryman Sid Cox angrily recounted, "We lost so many from this gas through ignorance ... If we had sent them back to the hospital they would have been all right ... but when we marched out of Ypres to Bailleul ... we must have lost ten or fifteen men" to the strain of marching under a full pack. "Their hearts just gave out."[16] Within days of arriving in Bailleul, the 1st Division was equipped with cotton gas masks along with instructions on how to use them. This was the Canadians' first in a long series of instructions concerning the development of gas discipline. The Routine Orders were to be "carefully observed," as they impressed on the infantry (the only arm to receive the cotton masks at first) that "experience shows that the effect [of gas] can be successfully combatted if certain simple methods are carefully carried out." One Canadian survivor of the first gas attack remembered with interest that the cotton masks were to be dipped in a deep-blue liquid that had been prepared by the battalion medical officer and that stained the wearers' hands and faces. He and others were surprised that their lieutenant-colonel was watching with concern the seemingly mundane task of testing the liquid, but they later realized that he had a vested interest in seeing his men and new reinforcements receive some form of protection against gas. To the Canadians who had withstood the chlorine gas less than two weeks earlier with even cruder "respirators," one battle-tested veteran of the 1st Battalion remarked how he was simply glad to have anything that "gave a certain feeling of security."[17]

Although the cotton masks were partially useful against the lachrymatory or "weeping" gases, questions remained about how a man could fight in such a thing. Even the Black Veil respirators, issued on 20 May, which had a pouch for the pad to sit in and a string to hold the mask in place, forced the men to remain almost stationary lest the respirator be jarred from its position covering the mouth and nose. One Canadian report alluded to the fact that the veil was "good against chlorine," but "only gave good protection in the hands of an expert who had plenty of practice."[18] One of the reasons why the Hypo helmet, a chemically treated bag that fit over the head, was introduced in the summer of 1915 was its simplicity in comparison to the Black Veil mask.

The idea for a gas mask in the form of a helmet originated with a Canadian sergeant who was gassed at Ypres and had seen some of the German gas pioneers wearing what looked like flour bags over their heads. A Newfoundland medical officer, Captain Cluny Macpherson, experimented with the idea and eventually developed the Hypo helmet. Some 2.5 million were issued during the war, and by 6 July 1915 every soldier in the BEF was equipped with one.[19]

The Hypo or Smoke helmet was a chemically treated flannel sack with a single mica window, worn over the head and tucked in at the neck during gas attacks.[20] The poison gas was neutralized by the chemicals in the helmet as the man breathed through the fabric. Yet not only did the Hypo smell, as one Canadian soldier lamented, "like last year's bird seed," but it was cumbersome, stifling, and blinding. The importance of having the gas helmet tucked in appears self-evident, but one British officer of the 2nd Royal Welch Fusiliers caught taking a bath during a gas attack simply "pulled on his gas helmet and stood waiting for the 'all clear,'" forgetting that he was defenceless because he had no garment into which to tuck the free end of the helmet. The addled officer, whose gas discipline had not yet reached the stage of an automatic, drill-like response, was saved by his quick-moving and embarrassed servant, who quickly rushed him some clothing.[21]

Further instructions were accordingly supplied, and in the summer heat of June 1915, the Canadian Corps ordered that all men had to wear their great coats during gas alerts in order to have something into which to tuck their helmets. Despite the improvement in the gas helmet, it brought its own complexities and confusion. In a flurry of orders from Canadian Corps and British Army headquarters, soldiers were ordered to keep their gas helmets clean and away from water.[22] Living in trenches thick with mud and debris, this was not always an easy task. In addition, eyepieces had an unfortunate tendency to crack with even mild use – not ideal for infantrymen enduring the subterranean world of the trenches. Perhaps worse in winning the confidence of the men, the Hypo helmet's chemical "dip" burned the forehead and irritated the wearer's eyes whenever he sweated, which turned out to be a constant occurrence in the stifling head bags. Along with these impracticalities, the alien nature of the gas helmets was initially bizarre for soldiers. Lieutenant D.E. Macintyre remarked how he made his men "practice breathing with our gas helmets on and the men surely do look a weird sight when they are wearing them. Great goggle-eyed things like a false face." The strange sight of men wearing these ghoulish masks, combined with the simple inability to communicate and the constant intake of breath rushing in one's ears, left men feeling alone and isolated from their comrades. Finally, although effectively protecting against chlorine, the Hypo helmet was opposed by physiologists in England on the ground that the excess build-up of carbon dioxide would eventually cause unconsciousness and death to the wearer, although this information was not passed along to the front-line soldier.[23]

With scientists scrambling to fix the defects before the Germans introduced a deadlier gas, the next and improved stage in the evolution of gas helmets was the P-helmet (popularly known as "the goggle-eyed booger with the tit").[24] Issued in November 1915, after the Russians warned the British that the Germans were employing a new lethal gas that was wiping out their soldiers by the thousands, the P-helmet, with its shapeless hood, two eyeholes, and a rubber tube hanging down from the mouth, had a nightmarish quality to it. Along with eyeholes that still clouded up or shifted around so that the wearer was trying to look through the nose or forehead, the P (for phenate) helmet was impregnated with a new chemical to protect against phosgene, the agent the British suspected the Germans were using to such deadly effect on the Eastern Front. In addition, a special valve that was clenched in the mouth was added to remove the carbon dioxide build-up within the helmet; unfortunately, it cut the corners of the mouth and resulted in a continuous flow of drool down the chin. Though

Canadian soldier wearing a P-helmet.

the helmet was more effective than a cloth tied around the face, it remained a stifling and fearful thing to wear. One Canadian soldier described the gas helmet in the following way: "Most everyone was loath to put on the mask because it was so uncomfortable. The sack kind of material that the mask was made out of had been treated chemically and had a pincher type clamp that clamped over the nose with an elongated mouth piece that fitted in the mouth."[25]

By pulling a flannel sack over one's head to protect against gas, one essentially pulled a blindfold over one's eyes. The helmet, if correctly used, partially protected against chlorine and tear gas, but what about the fear of the enemy attacking behind the poisonous cloud? Soldiers were taught that gas attacks, like artillery barrages, were often the precursor to large-scale offensives, yet how was a soldier to defend his section of trench with a bag over his head? The awful anxiety of donning a mask, and peering with weeping eyes over the parapet through the gas in hope of glimpsing when the Germans were coming over the top, was, to say the least, terribly distressing. Canadian Sergeant G.S. Twigg of the 4th Battalion remembered the P-helmet with disgust: "My God, it just steamed up and you couldn't see a thing."[26]

Even a "secret" memo reported that "These men must be warned that they may expect to experience not only slight discomfort but very serious discomfort in some cases almost amounting to a feeling of suffocation." The solution, as espoused by the Army, was to "avoid movement." Not only was the infantry's anti-gas training sporadic, but during a gas attack, with adrenaline pumping, gas enveloping the trench, and German troops following, soldiers felt like they were stifling in these nightmarish bags and that they were unable to move without suffocating themselves. Many soldiers had already realized this, as Canadian artilleryman Wilfred Kerr remarked: "The masks ... did leave something to be desired if one had to perform any strenuous manual labour; in those circumstances one could not draw breath fast enough through them."[27]

Although the Germans could not closely follow their own gas, for they had the same inadequate protection as the Allied soldiers, those on the receiving end felt like rabbits trapped in a warren, and blind rabbits at that, waiting, isolated and terrified, to see if their gas helmets would work this time. Forever hearing whispers and rumours of men "up the line" suffocating to death in dense clouds with their helmets attached, soldiers lived in fear of being caught in the direct path of a chemical attack. The warning that their gas helmets would last only twenty minutes in a dense gas cloud did little to ease their apprehension.[28] Canadian infantryman Richard Adamson recounted the dread he felt during a gas cloud attack:

As I lay there I wondered if my gas mask would protect me. The only tests my mask had was in a building [where] the volume and density of the gas had been controlled. From the colour of this poison gas cloud bearing down on us it looked like it was a very strong mixture ... All these thoughts raced through my mind as I lay there waiting for the gas to pass over us. Would my mask prove to be good or would I die a most horrible death. There was nothing to be done but wait and see. So I took to praying.[29]

Others cursed those who made them suffer: "If this is the only thing that is to keep us from inhaling Jerry's terrible gas," Canadian gunner Frank Ferguson wished, "I for one hope all his chemists die of some terrible disease." Lieutenant Armine Norris, who served with the Machine Gun Corps, who won the Military Cross and was later killed during the battle of Canal du Nord, remained convinced that gas was immoral, and his attitude had not changed with the issuing of the gas helmets. He wrote to his mother in the summer of 1915, that "Submarines and gas are murder, not war."[30] Gas remained universally disliked by the common soldier, but some began to replace the terror they had felt with simple disgust after they were issued their protective devices. The frenzy of activity in developing new gas helmets must be measured against the very little gas being employed on the Western Front due to the awkward and uncontrollable weapons system. When it was used, however, it continued to have devastating effect.

Along with the periodic use of lethal chlorine gas, the Germans plagued the Canadians with lachrymatory gas shells. Although not lethal, lachrymatory gases had the advantage that even a small quantity would force soldiers to wear their masks and reduce their fighting efficiency.[31] Soldiers were left temporarily blinded; Canadian medical officer and later member of Parliament R.J. Manion described his "eyes [being] as red as uncooked beefsteak and they felt as if they had been sandpapered" after he was affected by German tear gas. Another Canadian remarked that the gas, although not lethal, "affects my breathing and stomach, in fact, it makes you dizzy and senseless and pains in the head."[32] Lachrymatory shells continued to be used throughout the war, not to kill but to harass the enemy. The gas contributed to the misery of the soldiers and often provoked a breakdown in gas discipline. Due to the restrictive nature of gas masks, soldiers often wore gas goggles, which protected only the eyes. Such actions resulted in future gas casualties when lethal gas, like phosgene and diphosgene, was added to gas shells.

Tear-gas shells were used against the French in late July in conjunction with an infantry assault. The Germans were experimenting with combining and interspersing gas and HE shells in order to cause confusion and disrupt activities in the French lines. In September 1915, on a front of two miles, the Germans, using tear gas to bombard the support trenches and command posts, successfully hindered communication by runners from the front to the rear.[33] The Germans, the first to employ gas shells, were beginning to see further uses for the weapon they had unleashed.

One of the few truths about the nature of battle is that soldiers die in largest numbers when they run away, because it is when they turn their backs to the enemy that they are least able to defend themselves.[34] Proponents of gas warfare hoped to repeat what the Germans achieved on 22 April 1915. The panic and rout of two French divisions not only opened up a gap in the Allied lines, which could have been exploited if the Germans had the necessary reserves, but almost induced a form of contagious hysteria among the remaining soldiers. When the defenders saw their fellow soldiers running, it at the very least invoked a sense of uneasiness; in the worst scenario, it caused soldiers to turn and break. That there is an angry mob attempting to break free of all armies is a truthful adage, and the Germans hoped to exploit this possibility in the less disciplined Russian Army on the Eastern Front.

After the cloud attack at Ypres, the Germans transported large quantities of chlorine cylinders to the Eastern Front where the German High Command expected the poison gas to be a major tactical success. Erich Ludendorff, first quartermaster-general to Field Marshal Paul von Hindenburg, wrote in his memoirs: "We had received a supply of gas and anticipated great tactical results from its use, as the Russians were not yet fully protected against gas."[35] When the gas was released it was effective in causing heavy casualties but failed to allow a strategic penetration of the front, as the Russian artillery and small arms fire on the flanks broke up the attack. Applying the lessons learned from several gas cloud attacks, the Germans realized that gas alone was unable to create a situation where the infantry would be able to fully break through the enemy's lines.

As a weapon, gas was successfully used only in dense concentration or against those who were unprepared or unequipped. The great drawback of gas remained the inability to deliver it accurately and directly to the target at a specific time. Nonetheless, it was effective against the Russians, who were plagued by underdeveloped industries that could not meet the demand for even basic weapons like rifles and ammunition. Such auxiliary devices as gas masks were out of the question for all but a few lucky divisions. Their poor design and the suffocating feeling experienced by the wearer sparked a saying among the Russian soldiers: "If the German gas doesn't kill us, then the Russian mask will." Between 22 April and 6 August 1915 the Germans released 1,200 tons of gas, of which two-thirds was used on the Eastern Front. The Russians suffered almost half a million gas casualties during the Great War – almost as many as France, Germany, and Britain combined – as their industrial weakness was exploited.[36] Gas was the ideal weapon against the more technically backward Russians until the British and French supplied them with suitable protection. But it was the war on the Western Front, with its static nature, where the production of gases, defensive masks, and delivery systems came to fruition.[37]

A FOUL WAY TO KILL

> *It was a foul way to kill human beings but the Germans started it.*
> —DR. H. COTTON

On 27 April 1915 the British Cabinet discussed the German use of gas. Prime Minister Asquith's letter to the King records: "Enquiries and experiments are being made as to the best way of dealing with the resort by the Germans to asphyxiating gases." During the frantic days of April and May, the British looked to retaliate, but, more important, to teach their soldiers how to use the pads and masks. At General Army Headquarters, the director-general of Medical Services appointed chemical officers – later renamed chemical advisors – to each army. One historian remarked that these officers knew about as little as the frightened men they were teaching and went about dispensing such valuable information as it being a good idea to change pads "when respirators no longer stopped the entrance of gas." By the first months of 1916, however, the British had organized formalized schools to instruct officers in anti-gas drill in a more consistent and sophisticated fashion.[38] Despite these measures, it was apparent that further assistance was required to administer the anti-gas doctrine at the divisional level and lower.

On 26 May 1915 the British formally decided to enter the offensive gas war by appointing Major Charles A. Foulkes to the grade of lieutenant-colonel in the role of gas advisor to the General Headquarters. A field engineer, Foulkes had no knowledge of gas or how it was to be used in warfare, but nonetheless pursued his task with vigour.[39] The British High Command wanted gas to be ready as a weapon for an autumn offensive on the Western Front.[40] Foulkes had only a few months in which to recruit and train men to discharge the gas as well as devise some sort of doctrine to incorporate gas into the fighting mechanism of the BEF. That was asking too much. Moreover, Britain could not manufacture anything close to the amount of gas produced by the Germans. The Castner-Kellner works at Runcorn started production of chlorine on 4 June, but produced only five tons of gas a week. While a fraction of what the German factories were producing, it would be enough for an assault in September. With characteristic energy, Foulkes recruited, stole, and tricked chemists in other parts of the army and on the home front to join a special organization that would "give some of the Bosche its own medicine." Unlike the French Z (for gaz) gas companies, which were filled with men considered unsuitable for active combat, the British Special Companies were almost all totally fit and had some form of chemical training.[41] By mid-July there were seven Special Companies (later the Special Brigade) made up of four hundred men to carry out gas attacks.

Due to their unusual jobs, the men of the Special Companies were appointed the rank of corporal. Yet they made little use of their science backgrounds and more felt akin to plumbers in their application of the gas canisters. There was almost no analysis of the actual chemicals employed but simply continuous training in removing and quickly applying hoses to the gas canisters. After much complaining, they were finally told that chemists were needed to "give confidence to the infantry." The corporals found that not only were their jobs dangerous, they were also spurned by their own infantry, who derisively referred to them as "gas merchants."[42] The notion of gas as a dirty weapon remained strong among the infantry, who were its chief victims, but paradoxically, it was these gas merchants whom the Canadians would eventually rely upon to deliver their canistered gas.

THE BATTLE OF LOOS:
BRITISH GAS OFFENSIVE AND THE LESSONS LEARNED

After subsequent gas attacks by the Germans, the British retaliated with a chlorine attack of their own. To answer critics of gas, Foulkes was fond of quoting the Duke of Marlborough: "In the long run the pursuit of victory without slaughter is likely to eventuate in slaughter without victory."[43] Although many saw it as an evil, it was a necessary evil if they were to battle the Germans on a level playing field. And that playing field was to be the ground around Loos.

Although the Battle of Loos did not directly involve the Canadians, news of the fighting soon spread to them and influenced their thinking about chlorine. Before the battle, gas was viewed as a weapon of retribution. Afterward, it was associated with disaster and fear.

From March to June 1915, the British fought a series of unsuccessful and costly battles at Neuve Chapelle, Festubert, Givenchy, and Aubers Ridge. The Battle of Loos was one more in a series of engagements, and it occurred at neither the time nor the location the British wished for. Attacking in an attempt to support a French offensive against the Noyon salient, the British were to press their attack through flat ground dotted with rock quarries and slag heaps. Within the heaps and heights, the Germans had strongly fortified themselves with wire and machine-gun emplacements. As the earlier battles of 1915 had shown, attacks launched without adequate artillery support failed with high casualties. Once again the British were without proper high-explosive shells, but this time they had a new weapon that they hoped would deliver victory.

In the initial part of the war, Sir John French was chronically short of artillery and shells; in desperation, he turned to chlorine gas. French and his army commander, Sir Douglas Haig, hoped gas would produce results like those at 2nd Ypres, despite the fact that the Germans had been unable to replicate that tactical success. Their ignorance of gas combined with an inaccurate expectation of its use led to what one historian has called "a curious process of self-deception" among the British High Command. "Indeed," wrote Brigadier

General John Charteris, Haig's director of intelligence, on the status of using chlorine gas, "everything seems to point to success; we count and recount the chances, and all seems to point to the same [successful] conclusion."[44] On the morning of 25 September 1915, the first British gas cloud was to be released in a surprise attack at Loos, where it was hoped that the gas would sink into the German dugouts and trenches, killing or incapacitating the defenders.[45]

In great secrecy, the Special Companies supervised the digging of pits at intervals along the front line as soldiers struggled to bring up the heavy metal canisters. J.C. Dunn of the 2nd Battalion, Royal Welch Fusiliers, noted: "The official name for the content of these gas cylinders was accessory. It was a crime to call it gas. No printable vocabulary could repeat what the men called it as they struggled and sweated [to carry the heavy canisters] up the narrow angular trenches." With the units forced to wear the sweltering Hypo helmets because of gas leakages, the 150 pound containers were a despised fatigue. It did not end there, however, for after they were transported over miles of broken terrain, the canisters were planted in the front lines where many a man stared at them with unease, especially with the German guns searching up and down their front lines. Foreshadowing the upcoming tragedy, General Sir Herbert Gough had conjectured that "gas might be a boomerang ally – a tremendous but treacherous friend."[46]

Of course, the front-line troops knew only the positive. Officers of the 2nd Royal Welch Fusiliers were told, "According to the official forecast and programme the gas is to lay out all the Germans, the leading battalions have just to walk over [and occupy the positions]." As well, troops were emphatically told over and over again that their gas helmets would properly protect them from whatever residual gas they encountered while going over the top or while consolidating the enemy's captured trenches. Strangely though, the British High Command had no qualms about having the infantry fight in conjunction with the gas, a weapon that many of the new troops had never even seen before. This was in contrast to the Germans, who had decided by August 1915, because of their experience in the East, that "although the gas clouds were useful tools, they were entirely dependent on wind direction and thus impossible to coordinate with infantry attacks."[47] Without the German experience in gas discharges, the British would have to learn that lesson the hard way.

On the morning of the attack, periodic changes of wind direction led Haig to worry if the gas could be used: "I went on top of our wooden look-out tower. The wind came gently from SW and by 5:40 had increased slightly. The leaves of the poplar trees gently rustled. This seemed satisfactory. But what a risk I must run of gas blowing back upon our dense masses of troops!" Haig was assured by his chief meteorologist, the same man who would tell him two years later that he might expect a dry spell of weather during the Passchendaele offensive, that the weather would hold. If Haig were nervous about the use of gas, his junior officers were positively against it, as Robert Graves illustrated in his memoirs: "It's damnable. It's not soldiering to use stuff like that, even though the Germans did start it. It's dirty, and it'll bring us bad luck. We're sure to bungle it. Take those new gas-companies – sorry, excuse me this once, I mean accessory-companies – their very look makes me tremble. Chemistry – dons from London University, a few lads straight from school, one or two N.C.O.s of the old-soldier type, trained together for three weeks, then given a job as responsible as this. Of course they'll bungle it. How could they do anything else?"[48] That many of Graves's friends did not return from the "Loos show" was testimony that canistered gas could not be used in a combined-arms operation and was even more dangerous without a coherent tactical doctrine.

Historian Martin van Creveld has argued that the prerequisite for any weapon is a coherent doctrine for employment, giving basic rules as to how a weapon is to be used in conjunction with other weapons, arms, and services, in a mutually supporting fashion. In effect, doctrine is the accepted guidelines and framework by which training and war are conducted.[49] But at Loos there was no doctrine; worse still, there was even less understanding of gas by the senior commanders. General Haig did not recognize the limitations of gas as a weapon and, after ordering that it would be a key ingredient for victory, he left it in the hands of shunted-away gas companies. Gas was seen as a specialist weapon, used by chemists who understood its properties and better kept away from respectable generals. Such beliefs could result in nothing less then failure. It would not be until gas was accepted and developed into a coherent battlefield doctrine, along with new delivery systems, that it would become an effective tactical weapon.

In each section of trench there were dozens of gas canisters to be manned by the chemical specialist. It was his duty, when the signal was given, to attach a hose to the canister, release the gas, turn off the tap, and move the hose to the next canister to begin anew. While under fire it was a difficult and complicated task made worse by the fact that gas leaked from the pipes and that, initially, the pipes were rigid and cumbersome and tended to crack, thereby flooding trenches, causing casualties, and invoking the continued vexation of the infantry.[50]

Equally important was the need to gauge the wind, as any reversal could have disastrous effects. General French ordered that gas had to be released irrespective of wind conditions, but with the infantry straining to go over the top on the morning of 25 September, the gas specialists were deeply concerned that there was only a weak wind as zero hour approached. Owing to the large attacking front, it was almost impossible to call off the attack, especially one planned for so long and desperately needed by the French to divert German reserves away from their troops. Seemingly not realizing that gas discharges were different from artillery barrages, which could be coordinated to the minute, gas specialists were ordered to release the gas at zero hour, and were even threatened with being shot if they did not do so.[51] As opposed to the Germans at Ypres, who had been able to wait for five weeks for the proper wind, the British commanders allowed themselves no such luxury. When the wind died, the British brass hats seem to have had some delusional hope that somehow the gas would still work – for it not to would result in carnage and was therefore unthinkable.

At zero hour the gas officers released the lethal clouds as the waiting infantry battalions huddled in the trenches ready to go over the top. British gas specialist John Thomas, who watched a British assault following the gas discharge, wrote that "The enemy reacted [to the gas], after a short pause, with violent machine-gun fire." One German described the terrifying nature of the British gas: "The bank of fog passed over our trenches, then came a low bank of black-green smoke creeping toward us, and then another bank of gas some ten minutes behind the first … Some men coughed and fell down. The others stood at the ready as long as possible. Behind the fourth gas and smoke cloud there suddenly emerged Englishmen in thick lines and storming columns. They rose suddenly from the earth wearing smoke masks over their faces and looking not like soldiers but like devils. These were bad and terrible hours."[52]

There is no doubt that they were indeed terrible times for the German troops. However, gas, although effectively immobilizing some of the German positions, was no substitute for an artillery barrage. And unlike an artillery barrage, it did not force men to hide for cover; rather, it encouraged them to stay above ground firing their weapons. Although some defensive positions were overwhelmed by the chlorine, enough riflemen and machine-gun posts remained to counter the onrushing British attackers coming across the flat killing ground.

Not only did gas fail to provide the promised British walk-over, but more distressingly on the left flank of the line it blew back on the British attackers. Many factors contributed to the blow-back. The wind had shifted direction and died down. The German artillery had broken open some of the chlorine canisters. Finally, under intense pressure, the gas specialists had made errors: one officer forgot to put the hose into No Man's Land and as a result the gas flowed along the British trenches.

One British officer described the confusion in the firing trench when the gas turned on them just as he and his men were straining to go over the top: "Come on!" "Get back you bastards!" "Gas turning on us!" "Keep your heads, you men!" "Back like hell, boys!" "Whose orders?" "What's happening?" "Gas!" "Back!" "Come on!" "Gas!" "Back!"[53] The disarray was complete: gas blowing back; German artillery fire raining down on the massed attackers in the front trenches; smoke and fear; gas masks coming on and off, muffling officers' voices and nearly blinding the soldiers. At best, the result was a chaotic scramble across No Man's Land. At worst, it was a senseless slaughter as soldiers trapped by gas in their trenches were cut down as they climbed out of the poison.

A witness to the British infantry going over the top, Bombardier J.W. Palmer, 26th Brigade RFA, described the battlefield in his diary:

> The field of battle to our front presented a shambles. There appeared to be bodies everywhere. When I saw the effects of the gas on our lads I realised what they had suffered when the Germans first used it. Then we were totally unprepared for it but here at least we had the masks. I heard later that the masks were quite serviceable but during the charge which was nearly 800 yards in places, they were unable to get their breath. Some were unable to see and many in panic just pulled the masks off. By the afternoon the faces of our lads who lay in the open changed colour and presented a gruesome spectacle.[54]

The débâcle at Loos resulted in many of the Tommies believing not only that their gas was inferior to that of the Germans but also more deadly to themselves than to the enemy.[55] Whether or not the gas was effective, once the average soldier lost faith in a weapon there was little to be done to regain it. This "betrayal" only strengthened the hatred and anxiety toward gas, and did little to endear those gas specialists who would continue to install it in their front trenches.

Although the British attack at Loos was a resounding failure, and resulted in the replacement of Sir John French with Sir Douglas Haig as commander of the BEF, the first British use of gas created unease among the German High Command. More important, it struck fear into the German trench soldiers. They had been told that the Allies did not possess the capacity to retaliate, but the hundreds of dead and thousands of gassed Germans proved otherwise. An immediate cry went up among the German infantry, who demanded an improved gas mask to replace their cotton-waste type. The Germans eventually developed a new canister – or drum – gas mask, which was much more efficient than anything the Allies had at the time, issuing them in October-November 1915.[56] For the moment, the new German drum mask quelled the fears of the *frontsoldaten*.

Any analysis of the gas war must take into account the mistrust and apprehension it evoked among the common soldiers. Initially, with the British, and later the Germans, the average trench soldier's feelings bordered on hatred. With the failure of gas at Loos, the British brigade and divisional commanding officers also became more restrained about using it. No longer were there talks about gassing the Germans back to Berlin. It was all too clear that canister attacks left much to be desired as a tactical weapon. Any weapon that depended on the weather – the wind in this case – was not an instrument on which an operation could be based. The Special Companies often waited agonizingly night after night for a favourable wind while hoping that stray German shells would not puncture the canisters planted next to them. To organize a large attack and then have to cancel it because the wind was blowing in the wrong direction left a bad taste in many commanders' mouths.

One British gas specialist reported that "the infantry were scared stiff of our gas."[57] If the infantry and their officers were scared of the gas, they had every reason to be. Trench soldiers were under tremendous stress at the front, so much so that they were rotated out, usually after a week, of merely surviving "life" at the front. Trekking through mud, working all night to repair trenches, and patrolling in No Man's Land contributed to the exhaustion of the infantry. With the introduction of the gas canisters, the "poor bloody infantry" were conscripted by the Special Companies to carry the heavy metal containers from a stockpile in the rear through winding narrow trenches in complete darkness to the front lines to help set up a weapon they feared and distrusted.

J.B. Platnauer, a member of the British Special Companies, detailed the bringing up of gas canisters in his diary: "[The canisters] were horrifying things to handle. They weighed 180 pounds and were slung on a pole between two men. Everyone had to wear his gas helmet all the time in case the cylinders leaked, and that meant that most of the time we were stifled and half suffocated."[58] Traversing the trenches was difficult at the best of times, but combined with the darkness and weight of the canisters it was a dreaded task. The staff officers seemed to take little notice of this added burden. One joke circulated among the infantry, following the failure of the gas attack, of a "staff officer who detailed twice as many men to carry empty chlorine cylinders than full ones because he believed that when they were filled with gas they would be lighter."[59] It was little wonder that the infantry in their mulish role despised the men of Special Companies.

Besides the physical strain of carrying up the canisters, the noise of transporting metal containers invited the enemy to shell the firing line. For instance, when the 2nd Canadian Divisional Train was asked to transport gas to a stockpile position at the rear of the forward trenches, the wary drivers tied all wagon wheels with canvas and all loose parts of harness with sacking to muffle the noise, and tightly secured the metal canisters. They carried out the operation successfully, but nonetheless suffered some casualties from a German barrage that was "searching" the front lines. Nervous defenders, wary of being gassed in their sleep, often called down artillery barrages on the enemy front lines to make sure there were no canisters planted there. One specialist remarked how dangerous it was not only to have the gas canisters in the front line but also to be anywhere near them: "[German shelling] had thrown the gas pipes back into the trench and smashed the gas cylinders ... They [British in the trench] had lost 58 out of 64 [men]."[60] Due to the extreme concentration of the gas, if a soldier were near a burst canister, he was likely to be overpowered and poisoned even when wearing a gas mask.[61] Finally, to add salt to their wounds, as Tony Ashworth has illustrated in his study of the "live and let live system," the use of Special Companies invited massive artillery retaliation, which the infantry were left to receive.[62] Given that the infantry at the front rarely saw the effects of their gas on the enemy and were only too keenly aware of their own physical discomfort and the disadvantages of having gas canisters situated right beside their positions, it is no surprise that most soldiers cringed at the very thought of gas being delivered from their trenches.

Prior to Loos the 1st Canadian Division had taken part in costly minor operations at Festubert and Givenchy, but generally they were simply holding their front line in the Ypres salient. During that time, on 13 September, the 2nd Division had joined the 1st in the field, and the Canadian Corps, under command of General Alderson, was formed. The Canadians had a small but indirect part to play in the Loos battle: they were to engage the enemy on their front and thus draw reserves away from the battle.

On the night of 24 September, Canadian soldiers carried straw sacks and smoke pots of pitch, tallow, and saltpetre into their trenches and at the appointed time lit them to simulate a gas attack against the German line. The Summary of Operations recorded that, "it is believed that the enemy was somewhat puzzled, and movement in his communication trenches was observed, thus providing a target for our artillery."[63] Unfortunately, Canadian George Bell of the 1st Battalion told a different side of what occurred, the infantryman's view from the trench:

> Having no gas, we brought up loads of straw during the night. This was spread along the trench and set on fire. As the wind was favourable great clouds of smoke drifted towards the enemy. He mistook it for gas as we intended he would. [Unfortunately] he got his wind up and signalled for artillery support. For hours his artillery pounded our front lines and we suffered heavy casualties, accomplishing nothing in return. I sometimes wonder whose bright idea it was. The British suffered tremendous losses at Loos and accomplished nothing. Neither did we in our [fake] gas attack.[64]

This was the first "gas attack" by the Canadians, and as indicated by Bell it was far from successful.

The failed employment of gas at Loos was instructive to the Canadians in so far as the British had learned some hard lessons. Infantry and gas were a dangerous mix – difficult to control and laborious to coordinate in an attack. Most important, the British use of gas at Loos illustrated the common soldiers' mistrust of a weapon that they viewed as being more deadly to themselves than the enemy. Brigadier-General Tim Harrington, General Staff Officer for the 1st Canadian Division, did, however, note in a memorandum at the end of November that the French had begun to employ gas shells to harass and disable the Germans while not feeling compelled to send their infantry over to join in the fight.[65] It appeared that poison gas did not have to be the focal point of a battle; instead, it could be used to harass the enemy before or after an upcoming operation. Alternatively, it could simply become one more weapon of attrition and thus wear down and kill soldiers holding static trenches. Aware of the lessons from Loos, the Canadians made no effort to establish their own offensive gas cloud specialists.[66] Yet with the developing gas shell tactics, there might still be a role for command and control of gas in future Canadian attack plans. Despite the hint of new uses for poison gas, it was a dangerous agent, and after Loos the Canadians were more interested in protecting their troops by defining their own defensive anti-gas doctrine.

GAS DISCIPLINE

The instigation of an anti-gas doctrine was initially similar to the measures needed in combatting trench foot. Trench foot was an inflammation resembling frostbite and was caused by standing in cold water for days on end. If not treated it could result in the amputation of the toes and, eventually, the feet. It threatened to cripple the BEF in the first year of the war. Colonel H.S. Cooper of the 3rd Battalion remembered that "if a man [under your command] had a case of trench feet you were for court martial ... you had to prove that you had done everything [and] your orders were properly carried out." Unnecessary gassing in a battalion was also blamed on the commanding officers. As one threatening report proclaimed, "officers at the front are now liable to be court-martialled if any of their men are gassed."[67] In terms of trench foot, the officers were given strict orders to watch the men apply smelly whale oil to the feet, but they had no definite orders about how to achieve a good gas discipline. However, with the impetus of a new gas being used on the Eastern Front, by early December 1915 the Canadian Corps began to implement a stricter anti-gas discipline. Up until December it was necessary only to make sure that each man had a P-helmet, which had been issued a month earlier. As of 5 December an order to all battalion commanding officers dictated that "every man under their command must understand the proper use and the correct method of adjusting the helmet and has actually done so once during the tour."[68] Now it was necessary for commanding officers to enforce gas discipline by making sure that each man had worn his gas helmet once during the stint at the front (about four to six days). But how was he to do so? The only method available was for the commanding officers to order their junior officers to enforce this gas discipline. Yet for subordinates with absolutely no training, this was a difficult task that met varied success. The concept behind gas training and discipline was beginning to emerge, but there was no consistent way in which to implement it.

Along with the development of gas helmets, a device was needed to remove the gas that clung to shell holes and dugouts. Long after the clouds had dissipated there were cases of soldiers being gassed after entering dugouts still infected with chlorine. Initially soldiers built fires in the dugouts to clear them of gas, but this method had an unfortunate side-effect of attracting artillery fire. Other unsuccessful methods revolved around Ayrton fans, looking like big fly swatters, which were to be used to blow the gas back and afterward to clear trenches. With the fans were boxes filled with a mixture of gunpowder, which would be exploded when a gas cloud was moving toward the trenches. Both methods were impractical, one resulting in too much exertion for men wearing the suffocating gas helmets (as well as the fans simply not working)

A novel gas vane made by a Canadian.

and the other tending to destroy one's trenches and anyone who was too close to the boxes. The Ayrton fans were highly regarded by infantry in the trenches – but only for firewood. Foulkes remarked that more than 100,000 of these "useless" tools were produced.[69] Neither the short-lived fan nor the explosive box had any effect on the initial half-mile-wide gas clouds or in clearing the trenches afterward.

More productive were the Vermorel gas sprayers. These had been adapted from orchard sprayers and used the same chemical compound, although diluted, that the Hypo helmets were dipped in. They were not effective in dispersing a gas cloud, but they were beneficial in clearing the lingering effects of poison gas in dugouts following an attack. The solution for the sprayers was carried up to the trenches in corked rum jars. One soldier remembered how a few of the men from a unit mistook the chemical solution for army rum. Some of the more adventurous tried mouthfuls of the foul stuff before realizing what it was. Indicative of the trench soldier's hardships, after their two-day stint in the line there was not a drop of Vermorel liquid left in any of the trenches, as they had drunk it.[70] On the whole, however, the sprayers were useful for clearing lingering gas, and their liquid was not generally imbibed in lieu of alcohol.

It was realized that, along with anti-gas equipment, there was a need for some sort of early warning system of an impending attack. Without someone yelling or banging on a shell case to warn those that were sleeping or out of sight, gas helmets would be useless. But there was no organized alarm system, nor was there yet a fixed gas sentry as there would be later in the war. By December 1915 such an assignment was left to individual officers in their respective areas; some opted for gas sentries while others did not. At this stage in the gas war, the Canadian Corps' reliance on gas discipline was very individualized and unstructured. The need for a good anti-gas doctrine was understood; how it was to be carried out was not. That would begin to change with the introduction of phosgene gas by the Germans.

Inflicting high numbers of fatal casualties on the enemy in the gas war after the introduction of the gas mask was largely based on catching soldiers unaware. The most lethal gas of the war, phosgene, was employed for the first time on the Western Front by the Germans on 19 December 1915 against the British at the ruins of Wieltje in the Ypres sector. The Germans broke their self-imposed moratorium on gas, and 1,069 British became casualties, 120 of them dying. The casualties would have been worse had the Russians not warned the British about the impending use of phosgene; consequently, the British were just narrowly able to issue the new P-helmet, which largely protected the wearer. Instead of a failure in the gas helmet, the gas casualties were caused by a faulty alarm system and the difficulty in detecting the new gas by smell.[71]

The British were caught by surprise on the night of the attack, with gas sentries unable to wake all the men in time for them to don their gas helmets. Those soldiers who were awake fumbled in the dark trying to adjust their gas helmets as the cloud drifted nearer. The speed of the gas outstripped the alarms at the front: one man was even gassed five miles behind the line.[72] The fear of being woken by a screeching sentry, and the resultant rush as men frantically searched through packs to find their masks as the seconds ticked down, demonstrated the need for improved gas discipline.

The German assault behind the gas was broken up by British rapid-fire and artillery support, but the British troops, without an effective gas discipline, suffered numerous casualties from removing gas helmets too soon, entering gassed dugouts, or having officers who were forced to remove their gas helmets to see the enemy or give orders. One medical report indicated that some victims, after putting on their gas helmets, became nervous because of the strain of breathing and the smell of chemicals that the gas helmet emitted. In some cases, men tore off the gas helmets, thinking they were being poisoned, and in consequence were really gassed.[73] The gas war was proving that it required more than simply handing out gas helmets to the soldiers; it was necessary to train them in their use. After the first gassing at 2nd Ypres, it was the British, not the Canadians, who suffered from the second innovation of German gas. Nonetheless, the fear of phosgene, a highly toxic pulmonary agent that was eight times more deadly than chlorine and that eventually resulted in 80 percent of all gas fatalities in the war, instigated a new set of gas discipline reforms within the Canadian Corps.[74]

CHAPTER THREE

A Higher Form
of Killing

DECEMBER 1915–DECEMBER 1916

*In no future war will the military be able to ignore
poison gas. It is a higher form of killing.*
—PROFESSOR FRITZ HABER, 1919

THE CANADIAN CORPS ADAPTS

In the first phosgene attack on the Western Front on 19 December 1915, the Canadians were mercifully not among the immediate victims. Yet they would be exposed soon enough, for phosgene was the second great innovation of the gas war.[1]

At the time of the December gas attack, D.E. Macintyre of the 28th Canadian Battalion was sleeping in a billet to the rear of the front line and south of the British position: "I was awakened about 5:30 am by a heavy wind which shook the house in gusts. After a while a baby began to cry upstairs and I heard the Colonel get up and tell someone that the baby was scared to death of the wind. Pretty soon we all noticed the smell and discovered it was GAS! ... We were seven miles away but the gas made us cough and our eyes water. We heard the attack was a complete failure, the Germans not getting a man across."[2]

Other Canadians, such as Gunner Leslie Catchpole of the 15th Battery, Canadian Field Artillery, remembered being awoken by a frantic officer, even though they were miles from the gas cloud: "[He was] yelling at us to get up. He sounded quite tragic, but we were kind of lazy, and didn't hurry ... As soon as I got outside, I could smell the gas which went right to my lungs, and I started to cough ... I made for the stables, and could hear all the horses coughing; I thought I should cough my interior up, before I got that team ready. I didn't

59

want to put my gas mask on, as it was awkward, and uncomfortable ... and very hard to see or do anything." Luckily, Catchpole and his men were able to drive their horses and selves out of the outer vapours of the phosgene cloud. As he remarked in his memoirs: "The gas was not thick enough to be visible, but it gave us a good idea of its effects. With the gasses that were used later, it would have been foolish not to have used our [gas] helmets."[3]

To the north of the Canadian position, the British took the full brunt of the death cloud. They were probably saved from the same routing of their soldiers as chlorine had done in the Ypres salient only because the new phosgene clouds were still heavily reliant on the quixotic direction of the wind. Not all the gas turned, however, as indicated by the 120 Tommies who suffocated to death and the 1,069 that were wounded by the gas.[4] Such fatalities foreshadowed the future gas war, and phosgene quickly transformed the nature of gas as a battlefield weapon. Soldiers and armies who did not learn from their own and others' mistakes, would probably find themselves as the next victims; the gas war, like the larger trench war that raged on, was learned on a blood curve.

As one after-battle report indicated, the British defenders had "lined the parapet with their [gas] helmets on within a minute of the signal" and broke up the enemy attack with rifle fire.[5] After several months of basic anti-gas training, the principal casualties were no longer inflicted on men in the firing line. Rather, most casualties were produced among soldiers not awakened by the gas alarms and from the infantry removing helmets too soon or entering gassed dugouts. The insidious nature of phosgene, more so than chlorine due to its potency and faint smell, made it difficult to realize that one was being poisoned. Unlike chlorine, which burned, phosgene caused no initial pain to the throat and lungs; yet a few breaths were enough to kill a man.

The phosgene inhibited the lungs from expelling water: the more activity a soldier carried out, the quicker his lungs filled up with fluid before he collapsed and died.[6] After the gas began to take effect, the victims looked much like soldiers affected by chlorine: their fingers and lips turned blue; they gulped short gaspy breaths and expelled gallons of mucous and liquid from their swollen lungs. Not only the men afflicted with such obvious symptoms were in danger: some victims continued to look healthy while their lungs slowly filled with liquid. There were numerous cases like the one reported by British Captain W.R. Adio of the 1st Leicestershire Regiment:

The gas travelled quickly, and was noticed in the support lines, and at Battalion Headquarters before any warning had been received from the front line ... I saw every man in the two companies ... Many of them complained of being short of breath, and feeling, "a bit sore in the chest," but almost without exception they said they were able to "stick it." I returned to Headquarters very pleased with what I had seen ... [when] the men began to go about their duties, some thirty or forty men left the trench to report sick ... by the time they reached the road they were exhausted, and were quite unable to proceed any further. One man feeling fairly well, was filling sand bags, when he collapsed and died suddenly.[7]

The hardships in the trenches were numerous and soldiers lived in squalor and terror. Most men grimly stuck it out and refused to let down their companions, tied by their own beliefs to duty and subject to the ever-present shadow of military law.[8] But with phosgene poisoning, "sticking it out" could now mean a creeping death. Was every soldier who got a whiff of gas to head for the rear? Such a breakdown could destroy the whole fragile system that kept soldiers fighting. As a result, the insidious and deadly nature of phosgene forced the Canadian Corps to react with strict orders to ensure that gas discipline was to be followed.

In a report passed on to the Canadian Corps by Lieutenant Colonel J.H. MacBrien, who was later to become chief of the general staff of the Canadian forces, the corps was urged to strengthen its anti-gas doctrine before it encountered phosgene. In an analysis of British casualties, the report concluded that the P-helmets had worked properly except when "very wet and soaked through," and that human error had caused most casualties. Due to the strength of the wind carrying the gas, some "men were slightly gassed before completing the adjustment of their helmets," while others "were simply not carrying their helmets" when the alarm went off. More frequent drills and the ability to don one's gas helmet within fifteen seconds were called for, but the more difficult questions of what gas smelled like, how to know when it had fully dissipated, or what to do with wounded men, were still left to individual officers to decide rather than articulated in a centralized doctrine. One day after the gas attack, corps headquarters ordered that two men from each battalion were to be in charge of the Vermorel sprayers and anti-gas equipment. More important, in January the Second British Army commander instructed the Canadian Corps to prepare three non-commissioned officers (NCOs) from each division to be sent to Army Headquarters, where the Army Chemical Advisor would direct them in anti-gas defence.[9] Although it was intended that these NCOs were to form a nucleus for anti-gas defence, they did not make any impression on their very large divisions, partly because of their lack of resources and organizational structure but also because of their low rank. Very few generals or brigadiers paid much attention to an NCO advising them to devote more resources for a new doctrine of gas training. Although the Canadian Corps thus attempted to gain some control over the protection of its troops in the gas war, there remained a great deal of uncertainty at Headquarters and among the men in the trenches. Making sure one carried one's helmet to the latrine or being able to gauge the strength of the wind became factors that weighed heavily on each man at the front, as no one knew when or where the gaseous death would next strike.

The development of the defensive gas doctrine was essential for teaching soldiers how to survive in the increasingly chemically saturated battlefield. But doctrine does not evolve in a straight course, always building on past experiences. It can leap frog, converge, or diverge along separate paths, sometimes taking illogical or damaging turns. It does so because, although one person or agency attempts to instigate the set of rules, there are always many factors working against the process. Institutional and national learning styles and traits, rivalries and jealousy, lack of materials or resources, and an assortment of inhibiting external factors common in war – everything from the enemy's actions to moral pressure from the home front – affect the outcome and form the fluid nature and relationship of war, weapons, technology, doctrine, and men. It was in this conflicting environment that the Gas Services eventually had to carve out a workable doctrine.

When the Canadians in 1915 spent their first Christmas in the trenches, there was no fraternization with the enemy as there had been in some celebrated cases a year earlier. After the German use of gas at Ypres, reinforced in their minds by the recent phosgene attack, one Canadian officer grimly remarked that there "will be none of that this year for two reasons – One is that fraternizing with the enemy is forbidden and nobody wants to shake hands with the blighters anyway."[10] The men in the trenches were not about to thank the Germans for their added discomfort and the ever-present spectre of gas.

Following the terrible casualties involved in the Allies' failures to crack the German lines in 1915, the British War Office asked Canada to contribute another division to the Canadian Corps. The 3rd Division came into being in December 1915 and was ready for combat by March 1916. It was commanded by Major-General M.S. Mercer, a regular British officer who was former commander of the 1st Division's 1st Brigade. By the end of January 1916, there were 50,000 Canadian troops in the field. The Canadian Corps was once again deployed south of the Ypres salient. Not content to simply man the bulwarks, the Canadians continued to harass the German lines with trench raids, for which they were recognized by Haig in a 19 May 1916 dispatch.[11] The dominion colonials also worked toward improving their gas discipline in preparation for the day when they would hear the enemy's canisters being let loose.

A 9 January 1916 order from British High Command authorized individual officers and battalion commanders to practise gas warnings as well as to conduct investigations into how to notify those in the rear during a gas attack. Although it was not a formal order, the need for more efficient alarms had been illustrated by the December phosgene attack, when trench sentries, who without training were doubling as gas sentries, could not arouse the sleeping infantry before the cloud had overtaken the line. The sentries had been told to blow bugles to warn those in reserve. Yet due to the quickness of the gas, they were forced to don their gas helmets and thus were unable to sound the warning for troops in reserve, who woke up to find they were about to be or had been poisoned. There simply was not enough time for the gas sentries to blow their bugles to wake up their companions and to get their own gas helmets on.[12] The Canadians, realizing this failure in the British alarm system, attempted to devise their own.

Canadian staff officers puzzled over how to create an effective gas alarm. Within the first months of 1916, they had ordered that both divisions be issued electronic klaxon horns, six to the 1st Division and nine to the 2nd. The fog-horn sound, which could be heard up to a mile in the rear, was to be regarded as indicating an imminent gas attack, and all helmets were to be immediately adjusted. Along with the horns, individual battalions set up gas alarms made from whatever could be found within the trenches. Pots and pans were slammed together and shell cases were frenziedly banged to arouse exhausted soldiers. Canadian infantryman Alexander McClintock described his unit's crude anti-gas system: "hanging on a string, at the elbow of each sentry on the fire-step was a siren whistle or an empty shell case and bit of iron [with] which to hammer on it" if gas were seen coming over.[13] Such improvised gas alarms were useful for the front trenches, but during a prolonged artillery barrage (which usually accompanied gas attacks) they were usually drowned out. Thus, although there were not nearly enough horns for the entire area covered by a division's frontage, this problem was addressed by the additional precaution of creating a special Alert Zone.

The Canadian Corps Headquarters, which still did not have a separate gas section, was to advise divisional staff when the wind was blowing favourably (less than fifteen miles per hour) for the Germans to release a gas attack. All battalions in the Alert Zone (usually three miles back from the front line) were to have "gas guards" posted, were to "thin out areas of line which were very close to the Germans," and were to force the infantry to "travel or sleep with their gas helmets within reach at all times." Behind the Alert Zone came the Ready Zone (from three to eight miles to the rear), where all soldiers were to be aware of the possible use of gas, but were not forced to keep their gas helmets in the alert position. Despite these precautions, erected along the major trenches to the front lines were sign posts demanding that soldiers be alert. One read: HAVE YOU GOT IT? / YOUR BOX RESPIRATOR / IN THE ALERT POSITION.[14]

By having higher formations tell them when everyone had to be ready to expect gas, the Alert Zone removed some of the burden from front-line officers, who were saddled with having to cope with gas while knowing very little about it. Integrated into a system that also called for practice drills and shared knowledge, the Alert Zone provided psychological safety to the soldiers who knew that they had to be ready for gas when the alert was ordered. It allowed them some relief from constant apprehension about gas attacks. More important, without the zone, they would not have been as equipped to deal with the quick flowing poisonous vapours when they came. If a gas attack were observed, front-line companies used klaxon horns, wireless radio, or flares to warn their battalions, who in turn warned the next higher echelon, with the alarm rising up to division level if necessary. As one Canadian machine-gunner noted in a letter to his mother about his role as "gas-guard": "it's among the German refinements of this war that we can never lie down within a mile of the line save under protection of a guard lest we be gassed in our sleep."[15] It was a heavy responsibility for the exhausted and frightened soldiers, and of course with the real alarms came the annoyance of false ones.

With exhausted sentries, left alone to guard a section of the trench in the dead of night, nerves straining for fear of being snatched or dispatched by German raiders, there were invariably false alarms. The Canadian official historian, G.W.L. Nicholson, depicted the psychological strain of gas alarms: "There [were] as many as three in a single night. It mattered little that these might be false alarms: there would be a general stand-to, and all had to pull on their gas helmets and wear them in discomfort for upwards of an hour at a time."[16]

Sleep was a precious commodity on the Western Front, and all soldiers in the front lines suffered from the lack of it; men were known to grab it anywhere they could, by curling up in the side of a trench wall or even while waiting in line for dinner. British trench warrior C.E. Montague wrote this of the man in the trenches: "For most of his time the average private was tired ... If a company's trench strength was low and sentry-posts abounded more than usual in its sector, a man might, for eight days running, get no more than one hour off duty at any one time, day or night. If enemy guns were active many of these hours off guard duty might have to be spent on trench repair ... So most of the privates were tired the whole of the time; sometimes to the point of torment, sometimes much less, but always more or less tired."[17]

One result of soldiers being constantly exhausted was, as one Canadian Brigade report indicated, that there was great difficulty in waking the sleeping men, as "this duty cannot be rapidly carried out" due to their debilitated state. Any disruption of sleep was despised; as one Canadian wrote in his diary: "I was awakened by a hideous row made by Klaxon Horns, bells, gongs, etc., and men calling 'gas.' Of course, we all had to get up and dress and get our ready gas helmets within easy reach. It was a false alarm, however, and in a little we went back to sleep. Naturally everyone hates gas, and when the wind is with the Germans, as it nearly always is in fine weather, the whole army has to keep on the 'Qui vive.'"[18]

The stress of the blaring and clanging anti-gas horns was truly shocking. Private R.A. Rigsby, a signaller in the 47th Battalion, remembered the terror of being woken out of a dead sleep by a gas alarm, only to reach for his respirator and find that someone else had snatched it.[19] Despite the false alarm, he did not return to sleep that night. The disruption of gas alarms was just another in a long string of reasons why the infantry hated gas. It continued to wear down the already exhausted soldiers at the front, plaguing them during the day and even in their sleep.

As the Canadians struggled to instigate an effective system of gas defence, the British were creating an organizational structure of control. Transferred from the director-general of Medical Services, the British Gas Services were formally established as a distinct entity under Major-General H.F. Thuillier in January 1916. Colonel C.H. Foulkes continued to retain control over the Gas Companies and attack operations while Dr. S.L. Cummins of the Royal Army Medical Corps was appointed to organize the defensive aspects of the gas war.[20] Under a central authority the Gas Services hoped to craft and refine both the offensive and defensive aspects of gas warfare. Still, although a structure was in place there was no effective means of working with lower command structures and especially in actively training the soldier at the front.

VERDUN AND THE INTRODUCTION OF LETHAL GAS SHELLS

In long wars, both sides tend to leapfrog each other technologically; but with gas warfare, a decidedly different pattern emerged. The Germans almost exclusively introduced new and deadlier gases, while the Allies were forced to react against them by devising the opposing protective gas mask. This trend reflected Germany's initial advantage of having large chemical industries to augment this type of warfare, while the British and French were forced to catch up.

For the short term, the expanded Canadian Corps remained unscathed by any large-scale German gas attacks, as the wind was generally blowing against the German lines from the Canadian positions. That did not stop the use of lachrymatory gas shells, a terrible annoyance that only added to the misery of the exhausted infantry. As one Canadian recounted in a letter home, "The Huns sent over a bunch of Lyddite shells the other night and it is fierce stuff. The stuff is not poisonous but makes your eyes smart and run water. It will blind you for a couple of hours if you get much of it."[21] Many of the Canadian infantry, abhorring their gas helmets, continued to simply use their gas goggles (which were separate from their helmets) to ward off the tearing effects of the lachrymatory gas shells. In the winter of 1915-6 the gas war consisted of chlorine and phosgene gas clouds and various types of largely ineffective tear-gas shells. But all sides anticipated an increase in the use and lethality of battlefield gases.

As the Canadians continued to hold their sector south of the Ypres salient near the ruins of St. Eloi, the Germans launched a massive campaign against the French at Verdun. The success of Hindenburg and Ludendorff on the Eastern Front in virtually destroying two Russian armies at Tannenburg, the failure of the Allies at Gallipoli, and the removal of Serbia from the war left General Falkenhayn ready to engage in a major offensive. Understanding the true nature of the new warfare, Falkenhayn decided to annihilate the French army and "bleed it white" in a battle of attrition. His plan was to attack in the direction of Verdun and destroy the French Army as it counter-attacked time and time again to retake the valued ground. On 21 February under a blizzard of steel the Germans launched the operation in what was to become one of the bloodiest battles of the war.

J.F.C. Fuller, British military writer and proponent of tank and gas warfare, wrote that "weapons, if only the right ones can be found, constitute ninety-nine percent of victory." Gas had already shown it could be a deadly if not decisive weapon. Could it be improved to deliver final victory? The British, more interested in keeping up the steady demand for high-explosive shells and having the wind at their backs, decided to stick to gas cloud attacks released from stationary canisters. By contrast, the French and German commanders quickly became disenchanted with large-scale cloud attacks, and moved toward developing lethal gas shells that could be fired from artillery and thus be independent of the wind.[22] The French were wary of the gas indiscriminately killing their countrymen trapped behind enemy lines, and the Germans realized that the natural prevailing winds were more often than not against them. With more dangerous gases and more advanced delivery systems, both sides attempted to catch each other off guard and exploit the situation before a new gas mask or filter could be introduced to counter the advantage.

During the massive artillery duels that characterized the battle of Verdun, lethal gas shells were introduced for the first time in the war. Up to now, gas clouds had not only been visible but also audible when the canisters were opened and the chemical liquid hissed forth to cool and turn into gas. The lethal gas shell – introduced by the French but quickly perfected by the Germans – not only facilitated a deadlier gas war but made it more prevalent in the later stages of the war.[23] The use of gas shells, although directly contravening the 1907 Hague Convention, was accepted without the slightest protest. As soldiers encountered gas more frequently, it was transformed from a terror weapon to one viewed with antipathy and caution based on learned experience. This change in perception, moreover, was directly linked to chemical shells turning gas warfare into a more lethal and common occurrence.

With the development of lethal shells filled with diphosgene and marked with a Green Cross on the head, the Germans inflicted on the French large-scale gas bombardments, such as the one at Fleuy on 22 June 1916 when 110,000 gas rounds were fired in six hours. When the shells began to land among the French gunners, they barely realized what was happening. There was no massive chemical cloud rolling toward them, merely shells that hit the ground with a soft "plop" – the same sound dud shells made when they hit the ground. By the time the soldiers had donned their masks it was often too late. Even a small dose was enough to affect a man. Gun crews were reduced to one or two men, many of them tinted green like the corpses around them.[24] The Germans had achieved an enormous tactical success over the French artillery, but it was not enough to allow the German infantry to capture Verdun. The lessons learned at Verdun proved that gas shells were more effective in deterring enemy batteries than in clearing safe passage through the entrenched front lines. They could, however, still be devastating when used against the dug-in infantry.

After initial, withering losses, the French artillery grasped the use of gas and retaliated against the German attack with its own lethal shells. *Frontsoldaten* Arnold Zweig had been stunned by high explosives and then gassed by a French shell:

> I had been choked by the poisonous gases; and, subjectively speaking, I was dead. So long as a man can feel fear, it's awful – you gasp for air and breathe in more and more of the poisonous muck, your gullet burns, and there's a roaring in your ears; but oblivion was deliverance ... I never want to be hanged, and I never want to be choked, and I'll never turn on the gas tap. The very thought of a gas attack makes me vomit. No, a shell-splinter in the head, or a clean shot through the heart – that's good enough for me.[25]

The Germans held the upper hand in the gas war, but it was not their exclusive domain. As gas became more common on the battlefield and no longer entirely reliant on the weather, all soldiers had to be trained in how to avoid becoming victims.

With gas masks becoming more efficient, it only followed that gas tactics would also have to improve or change their objectives. In an attempt to make the enemy more hesitant in putting on their masks, gas shells were concealed. One could not wear a mask all the time, so the goal would be to hit the enemy when they were unaware – at night or under an HE bombardment when they had other concerns to worry about.

Gas was not the most deadly weapon in the Great War: the massive HE bombardments were the greatest killers, causing close to 60 percent of all wounds.[26] During one bombardment, Robert Graves was stunned by a close-hitting shell: "My ears sang as though there were gnats in them, and a bright scarlet light shone over everything. My shoulder got twisted in falling and I thought I had been hit, but I hadn't been. The vibrations made my chest sing, too, in a curious way, and I lost my sense of equilibrium. I was ashamed when the sergeant-major came along the trench and found me on all fours, still unable to stand up straight."[27]

As the infantry were being thrown left and right, up and down, having their bowels liquify and their brains numbed, a few well-placed lethal shells could wipe out a whole company.[28] The concussions of the large shells were known to kill men simply from the shock. Victor Wheeler, a signaller for the 50th

Battalion, remembered how the "explosions made it difficult to keep the respirators between our teeth, and in many instances respirators were blown completely off our faces."[29] As well, HE shelling following lethal gas shell bombardments was common: soldiers gassed by phosgene or diphosgene would be forced to move about, thereby causing their lungs to fill up with their own fluids. The mixture of HE and gas shells was a deadly combination that would be exploited by both the Germans and the Allies to confuse the enemies' infantry and artillery.

The smell of the gas was one of the methods by which soldiers distinguished between HE and gas shells. The soldiers figured out and were told by their officers that phosgene by itself smelled like ripe corn or musty hay. Of course this was a good warning if one were sitting on one's back porch, but in the middle of an artillery duel in No Man's Land, the pervading smell of garbage and rotting corpses could dampen even the most distinguished olfactory sense. Soldiers could not rely solely on their sense of smell and had to be constantly alert. L.W. Burns of the 44th Canadian Battalion was employed as a stretcher-bearer and was in the process of carrying a wounded mate back to the rear when he heard a shell coming: "Then we heard a thud. I said to the other guy, 'Oh, hell, it's just a dud.' So we picked the stretcher up and started to walk. Then we smelled gas ... We put the respirator on the wounded man, then we put them on ourselves. But it was too late for us and too late for the wounded man for we had all inhaled the gas. We finally got him in and laid him down. Then we both collapsed."[30] Soldiers were forced to cock an ear and pay attention to the most minute details. A discoloured patch in a shell hole or a tickling in the back of one's throat, if ignored, could lead to an agonizing death.

One of the ingenious methods through which soldiers tested to see if they had been gassed was the "tobacco reaction." Cigarettes, even more so than rum, were the distraction of choice for the infantry in the trenches, and almost everyone smoked.[31] One of the indications of phosgene poisoning was a strange taste to the tobacco. It certainly must have been a shock to any soldier who took his first intake of smoke only to find that it had an acrid flavour. The soldiers learned to adapt, but gas from shells that insidiously landed behind the lines could elude gas sentries and be difficult to detect until it was too late.

With the arrival of the gas shell, the chance of encountering gas rose dramatically. The development of the projectile shell allowed chemical agents to be delivered more accurately and during adverse weather conditions. No longer was gas reliant on exhausted infantrymen arduously bringing up metal canisters or on the direction or strength of the wind; shells could be fired at any time and allowed for greater tactical mobility. Shells could be employed by commanders wishing to use gas in some coherent tactical operation in combination with other arms of the military. This new flexibility allowed gas to be subservient to the infantry rather than the other way around. Although the dense gas clouds from canisters and later projectors were deadlier and inflicted more casualties because of their high concentrations, gas shells were more effective in causing a constant trickle of casualties as well as psychologically harassing all soldiers at the front.

Haig was impressed with the potential of the gas shell, especially after the débâcle at Loos. On 16 May 1916 he demanded the production of 40,000 rounds within the next month and 10,000 rounds per week thereafter. Unfortunately, such a request was out of the question, for the British munitions industry was still desperately trying to meet the demand for HE shells. By the end of 1916, Britain possessed only 160,000 gas shells and discharged less than one-third of its toxic gases by artillery. The Germans, French, Austrians, Hungarians, Italians, and even the Russians, by contrast, used artillery to deliver 75 percent of their gas.[32]

Although Loos had led many commanders to question the role of poison gas, General Haig continued to see gas as an effective weapon, another tool in his arsenal to wear down the enemies' morale. This was the cornerstone of his strategy for winning the war – a policy of attrition that would steadily exhaust the enemy until a final decisive blow could be delivered. Haig's seemingly inhumane policy, so heavily criticized over the years, was not as clear-cut as is sometimes flippantly recorded by historians. The Great War could not be won on the cheap, and by end of 1915 all sides had realized that. It would be a brutal slogging match between titans; and because each side could afford it, millions of men would be expended until the armies disintegrated under the strain. High-explosive bombardments and infantry assaults were the key to breaking the enemy, but Haig also realized that poison gas could also weaken morale and hasten the decisive blow. That this strategy took three more years was partly the responsibility of a failure in tactics and command in the British Expeditionary Force, but much more it was the nature of trench warfare that blocked all attempts to introduce manoeuvres and instead forced battering frontal assaults. As is sometimes forgotten, the Last Hundred Days gave some vindication to Haig's strategy of attrition – a strategy that incorporated poison gas into the push to victory.

THE BATTLE OF THE CRATERS AND
ESCALATION OF THE GAS WAR: APRIL 1916

As the battle for Verdun raged on, the 2nd Canadian Division was mauled at the beginning of April in the ill-fated battle of the St. Eloi Craters. Displaying a high level of confusion and incompetence, the 2nd Division's staff officers, led by Sir Richard Turner as division commander, caused needless casualties among their own men when they failed to prepare and support front-line troops, who were found to be holding the wrong trenches. It was a case of the "blind leading the blind." By the time the fighting died down on 19 April, the 2nd Division had suffered 1,373 casualties and even greater embarrassment as a result of the inadequacies displayed by Turner and his brigadiers. Many senior commanders believed that he should be let go, but due to political meddling, Turner was retained and the British-born corps commander, General Alderson, was replaced by General Julian Byng, also British. As embarrassing as the affair was, the Canadian infantrymen in the trenches, suffering under the German onslaught for more than two weeks, remembered St. Eloi as nothing more than a "murder hole."[33]

Recently equipped with newly issued PH-helmets, which gave better protection against phosgene than P-helmets had, the Canadian Corps continued to hold the area around St. Eloi. On the night of 27 April, the Germans released a gas cloud against the Canadian lines.[34] With the squealing and rush of whirling bodies, thousands of rats scurried over to the Canadian lines, falling in the frightened soldiers' faces and laps, as they instinctively fled from the poison following them. A light chlorine gas cloud moved through the Canadian lines, but the men were able to withstand it, having been roused by alarms, rats, and shouts of fear. Even though they could barely see through their clouded-over plastic eyepieces, they beat back a small raiding party of Germans. The shock of the rats and gas combined with the adrenaline rush of defending a trench against enemy attackers left the Canadian defenders drained as they slumped to the ground, smoking cigarettes or sleeping. Within minutes the Germans released a second gas cloud, which was "very thick," catching many Canadians who had "thrown their helmets away" when they had "thought all was over."[35] Such displays of gross indiscipline testified to the need for constant training. On orders from British Headquarters, all soldiers in the Alert Zone were to wear their gas helmets rolled up on their heads during a gas warning. This was to become a hated precaution among infantrymen, who were dismayed at being forced to wear a medicated bag that burned their eyes and the skin of their foreheads.[36]

Due to the wind patterns, the gas attack had been most effective against the British units to the north of the Canadians, and they suffered 1,260 casualties, of whom 338 died.[37] The total Canadian gas casualties were not recorded, but among them were twenty cases of gassed new recruits who had joined their unit only three days earlier.[38] Although blame can be put on NCOs and junior lieutenants, who did not keep a better eye on the new men, the attack once again showed that it was the inexperienced who were the prime victims of gas. As in all other aspects of the war, soldiers required time to learn how to survive the gas war. As one artillery officer remarked, "Green troops always hated gas. Our first gas alerts were the worst." G.V. Francoeur of the 22nd Battalion concurred and noted that "new men were always getting killed within a week and we always said that if they could go through the first ten days, they were alright."[39]

Although it was clear that new troops were the most susceptible to the effects of gas, it was not decided until later in the war to devote more training to them. At this stage, green recruits' knowledge of the gas war came only from what they heard through rumours. Their more seasoned comrades generally offered insight into the "tricks of the trade" but some took perverse pleasure in giving the rookies a hard time. One malicious veteran was caught spreading rumours that, among other nasty things, gas "made [soldiers'] eyes drop out of their sockets or their fingers and toes drop off." Such thoughts were certainly not comforting to new men, and one sergeant-major was so afraid of gas that "on his first trip into the line [he] slept all night in his gas mask."[40]

Examining the ground following the gas attack revealed an absolute desolation. Whatever had been living in the area was dead; the gas had extinguished every living thing in its path. Small animals, including rats and even snails, were lying in various positions of death. The ground was a wasteland with all foliage turned brown and yellow. There was truly no place to hide.

THE GAS DEFENCE GETS STRONGER

Following the chaos of the April gas attack, the First Army ordered the Canadian Corps on 23 May 1916 to appoint a divisional gas officer (DGO) – the catalyst in the creation of the Canadian Gas Services. The order proclaimed that as a result of the increased use of gas by the Germans, "it has become necessary to decentralize the work of instruction in preventive measures against gas."[41] Prior to this each British Army had a chemical advisor, but he was hamstrung in his ability to administer the developing anti-gas doctrine as a result of being stationed at Army Headquarters in the rear and unable to associate with any of the troops in the line. As a 1916 Canadian manual on trench warfare tactics lamented:

> The more recent developments of trench warfare have introduced so many new conditions and surrounded us with an environment so entirely novel and unexpected that ideas tend to become fogged and the most nebulous and contradictory opinions exist with regard to the minor tactics of the form of trench warfare. Many who by their training and experience are fitted to make valuable deductions from these experiences, can only by the very nature of their duty obtain them at second hand; while of those who do obtain this experience at first hand, many are unable to make any such deductions, while of those who could so few return to tell the tale that little or no progress is gained towards the general elucidation of these problems.[42]

Mirroring the necessity of understanding the nature of trench warfare, gas imposed the same restrictions on trench warriors and staff officers in the rear.

The resulting contradictions required a new organization that was equipped to deal with the problems in the trenches as well as to instigate and enforce reactive policies to deal with it.

The initial Canadian DGOs had been trained in one of the four British Army gas schools and in turn were ordered to organize divisional gas schools in which to disseminate information to the division's officers and NCOs. The DGO gave lectures and demonstrations to the troops on defensive gas measures, was responsible for anti-gas appliances, inspected the troop's gas helmets, and gave advice for the protection of dugouts. Working in conjunction with the divisional commanders, the gas officers were to fashion an anti-gas doctrine for their men. In the Canadian Corps the introduction of the DGO signalled a major change in gas training: now there were officers who could actually carry out some of the orders passed from the army chemical advisor – or develop some of their own initiatives. Yet creating a defensive line was not an easy task, as unsophisticated youths poured into the army from all walks of civilian life; as one gas officer remarked, "gas was mysterious enough, but add to it the word chemical, and it became hopelessly beyond ... their conception." It was the difficult and often unrewarding job of the DGOs to make the intangibles of gas relevant to the soldier before he experienced them himself in a life-or-death situation. The gas schools were allotted only one gas instructor, two sergeants, and a clerk to carry out the enormous task of training a 15,000-man division, but it was, nonetheless, a beginning.[43]

The doctrine of gas defence worked its way backward from the front. The men in the trenches with urine-soaked rags had instigated the first effective anti-gas defence. But as gas became deadlier and more frequent on the Western Front, organizations of anti-gas defence became necessary. The events at the front drove the need to react from the rear. Originally soldiers had haphazardly picked up their anti-gas training in the trenches from the "old hands" of the battalion. As a system of gas defence began to form, the initial training of the soldiers moved out of the trenches. Such systematic training was geared to reducing the withering casualties among the untrained, but it also recognized that those well-versed in gas could fall victim because of a panicky companion as well. For instance, it was not uncommon, as one American report noted, for untrained men to go "out of their head," flail around, and thereby "knock off the masks of others."[44] However, because the use of gas was still sparse in the first months of 1916, the development of an anti-gas doctrine was a slow process. If gas were rarely used, there was little need for an efficient system. But with the advent and more frequent employment of gas shells, anti-gas training and good discipline were necessary before the soldiers entered the front lines.

The most important aspect of the gas training revolved around faith. Soldiers had to believe in their masks, and they had to believe that they could function in them. Gas was a physical and psychological weapon; if the average soldier did not think that he could survive in the growing gas environment of the Western Front, then he would not. Brigadier W.A. Griesbach was thinking of the Ross rifle, but it was equally applicable to the soldier and his gas mask, when he wrote: "It may be fairly stated that it doesn't make much difference whether a military weapon is good, bad or indifferent. If the men who have to use it all agree in thinking that it is bad, and that a better weapon can be had, the time has come for a change. This involves a question of morale, the most delicate and intangible of military factors." This question of morale was imperative for defeating the friction imposed by gas, and although weapons like the Colt machine gun or Ross rifle could be replaced by better ones, the gas mask could not. All gas masks – although some more than others – were off-putting, stifling, and exhausting to wear; but there was no other choice. To remove them meant death.[45]

In order to assist in anti-gas training, the position of brigade gas officer (BGO) was created. The BGOs were attached to their respective brigades and were given the authority to travel freely into the front lines to check on gas defences and discipline. The DGOs also ordered that all infantry and artillery officers would eventually have to attend a three-day course in gas instruction at the gas schools in order to better understand the role of gas on the battlefield and how to protect the soldiers under their command. The DGOs further decentralized the system in an effort to train one NCO from each infantry company, battalion machine-gun section, engineer field-company, battery of artillery, and signal section to enforce gas discipline for those troops in the line.[46] The gas NCOs were to carry out, among other things, gas drills, inspection of gas helmets and appliances, assistance to officers during gas alerts, and supervision of filling gas shell holes with mud. Part of what made the job attractive to some men was the order that they be "given the opportunity for the carrying out of their gas duties" without interference from other trench chores.[47] Thus, the hatred of gas was weighed against the expediency of not having to conduct night patrols or arrange working parties.

Such inducements were not always good enough for men who did not want to be associated in any way with gas and thus be segregated from their companions. Lieutenant Wright of the 4th Battalion, for example, fought "tooth and nail" against being appointed a gas officer. Eventually he was dismissed from the role after "insulting the colonel every day until he let me go."[48] Although still distrusted by most of the infantry, the new gas officers began to build an anti-gas discipline, which had been very difficult when there was no one and no place from which the information could be issued and explained to officers who were to carry out the orders. The divisional gas schools and the men trained in them were beginning to bring some control to the inherent chaos introduced by the gas war.

CANADIANS GASSED AGAIN: MOUNT SORREL, JUNE 1916

The Canadian Corps continued to be entrenched around Ypres. Within the sector the newly arrived 3rd Canadian Division held Mount Sorrel, the only British-held ridge left in the Ypres sector that gave an advantageous view over the German lines. The Germans remained busy during May by constantly harassing the Canadian lines with artillery fire and the occasional tear-gas attack. In late May the Canadian Corps received a pamphlet from General Headquarters entitled, "Defensive Measures against Gas Attacks." It described how to keep gas helmets in working condition and the importance of wind observation and general precautions against gas attacks. But most important was the need "to inspire confidence" in the troops to withstand gas.

After the introduction of efficient gas masks, the nature of the gas war was becoming not one of killing and maiming (although it was warned that this would certainly happen if gas discipline were not enforced), but rather a psychological battle in which soldiers had to believe that their helmets would save them.[49] As the gas war intensified, there was a marked tone of desperation in the countless reports, orders, and gas pamphlets issued by High Command and the Gas Services. All such gas orders contained within them some reference to "informing the troops that their gas helmets or masks are perfect protection against the gas." This constant reference came from the same officers who realized that the gas war could only be partly contained and never beaten.

With the 3rd Canadian Division holding the remaining high ground in the Ypres salient, the trenches of Mount Sorrel quickly gained the reputation, in the language of the soldiers, as "the dirtiest bit of the line."[50] Shallow and muddy, the trenches were known to attract artillery fire from three sides, as the whole position jutted out into the German-held lines. While the newly arrived Canadians learned the nuances of surviving on the Western Front, the forward battalions were attacked in a whirlwind blitz of high explosives and gas on 2 June 1916. The War Diary of the 4th Canadian Mounted Rifles recorded that the "bombardment increased, and we were bombarded in the front line, supports and reserves, by thousands of shells of every description." On the ridge of Mount Sorrel, "whole sections [of trenches] simply vanished, and the garrisons in them were annihilated." The battalions holding the line were decimated. In the 4th Canadian Mounted Rifles (CMR) they suffered an 89 percent casualty rate: only seventy-three of the original men answered the muster roll the next morning.[51] Although the 4th CMR took the full force of the assault, other Canadian battalions suffered heavy casualties as well, with General Mercer, commander of the division, killed while reconnoitring the front lines.

In the barrage, tear and lethal gas shells were interspersed in order to force the Canadian infantry to wear their debilitating gas masks; the infantry at the front and those that later marched forward to reinforce the remaining trenches undertook their already difficult tasks with clouded vision and strained breath.[52] Sergeant J.A. Caw of the 5th Battalion wrote in a letter home that "Gas alarms were the thing of the day, and, believe me, it is not pleasant business to 'stand to' with gas helmets on for a matter of two hours or so, every minute expecting the Boches to come over. They gave us all kinds of tear gas, and at the end of the week my eyes began to feel as if they were stuck on the end of poles like crabs' eyes." The Germans were planning not only to wear down the fighting strength of individual men in the line, but also to deluge the rear areas to sow confusion there. A.Y. Jackson, who shortly after the war helped to form the famous Group of Seven painters, remembered that the Germans "soaked the whole country with gas" and that, as a result, his unit was late in counter-attacking. Another Canadian, one of the casualties of the gas, Private W.G. Winslow, was only sixteen years old when he was wounded, gassed, and taken prisoner. He survived the war and returned to Canada only to die at the age of twenty-three from tuberculosis, diagnosed as being brought on by the effects of his gassing.[53] The German use of gas shells was not concentrated, but many fell victim nonetheless. After being driven from the position, the Canadians failed to recapture the lost ground in a hastily prepared counter-attack that night.

Yet the Canadians refused to be cowed, and on 13 June the 1st Division retook Mount Sorrel in the first in a long string of victorious set-piece battles where the infantry advanced behind a smoke and artillery bombardment. At 2.05 a.m., a message was dispatched to the 1st Brigade by the 3rd Battalion: "We have Mount Sorrel."[54] The Germans viciously counter-attacked with infantry, artillery, and gas, but the Canadians were not to driven off the position again. The Canadian trenches were in terrible shape, caved in and inundated with corpses. It was only with luck that Private George Wadsworth of the 15th Battalion was found, unconscious and bright green, three days after being gassed.[55] Countless other Canadians were wounded, and later gassed, as they lay helpless and unconscious. One such example, Private Diggle, an ammunition driver for the Reserve Brigade of the Canadian Field Artillery, was thrown from his wagon, lost twenty teeth, and woke up to find he had been gassed.[56]

On the night of 16 June the Germans unleashed another gas-cloud attack against the Canadian Corps, but once again failed to dislodge them. T.B. Smith, an orderly with the First Canadian Casualty Clearing Station, recalled that there were so many gassed casualties that they could not fit into the hospital, so two hundred were placed outside the building. "By 8:30 am on the 18th 645 cases had been admitted, of whom some 420 were gassed ... Forty of them died." In afterbattle reports it was noted that the infantry should be equipped with gas-proof dugouts in order to escape from the worst of the gas attacks. As well, because the Germans had increased the concentration of the cloud attack, some wearers of the PH-helmet could take in oxygen only if they stayed absolutely still and did not exert themselves.[57] The gas war was intensifying in its role and scope, but the additional gas training had helped keep the gas from crippling the 3rd Division. Yet it remained that this division, following the pattern of the first two, experienced a harsh initiation to the grim reality of the Western Front.

THE BLOODY SOMME: JULY 1916

As the slaughter at Verdun raged on, the French government pleaded with Haig to launch an attack in order to relieve the pressure on their armies. Upon General Joffre's suggestion, the British general looked to the Somme area in which to achieve his breakthrough. Haig and his staff officers hoped that a massive barrage would annihilate the German defenders so that the infantry could simply walk over and occupy the trenches, with his cavalry driving through to exploit the gap. Since Haig's armies were, in the words of one general, engaged in "open warfare at the halt," his solution to the stalemate of the Western Front was one word: more. After the failure of the 1915 attacks, it was believed that more men, more guns, and more shells by a factor of three or five, would surely lead to victory. Although it resulted in a terrible blood-letting, leaving the dour general roundly condemned by a whole school of Haig-bashers, he had hit upon the right artillery tactics. As the British armies showed in 1918, massive hurricane bombardments of high explosives, shrapnel, and gas were the key to victory; however, this "storm of steel" was combined with more sophisticated fireplans, near-unlimited shells, accurate counter-battery work based on scientific principles, better intelligence and communications, vastly increased training, and new tactics among the infantry, who attacked in small groups under supporting fire from flanking units. None of this was part of the British attack doctrine in 1916, and they suffered accordingly.

The seven-day bombardment on the German lines before the opening day of battle was the heaviest in the history of warfare. Poison gas was employed to cause further casualties and wear away at the morale of the enemy. Following this policy of massive assault, the barrage was interspersed with various gas discharges to catch the enemy relaxing and recovering in their dugouts from the bleeding ears and the constant concussion of shells. But the thousands of tons of high explosives failed to kill the majority of the German defenders, who were holed up in deep dugouts that could be destroyed only with direct hits.[58] The result was the most infamous event in British military history, the first day of the Somme in July 1916. Within hours of the first troops going over the top in rigidly spaced waves, the BEF suffered 57,470 casualties.[59] The battle raged for another four months – the Canadian Corps would not be sent into the maelstrom until September.

The Somme had failed to be Haig's breakthrough battle. Instead, it had led to grinding, attritional fighting that gobbled up men faster than they could be sent into the line. Although still distrusted by many senior officers, gas remained a key component in wearing down the deeply entrenched defenders. By late July the British Special Gas Companies had released more than fifty separate gas attacks involving 38,500 gas cylinders.[60] Colonel C.H. Foulkes argued that the use of gas, along with the massive artillery barrages, was an excellent precursor to attack, but most line commanders, remembering the débâcle at Loos, refused to allow it be used in conjunction with any large-scale infantry assault. The combined effects of fear and unreliability had a divisional commander bark to a gas captain attempting to organize a canister attack during the Somme campaign: "Take your bloody gas away. I'll have nothing to do with it."[61] Despite his misgivings, gas was still employed; but for the average soldier, gas continued to inspire a mixture of uncertainty and fear, as Captain Geoffrey Boles Donaldson of the Warwickshire Regiment noted when waiting to go over the top on 16 July, just three days before he was killed:

> I can tell you that in that ½ hour before the attack started, I came nearer to "having the wind up" or in other words losing my nerve than has ever been the case before ... At 8.30 pm the show started. I had all the men in the trench out of dugouts and we all had our gas helmets on. It was like an appalling nightmare as you look like some horrible kind of demon or goblin in these masks ... In the next bay to me, one idiot sapper turned the jet in the wrong direction, and filled our trenches with gas.[62]

Regardless of what the infantry thought, the Special Companies continued to release their gas. In this, they generally followed two tactical strategies: the surprise and the wearing-down attack.

The object of the surprise effect was to release all canisters simultaneously and hope that a strong breeze would carry the gas over the enemy lines before they could react. The shape of the cloud leaving the canisters flowed like a wedge cut along its length – the pointed end near the cylinder with the broad end nearest the enemy lines. The gas clouds were not uniform in strength – the edges were less dense then the centre – and the farther away the target the less potent the cloud became. Variations in wind speed, rate of discharge, temperature, precipitation, and terrain also reduced the effectiveness of poison gas. In addition to these considerations, another tactical question of canistered gas was the audible hissing it made when released. To mask this sound and distract the enemy, at the same time as they released their gas the British fired a heavy artillery barrage on the German lines. The British, along with the Germans and French, recognized the importance of releasing gas at night. With the cold air above the warmer soil, the gas hugged the ground in greater concentrations. More important, at night there was a greater chance of causing friction in the enemy's lines as alarms went off, sleeping soldiers lurched to their feet in the dark, and everyone scurried about in fear and disorder.

In conjunction with the tactical surprise was the attritional method of the gas war. If one could not kill the enemy outright, then the other option was to harass him all night to exhaust his fighting efficiency. In such instances, generally five cylinders (as opposed to the regular fifteen to twenty) were discharged in each bay at zero hour, and a continuous discharge of one cylinder per bay was released for an hour following zero hour. Combined with this discharge, smoke was used to prolong the time the enemy spent wearing their masks.[63] When the British interspersed smoke and started and stopped the discharge, the Germans were left with no hope of removing their suffocating masks and were forced to wait in dreadful anxiety at the firing line in case troops were following behind the cloud.

The gas specialists closely watching the effects of their gas found that gas and smoke had to be released over a large front so as not to create too small an area within which the German artillery could concentrate its fire. It was eventually decided, after German retaliatory bombardments annihilated the better part of several Special Companies, that the surprise method was more effective than the attrition method. With attrition tactics, the German artillery typically found the British canisters, blowing them open and gassing the specialists and all those around them in the trenches. The infantry were aware of this drawback as well, and when the Special Companies placed canisters in the Canadian lines at the end of July, Victor Wheeler of the 50th Canadian Infantry Battalion fervently wished to get them out of there as quickly as possible before the enemy sent any shells over. Thus, for as long as the British continued to rely on the canister method, they generally refrained from employing the attritional strategy. With fifty chemical cloud releases by the British alone in a little more than a month, the gas war was beginning to develop into a more frequent and deadly occurrence on the Western Front.[64]

Under direct orders from Foulkes, who was constantly attempting to justify the use of gas to those detractors who believed it was both immoral and useless, the British Special Companies had a man present at the interrogation of prisoners in the hope of ascertaining the effects of the British gas discharges on the Germans. The results were not exactly what the gas specialists wanted to hear, as a series of prisoners remarked that on "most fronts [they] had been warned that gas was installed." Captured Somme prisoners reported numerous casualties, but most of them were slight, although one prisoner reported that he had seen two companions dead with their masks on. Gas could also have hidden effects, as one unfortunate prisoner found out. Interrogated by Foulkes, the prisoner ridiculed the ineffectiveness of British gas; twenty-four hours later he was found dead in his cell from the effects of phosgene. Official German reports indicated that the British gas attacks in June were largely ineffective but that they had the serious result of undermining good gas discipline so that later in the battle German soldiers fell victim through carelessness.[65]

In gas discipline the Germans seem to have been comparable to the Canadians, with lectures from anti-gas officers stressing that soldiers should "regard [their] masks as sacred."[66] But in a separate report, a captured German doctor who had worked on poisoned soldiers remarked that the Germans in 1916, "did not realize the danger of exertion in gas cases" and suffered unnecessary casualties among soldiers walking to the rear.[67] Moreover, gas seemed to be an effective psychological weapon: prisoners reported "that they were afraid of gas either as gas [canisters] or in shells." Notwithstanding the caution of prisoners, who often told their captors what they wanted to hear, many captives reflected the statement of one German from the 60th Regiment, who remarked "that the German soldier is sorry that they ever began to use gas, and he had frequently heard that the German Army has come off worst in the gas war."[68] Such sentiments notwithstanding, the Germans continued to hold the upper hand with their lethal gas shells and the failure of the British to develop a better delivery system.

The counterparts of the British gas specialists, the German gas pioneers also attempted to collect information regarding the effectiveness of gas. In a captured German document, German gas specialists claimed to have "killed thirty to thirty-five thousand enemy [soldiers] between March 1915 and August 1916."[69] Although the number was certainly inflated, the German Gas Brigade had killed more men through gas than the British and French combined, due to the success at 2nd Ypres, the four May attacks on the Western Front, and, most important, the wide success of gas on the Eastern Front against the technically inferior Russians. Constantly aware of the necessity of justifying their existence to High Command, both the British and German gas regiments regularly exaggerated the importance of gas, although such inflation was probably due more to wishful thinking and the inherent problems of gauging success from across No Man's Land than to purposeful lying.

Due to the increased us of gas, it became imperative that soldiers be ordered to keep their PH-helmets with them at all times; systematically drill in their use was also implemented. Lieutenant Claude Williams, a nineteen-year-old machine gun officer, remarked in a letter home to his mother that the "whole secret" to the gas helmets was "in breathing properly. If one breathes wrongly[,] one's name may likely come out on the roll of honor [the] next day. One has to breathe through one's teeth and then out through the lips. It is very hard to do at first because one's throat becomes very dry and is irritated. It is a grave temptation to breathe through one's nose. The chemical too makes most sick."[70] Despite the time allotted to properly donning and enduring the strains of the gas helmets, anti-gas discipline was still not firmly established among trench warriors. They may have looked smart on parade, gas helmets at the ready, but without the threat of gas, discipline could degenerate. New units arriving at the Somme quickly realized, however, that to be without a gas helmet at the wrong time could usher in a slow death. Canadian Private Richard Adamson recounted a situation when he was surprised by ringing gas alarms:

> The latrine was located about fifty yards behind the line. I had been foolish enough to leave all my fighting gear in the Front Line including my gas mask. This removal of one's fighting gear in the Front Line area was strictly a "No No" with the Army and if caught without it on we were subject for a court martial. Here I was half undressed and fifty yards away from my gear. I had almost as far to go for my gas mask as the poison gas had to travel. I am sure that I set a new world's record for the fifty yard dash.[71]

Others did not move as fast. Private Donald Fraser, who was later crippled at Passchendaele, wrote in his diary that the Germans had gassed the Imperials near the new Canadian lines and that "It is understood that between 600-700 were gassed, including a working party of about 100 men who were caught unaware a considerable distance from their gas helmets."[72] Because of the infrequent use of gas, the gas discipline of the soldiers was still haphazard; yet with incidents like the above, the persistent training by DGOs and their subordinate

No Man's Land.

gas officers, and, perhaps most important, the obvious increase in the deployment of poison gas, the Canadian soldier was eventually convinced that gas discipline was necessary to keep him alive in trenches increasingly permeated with gas. At this stage, some soldiers of the BEF still remained largely ignorant of gas, but those regiments and divisions that were unable to instill effective gas discipline were liable to be crippled within the later stages of the gas war when chemicals permeated the battlefield.

GAS-TESTING EXERCISES

When the 4th Canadian Division was created in England, its soldiers were given basic anti-gas training, but it proved to be terribly deficient.[73] The 4th Division reached the Canadian Corps in France at the start of August 1916 to receive additional instruction. For training purposes, its brigades were attached to the other Canadian divisions in the line for seven days, and were given "special emphasis on instruction in anti-gas measures." The "special emphasis" was more training than had been allotted to earlier units, but it remained insufficient for the growing gas environment of the Western Front. Each battalion was put through a real gas cloud in an attempt to duplicate battlefield gas conditions. Gisli Norman described the experience: "We were told to under no circumstances breathe except through the masks but two oafs (I suppose they figured to go to some hospital) slipped out of their mouthpieces (by accident they said). They sure were sick. They got away all right but none of us wanted to be in their shoes."[74] This was a terrifying event in a new recruit's training, and men were known to faint as they waited in line for their turn in the gas hut. As one Canadian gunner remarked in a letter home after passing through the gas, "it turned my brass buttons black, destroyed the illuminated dial on my watch and turned my khaki uniform a reddish brown. Say! What would it do to your lungs without protection?" Others, like the unfortunate Private Edward Pett at a gas-testing station at La Havre, had less educational and more tragic experiences: "I was going through a test gas attack and one of the men turned back and I was knocked down and broke the glass in my helmet; I was in the gas for two minutes before I was dragged out."[75] Pett was sent to a hospital, where he developed pneumonia, and was eventually invalided home. Generally, the effects of the first pass through a gas-testing station were not this serious; nonetheless, they were always traumatic, as soldiers were herded into the dark chambers to be enveloped by poison. If the training did not mirror exact front-line situations, it was the beginning of the soldier's faith in his gas mask.

Such events became more common in the infantryman's life later in the war, as more gas-testing stations were created due to the increased frequency of chemical agents. If a soldier were gassed only once every month or two, it was not as important to train him in the use of his helmet rigorously. In fact, there were so few gas shells used against the Canadian infantry that Signaller Ted Garrison of the 44th Battalion had a difficult time convincing his officers and then the doctors of the Canadian Army Medical Corps that he had indeed been gassed in the fighting after Mount Sorrel in the Ypres salient. All of that would soon change. An ominous report issued in August 1916 by the 1st Canadian Division warned the infantry, and especially the artillerymen, that "the enemy now has a very large supply of [lethal gas] shells and uses them extensively against our ... positions."[76] With the increase in the number of gas shells, the Canadians were threatened with a situation where they could be gassed anytime.

The Germans released their last cloud gas attack against the British on the night of 8 August 1916. The 4th and 23rd British Divisions were blanketed by the dense cloud of phosgene and chlorine, which the gas pioneers had timed to arrive when several front-line British battalions were relieving each other. As a result, the exhausted soldiers leaving the front were caught in complete darkness moving to the rear, many with their gas helmets inside their coats or packs. It was later found that some of the inexperienced British Tommies, suffering through their first "real" gas attack and never having worn their gas helmets while marching, in some cases did not understand the ringing alarms and were more concerned with the HE shells falling around them than with getting their PH-helmets on.[77] There were 804 recorded gas casualties that night, and because the Germans had increased the phosgene content of their gas clouds in April 1916 from 20 to 50 percent, 44 percent of those were fatalities.[78] The British generals were shaken by the devastating effects of the German gas, and the attack resulted in a series of orders being passed calling for increased anti-gas training. General Byng, who had received a damning report on the poor gas discipline of some Canadian units, was furious with the apparent "glaring instances of slackness" and commanded that the instruction of gas discipline be intensified. As he stated in an order to all unit commanders, if "this attack had been made on our front the casualties would have been disastrous." More stringent anti-gas measures were immediately introduced within the Canadian Corps regarding increased drill with gas helmets, repeated clarification of the necessity for gas alerts, and the posting of gas sentries. But once again, the process of trench learning was based on past mistakes and lost lives.[79]

Canadians on the Somme: September-November 1916

Ordered to the Somme, the Canadian Corps relieved the 1st Anzac Corps near the Pozières Ridge in early September. In the process, the colonials tried to acquaint themselves with the horrendous battlefield conditions. There had been rumours of the corps being sent to the Somme, and the Canadians had consequently undergone training in open warfare tactics, combining the movement of artillery with quick advancing infantry. Unfortunately, the prospect of fluid, open warfare had long been replaced by ponderous, attritional fighting once the German defenders proved that they would not break. In this wasteland the Canadians faced the constant horror of digging new trenches and uncovering decomposed bodies, turning to a new area and uncovering more. The stench of sitting, sleeping, and shaving on top of rotting flesh was a most trying experience for Canadian infantrymen.[80] They, along with all soldiers at the Somme, were living in an open graveyard.

The Canadian Corps took part in a series of battles: Courcelette, Thiepval Ridge, Regina, and Desire Trench. In numerous instances, the Canadian artillery employed tear-gas (SK, for South Kensington, where it was created) shells in counter-battery work to help get the infantry across the firezone of No Man's Land, but the initial success was often reversed by fierce counterattacks by the Germans, who drove the exhausted and depleted Canadians from their newly won ground.[81] The production of lethal gas shells was still being perfected in England, and no such shells had filtered down to the corps level. This hampered the development of the lethal gas attack doctrine. At the same time, it was discouraging for Canadian infantrymen to find out that their gas caused eyes to water while the German gas burned out the lungs.

To make up for the shortage of lethal gas shells, gas grenades were introduced as an experiment. The White Star hand grenade, filled with a mixture

Canadian soldiers returning from the trenches during the Battle of the Somme.

of chlorine and phosgene, was issued to soldiers for the clearing of dugouts. The infantry's dislike of handling gas, combined with the dubious value of the weapon – explosive grenades were equally effective in "removing occupants" of dugouts without leaving behind a death cloud that took hours to clear – made gas grenades highly unpopular. Dubbed "chemical hates," gas grenades remained a mistrusted weapon and, if possible, unused by the infantry.[82]

The Canadian Corps suffered 24,029 casualties on the Somme; one survivor remarked, "quite a few chaps I knew, have just been missing ever since, never heard of." Colonel Mason of the 3rd Battalion observed how morale was low following the end of the battle, for "we had really been cut to pieces [and there was] not very much of it [the battalion] left." Still, the Canadians had learned from their mistakes. They had shown that they fought tenaciously at the sharp end and often came out on top in battling even the best of the German divisions. In a 5 November 1916 letter home to his aunt, Canadian medical orderly Frank Walker described his impressions on the Somme campaign: "Things are vastly different to what they were when first we came to France. The Germans had it all their own then. They sowed their little wind, and now they're reaping a whirlwind. Canadians have not forgotten Ypres, and the Huns are now paying dearly for everyone they killed with their infernal gas."[83] Even after the hard pounding they endured at the Somme, some Canadians believed that what they inflicted on the Germans was a partial payback for 2nd Ypres.

On the Somme, unlike at Ypres, both sides employed gas with increasing severity. After Verdun the German artillery recognized that gas played an integral part in paralyzing the enemy's guns and getting the infantry across the killing ground of No Man's Land; they had subsequently proposed to create special gas batteries controlled by highly trained staffs. To ensure that the artillery could adapt to various situations, and to prevent the marginalization of gas, the German High Command decided that all gunners should be trained in firing gas shells. Although it would eventually prove to be the right concept in practice, the German batteries had very little guidance in preparing the offensive doctrine of gas, and much of that knowledge went to the grave with the men who had pioneered it at Verdun. This lack of guidance combined with an overestimation of gas's effectiveness, resulting in Green Cross shells not being concentrated enough to cause sufficient casualties. But as the Battle of the Somme petered out, the Germans refined their artillery attack doctrine, and special artillery gas schools were established to study the use of gas.[84]

Looking back on the Somme fighting, American Herbert McBride, who served as a sniper in the 21st Canadian Battalion, remembered that "gas did not cause us any great amount of trouble." Bearing out that observation were the slight casualties among the Canadian Corps – only 180 recorded cases. Although there were no doubt more gas victims who either went unreported or simply died on the battlefield, that figure bothered commanders because it was made up of an excessive number of officers and NCOs. The junior leaders' high casualty rate stemmed from two important tasks they had to carry out. First, amid the confusion of a gas bombardment, officers and NCOs had to rush to and fro making sure that their men had their PH-helmets on and also giving orders to man the parapets and watch for any German attacks. The extreme lethality of phosgene meant that in anything above mild concentrations it could overwhelm the PH-helmet's absorption, and it was necessary for soldiers to be still if they wanted to survive. During the bedlam of a gas attack, those in command, who had to move about rapidly and shout orders, were clearly exposing themselves to the greatest danger from gas. Indeed, one soldier remarked that the officers shouting orders sounded "as if [they were] strangling."[85] As well, many officers thought it beneath themselves to wear the baggy gas helmets, cowering as gas flooded over them. Officers have always had to hold themselves to a higher level of bravery, leadership, and action than the men they command. Perhaps at a deeper level, though, within the hierarchical system of officer and men, when everyone donned a helmet, officers not only lost their uniqueness in appearance but also in action. The gas mask homogenized the men – the leaders were indistinguishable from the led.[86] Whatever the reason, the need for leadership often overpowered any thoughts of self-protection and led officers to remove their gas helmets.

Secondly, it was very difficult to ascertain when the gas had dissipated from an area, especially when one was wearing cloudy gas goggles and was surrounded by smoke in an area under fire. The common practice was for officers and NCOs to lift their gas helmets and sniff the air. Of course this rarely worked, because the chemical smell of the PH-helmet itself and the smell of gas permeating one's clothing warped any such olfactory test for lingering gas.[87] Caring for their men, many officers took off their helmets completely and were occasionally gassed.[88] The friction caused by gas directly resulted in the loss of many officers and NCOs, just the men who could not be replaced, thereby reducing the efficiency of whole fighting units.

The chief victims of gas on the Somme, besides officers and NCOs, were the animal transports of the Canadian divisional trains. Horses were gassed as they brought up food and ammunition to the troops in the line. Tactically the Germans had hit upon two important aspects of the new gas war at Verdun and the Somme: the use of shells against artillery batteries and the disruption of the lines of communication behind the trenches. Enemy infantry could not break through one's line without artillery support and supplies. Therefore, the use of gas shells to disrupt and injure gunners, drivers, and horses was an indirect but very effective way of spoiling any such breakthrough. The effects of the various chemical agents was felt by the Canadian Army Service Corps, which had one in seven casualties fall victim to gas by the end of the war.[89] With additional and varied tactical applications, German commanders realized the potential for gas to be a useful addition to their arsenals, and one captured German document forced a BEF-wide warning that enemy "future bombardments with Gas Shell[s] will probably be prolonged and concentrated." The powerful German ammunition and chemical industry was eager and able to respond to the army's plan for more gas, and the resultant output of gas shells became known within German munition reports as the Hindenburg program.[90]

The growing chance of being caught within a phosgene cloud, delivered by canister or by the increasingly common gas shell, meant that all officers and staff officers had to actively incorporate the danger of gas into the preparation of battle. For the soldiers in the trenches, the front-line troops often took pro-active anti-gas action into their own hands. On the night of 14-15 December 1916 the 2nd Canadian Infantry Brigade carried out a night raid against an advanced German position across the Messines-Ploegsteert road to destroy a strong point in the Ypres sector. As the Summary of Operations reported, "It was considered that in the event of an enemy gas attack this barrier would be of considerable advantage to the enemy," for the Germans could bury cylinders in the advanced position without fear of them being cracked open to gas the rest of the German unit. A previous failed raid on this position had resulted in one officer and two men killed and eight wounded. The Brigade Headquarters feared the potential of this point as a forward area for the release of gas, and during three nights and days prior to the raid the artillery bombarded the area. The barrage kept "them in a state of uncertainty as to the real night of the attack" and also forced the German defenders to thin out the front lines. During the dark hours, a raiding party from the 5th Battalion carried out the operation, capturing two German prisoners. To deliver a final blow, a mine was placed under the strong point and blown when the Germans cautiously re-entered their abandoned position. For the loss of two injured raiders, the Canadians had eliminated the very real danger of the advanced German "gas" location. The Canadians' aggressive policy of raiding was carried out to impose their will on the enemy, cause casualties, gather information, and ease the psychological fear and physical danger of gas canister emplacements.[91]

REORGANIZATION IN THE GAS SERVICES

During the bloody Somme battles, the Canadians stumbled upon two important observations and innovations with regard to the gas war. The first was an attempt to determine more accurately the extent of gas casualties. Following the death of Private J. Dean, who was gassed on 24 April 1915, Medical Services in Canada requested of the Militia Council on 27 June 1916 that the British follow the Canadian lead of investigating discharged gassed victims.[92] The letter was produced because Private Dean had died at his home in Brantford, Ontario, on 25 May 1916 after being released from the expeditionary force. How many more gassed soldiers had been invalided out of the army, only to die months or years later after suffering quietly at home? Such victims did not fall under any fatal gas statistics, yet their early deaths were a direct result of gassing. Various government departments attempted to evaluate and record the gassed Canadians who were sent back to hospitals – for reasons of pension claims, certainly, rather than to ascertain true statistical casualties incurred in the gas war – but as will be seen later, they were often negligent in the matter. Still, such reports are glimpses into the hidden effects of gas in the First World War.

The second innovation – and the more important one to the soldiers in the field – was the creation by the Canadian Gas Services, as the collection of gas officers was now called, of the position of battalion gas officers in October 1916.[93] The Canadians, perhaps wary of how gas had already been successfully used against them, and recognizing their unique organization in the more stable Canadian Corps as compared to their British counterparts, were able to instigate fundamental changes quicker than the rest of the BEF.[94] The introduction of battalion gas officers, filling the gap between the brigade gas officer and the gas NCOs of the companies, played an important role in coordinating the application of gas discipline.[95]

Lieutenant W.J. Wright, who after a four-day gas course had become the 19th Battalion's gas officer, described in a letter home to a curious friend his role on the battlefield: "I have no duties as a Platoon leader but have charge of defensive gas appliances, inspect gas respirators, help to drill men in use of respirators and patrol front line; also inspect gas-proof dugouts, wind-valves, sprayers and horns." Along with these roles was the job of collecting soil and gas samples of heavily gassed areas so that they could be analyzed. To collect air samples the gas officers used gas sampling bulbs, which looked like glass bottles tapered off to a fine point. The pointy end was broken off and air was drawn into the glass tube, which was then quickly stoppered.[96] But the battalion gas officer's most important role was to continually teach – or enforce through drill and fear, as the case may be – the need for good gas discipline. One trench warrior remembered how his unit's gas officer carried out his mandate: "It is late when a little fellow flits like a ghost through the trench, creeps up behind the posts and shouts 'Gas attack!' in their ears, and then quietly ticks off the seconds it takes them to get their masks on." Taking over many of the roles carried out by the four company gas NCOs, the battalion gas officer now coordinated and supervised their activities. The gas NCOs were relegated almost exclusively to checking their men's PH-helmets and newly arriving respirators to make sure they were in working order and to assisting in any other anti-gas tasks that were deemed necessary. Following the Canadian lead, the British instigated battalion gas officers, but not until September 1917.[97]

In August 1916 the British introduced the best gas mask, the small box respirator (SBR), which would be used until the end of the war.[98] Lighter, more comfortable, and able to withstand higher concentrations of gas than the previous gas helmets, the SBR was almost entirely effective in protecting the wearer from gas. The SBR had chemical granules packed in a metal container and carried in a satchel. From the satchel a rubber tube led to the mask, which covered the mouth and nose. As air entered the valve in the bottom of the satchel, it passed through the chemicals and was taken in through a metal mouthpiece. To ensure that the wearer did not breathe through his nose, a nose clip was worn. Although the device was effective, it imposed an unnatural method of breathing that was difficult to maintain during heavy activity. But as the War Diary of the 3rd Battalion, Special Brigade, remarked after a gas attack on 21 August 1916, "there were practically no cases of slight poisoning. If men put their masks on quickly enough and in the right way they were unharmed. If a mistake was made it cost a man his life."[99]

British units were issued with the SBR between August and December, and the Canadian Corps began to receive their SBRs in late November.[100] W.J. O'Brien of the 1st Battery, 1st Brigade, Canadian Field Artillery, did not receive his SBR, which he described "as a dandy," until 11 December 1916. While the SBR was the first line of defence, PH-helmets were still to be kept in case of damage to the respirator.[101]

Once the Canadians began to train with the SBR, they, like all soldiers of the BEF, realized its advantage over the gas helmet. The gas officers of the Canadian Gas Services instructed the soldiers in how to wear the SBRs properly and, more

Two soldiers with small box respirators examining a Lee Enfield rifle.

important, how to get them on quickly. There were to be five steps in adjusting the respirator, but these were not easily accomplished with nerves straining as poison gas drifted closer. As George Maxwell of the 49th Battalion described:

> Every man hustled to get his mask adjusted. To do this, the steel helmet had to be jerked off; the mask had to be pulled over the head; the clamp had to be fastened on the nose to shut off the breathing with that organ, forcing one to breathe by mouth through the chemically prepared canister attached to the mask. After the beastly mouthpiece was inserted, the helmet had to be readjusted on the head. I forgot to jerk mine off; the chin strap got entangled with the straps of my gas mask. Fortunately, Lieutenant Wyndam was standing beside me and saw my predicament. He came to my aid, but not before I had inhaled some of the abominable gas.[102]

It was eventually observed by gas officers that men would instinctively take a sharp breath upon hearing the gas alarm and before putting their gas masks on.[103] Such an action could result in the inhalation of poison gas into the lungs, and it was quickly ordered that soldiers should stop breathing, as opposed to taking a deep breath. Such actions and corrections, although seemingly insignificant compared to the enormity of the war, saved countless lives and epitomized the important debt owed to the Gas Services. Nonetheless, the respirator remained a frightful thing to wear, as one trench soldier lamented: "The mask is safe but is the most uncomfortable thing I have ever experienced. If [anyone wants to] know how a gas mask feels, let him seize his nose with a pair of fire tongs, bury his face in a hot feather pillow, then seize a gas pipe with his teeth and breath through it for a few hours while he performs routine duties. It is safe, but like deadly poison [gas] which forced its invention, it is not sane."[104]

The year 1916 was marked by the bloodbaths at Verdun and the Somme, where more than a million men were churned up within the holocaust of machine-gun bullets and high explosives. The number of gas casualties was insignificant when compared to the slaughter wrought by conventional weapons – a thimbleful in a sea of blood. Yet it was the genesis for a new gas attack doctrine based on gas shells. With refinement, practice, and greater manufacturing outputs of gas shell stocks, the lethal agents took a large step toward creating a new type of warfare on the Western Front.

CHAPTER FOUR

Tough Guys

JANUARY 1917–JUNE 1917

NEW GAS TACTICS

After the battle of the Somme wound down to an inglorious end, the winter of 1916-7 was a period of recuperation and training for the battered divisions of the Canadian Corps. Notwithstanding their losses, the Canadians continued to pursue a policy of vigorous patrolling and raiding in No Man's Land. In conjunction with this offensive-minded plan, the Gas Services continued to refine the implementation of an anti-gas discipline.

The aim of the Gas Services was damage control. Gas officers readily admitted that "no precautions can be taken which will render our troops immune from the first shell which falls among them ... but what [we] must aim at is to prevent others from suffering in the same manner."[1] The goal was to impart a realistic understanding of what would be confronted at the front, control a possible epidemic of gas casualties, and ease the fears of all soldiers regarding the expanding gas war by developing an active defence against it.

After the relentless fighting on the Somme, some Canadian battalions had lost half their men. The gaping holes in the infantry were to be filled by raw Canadian recruits. If these young men were to fulfil their roles, they required specialized training. Musketry, hand grenades, rifle grenades, bayonet fighting, Lewis gunnery, anti-gas precautions, entrenching, and construction of barbed wire entrenchments were all part of the instruction at the reinforcement camps in England. As early as August 1916 the general officer commanding-in-chief, of the British Expeditionary Force had ordered General Headquarters, Home Forces, that "no officer or men shall leave England for this country [France] without having actually passed through gas in a helmet or other anti-gas appliance." Although recruits were supposed to be drilled in anti-gas procedures, one investigation found that in nearly every case new drafts had received no such training prior to their arrival in France. In 1916, instructing officers were often reluctant to devote precious time to anti-gas discipline instead of a host of other trench skills that new recruits were lacking. The old notions of practising rifle marksmanship and close-order drill, as well as the growing realization that a knowledge of bombing was needed, were augmented by the belief in the "cult of the offensive." All of this meant that defensive skills were often overlooked. The Canadians, still very acquiescent to the British, did not even have a gas officer placed in England.[2]

Although it is unclear from the records why there was such a neglect of anti-gas training in England, the fledgling Canadian Gas Services was expanding only very slowly and was never able to get across the English Channel from the front. Also, as the instructors were often out of touch with the realities of the battlefield and the quick changes wrought in the gas war, their lessons were frequently outdated and inaccurate.[3] The Seventh (McGill) Siege Battery's regimental historian noted that the issuing of gas helmets during the final stage of training indicated that the battery would finally, after several false hopes, be sent overseas; still, its anti-gas instruction from the hastily appointed NCO was desultory.[4] Under the watchful eyes of the divisional gas officers (DGOs), and later the chemical advisor, the Gas Services preferred to train their new recruits in France.

At the Canadian Reinforcement Camp in France, new drafts and soldiers returning to their units were forced to perfect the donning of their SBRs in less than six seconds from the alert position, which was having the SBR worn on the chest. "In the case of gas attacks, there are only two classes of soldiers, the quick and the dead," was just one of the motivational phrases spouted by gas officers. In the process, soldiers were drilled, in the words of one historian, so "that even the stupid could master the routine effectively."[5] Training, no matter how monotonous, built self-confidence in handling the respirators. After hours of practising to get the mask on in time, soldiers were marched into gas chambers – masks attached – and gassed with chlorine. New recruits without their respirators on were also exposed to tear gas for thirty seconds in order to frighten them into recognizing the unforgiving character of the gas war. After completing the ordeal, soldiers received the letters PTG (Put through Gas) in their pay books to indicate that they had passed basic gas training. Historian Denis Winter has remarked that the whole process left soldiers "with an aggrieved feeling of the unfairness of gas," but it instilled a healthy awareness of the deadly nature of chemical warfare and the need to follow anti-gas precautions.[6]

Although drill was essential, some commanders were apprehensive that attempting to familiarize soldiers with this new weapon would generate additional fears and rumours. Yet fear was better than apathy, a trait not unknown among some of the British and, especially, the French troops.[7] The notion of soldiers who knew too much or were asked to think for themselves was antithetical to the old top-down style of leadership still embraced by some British commanders, but it did not present a problem under General Byng. Certainly there were officers who initially paid only lip-service to establishing an anti-gas doctrine in their units, but the continuous diligence of the Gas Services, when combined with the complete backing of both Byng and later Currie, eventually solidified a strong gas discipline within the Canadian Corps.

As the fledgling Canadian Gas Services was attempting to create an effective anti-gas doctrine, an order issued by the British First Army on 26 January 1917 allowed troops to continue using their gas goggles to combat the lingering effects of lachrymatory gas shell vapours. The order was issued despite some apprehension that gas goggles ruined good gas discipline. It was emphasized, though only haphazardly, that these "goggles will only be used after a bombardment."[8] Unhappily, soldiers were inclined to take this freedom too far. Never liking their gas masks, and more comfortable in goggles, they wore the

Exiting the gas chamber at gas drill.

latter in situations when their respirators should have been attached. As a result, not only was firm gas discipline eroded, but there were unnecessary gas poisonings as well.

To supplement the hours of practising the quick donning of masks, gas officers were issued new orders on what to do during a German gas attack. Instead of Divisional Headquarters sending out a "gas alert" warning, battalions, with their gas sergeants gauging the wind factor, were empowered to order alerts and to warn the next higher formation of possible danger.[9] With the new danger of gas shells landing behind sentries, it was important to have gas alarms not just at the front but throughout the multilayered defence-in-depth, from front lines to the reserve trenches in the rear.

The new SBRs were much valued by the Canadians, for they hung loosely on the chest and thus were very accessible during a gas alert. Because an alert could last for a day or two, it was important that the SBR was less cumbersome and safer than the old PH-helmets, which had to be worn rolled up on the head. Within the first weeks of their arrival, when there were not enough to go around, the SBRs were sometimes passed to relieving battalions. This practice was stopped when several cases of trench mouth were brought to the attention of the medical officers of two unfortunate battalions.[10] Although such actions were unsavoury, it indicates both the benefits and the popularity of the SBR.

Soldiers were drilled that in the event of a gas attack, by canister or shell, infantrymen were "not to move or talk" and were "forbidden to move to a flank or to the rear." Troops were to counter the attack with a slow, steady fire on the enemy trenches, quickly followed by all available artillery. Such a strict gas discipline and coherent doctrine of defence made it suicidal for the Germans to combine gas and infantry tactics. As a result, until an attack doctrine could be developed, poison gas was relegated to the mental and physical harassment of soldiers rather than employed in combined-arm tactics. Reflecting this, the increasing use of gas would no longer be directed solely at the infantry, but also at gunners and soldiers operating supply lines leading up to the front, in the hope of disrupting their contribution to offensive or defensive operations. The attack gas doctrines began to diversify and gain new tactical objectives, but it was only through field experience that results could be recorded and problems corrected. A captured German document, which outlined the employment of gas shells, stated that "no favourable opportunity should be lost of hampering the enemy's working parties and of shelling reported concentrations of troops."[11] Working parties consisting of trench soldiers engaged in activities that might slow or otherwise inhibit the response to a gas attack were most vulnerable to gas.

To the Canadians holding the close-proximity trenches, raids and counter-raids made it imperative that resulting gaps in the wire be repaired, that listening posts be manned, and that the parapet be kept in good defensive order.

Thus, every night the exhausted infantrymen were sent to work along the trenches or, more often, into No Man's Land to prepare new defences. Ian Mackenzie, an officer of the Canadian Railway Troops and future minister of national defence, remarked how most nocturnal work on the trenches was "done under great difficulties." Just a few well-placed lethal and lachrymatory shells compelled the soldiers to frequently wear respirators. Mackenzie noted that it "was particularly trying to lose all rest at night after a day's hard toil" while having to stand in the dark waiting for gas to dissipate.[12] To some, gas was an inconvenience; to others, it raised the spectre of a slow, painful death. Albert West of the 43rd Battalion described how he was sent into No Man's Land to dig a trench:

> It rained all the time and was so dark you could not see anyone else ... One half hour or so before I finished I discovered I had left my gas mask in the camp. I was never so frightened before. There I was three to four miles from camp in a strange part of the line and the enemy liable to put over gas any time and I with no protection. I did not know the way "home" or I should certainly have "beat it" and I dare not report it for I should have been punished. I did not feel safe again until I was beside my mask in the hut again."[13]

West's intense fear of gas and his "feeling naked" without his respirator were not uncommon among soldiers at the front. Such responses only became amplified when the men went outside the physical and psychological safety of their trenches into No Man's Land.

Louis Keene, a sentry in reserve early one morning, remembered watching a working party return to their billets:

> They were wet through and wrapped up with scarves, wool helmets, and gloves. Over their clothes was a veneer of plastered mud. They marched along at a slow swing and in a mournful way sang –

> "Left – Left – Left
> We – are – the tough Guys!"

> Apparently there are no more words to this song because after a pause of a few beats they commenced again –

> "Left – Left – Left"

> They looked exactly what they said they were.[14]

It took "tough guys" to survive in the front-line trenches, among the mud, lice, and corpses, not to mention the shells and snipers' bullets that were fired at the infantry, but it took "trained guys" to survive the gas war.

Let the "Rats" Loose: Toward Vimy

After being continually subjected to gas, the Canadian Corps decided to retaliate on 16 January 1917, when it attempted a gas attack against the German lines. Lacking gas shells, the 8th Canadian Brigade proposed to have a gas cloud released in its sector, to be followed by a smoke attack and then a series of raiding parties.[15]

For weeks before the raid, the Canadians organized eighteen carrying parties of forty-eight men each to bring the canisters from the rear on toboggans and then drag them the final distance overland during the night to the front-line trenches.[16] When the "rats" (as the canisters were code-named) were brought into the front-line trenches, men of the Royal Engineers Special Companies set them into specially prepared "rat traps." They were buried halfway into the trench floor, with sandbags surrounding them; flexible hoses attached to the nozzles ran into No Man's Land. They appeared innocuous, except of course to the men in the trenches, who were continually praying that the Germans did not open an artillery strafe and crack any of the half-buried canisters.

The Special Companies, as already mentioned, were groups of trained gas specialists whose job was to gauge the wind, make sure all of the hoses were emptying gas in the right direction into No Man's Land, and then release the gas at the appropriate moment. The gas specialists were generally viewed with distrust by the infantry, who knew that once the gas was released, the specialists retreated to the rear "before all hell broke loose." The regimental historian of the Newfoundland Regiment noted that there was almost always intense retaliation for the release of gas, so experienced officers sent their men into deep dugouts to escape the expected barrage. British infantryman Edmund Blunden echoed the same sentiments when, upon hearing a German gas alarm while out in No Man's Land, he hurried back to his own line and "shook in the prospect of a retaliation." Notwithstanding the awareness of the likely German response, the Canadians were set on their gas retaliation.[17]

An uncooperative wind remained a problem. From 14 January onward, the brigade gas officer had been forced to give the gas alert because the wind was blowing from east to west, that is, from the German to the Canadian lines. All soldiers were required to keep their SBRs on their chests, anxiously awaiting any indication that the Germans might pre-empt their gas strike. The delay was even more intense for the battle groups, made up of two officers and thirty-five other ranks from the 4th and 5th Canadian Mounted Rifles, who were to go over the top following the gas and smoke releases.

The careful plan called for the Canadian front-line soldiers to increase their activity in the trenches by firing their machine guns, shooting flares, and moving into the trenches to give the impression that they were nervous and anticipating a raid from the Germans. This was to be carried out from sunset to zero hour at 8 p.m. on 16 January. At zero hour the Canadians were to blaze away with their machine guns and throw hand bombs into the gaps in the wire in front of the Canadian line. It was hoped that this would impress upon the confused Germans that the Canadians thought the Germans were raiding them. Amidst this confusion and noise, the field artillery was to lay down a barrage on the enemy trenches and the heavy guns were to bombard the reserve trenches, thereby isolating the Germans in the front lines, who would head into their dugouts to escape the HE barrage. As this was happening a strong wind was to carry the simultaneously released gas over into the German lines to seep into the trenches. Artillery shells would continue to fall back and forth over the German lines to cause more friction among the German soldiers and would stop only at sixty-five minutes past zero. At zero plus one hundred and twenty minutes, a smoke wave would be put over by the Special Companies using smoke candles, and the raiders were to follow into the German lines.[18]

As the infantry, artillery, Special Companies, and their commanders waited with SBRs attached, hour after hour ticked away. Due to an unfavourable wind, zero hour was missed. The forward battalions of the 8th Brigade, which had been in the line for over a week, were scheduled to be pulled out the next morning. Clinging to the hope that the wind would change, everyone involved was relieved by the 26th Infantry Brigade (British), but the Canadian raiding parties were left in the line. After two days the raiding parties returned to the reserve trenches with the intention of carrying out the operation even if they had to stay behind to do it. For nearly a fortnight the raiders were moved up the line and then back again as the wind remained temperamental, constantly changing direction or strength and leaving all involved thoroughly frustrated. By 4 February the 8th Brigade was moved to a different sector of the front, and the battle groups rejoined their units, having left the gas canisters to the British occupying that sector.[19]

Having a planned raid delayed and eventually cancelled because of meteorological factors should have ruled out the future use of gas. Yet as one soldier-journalist who associated with both front-line troops and staff officers noted, the Canadians had begun to underplay the inherent dangers of the Western Front and compete among themselves and other units in the BEF for the most daring raids and biggest payoffs. As the youngest of the Canadian divisions, the 4th was also looking to distinguish itself. The nature and failure of the 8th Brigade's 3rd Division gas raid had not been formally conveyed to the other Canadian divisions. Thus, unaware of all the problems and frustrations of including gas as a tactical weapon, the 4th Division's staff officers began planning for a large assault – one that would also hinge on chemical agents clearing the trenches protecting the German-held Vimy Ridge.[20]

On 31 January 1917 the Germans released a massive gas cloud of very dense concentration and long duration against French units between Marquises and

Auberive. Although the French were aware of the impending gas attack, which was delivered in daylight, they suffered 1,900 casualties, including more than 500 dead.[21] News of the disquietingly high casualties and the shocking lack of French anti-gas discipline was passed on to all Allied armies in the hope that such a disaster would not happen again. The success of the canister attack further strengthened the 4th Canadian Division's resolve to incorporate gas into its forthcoming raid.

The Canadian Corps continued a campaign of raiding in February and March 1917, which not only cowed the German defenders but taught important battlecraft tactics to the Canadian infantry. The raiders were forced to devise new methods of getting across the firezone, learned the importance of having every member know his role in the operation, and mastered the difficult task of coordinating the infantry and artillery to work in combination. A series of raids by the 4th Brigade on 17 January and the 10th Brigade on 13 February were very successful in capturing prisoners, obtaining information, and killing Germans.[22] The raids were not without their costs, and it was usually the best officers and troops who suffered when things went wrong, as they sometimes did. Yet as the Canadians were gaining confidence in their superiority over the Germans, the 4th Division was putting the finishing touches on its operation against Hill 145, one of the highest points on Vimy Ridge.

The oversized raid was to consist of 1,700 officers and men from the 54th, 72nd, 73rd, and 75th Battalions, preceded by a bombardment and a release of canister gas to achieve surprise and overcome the German defenders.[23] The fact that the assault against Hill 145 would be moving uphill does not appear to have worried General David Watson or his General Staff Officer 1 (the highest ranking staff officer) Edmund Ironside. The bristling fortified defences and interlocking machine gun nests that the Germans had reinforced for two years were deemed a powerful position, but it was assumed that the poison gas would paralyze the defenders so the infantry could close and do battle. Despite the largely unsuccessful use of gas clouds in this way to date, the DGO, Lieutenant Henry V.L. Beaumont, gave little if any warning that the gas, which followed the contours of the ground and sank into crevices and shell holes because of its weight in comparison to air, would require a stiff breeze to move it up the hill. Gas remained a misunderstood weapon and, because of its technical and scientific nature, it was shunted to the periphery, to be used by "specialists" who were seen more as chemists than soldiers. Bent on a "raiding mentality," the 4th Division's staff officers overlooked the obvious disadvantages of their plan, perhaps because their gas specialist gave no reason for concern. More likely, they assumed that it would work because they needed it to. The raid's planners proceeded to place their faith and their men's lives behind a wave of gas.

There was little understanding of chemical warfare by senior commanders. When gas was implemented, senior officers always hoped that it would emulate the first gas cloud release of the war, when two whole divisions were routed. Although poison gas was still a weapon that inspired terror, better gas discipline and respirators ensured that no such rout would occur again. Equally detrimental, the Canadian staff officers and commanders had neglected training their soldiers in any doctrine on how to work in conjunction with the gas. Yet given the formidable position of the hill and its defences, gas was needed because other, more conventional weapons could not guarantee success. Gas was not the armament of choice, but of desperation; ill-placed hope created delusions that outweighed all logical assumptions.

It fell to the pack mules of the army – the infantry – to once again lug up thousands of hundred-pound metal cylinders. Although everything was organized by the night of 25-6 February, the wind remained uncooperative and the British attack gas specialists of Company "M" were forced to delay the release. As the raiders waited for the signal, one wonders how much faith they put in their orders, which had told them that "fifteen tons of gas was to be sent over to strike terror into the black heart of the enemy. The first wave was to be of deadly poisonous gas that would kill every living thing in its path: while the second would corrode all metal substances and destroy guns of every description."[24] This was the official line from both commanders and gas officers, which, when combined with the constant rumours that percolated at the front with regard to new, lethal gases being introduced, continued to foster the belief that poison gas would be the catalyst to victory.

Some had a better tactical appreciation of the situation, and at least two of the four battalion commanders argued that the raid was impractical. Lieutenant-Colonel A.H.G. Kemball, the commander of the 54th Battalion, objected to Brigadier-General Victor Odlum, commander of the 11th Brigade, that because of the unpredictable wind the raid should be postponed and more artillery should be brought to bear on the German lines. Equally concerned, Lieutenant-Colonel Sam Beckett, the commander of the 75th Battalion, not only believed that the surprise attack no longer a secret but also feared that his troops had insufficient training with gas. Aware that two of his experienced and decorated battalion commanders were unhappy with the plan, Odlum questioned his orders by writing to and visiting Lieutenant-Colonel Edmund Ironside. Despite getting into a heated argument with Ironside – bordering on insubordination, as one officer later reported – Odlum received no definite answer to his central concern about how, if the gas failed, his men were to get across No Man's Land before the enemy barrage opened up. A future chief of the Imperial General Staff of the British Army, the massive Ironside, who stood six feet four inches and weighed 220 pounds, had a firm hand on controlling the division, and, as some junior officers noted, had undue influence over Divisional Commander David Watson. Ironside, possibly on orders from Watson, refused to entertain ideas about postponement – too much planning and hope were riding on the raid. Hoping for the best, the attack groups remained at the ready. Thus, two experienced battalion commanders, who were close to the front and saw the formidable defences their men were up against, were ignored by staff officers who relied on a dubious weapon to overcome defenders who had spent two years fortifying their position. Such actions did not bode well.[25]

The inconsistent weather, a superior German position, and the normal difficulties associated with a large-scale assault, especially one that involved hundreds of men carrying clanging metal objects to the front, meant that the surprise of the attack – the fundamental aspect for the gas component to succeed – was lost. Nerves began to fray as the interconnected infantry, artillery, gas specialists, and commanders waited hour after hour for the start signal.

The waiting also took its toll physically: the 12th Brigade had three killed and twenty-two wounded in stray shelling alone. Moreover, during the wait at least one German artillery barrage searching the Canadian lines punctured some of the canisters. A sentry noticed the gas and awoke his platoon, but not wanting to alert the Germans they could not raise a gas alarm. Word was quietly passed along the trenches, but it failed to reach a small group of infantrymen in the path of the wayward cloud. All were poisoned and one man suffocated to death. The Canadians were learning the hard way that employing infantry and gas was a dangerous proposition. Still, the attack remained unchanged; the raiders were to follow behind the second of two gas clouds into the German trenches. It was planned that the second release would catch many of the Germans unprepared, exhausted and lethargic from the ordeal of the first gas cloud.[26]

The hours of waiting turned into days – a full three days passed before the 4th Division's Headquarters received the code word "CAT" from the British gas specialists to indicate proper weather conditions. Finally, at 3 a.m. on 1 March the Special Companies' gas sergeants, wearing red, white, and green brassards for identification, released 1,038 cylinders of White Star (chlorine and phosgene) gas into a stiff breeze of nine miles per hour, which in some areas carried it quickly over to the German lines. Unfortunately for the Canadians, the German defenders had only recently been issued orders to combat a gas attack: "As soon as the alarm is given shoot up red and green flares. Our artillery will fire into the gas cloud and on the hostile trenches." True to orders, the German counter-barrage fell on the Canadian lines and immediately punctured three canisters, gassing several Canadians and gas specialists and further lowering the infantry's impression of their chemical agents.[27]

Messages sent back to divisional headquarters by forward observers noted that the Germans, adopting the new gas defence, immediately fired red SOS flares and kept their rifle fire "fairly regular" until the gas had moved past their lines. The raiders were to go into No Man's Land at 5:40, forty minutes after a second discharge of gas. But minutes before the second gas cloud was to be released, the wind changed and the second wave of gas could not be liberated. In the 12th Brigade's sector, however, the message to hold off was not received, and when the gas was released it slowly moved up the ridge only to stop and lazily float back toward the Canadian lines, eventually drifting through the waiting soldiers of the 11th Brigade. A private from the 102nd Battalion, Maurice Bracewell, remembered with terror as the gas turned and seeped into the Canadian lines: "Our front lines got all the gas, the front trenches were saturated with it." Although, in the confusion, the gas casualties suffered by Canadians were not recorded, they were probably light, considering most men were equipped with the very effective SBR. Yet because the gas was so dense in the crowded trenches, the raiding parties, mostly from the 73rd Battalion, were forced to leave their safety, suffering additional casualties from conventional weapons as they proceeded overland until they found their assembly points.[28]

Mistakenly thinking that the second gas attack had blown through the German ranks, one officer of the 50th Battalion remembered years later that he and his men, who were acting as a reserve on the flank of the 75th Battalion, believed the orders passed down from higher commands that "we were just going to jump over the top and pick up all these gassed Germans." When he looked across the 250 yards of No Man's Land, just minutes before the first wave of 75th Battalion men were to go over, he was shocked to see the Germans tightly packed in their trenches, bayoneted rifles aimed at his lines.[29] The Canadian raiders, already committed to battle and spurred on by their earlier dominance, continued with the plan and hoped that the Germans had been sufficiently overcome by the first wave of gas. They were not.

The Battle of Vimy Ridge.

THROUGH FIRE AND GAS

At zero hour the Canadians went "over the bags" in a headlong assault into massed enemy fire. The gas had been expected to paralyze the enemy, and white flags had therefore been set up to mark the gaps in the wire. They drew the Canadians into natural killing zones as German machine-gunners were drawn to those hard-to-miss targets. In order not to alert the enemy, there had been only a sporadic attempt at clearing the barbed wire with explosives. Hundreds of Canadians were mowed down as they struggled through the ill-cleared razor-wire of No Man's Land. In less than five bloody minutes the 54th Battalion alone lost its commanding officer, two of the four company commanders (the other two injured), and close to 190 men, remembered Sergeant Major Alex Jack. Other attack groups made up of the other three battalions suffered similar fates.[30]

The futile assault degenerated into a mad scramble, but throughout it the Canadians displayed their reputation for dogged tenacity that they had won on earlier battlefields. Despite their relentless push forward, it was a grim time as friends and companions who had survived the horrors of the Somme were cut down in swaths. Added to the confusion of losing most senior commanding officers, vapours of the first and second waves of gas clung to shell holes in No Man's Land so that the attackers had to advance through their own lethal agent. In addition, the Germans fired gas shells into the assembly trenches of the attacking Canadians. Although this caused few casualties, it forced the raiders to don their respirators, which left them almost blind as they ran through the lingering gas, desperately searching for gaps in the wire as bullets and shells rained down.[31] Despite this frontal attack, the Canadians cleared a 500-yard section of the German trenches in hand-to-hand fighting. The inability to reinforce the raiders and the general breakdown of the assault meant the retreating Canadians, jumbled together from the four battalions, fought a running battle with the Germans. Cut off from their own lines by counter-attacks, the Canadian infantry risked having all survivors captured. A successful rearguard action by several officers allowed dozens of men to escape, but as one trench warrior observed, "we had very heavy casualties, especially among the officers."[32] As the futility of the attack became apparent, front-line officers, from battalion commanders to the lowest lieutenant, sacrificed themselves for their men.

Those soldiers wounded in No Man's Land crawled to shell holes for safety and in the process often fell victim to their own gas, which pooled in the mucky depressions. Stuck in a crater while the Germans sniped at anything that moved, private Stanley Baker remembered watching the men in his large hole slowly being killed as exposed heads and backs were blasted by sharpshooters. Employing one of the corpses for cover, he used his helmet to dig a shallow trench through the muck to reach another hole in the rear. The lingering gases made him cry and vomit, but he finally wormed his way back to the Canadian line later that night.[33] As soldiers dragged themselves into the trenches, their chlorine-tarnished brass buttons were just as noticeable as their ashen faces and bluish lips. The chaos of the battle, with smoke and fire obscuring vision, and gas masks clouding up and reducing the intake of breath, had forced many of the soldiers to remove their respirators for periods of time in a desperate need to locate the gaps in the wire. Masks could not be worn all the time. Any heavy exertion, like running up a ridge while under fire, provoked near strangulation effects, as not enough oxygen entered through the filters. The nature of enemy fire forced all to take cover; many who did not quickly move from their corrupted shell holes never left their informal graves.[34]

When the roll was called the next day, the full extent of the disaster was known; the four attacking battalions suffered 687 casualties. Those men who were not too numb with exhaustion or suffering from the lingering effects of gas began to question the whole raid. The War Diary of the 54th critically remarked that the "first discharge of gas apparently had no effect on the enemy," but more important, the question arises as to why anyone would have thought any differently. By this point in the war, both the Canadians and Germans were equipped with very good respirators that made the use of canistered gas almost useless unless employed against poorly trained or surprised opponents. The distance of 200 to 250 yards between the lines meant that the enemy had one to two minutes before the vapours reached them. That was certainly enough time to don respirators, especially if they were aware of the possible use of gas. The series of delays, combined with German intelligence gathered from raids, prisoners, and simple observation, had already cancelled the surprise factor. As the full results of the débâcle circulated, gas was viewed with loathing; it was supposed to be a super weapon that was to have made the raid a walk-over; instead, it had led to an absolute disaster.[35]

If despised by the front-line troops, gas was also universally condemned by the commanders in the rear. In an after-battle report, Brigadier-General J.H. MacBrien, commander of the 12th Brigade, noted that the initial "discharge brought the enemy up out of his dugouts and made him suspect and prepare to resist an attack or raid." His equal, the commander of the 11th Infantry Brigade, Victor Odlum, was more emphatic and raged that the infantry should never have been sent over for it was obvious with the rifle fire coming from the German lines that the defenders had not been incapacitated by the gas. Major-General David Watson, commander of the 4th Division, echoed his brigadiers – despite his earlier dismissal of Odlum's concerns – and later wrote that "gas was overestimated, and too much reliance was therefore placed on it." Such comments were correct in exposing the limited role of gas clouds as tactical weapons, but it did little for the hundreds of Canadians who were rotting on the battlefield due to faulty planning.[36]

Gas remained a double-edged sword that, when employed properly, could be a very useful weapon. However, the infantry hoped to never see the vile stuff again. General Byng, always a favourite among the rank and file, recounted later: "I consider I was wrong in thinking the gas would be more effective on the morale of the enemy than events proved. I was under the impression that this gas used in large quantities had the effect of placing men temporarily out of action."[37] As a result of the failed raid the Canadians decided, and rightly so, against combining gas and infantry attacks for the rest of the war. This did not preclude the use of gas shells in barrages or counter-battery work, but the infantry commanders chose to return to proven methods of combining artillery, mortars, and machine guns.[38] When the Canadians went "over the top" at Vimy, they would not be blind cattle mounting the slaughterhouse ramp like the men of the 4th Division five weeks earlier. They were to be thinking, reacting soldiers, whose commanders relied on the polished policy of soldiers leaning into massive artillery barrage, rather than an untrustworthy gas cloud.

The devastated 4th Division did not have enough time, or enough experienced officers, to train and integrate new soldiers into the units that had been so damaged in the raid. Not only were the results of the raid destructive to those four units and the morale of the division generally, but, more important, it illustrated the exceedingly poor leadership from the Canadian commanders. The naïveté of the 4th Division's staff officers was shocking, and their flimsy understanding of the concept of poison gas resulted in needlessly wasted Canadian lives. Perhaps the use of this exotic weapon stemmed from a desire to distinguish the most junior division from the rest, but the operational disaster that resulted left the survivors wary both of gas and of the fools in their comfy camps behind the line who believed in it. Gas had clearly been overestimated, yet it was a weapon that had been used on the Western Front for almost two years. The success of gas in several sensational battles perverted its true role and allowed the staff officers in the rear to trick themselves into believing that they had found the solution to the tactical problems of their raid. Some of the blame must also fall on Lieutenant Henry V.L. Beaumont, the DGO who pushed to have the gas incorporated into the assault. Corporal A. Selwood of the 72nd Battalion remembered seeing Beaumont "feeling sorry for himself" when the news of the gas-induced disaster began to seep back to the front and Selwood remarked that the raid destroyed his hope of winning a Military Cross, which he had been talking about before the battle. Equally grievous, the failure to heed the advice of experienced front-line officers showed a dangerous rigidity within the division. The success of the 4th Division in later battles, after they had recuperated from their lashing during the March raid, proved that they had learned the requirement for meticulous planning, the need for accurate battlefield intelligence, and, finally, the necessity of a combined-arms doctrine based on artillery and infantry working in close conjunction. Still, for the poor bloody infantry in the trenches, gas was further distrusted and feared, and there were few survivors in the 4th Division who would not have agreed with Lieutenant Howard Green of the 54th Battalion, who remarked that the raid "was just a proper slaughter."[39]

Shortly after the failed battle for Hill 145, on 3 March 1917, the Canadian Corps took the last step in the organization of its Gas Services by appointing a Canadian Corps chemical advisor, Captain W. Eric Harris. Prior to the war, he had been an instructor in chemistry at Ridley College, and before his current position he had been assistant chemical advisor at First Army Headquarters. Harris was now attached directly to the Corps Headquarters as the most senior officer of the Canadian Gas Services. His job was to work directly with the general staff at Canadian Corps Headquarters in organizing and managing the dissemination of gas information, while also "standardiz[ing] the work of the Divisional Gas Officers." Harris was to play an important role in entrenching effective gas discipline in Canadian troops. Throughout the war he campaigned against the slackness of commanders and junior officers in failing to enforce the gas discipline needed to ensure survival on the battlefield. In addition, he became a figurehead through which the Gas Services could implement vital changes. Although the four DGOs were generally effective in carrying out gas discipline, not one of them could organize reforms for the whole corps. The creation of a chemical advisor changed all of that. Harris arrived at the Canadian Corps on 26 March and found to his dismay that the Canadians were about to undertake their most ambitious attack of the war to date.[40]

New Gas Technology

In May 1916, Haig had requested poison gas shells, but the slowness in research and difficulties achieving production priority compared to HE shells resulted in lethal chemical shells not being readily available until March 1917.[41] Throughout the war, thirty-three different British laboratories tested 150,000 known organic and inorganic compounds in order to develop deadlier poisonous gases.[42] Yet within this flurry of activity there continued throughout the different chemical research departments a terribly unorganized system whereby scientists worked aimlessly and without knowledge of what was being done in other parts of the country. Ideas ranged from developing machine-gun bullets filled with gas to dispersing coal dust over the German lines and then igniting it to burn the whole German Army in one single apocalyptic fire. The most prominent historian studying poison gas, Ludwig Fritz Haber, the son of the mastermind behind the German gas program, has argued that "the Germans never had any trouble making gases, the French a good deal, the British (except for liquid chlorine) all the time."[43]

Initially most of the research was directed toward anti-gas measures, but by

1917 the balance shifted and the belligerents looked to develop deadlier gases and more efficient delivery systems. Although the scientists' work was often uncoordinated, and sometimes was even subject to active meddling by High Command, the British innovators Wilfred Stokes and Charles Livens eventually perfected the four-inch Stokes mortar in 1915 and the Livens projector in 1916-7, which together revolutionized British gas warfare. These two delivery systems would be combined with the old method of canistered attack and the emerging production of British lethal gas shells – the CG phosgene shell and the PS chloropicrin lethal/irritant shell were soon to be issued – to achieve an effective attack gas doctrine separate from the growing artillery program.[44]

The Stokes mortar was a small and mobile three-foot pipe that could deliver a devastating rate of twenty rounds a minute. Although its range was only a mile, it was especially useful in establishing high concentrations of gas in designated areas. Colonel Foulkes, commander of the Special Gas Brigades, remarked how the Stokes mortar was very useful during the battle of the Somme in forming effective smoke screens to cover the infantry raiding parties. But due to the slow manufacturing pace of the British munitions factories, Foulkes, who asked for lethal shells in July 1915, did not receive any until the spring of 1917.[45]

The complement to the Stokes mortar was the Livens projector, the only delivery system that the British developed before the Germans. A remarkably simple weapon – it was just a tube with a plate at the base of the stand, from which a gas shell or drum was fired – it was first used during the Arras offensive in April 1917. The projectors were fired by an electric charge, rather than percussion, and each gas drum contained thirty pounds of gas, which burst in a great concentration on an unsuspecting position. One German prisoner remarked that "the enormous flash from the projectors looked like an ammunition dump exploding." But the weapon produced more than the pyrotechnics. The projector's deadly effects were illustrated in a captured German document, which frankly admitted that "The enemy has combined in this new process the advantage of gas cloud and gas shell. The density is equal to that of gas clouds, and the surprise effect of shell fire is also obtained ... Our losses have been serious up to now, and the [British] have succeeded, in the majority of cases, in surprising us, and masks have often been put on too late." The "man of steel," German storm trooper Ernest Junger, who survived over twenty wounds during the war, supported the claims of the document as he described the new method of English gas delivery: "Frequent gas attacks were unpleasant and claimed hundreds of victims. They were carried out by means of hundreds of iron cylinders buried in the earth and discharged electrically in a salvo of flame. As soon as the light showed, gas-alarm was given, and any one who had not his mask on and flap well tucked in found himself in a bad way. In many spots, too, the gas reached an almost absolute density, so that even the mask was useless, since there was literally no oxygen to breathe." Although laborious to install, the projectors were a saturation weapon that could deliver a powerful payload. As well, the infantry feared the mortars and projectors less than gas canisters, for they generally did not blow up and spew their deadly contents if hit by a shell.[46]

The projector's clear advantage in the static war was also its shortcoming. When the war of movement returned during the German March 1918 offensive and the Last Hundred Days, the projectors proved difficult to transport quickly into the shifting front lines. As well, the German practice of a flexible defence often made it difficult for the projectors, with their relatively small range, to reach the enemy. Despite these later problems, the Stokes mortar, Livens projector, and gas shells were to support the Canadian Corps in their upcoming battle to take Vimy Ridge.

Vimy Ridge: The Canadian Artillery Enters the Gas War

The attack on Vimy in April 1917 by the Canadian Corps was only a small part of the general offensive launched by the British in conjunction with a major French offensive that spring. The French commander-in-chief, General Robert Nivelle, who had replaced Joseph Joffre, promised a crushing victory, thereby winning the support of the French government and of David Lloyd George, the newly elected British prime minister. But in early 1917 the Germans disrupted the French plans by withdrawing twenty miles to the Hindenburg Line in an effort to reduce the section of line held by them and thus strengthen their position. This, in conjunction with the German adoption of a flexible defence, which relied on lightly holding the front line and then vigorously counter-attacking to drive the weakened attackers from the lines, made it very difficult for attacking troops to exploit success.[47] Despite these factors, Nivelle refused to be put off. He carried out his attack, but failed to live up to his promises of a breakthrough. Instead the move resulted in horrible casualties among his troops and eventually mutiny in the French army. Within this overall context, the Canadian Corps attack on Vimy Ridge took place.

Vimy Ridge had been the scene of desperate fighting throughout the war, and the French had twice unsuccessfully attempted to take the ridge, losing 100,000 men in the process. As one Canadian infantryman later remarked, "It was the central point of an immense graveyard."[48] And within this open charnel house, all four Canadian divisions fought together under the command of the Canadian Corps Headquarters for the first time in the war. It was an almost perfectly executed set-piece battle planned so that everyone, down to the lowest private, knew their objectives. While the British were reluctant to give maps to any soldiers below the rank of colonel, the Canadians, by contrast, had a slogan, at least among the 1st Division, of "Maps to section leaders."[49] The success of the battle relied on the infantry closely following a moving artillery barrage as it crept up the ridge and devastated everything in its path. The central importance of high explosives has obscured the fact that, for the first time, gas was used by the corps in a set-piece battle.

On 2 April the divisional gas officers of the Canadian Corps met with the newly appointed Canadian chemical advisor, W.E. Harris, and together they discussed the role of gas in the upcoming assault on Vimy Ridge.[50] Canadian staff officers had been furnished by British intelligence with information extracted from a captured German gas NCO, who had described the average German soldier as incapable of understanding the intricacies of his gas mask. Such a statement seems at best inconsistent with the success of the Germans in surviving previous canister gas attacks. But when combined with a series of raids carried out by Canadian units, especially one on the first night of April by the 10th Canadian Infantry Brigade in which eight prisoners were taken, the Canadians inferred that the German defenders were not of the highest quality. In order to cause more confusion in the German ranks at the time of the attack, it was thus decided that, along with the intense artillery bombardment, there would be a series of gas bombardments with newly acquired gas shells.[51]

In conjunction with the warning to all troops in the vicinity of Vimy that during the month of April enemy gas attacks might be expected and troops must be on gas alert at all times, the first lethal gas shells were being delivered by wagons to the waiting Canadian artillery on the last day of March.[52] Given the failure of using canister gas in coordination with infantry attacks, the Canadians had wisely decided that, while gas could still be useful, it would largely be limited to a counter-battery role.

A significant component of the success at Vimy and the subsequent string of Canadian Corps operational victories was the corps' qualitative advantage over the German system of counter-battery work. The Canadians were among the first to use sound-ranging techniques. Moreover, under senior Counter-Battery Staff Officer (CBSO) Colonel Andrew McNaughton, the meteorological conditions were also rigidly observed. These methods were combined with air photographs, unit patrol debriefs, information from prisoners, and hostile battery reports to create an overall picture of where the enemy guns were located. The artillery's basic principle was one of "see first, hit first and keep on hitting." Accurate staff work, vectoring many guns on one target, firing from map references, and employing high explosives, shrapnel, and poison gas shells at a prolific rate, all led to a hurricane of fire that dampened the enemy rate of return. Much had been learned from the experienced French and British gunners, but the Canadians were not afraid to take chances with new technology and equipment. The self-contained nature of the Canadian Corps allowed them to experiment with new artillery techniques while other British units had to carry out such reforms either at the divisional or army level. Scientific gunnery was a large component of the corps' successful attack doctrine. As the Counter-Battery Office further honed its life-saving tactics and doctrine, greater protection was afforded to the attacking infantry battalions scrambling across the killing ground before the enemy's counter-barrage caught them in the open.[53]

The position of counter-battery staff officer (CBSO), attached to the staff of the general officer commander of the corps artillery, had been created in early February 1917.[54] The CBSO was responsible for collecting information on and neutralizing enemy guns, recommending artillery plans to the general officer commander of the corps artillery, requisitioning artillery to carry out the task, and allotting ammunition to the artillery units. It fell to Colonel McNaughton to introduce gas into the artillery of the Canadian Corps. Although intrigued, McNaughton had no established battlefield doctrine on how it was to be used within the artillery.

The British had been employing lethal gas at the Army level only since the beginning of 1917, and the increased production of lethal gas was just beginning to get its footing in Britain in March. The British were slowly working out the integration of lethal gas into their own attack doctrine. Given the lack of Allied experience in this area, it was Captain Harris, as the chemical advisor to the Canadian Corps, who had the important job of working with the artillery, and especially McNaughton, to coordinate the use of gas shells. Harris issued a report entitled "Instructions for Firing Gas Shells," which described the decisive role of the weather, the need to fire shells to the windward side of the target, and the importance of surprise and rapid fire in the first five minutes of the bombardment. It was stressed that the humidity, temperature, wind speed, enemy terrain, and type of gas used would affect the cloud burst. While this information was disseminated among the batteries, on the night of 7 April No. 2 Special Company attempted to fire lethal gas into the German lines by Stokes mortars. The action was cancelled due to driving snow and strong winds, and the company was nearly wiped out when a stray shell found their dugout, killing fourteen and wounding forty-one. Despite yet another demonstration of the inherent shortcomings of gas as a weapon, both McNaughton and Harris hoped that the wind would die down and allow for a counter-battery gas bombardment by their artillery on the morning of the attack.[55]

When the first troops went over the top at 5:30 a.m. on 9 April, they moved up the hill following their barrage in the cold morning's first light.[56] Through snow and sleet the Canadians, heads bent, took their first objectives with little resistance, but the slogging got progressively harder as the initial surprise was lost and the Germans tenaciously held on with machine guns and small pockets of resistance.

After the shock of having the Canadians overrun their forward trenches, the Germans fired HE and Green Cross gas shells in order to slow the Canadians' quick rate of advance. Private Donald Fraser was saved from breathing a lethal dose of gas by his good gas discipline: "I was on the point of climbing out of the trench when a shell with a dull pop burst on the parapet almost in my face. My breathing stopped at once. With my mouth open I could neither breathe in or out ... In a flash I knew it was a gas shell and it completely fouled the air. In a fraction of a second, in fact my quickness astonished me, I had my respirator on and was breathing freely." With dogged determination and superior training, all but the 4th Division, on the far left and having the highest portion of the ridge to take, had made it to their objectives on schedule by noon on 9 April.[57]

As the other three divisions were hastily digging in for the expected counter-attacks by the Germans, the 4th Division was having difficulty taking the strongly fortified Hill 145 against which the Canadians had been unsuccessful five weeks earlier. Tenaciously advancing through a driving snow storm and their own smoke screen, the 4th Division finally dislodged the Germans from the top of the ridge on 12 April. While many of the infantry were simply shocked to be there, others went about collecting souvenirs (for which the Canadians were infamous) to mark the occasion; one officer stumbled upon a "youngster who had ten revolvers" in his possession.[58]

The Canadians had taken a length of 7,000 yards, and they had pushed 4,500 yards deep into the German lines – the greatest advance by the Allies up to that point in the war. A success it remained, but the fighting had cost the corps 10,602 casualties, 3,598 of which were fatal. It was a serious strategic loss for the Germans, and Crown Prince Rupprecht wrote in his diary that "No one could have foreseen that the expected offensive would gain ground so quickly." The Canadian success was, not surprisingly, a very welcome development to the Allied generals and politicians in what was otherwise a very bleak year. Nevertheless, to the average infantryman, Vimy Ridge was remembered as hours of pure terror, watching their comrades being killed and maimed, suffering without blankets or hot food, nervously waiting for the counter-attack they expected to be unleashed on them at any moment, and all while attempting to consolidate ground that during the battle had been churned up into a viscous mess.[59]

As the Canadians dug trenches on the ridge, fresh troops rushed up to the top of the newly won position. The Canadian Corps' gas officers, wearing the distinctive black and green band on their arms, scoured the hill looking for their units, praying that not too many of their chums had become casualties during the spectacular advance. At the same time, they set about establishing the anti-gas dugouts for the new positions. For example, Sam Hewit, a gas sergeant for one of the 15th Battalion's infantry companies, brought up klaxon horns, buckets of chloride of lime, and gas curtains (chemically treated curtains that would hang from dugouts to provide a relatively gas-free area) for the vulnerable troops on the ridge, who had attacked with as little kit as possible.[60]

To the disappointment of Harris, the harsh weather – which probably helped the attacking Canadians as the sleet and snow blew into the Germans' eyes – forced a cancellation of the artillery gas shoot against German battery positions on the morning of the attack. The targets were to have been artillery pieces that had been deemed unhit by HE shells, as well as the general harassment of enemy gunners, who would have had to wear respirators while they manned their howitzers and guns.[61] Although there was no use of gas on 9 April, the preparation provided valuable technical knowledge to the artillery, who were always wary of being instructed by anyone outside of their arm on how to use their guns. The artillerymen were forced nonetheless to learn some of the basic premises about gas shells and how to employ them effectively.

Being able to use gas shells, or any shells for that matter, required laboriously transporting the heavy guns up the shell-marked ridge. The terrible bombardment on 9 April had reduced all the roads to quagmire, where horses sank to their bellies in slime. The few light artillery pieces that made it up the ridge were forced to do double duty in both conventional and counter-battery roles. Working closely with forward observers equipped with wireless sets and the Royal Flying Corps who were photographing the German lines, the artillery organized defensive barrages to harass any suspected German counter-attacks. Yet without more artillery, the heroically won ridge might be lost to counter-attack, so, with much determination, men and horses dragged the guns up the hill. German artillery harassed them the whole way, and one working party under the command of Major Harry Crerar suffered casualties to more than 50 percent of the men while they were laying a road. Still, the Canadian gunners succeeded in getting their artillery up the pock-marked ridge.[62]

With more guns on the ridge the next morning, the Canadian artillery was able to use their first lethal gas shells as they, on advice from the chemical advisor, fired on the village to "cause panic, lower morale and prevent any organized attempt to counter-attack" from the gathering German troops. Issued 17,000 lachrymatory shells and 14,500 lethal shells to concentrate against the German lines, the Canadian artillery saturated the enemy positions. Captured German guns and gas shells were also gleefully turned on the retreating German troops by Canadian artillery specialists.[63]

Canadian units advancing down the eastern slope of the ridge to take the villages of Vimy and Farbus on the morning of 13 April were held up and suffered casualties from German howitzers pounding the area with HE and shrapnel. To silence them, the Canadian artillery fired two hundred 4.5 inch lethal and lachrymatory gas shells against the German artillery; less than five minutes later the German gunners were reported as running away from their gassed guns. In a captured German report, the German First Army lamented that "Counter battery work was carried out by the enemy with considerable success ... The fighting resistance of the men suffered considerably from the wearing of the mask for many hours. Horses were greatly affected by the gas. In many cases the failure of the ammunition supply is attributed to this." The success of the gas shell in counter-battery work was not lost on McNaughton, who added it to the ever-refining doctrine of the Canadian Corps artillery.[64]

The relatively light casualties incurred by the Canadian Corps in taking what was thought to be an impregnable position demonstrated thoroughness of preparation and brilliant execution by both infantry and artillery in combined arms tactics. Some of the success of the Canadians rested, to be sure, on the Germans' uncharacteristic oversight in not keeping their reinforcements close enough to the front so they could have immediately counter-attacked the exhausted Canadian troops. The success also had much to do with the commitment and determination of the Canadians, whom the Germans acknowledged as "first-class troops." Vimy had fallen to the colonials, and it became an integral national symbol for the young country and enhanced the reputation of the Canadians as elite troops.[65]

Post Vimy: Retaliation by Gas

In the following days the Canadians, who vigorously patrolled the new No Man's Land on the eastern plain of Vimy, were bombarded mercilessly by both gas and high explosives. In a passage to his wife, former Ottawa Valley lumberjack Frank Maheux described the experience of probing the new German defences: "I forgot to tell you before the Germans attacked us the 3rd time, they sent gas we had our respirator for 3 hrs in one time that what save our life." Maheux later characterized the effects of such gas attacks on his companions, "We got a bad dose at Vimy – when the gas comes it is like pineapple it smells so good if you smell a lityle [sic] you die choke and you can't get your wind I saw many dying like that healthy young men the best in the nation just kids." Echoing Maheux, Private Donald Fraser suffered through a different gas bombardment, and wrote in his diary that it was "a night to be remembered and it stirred more hate in us than at any other time." Wary and more than willing to punish the colonials for their success, the Germans continued to drench the corps' forward positions in gas. Attesting to the accounts of the front-line soldiers, the Canadian Corps War Diary indicated that gas was used almost every day against the Canadian Corps front during the last three weeks of April and all of May.[66]

Responding to the German lashing of gas, the Canadian artillery attempted to protect the infantry despite being desperately short of ammunition, in some cases receiving less than one-fourth of its needs for the heavy batteries. With only one day of counter-battery ammunition in reserve, the reliance on gas shells became more important. Gas helped to interrupt or stop the enemy's rate of fire and bought time for more ammunition to be brought up from the rear. Incorporating a new attack gas doctrine, which combined the Canadian chemical advisor's earlier instructions with new tactics developed by the French, the artillerymen were instructed to use their gas shells only against "fixed objects so that the personnel against whom the shells are used cannot escape by flight from the action of the gas." Working with the chemical advisor – who determined the effect of the weather on the shoot and chose the type and ratio of gas to be used as well as the number of shells required – the commander of the artillery, Brigadier-General Edward Morrison, and his staff retained control over the choice of targets and the program of fire. Noting the separation of control, one First Army report noted that "the secret of success lies in the closest liaison between Corps Chemical Advisors and Artillery." From Harris's war diary it seems that there was very little friction. His expertise was needed in technical matters relating to gas, but the artillery was still able to keep control of target selection. This union produced fireplans that called for a constant barrage of six shells a minutes so that the target was under a continual poison cloud. Although the Canadian gas response brought the gas war to the Germans, the Canadian infantry continued to be plagued by living within the gas environment as they inched their way across the Douai Plain.[67]

The fighting was hard and merciless. On 26 April, while holding the line east of Vimy Ridge, the Germans blew a mine underneath a trench held by one company of the 38th Battalion. Shortly after the explosion, the Germans saturated the area with Green Cross shells to poison those who were buried, injured, or trying to dig out their companions. Seventeen men were badly gassed, and seven died before they could be extricated to the rear.[68] Once again, gas had proved to be most deadly to those who were the most helpless.

The Canadians responded in kind. Supporting a much larger British attack by the Third Army astride the Scarpe River, a successful attack by the 2nd Canadian Infantry Brigade on 28 April was launched against the Arleux Loop, which bulged westward around the village of Arleux-en-Gohelle, two miles in front of the heavily fortified German Drocourt-Quéant Line. The attacking infantry were assisted by the drowning of the German rear areas in gas shells. After taking the enemy trenches, McNaughton ordered all allocated artillery to blast the German-held woods of Fresnoy and the Oppy-Mericourt Line with HE and gas to pre-empt an expected German counter-attack from these areas. The harassing and negating of assembly areas for counter-attacking infantry, the disruption of reinforcements, and the prevention of working parties from building new defences were all achieved by the ample use of gas shells.[69] The aim of the gas was not to kill the enemy – although that certainly occurred – but, rather, to delay and encumber him so that attacks were slow and uncoordinated, soldiers arrived at the front exhausted from having to wear respirators, and artillery support was desultory. Despite encountering uncut wire, the Canadians took and held the German position on the loop, an assault that the British Official History described as "the only tangible success of the whole operation."[70]

Gas was employed by the Canadians in the offensive break-in, in conjunction with holding the newly won weak ground from counter-attacks, and to retaliate against the enemy. "As far as the tactical employment of gas was concerned," wrote Lieutenant Colonel Pascal Lucas, a French officer, "it took us a long time to realize that the neutralization of personnel [by gas] could supplement the always incomplete destruction of defensive organizations" by high explosives.[71] The British remained obstinate in their use of canistered gas, and because much of the knowledge was in the hands of specialists who wished to keep the offensive use of gas under their control rather than hand it over to the artillery, there remained great tension and confusion over the use of chemical agents by the British. Their misplaced conviction on the use of gas clouds impaired and diluted the development of an attack gas shell doctrine that welded infantry, artillery, and gas in combined, mobile operations. Although this type of fighting was still in the future, the basis of knowledge needed to be developed over a period of time, and the British deliberately placed themselves in a subservient position with their avoidance of gas shells. The Canadians, undoubtedly driven by the ingenuity of McNaughton and Harris, incorporated gas into all of their fireplans for the rest of the war; Hill 70, Passchendaele, and the Last Hundred Days proved that poison gas could be used in a myriad of tactical operations.

The Canadians fought in the area of Fresnoy, less then a thousand yards east of Arleux-en-Gohelle from 3 to 8 May in association with the British offensive to capture larger objectives between Vimy and Lens. To support the infantry, the artillery placed two and even three guns on every known enemy field piece, and each heavy battery was issued a thousand gas shells to carry out its task. Despite the ample issue, there were limitations on gas shells that gunners had to acknowledge. The weather remained the key concern – winds over twelve miles per hour made gas all but ineffective. Extreme cold, rain, and terrain also had to be considered. Gas shells held only a small amount of chemicals in them and it took a concentration of chemical shells to create lethal gas clouds over a large area. However, gas shells proved ideal agents against enemy batteries that might not have been hit by pinpoint conventional fire and thus simply caught in the blanket gas cloud. Yet the gas war went both ways, and those German positions that were unscathed, or were able to keep firing within the Canadian-produced gas cloud, responded with their own chemical shelling. Canadian artillery positions were deluged in return and suffered accordingly. The 11th Battery, Canadian Field Artillery, for example, had thirteen men knocked out by phosgene as well as the rate of fire severely reduced in the fighting. In his small pocket diary, artillery lieutenant Warren Skey detailed the retaliatory German gas attacks that lasted on and off for three days: "Fritz started a show with gas shells ... Gas all night, up all night & cursing Fritz some – believe me ... More gas last night but we got a bit of sleep thank goodness ... The old Hun is an —— ——!!! Damn his hide!" Where gas was used nightly, supply trains were disrupted, firing was hampered, and men fell victim. Gas was also used on the roads leading to the front to slow and harass ambulances ferrying men to the rear. In the words of one regimental historian, such shelling made the roads "almost impassable." Driving an ambulance in the dark along shell-pitted tracks while wearing a respirator was, to say the least, challenging. Just as the Canadian gunners were employing poison gas in counter-battery work, so too were the Germans relying on chemical agents to saturate the Canadian newly won position and isolate them from their old trenches and lines of logistics.[72]

The dominion troops had taken another fortified position, and one wounded German officer remarked to General Currie that the Canadians "must be a special assaulting division." If a reputation was being forged in the Armageddon of battle, it cost another 1,259 men who fell to gas, shell, and bullet. Although it was unclear what number of Canadians were gassed, many, like Brigade-Major D.E. Macintyre, had their positions "drenched with gas shells." As he wrote in his diary after the battle, "I find I tire easier than I used to ... Of course, down here the back area is drenched in gas shells all night and all next day the fumes – sickly sweet – hang about the ground and in the shell holes and get into one's throat. Isn't it a filthy war?" It was a filthy war, and the use of gas made it even more difficult for the soldiers, both physically and mentally. Moreover, gas disrupted communications, logistics, and fighting efficiency as both sides incorporated chemical shells into their artillery doctrines.[73]

During these skirmishes with the German troops, the Canadians were issued further warnings against wearing goggles instead of their SBRs to combat the effects of lachrymatory shells during gas alerts.[74] Although the practice of wearing goggles had been approved before the advent of lethal shells, the point was raised by some gas officers that "goggles only" habits would obviously deter good gas discipline and might result in fatalities if lethal gas shells were mixed in with lachrymatory.

In May 1917, the Germans manufactured a new gas shell, which contained 65 percent diphosgene (the substance used in Green Cross shells) and 35 percent chloropicrin (an irritant gas).[75] The result was a gas shell (called Green Cross II) that contained both lachrymatory and lethal properties. Those Canadians who had been using their goggles to protect their eyes from the irritation of the tear gases were now becoming victims to the lethal aspects of the shell. Private William Woods of the 1st Battalion remembered that his unit encountered some of the new gas in late May: "A man a little behind me fell into the ditch. [His commanding officer] ... said in a rather nasty tone the one word, 'Drunk.' I said without the SIR niceties, 'I do not think so, I think he is gassed, they put over a smoke screen mixed with tear gas and poison gas, I put my mask on, some of the boys put their tear-gas goggles on.'"[76]

When the news of the gas casualties and, in the words of one Canadian Gas Services report, the "false sense of security" instilled by the goggles came to the attention of the Gas Services, it was decided to withdraw the eye wear from Canadian troops. By 10 June it was ordered that all goggles be returned to the ordnance for the protection of all ranks in the Canadian Corps. The Canadians were the first in the BEF to withdraw the goggles, with the rest of the BEF following suit in September 1917. Despite such ingenuity, the Canadians were still very much influenced by the higher British formations. The implementation of a doctrine through training and relentless concern nevertheless meant that the Canadians would later distinguish themselves by successfully advancing through the gas environment of the Western Front, while so many others were floundering in the chemical wasteland.[77]

NEW RECRUITS

After the casualties suffered at Vimy, thousands of reinforcements had to be integrated into the corps before it was sent back into another set-piece battle. The new troops arriving from the base camps were understandably nervous about their chances of survival in the trenches, and one of their greatest fears (as for all recruits before them) was gas. The whole nature of trench warfare was foreign to them; most knew only to keep their head down and listen to veterans who would give them tips on survival. New soldiers were told not to seek Victoria Crosses, unless they wanted to end up with wooden ones.

The basic training for soldiers in England still largely revolved around bayonet practice, trench construction, and the role of hand grenades in trench warfare. New recruits coming from Canada were generally deposited and given basic training in one of the four Canadian command areas in England: Bramshott, Witley, Shorncliffe, or Seaford. Their skills were further honed at the Canadian Trench Warfare School at Bexhill. Yet soldiers were still receiving only half-hearted anti-gas training in England. In July 1917 Canadian Headquarters in England, commanded by General Richard Turner, acknowledging that it was inexcusable for recruits not to have passed through the gas chamber before being transported to France, ordered that all men must be instructed in anti-gas measures.[78] The theory was good, but the problem remained that there were very few well-trained or well-informed gas officers in the Canadian bases.

Little anti-gas training had permeated back to England, and the Canadian Gas Services still did not have any senior gas officers in that country. Giving overall direction in promoting gas discipline to all forces in England was the British chemical advisor, GHQ, Home Forces. Despite his wide mandate, the Canadians were largely ignored. One suspects that this was because they were very small in number compared to the British and, more important, were in the throes of emerging nationalist sentiment and not always receptive to British control. The actual gas officers – sometimes known informally as "canaries" after the birds that miners used to detect poison gas in mine tunnels – who instructed the Canadian units were permanently attached to reserve brigade units; they were not a component of the Gas Services but a fixture at their unit or base. By many accounts their proficiency and their knowledge were low. They were consistently criticized by observers from the Canadian Corps Gas

Services sent to investigate why soldiers were being shipped to France with faulty and ill-fitting respirators and not knowing how to identify gases or understanding the true consequences of fighting in a gas environment.[79]

More detrimental was a documented case that so disturbed the British chemical advisor in England that he instigated a full investigation of the Canadian training services. A gas instructor in an unnamed training area had been teaching his new recruits that it was "unnecessary for men to protect themselves from Gas Shells if at a greater distance than 300 yards from the *Area of Bombardment*."[80] Such a blatant error, especially from an officer whose job was to establish a rigid anti-gas doctrine, led the Gas Services in the field to view new recruits with suspicion. The perception of faulty practices was only reinforced by the continual evidence that, without further training, soldiers coming to France were ill-equipped to fight and survive in the growing gas environment of the Western Front. A series of reports from July 1917 to the end of the war indicated that soldiers were not being properly trained. For instance, during a period in July and August 1917 medical officers and other ranks received no anti-gas discipline; in October 1917 members of the Canadian Army Veterinary Corps missed several key components of their training. In addition, dozens of reports indicated that the instruction had to be improved in everything from forcing men to wear their respirators more often to adding night marches to prepare for the prevalent use of gas shells at the front.[81]

Most problematic, anti-gas training in England had an aura of unreality. Men were taught to stand at attention in two lines when a gas alarm went off and to adjust their respirators quickly but calmly, or not to enter a dugout except under supervision of a gas officer. Such actions may have seemed correct in England, but anyone who had been in France and scrambled to rip open his respirator in a trench while under fire or who had stood sentry for two hours on a bitterly cold night was not about to accept those parade-ground drills. Although they were a start, the key lesson remained that each man had an individual responsibility for his own protection. Elaborate drills or emphasis on speed in adjusting SBRs were preached by gas officers in England as all that was necessary to establish a good doctrine. As Major McCombie, a DGO in France, noted, a more holistic view had to be taken in England.[82] Men had to be taught more than simple drill; they had to understand the new environment they would soon be entering, and they had to be able to act and react to the changing nuances of the gas war.

To be fair to the training officers in England, they consistently asked for more information and more help from the Canadian Gas Services in France. As well, the calibre of gas officers the reserve brigades had allotted to them was poor. The instructors were generally unfit for active service and did not have the energy, drive, or knowledge to encourage an interest in the important yet seemingly mundane aspect of anti-gas discipline. The gas officer at Shorncliffe, for instance, who had been deemed unfit for active service, went through an intensive gas-training course to certify him as a gas officer, and was then removed from the training brigade and sent home to Canada without a suitable replacement specified. As a result, all reserves trained at Shorncliffe in November 1917 received no gas training. More often, the sporadic knowledge of gas resulted from soldiers coming and going from training regiments, being posted to a unit only a week before the draft was sent to France, and thus missing out on certain aspects of their training. The issue became so problematic that Chemical Advisor W.E. Harris left France at the end of December 1917 to see whether the gas work in England and France might be coordinated. Harris hoped to create a director of Gas Services for the Canadians in England but was, for unknown reasons, denied the organizational restructuring. The problem remained unsolved, and soldiers were required to learn much of their gas training in France for the rest of the war.[83]

Fearfully clutching their newly issued SBRs, green troops arrived in France at the Canadian Corps Reinforcement Camp wondering how they were to survive this new form of warfare. One of the first apparitions of gas was an order read to all recruits: "Your life will often depend upon your respirator. You have nothing to fear from gas, if 1) Your respirator is kept in good order, 2) You have learnt your drill thoroughly, 3) You know how to recognize gas shell and cloud gas." To recruits who had little knowledge of what gas was and could scarcely comprehend its effects, this was a harsh jolt of reality. One Gas Services report underscored this fear and warned of fresh troops arriving "with wild stories about the effect of German Poison Gas, and that the men have no confidence in their respirators, but are, in fact, frightened of gas." Even when drilled in the use of the gas mask in the infamous Bull Ring training area, many recruits felt anxious at the prospect of wearing such a contraption. Victor Wheeler described their reactions based on his own experience: "Many a recruit, when he read [the gas instructions], was very uneasy, and the thought of going into battle with a gas mask over his head, his vision reduced, unsure whether he had correctly remembered all the 'directions for use,' did nothing to fortify him with a sense of relief, much less a desire to go over the top."[84]

It was the role of the divisional gas schools and the gas NCOs to try to quell the fear among the new recruits and have them rely on their SBRs as protection rather than view them with apprehension. In case they were quickly shipped off to their depleted battalions, anti-gas instruction was taught within twenty-fours hours of new recruits arriving in camp; the need for good gas discipline was too important; it had to be drilled into soldiers before they left for the front lines. New soldiers were told to forget about poison gas as a separate function of warfare; now it was all-encompassing and affected all aspects of battle: "War, being based mainly on offensive action, calls for instruction mainly in the subjects meant to inculcate the offensive spirit. But present conditions have shown that in order to be in a position to carry out this offensive action, a unit must be able to successfully resist all forms of gas attack."[85]

Apart from the lectures, soldiers were subjected to fake gas attacks in the middle of the night, had to perform mundane duties and even play soccer games with their SBRs on in order to increase their confidence in their respirators. One report reminded instructors to try to make gas lectures interesting, and reiterated that it was of the utmost importance to get the new soldiers feeling comfortable wearing their SBRs, especially as gas was being used in every large-scale battle, as well as in raids and for harassing troops at night. Finally, when possible, before troops were sent off to the reinforce their units they visited a base hospital to view gassed men; as one instructor noted, it "furnished a great stimulus to general gas training." It was hoped that a combination of education, training, and fear would stimulate a firm anti-gas doctrine.[86]

The need for specialized training of the artillery and auxiliary components of the Canadian Corps also fell to the individual unit gas officers. Particularly vulnerable to gas shells were the artillerymen. Weary from feeding their guns, breathing heavily from the exertion, partially deaf from the constant roar of their own firing, and even possibly under a barrage of HE shells, they were susceptible, unless properly trained, to miss the fall of "dud" gas shell. Both the Germans and the Canadians realized the importance of gassing an enemy's batteries to kill men and to impede the rate of fire. Battery gas officers trained their men to fire with their masks on during the day and at night. Officers were trained to improvise signals that were needed when their whistles could not be used because of gas, and the men were forced to practise fuse setting, which was particularly difficult to accomplish while wearing an SBR.[87] When one gas officer found that troops in reserve, such as cooks and wagon riders, could not adjust their respirators in less than a minute, they were forced into intensive anti-gas drill to bring them up to speed.[88]

Realizing that all the training possible could not save soldiers who were forced to live in a constant gas environment, the Gas Services insisted by mid-1917 on the creation of numerous gas-free dugouts. Initially, the innovative troops used wet blankets, which kept out some of the gas. Later, battalions were given chemically treated blankets to protect the dugouts, so that soldiers could be removed from a gas bombardment if wounded or could escape if facing high gas concentrations in the trenches.[89] By the summer of 1917, the common use of gas shells meant that periods of readiness were abolished and gas alerts were more stringently adhered to. Within three kilometres of the front, all soldiers were required to keep their SBRs at the ready position on their chests.[90] During gas alerts, gas sentries were posted, and the general level of anxiety rose for all soldiers in the forward alert zone.

The gas war thus continued to intensify with the interplay between offensive gas tactics and enforced defensive anti-gas doctrine. It would get worse; in July 1917 the Germans introduced a new gas, the most effective casualty-causing chemical agent of the war.

CHAPTER FIVE

Mustard, King of the War Gases

JULY 1917–DECEMBER 1917

Hollow-Eyed Zombies

By early 1917 Sir Douglas Haig thought that he might finally be able to launch the offensive he had been planning ever since the disastrous Somme battles the year before. The field marshal was planning a massive attack in Flanders in late summer that would break through the German lines and force the enemy to retreat or be enveloped. That fighting was to be some of the bloodiest of the war, under conditions that made Hell look welcome. The first soldiers went over the top at the end of July, and the battle raged until November, with both the British Expeditionary Force and the Canadian Corps clashing with the Germans for months in a huge muddy grave surrounded by a blasted and desolate landscape. But before Haig could unleash his long-awaited operation, the Germans forever changed the tactical nature of gas warfare with their introduction of the new mustard-gas compounds in the Ypres salient on 12-13 July 1917.[1]

Up to July 1917, gases could be classified under two broad headings: non-persistent (chlorine, phosgene, diphosgene) and harassing agents (lachrymators or tear gas). The cloud attacks of chlorine and phosgene gases that had been effective earlier in the war had largely been negated by better respirators. Although gas tactics using Green Cross shells still surprised the enemy, and thereby caused casualties before respirators were donned, they did not linger more than a few hours and could be negated by Vermorel sprayers, rain, and strong winds. But the new battlefield mustard gas, which was later labelled by one contemporary as the "King of the War Gases," was unlike the previous agents, because it was a persistent gas.[2] It did not disappear, but polluted the battlefield for days or even weeks as it lay, dormant and deadly.

New gas shells were filled with an oily liquid; when the charge burst in the shell the mustard gas evaporated and was scattered over the ground or anybody nearby, where it slowly evaporated. Unlike chlorine, which had an almost immediate effect on terrified soldiers, this new gas was difficult to detect: the first symptoms of poisoning were an initial tendency to sneeze accompanied by the light smell of mustard, giving the gas its name. Initially, thousands fell victim because they associated gas with violent chocking, raw throats, and suffocation – a slight tickling of the nose and throat by this new agent was among the least of a soldier's worries at the front. In addition, mustard gas was a slow-acting agent that killed the nerve cells so that the victim would only start to feel the effects hours after being gassed. Eyes became inflamed and swollen, skin blistered, and men vomited uncontrollably. Upon being taken to the clearing stations, the gas cases became hoarse, coughed harshly, and went blind. On the second and third days the victims began to die. The effects were traumatizing, and many soldiers must have wondered to what further levels of horror the Germans were willing to stoop. As one recorded: "The vile mustard gas, that turned lungs to fluid, and burned skin from the body, now permeated the light summer clothing, and the men writhed at the scorching touch. Around the neck and throat and upon the hands it seemed as though hot irons seared the flesh ... Eyes swollen and sore; faces and hands seemingly scalded; ears deafened; throats parched." Within three weeks of the introduction of mustard gas, such casualties reached 14,000 – more British gas cases than in the whole previous year. Although the death count was low – about 500 – the gas incapacitated large numbers of men and clogged British clearing stations and war hospitals.[3]

More insidious than the slow-acting nature of the gas was the ability of enemy gunners to make an area almost uninhabitable by firing only a small number of mustard gas shells. The problem with non-persistent lethal shells was that many shells had to be fired in order to gain the high concentrations of gas needed to kill or incapacitate. For instance, British estimates thought it would take between 5,000 and 8,000 gas shells to smother a small fortified village.[4] But with mustard gas, even if the contents of the shells were not initially inhaled or sprayed on anyone, they still lurked within the mud and water of the battlefield, where the unfortunate soldier made his home.

Not only did mustard gas kill, burn, and incapacitate, it also consigned the soldier to a permanent state of unease. With every puddle an imagined trap, with every patch of ground possibly containing a substance that burned and blinded men, it left the already exhausted and strained soldiers with no rest, physically and mentally, from the horrors of war. "Gas condemned the soldier to a state of unendurable helplessness," one postwar writer noted.[5] Although that might be overstating the case, soldiers forced to hold an infected mustard-gassed area took on a zombie-like state. There was no escape: men were hollow-eyed from lack of sleep and were afflicted with continuous headaches, bouts of vomiting, and voices raspy from minor gassings.

As the Germans continued to refine their attack gas tactics, the Canadian Gas Services were undergoing some changes as well. At a conference between the chemical advisor and the divisional gas officers on 19 July 1917, it was decided to disband the divisional gas schools and replace them with one Canadian Corps Gas School. On 26 July 1917, Lieutenant N.C. Qua, as the new commandant of the school, took over a mining building in northern France and began to design a course on gas. The Corps Gas School would facilitate the standardization of gas training and relieve some of the workload of the divisional gas officers. Officers and selected NCOs would remain the school's students, and it was mandated in October 1917 that because "many of the failures in gas defence have been traced to the lack of training of officers," all staff officers, commanding officers, company commanders, and adjutants were now forced to attend a special two-day course.[6]

At the same time, a meeting of senior Canadian gas officers was organized to discuss the German introduction of mustard gas onto the Western Front battlefield. Questions arose about how to defend against a gas that was difficult to smell, lurked in shell holes and dugouts, and continued to present a danger days after it was fired. There was a frenzy within the BEF as High Command urgently required information to combat this new gas. The 1st Canadian Division received a message from the Canadian Corps Headquarters asking for any information on the "means adopted by them [Germans] to safeguard their own troops against its effects."[7] There was no adequate response from the 1st Division, however, and the only answer lay in education and training. The analysis of spent gas shells, mustard-gassed victims, prisoners of war, and captured German documents produced varied levels of information on the new gas. But it remained a slow process that was significantly furthered only when the agent was actually encountered and accurately reported upon. More dangerous to the evolution of gas discipline, the men of the Canadian Corps had accepted the proven protection of their respirators only to find that the Germans' newest gas could burn soldiers who followed the directions of the Gas Services.

Canadian gunner Ernest Black remarked how he had returned from leave only to hear that the Germans had introduced a new gas from which there was no defence. As a result, in the colourful words of Black, "the morale of the whole army was lower then a snake's belly." Wilfred Kerr of the 11th Battery, Canadian Field Artillery, agreed with Black about the "sensational reports" of mustard gas and described some of what he heard in the rumour mill: "that it would burn one's skin if the liquid fell thereon, that it would lie in dugouts and shell-holes for a week, that it would be proof against the chemical contained in our masks, that it possessed mysterious qualities beyond number." It was only through education by the Gas Services that the wild rumours concerning mustard gas could be quelled. The goal of the Gas Services therefore was first to dispel the mystery surrounding the new German weapon.[8]

In August 1917 the First Army desperately ordered that "it is essential, if casualties are to be avoided, that the properties of the gas and the means of combatting it should be explained to each individual, and in many cases immunity depends on the action of the individual." The Gas Services were in a quandary. Up until the introduction of mustard gas, they had attempted to instigate a gas discipline that removed all individuality on the part of the soldier; if he followed the rules then he would most likely escape the effects of the gas. Drill, in the words of one British cynic, was to place the recruit "into a state of routine coma," where every command was automatically carried out and the brain's reason effectively muted. But now the rules had changed, and a more progressive pedagogical approach was required. It was ordered that all soldiers must take their own precautions. Lectures by Canadian gas officers and sergeants stressed that "each man is responsible for his own proper protection against hostile gas." The SBR still protected the face and lungs perfectly against mustard gas, but the rest of the body was vulnerable. The best precaution was to be constantly aware of one's surroundings for any hint of gas and react accordingly. This level of readiness required a thorough knowledge of gas and all of its effects and symptoms. What eventually developed was a combination of rigid rules, individual training, and self-preventative measures – all of which were instilled by the Canadian Gas Services.[9]

The teaching of gas discipline to the Canadian Corps officers was accomplished at the new Canadian Corps Gas School. The advantage of having the Canadian Corps as a self-contained unit, rather than as part of the British Corps – which more or less fought on one sector of the front and continually had divisions posted to and away from it – was that the Canadians could instigate gas discipline in a continual and consistent manner for its troops. As one Canadian Corps report noted, "The units under it were accustomed to living and fighting together, the Corps and Divisional Staff were accustomed to working together, and the Canadian Corps thus became a homogeneous, self-contained and mobile whole." The importance of the self-contained Canadian Corps should not be underestimated. As General E.L.M. Burns, then a lieutenant commanding a signals section in the 4th Division, remarked after the war: "Under a corps commander and staff whom they could trust, and whose methods and abilities they knew and understood [the Canadians prospered]. In contrast, British divisions moved about from one corps to another, and sometimes differed from misunderstandings arising from different operational and administrative practices in the different corps, and personality clashes between officers on the divisional and corps staff." A more simplistic analysis by a Canadian colonel after the war noted that, "We just felt that we were getting better all the time, chiefly because we weren't being separated." For Canadian commanders it was like being a teacher and having the same class all year long; in contrast, the British had their classrooms change every few weeks with the addition of new students. The advent of a centralized Corps Gas School freed the DGOs from their individual schools in order to be closer to their men at the front, an advantage the British eventually acknowledged when they followed suit months later.[10]

In the first Canadian Corps gas course, which opened on 5 August 1917, the officers and NCOs were instructed on a myriad of gas subjects. The students attended nine gas lectures, covering topics ranging from anti-gas defence and how to care for gas dugouts to gas shell tactics and a history of the gas war. The climax of the course was subjecting the men to a gas attack. Canadian infantry officer James Pedley enjoyed his gas course up until the last day, when "the demonstration put three officers in the hospital through carelessness with the gas-masks ... [but] I suppose the rest of us were duly uplifted." The courses were useful in teaching officers and NCOs about the gas war, and, as was a function of instructive schools away from the fighting, were also a chance for commanding officers to give some of their tired officers and NCOs a break from the crushing pressure of the front. The men attended lectures and demonstrations during the day, but in the evenings it was free time, and most officers emulated the actions of Canadian Lieutenant Albert West, who spent his four days relaxing and catching up with an old friend from home.[11]

Within the learning environment of the gas school, the gas instructors and DGOs frantically processed all information they had received from the Canadian Corps chemical advisor. It was initially a difficult task, as the gas officers had no direct contact with mustard gas, but most were able to pass along the basic characteristics, gleaned from hastily published army-level pamphlets, during the gas courses. Officers and NCOs, after taking their courses at the Corps Gas School, augmented the teaching role of battalion gas officers by ensuring that proper gas discipline was followed by their troops.[12] A Canadian stretcher-bearer wrote home to his wife about what his battalion gas officers taught him: "We have had a small lecture on the Huns' new gas ... It has already been christened the 'Mustard' shell, as it leaves the ground, where it hits, yellow, and tickles the nose like mustard. It remains effective for as long as thirty hours. You can absorb it through the skin by rubbing your clothes with your hands; in fact, any old way. It seems to be made so you can get gassed with the least possible trouble on your part."[13]

Such lectures helped to somewhat ease the soldiers' minds against the unknown, but it was impossible to feel secure until mustard gas was encountered and successfully overcome. The expectation of Yellow Cross shells (the sign painted on mustard gas shells and the name given to the shells by soldiers) being used revolutionized the Gas Services. It was now imperative that every man in the Canadian Corps have a thorough knowledge of mustard gas and the resulting changes in the gas war.

An understanding of the new German artillery fireplans of hiding gas shells among high-explosive bombardments raised the level of apprehension as the 2nd Canadian Division's staff officers, wary of losing able troops to this new gas, overreacted to the German tactics. On 3 August H.E. Burstall, the divisional commander, ordered that "in future, whenever the enemy opens an Artillery or Trench mortar bombardment, box respirators will be worn by all ranks in the vicinity or where the shells are falling."[14] Such overcompensation was due to the lack of control that commanding officers felt they had in terms of this alien weapon. It was also unrealistic. Soldiers hated their claustrophobic masks, and they could not possibly wear them all day and night and still function as soldiers. It is unclear when the order was rescinded, but it surely would have been a result of open hostility from the trench warriors.

Besides such overreaction, Canadian troops were given useful warnings that mustard gas could be delivered from both shells and trench mortars, and that the Germans would most likely soon develop a gas projector due to the success of the British Livens projector. More important, a report entitled "Organization for Defence against Gas," issued on 10 August, just as the corps was preparing to carry out its long-awaited attack on Hill 70, warned that "it is not unlikely that in the near future all assaulting troops may be compelled to operate with respirators adjusted, and it is certain that all troops will be exposed to gas more frequently than in the past." Much like the training before Vimy, the infantry rehearsed in advancing through simulated courses, but this time with their SBRs on. In connection with this, all dugouts were to have a gas blanket covering the entrance, SBRs were to be inspected daily, and gas sentries were to be posted to all working parties, dugouts, signal offices, and headquarters. Strict gas discipline was necessary, but it would take a while before the soldiers realized the insidious nature of the new weapon.[15]

One of the reasons why there were such high casualties in the British Army within weeks of the introduction of mustard gas was the surreptitious method of delivery employed by the Germans. The faint smell of mustard given off by the Yellow Cross shells, like phosgene, was usually lost amid the overpowering smells of decay, garbage, and body odour surrounding the trenches. The difficult-to-discern smell in combination with Yellow Cross barrages being "hidden" within HE bombardments meant that most soldiers barely realized they or their trench had been gassed. J.W. Lynch, an American serving with the Princess Patricia's Canadian Light Infantry, remembered the German artillery gas tactics: "We listened intently. Intermingled with the crash of high-explosive shells could be heard the dull 'plop' of bursting gas shells. Heinie thought to

catch us napping. There is just enough explosive in a gas shell to burst the casing and release the deadly stuff. During a heavy bombardment it is very difficult
to hear them. The gas is almost odorless and often goes undetected until too
late. The gas is heavier than air and seeks low spots, such as shell holes and
dugouts, where men are ordinarily safe." The wicked nature of gas left some soldiers questioning the morality of such a weapon, with one such trench soldier
actually believing that mustard gas embodied evil: "from the first velvety phut
of the shell burst to those corpse-like breaths that a man inhaled almost
unawares. It lingered about out of control. When he fired it, man released an
evil force that became free to bite friend or foe til such time as it died into the
earth. Above all, it went against God-inspired conscience."[16]

With the new gas, the role of the company gas NCOs rose in importance, for
it became their job to study enemy barrages and immediately indicate to the
battalion gas officer if any mustard gas shells had contaminated their area.
These saturated zones would then be roped off, indicating to the higher eche-
lons and the next relieving battalion to beware. Of course, to note where Yellow
Cross shells had fallen, a gas NCO had to stay out of the dugout during a bombardment, which was often a death sentence in anything but the lightest of
strafing. Thus, most NCOs waited in the protective dugouts with their companions and investigated the surrounding region after a bombardment for any
signs of contamination. This forward planning about mustard gas notwithstanding, the Canadians had thus far been lucky in avoiding the Yellow Cross
shells that had done so much damage to their British counterparts.

HILL 70: AUGUST 1917

With the success at Vimy Ridge, the Canadian Corps commander, Sir Julian
Byng, was given command of the British Third Army, and Arthur Currie took
control of the corps. Currie, who had not even been a regular force officer prior
to the war, was the first Canadian to lead the corps. His unmilitary-like
demeanour, with his pear-shaped body and lack of charisma, was overshadowed by his keen military mind and his devotion to his men. Eventually to
emerge as one of the most successful of the BEF's generals, Currie was about to
organize his first set-piece battle. The objective was the strategically situated
mining town of Lens, located north of Arras and the Scarpe River. And here the
Canadians would encounter mustard gas in great quantities for the first time.

The Canadian Corps' attack at Lens was to achieve two objectives: first, attack
and draw German reserves away from the Passchendaele battlefield, and second, kill as many Germans as possible according to the High Command's policy of attrition.[17] General Currie was given a detailed plan by Army Headquarters to attack the city of Lens in a frontal assault. Because the city was flanked on
two sides by hills, enfiladed fire would virtually ensure a costly failure if that

plan were followed. Seeing nothing innovative about a headlong charge into machine-gun and artillery fire, Currie objected to the plan and offered to stage an operation against Hill 70 to the north of Lens. The new Canadian commander argued that if Hill 70 were taken, then the Germans would be forced to counter-attack the Canadians in a situation similar to that envisioned by General Falkenhayn at the battle of Verdun. Moreover, the Germans position at Lens would be flanked and vulnerable if they could not regain the hill. General Haig agreed to Currie's plan, although he warned him "that the Bosche would not let us have Hill 70."[18] That was, of course, factored into Currie's set-piece battle.

The Canadians carried out a series of large-scale raids between late May and July using tactics that the corps had honed to an art. Despite the failed March gas raid, a number of raids were preceded with gas bombardments by shells and projectors to confuse the enemy and wear him down. Sergeant R.G. Kenter of the 46th Battalion remarked on the Special Company projector attacks: "A projector gas attack was launched against the enemy on the whole Canadian front. It was launched simultaneously by an electrical arrangement, and was accompanied by a terrific barrage ... We had the rare pleasure of witnessing it. The effect on the enemy must have been severe." A successful raid against La Coulotte, by the 44th and 50th Battalions on the night of 2 June, worked primarily because the exhausted and confused German defenders

Gas projectors used by Canadians at Hill 70.

had been drenched with more than 600 British gas canister projectors prior to the attack.[19]

But six days later, in a five-battalion attack involving the 3rd and 4th Canadian Divisions against Souches, some of the Canadian infantry were caught by their own gas. A group of projectors had been jarred by the concussion of a shell blast and had dropped the gas short into the Canadian lines. One of the results was an order passed from the chemical advisor that all soldiers at the front had to wear their gas masks an hour before all gas attacks. Good gas discipline removed the individual's responsibility in favour of general instructions that all had to follow, yet the final protection ultimately fell to the lowly soldier who had to be drilled in following those policies.[20]

The raid inflicted over 700 casualties and garnered 136 German prisoners. This success was a direct result of the artillery fireplan that used both HE and gas shells to neutralize hostile batteries. Lethal gas was fired intensely from zero to fifteen minutes, followed by lachrymatory shells, which were fired from fifteen to forty-five minutes, and finally intense lethal gas shells for another fifteen minutes in hopes of catching gunners who had removed their respirators to wear only their gas goggles. The Canadian artillery was becoming adept at the use of gas to neutralize enemy guns. Their skill would be needed in the upcoming August battle of Hill 70. As well, the infantry commanders seemed to have no problem with gas as long as it was used by the artillery in their fireplans, and if the infantry did not have to rely on working in direct combination with it, as during the 1 March 1917 raid.[21]

Poison gas was increasingly becoming more prevalent on the battlefield, and after the successful use of gas in both attack and defence operations it became necessary to exert operational control over it. Initially the use of gas was suspect by senior artillery officers, who were required and ordered to consult with the chemical advisor in implementing a fireplan. But with escalated use came more familiarity and a better understanding of the missions poison gas could support. The chemical advisor continued to play a role, albeit a less central one, in the artillery chemical fireplan; he chose the gas, the number of shells needed, and the best method to employ the chemical agents, but the actual target and intricate preparation fell to the corps artillery headquarters. Despite this central control, as early as July 1917 there was discussion between the chemical advisor and the brigade major at Artillery Headquarters that divisions should be allotted and trained in the use of gas shells. But at the upcoming battle of Hill 70 the role of gas still fell to the CBSO.[22]

Bad weather conditions continued to postpone the operation on Hill 70, leaving the soldiers fighting their nerves as time and again they prepared themselves for the attack only to have it cancelled. As the infantry waited for the battle, Canadian gunners and the sergeants of the Special Gas Companies continued to fire thousands of gas shells and projector gas drums into Lens to "demoralize" the enemy.[23] The obvious preparation for an attack made it impossible to achieve surprise, but General Currie hoped that the demonstrations against Lens itself would trick the Germans into believing that the main attack would indeed fall there. The key to the Canadian attack, and the subsequent Canadian operational way of war for the remaining year and a half, was to mass the enormous firepower of indirect artillery bombardment, machine-gun barrages, and gas attacks in order to take the enemy position and hold it against subsequent counter-attacks. This interaction between infantry and artillery was essential for victory. As Haig recounted in his personal diary three weeks before the battle, the Canadians were always clamouring for more guns and they "always open their mouths very wide!"[24] The dominion shock troops were about to show that their success at Vimy was not an aberration. They were looking to bite off another chunk of German-held strategically important territory.

The constant shellfire by the Canadians, and the British before them, had reduced the mining village of Lens to rubble, and Hill 70 had been severely battered, with only small tufts of vegetation here and there on a top of white chalk. The Germans, aware of an upcoming attack, fired gas shells into the Canadian lines in hopes of disrupting the preparations for battle. William Morgan of the 24th Battalion wrote in his diary during the days leading up to the battle that "the Germans [were] unable to find the exact location of the Canadians [with HE shells and] fired over gas shells to make sure [our] stay ... was uncomfortable." Likewise, as the 7th Siege Battery trudged up their battery positions, Signaller T.W.L. MacDermot spoke for all his men when he wrote that "the deadly thought of what lay over the top were [sic] deepened by the choking sound all around and among us of the gas shells that the Germans were throwing over." As the Canadians went into battle, many passed the famous padre, F.G. Scott, who gave each man a blessing, "which was not lost even when seen through the sweat-clouded windows of the masks, and the sombre atmosphere of the surroundings." Sensing the magnitude of the attack, Arthur Lapointe, a newly arrived reinforcement for the 22nd "Van Doos" Battalion, nervously asked a trench veteran who had been through some tough shows how this one looked. He was struck by the answer: "Lens will be strongly defended and the assault will be a hard one." The veteran was right.[25]

The deception by the Canadians gave them an added advantage, but they still needed to find a way to break the German defences-in-depth. In this superior defensive system that protected soldiers against concentrated bombardments and gas clouds, strong groups of counter-attacking reinforcements were held behind the lightly manned German front lines to drive the exhausted and depleted attackers from the newly won trenches. Although Haig had derisively called the German defence-in-depth system "simply the refuge of the destitute," it had inflicted heavy losses on the French and British since it had been implemented in the beginning of 1917.[26] The Canadians hoped to destroy the elastic nature of the German defences with crushing firepower, which would paralyze the "bounce-back" of counter-attacks and thus allow the troops to take and hold the enemy trenches.

The ten attacking Canadian battalions left their trenches at 4:25 on the morning of 15 August 1917 behind a smoke screen and a rolling barrage. Although the Germans laid down a counter-barrage of artillery, bullets, and gas, within twenty minutes the Canadians had overrun the defenders' machine-gun posts and taken their first objective, the Blue Line. As one astonished infantryman exclaimed, "It seemed a miracle that anyone could come through such shell fire alive." Those Canadians who made it up the hill through the fierce fighting immediately turned to the necessary ritual of frantically digging trenches, reversing parapets, laying wire, and preparing for the inevitable German counter-attacks. Additional protection was secured for the first assaulting battalions, as the Canadians had grouped all the machine guns from the reserve battalions and moved up ninety-six to strengthen the defence. This combined with the nine field artillery batteries, which were being guided by artillery spotters in the front lines, were intended to make the No Man's Land in front of the newly won Canadian trenches a particularly deadly killing ground.[27]

Supporting the arms set to sweep No Man's Land, the Canadian counter-battery artillery were furnished with more then 8,000 rounds of phosgene 4.5-inch and 6-inch shells in order to disrupt the German guns supporting their infantry's counter-attacks, thereby leaving them without adequate cover as they approached the Canadian lines. The chemical bombardments were to be a surprise, with intense bursts of lethal gas in order to catch German gunners at rest or unaware, followed by a mixture of lachrymatory and lethal gases and high explosives to "confuse the enemy and conceal the fact that gas" was being used. The Canadian artillery had learned that, despite its advanced counter-battery work, it could not be sure to hit every enemy gun with high explosives or shrapnel. Instead, chemical shells employed to keep the opposite gunners engulfed in poison gas and thereby slow or completely stop the enemy rate of fire. As one general staff report on counter-battery work stressed, "just as artillery forms the main support of the offensive, so also is it the strongest weapon of the defensive." And in completing this defensive counter-battery work, poison gas became paramount.[28]

Within two hours the Germans had unleashed four counter-attacks, all of which were broken up by the combined efforts of the Canadian infantry and artillery. Some attacks were stopped with concentrated fire held until the Germans were two hundred yards from the line, while others were beaten back in vicious hand-to-hand fighting, as described by Alfred Pike of the 26th Battalion: "The Germans would come and drive us a little ways, and we halted them and drove 'em back." The Germans brought seven more battalions to add to the eight they had in reserve and continued to launch themselves in a frenzy of attacks against the Canadian positions for the next three days. On 16 August, the Canadians attacked again and took all of Hill 70 before digging in again to stave off a dozen more counter-attacks that day. Arthur Lapointe, desperately fighting in the trenches, bemoaned the furious German counter-attacks, which had left his unit mauled: "Out of 117 men, our company now numbers less than fifty." The Canadians held on to the newly won trenches in a grim struggle and ultimately broke the German attacks, which were continuously annihilated as they struggled across the killing zone.[29]

Constantly risking danger as he carried the wounded back to the clearing stations, one Canadian stretcher-bearer remarked on the force of the Canadian guns: "Our guns – my God! This isn't war; it's murder ... the dead are piled in heaps."[30] A German soldier who survived the slaughter candidly attested to the firepower of the Canadians in a letter home: "I had always thought that our U-boats were working so thoroughly that our enemies were suffering heavy losses of ammunition, but it does not seem to be as bad as that."[31] The German attackers, valiantly offering their lives as they followed orders and counter-attacked, eventually realized that the hill could not be retaken by conventional means. If they were to retake their position they had to somehow neutralize the Canadian guns.

And so on the night of 17 August, the Germans turned to mustard gas. Between 15,000 and 20,000 Yellow Cross shells were fired, cut with diphosgene shells, heavily gassing the artillery, as well as the Canadian front line. The 1st and 2nd Artillery Brigades were the hardest hit, but the Canadian gunners, aware of the need to keep firing so as to protect the vulnerable infantry, removed their fogged-up respirators, refusing to be hampered in their ability to lay their sights and set their fuses. Working beyond the limits of endurance and aware that gas-shell fumes swirled around them, the Canadian gunners did not let up, and further German counter-attacks were broken up. But by morning 183 heroic gunners lay in agony, suffering from blindness and burns to their bodies. There was almost nothing left of the two batteries; as gunner K.B. Jackson of the 1st Divisional Artillery noted two days later, "We had only five Sergeants and cooks, and lord knows what, manning the guns." During an inquiry carried out following the affair, it was noted that the men "were keenly alive to the dangers of a gas bombardment" and the gunners conducted their actions "with a full knowledge of the probable consequences but determined to do what they thought was required of them at all costs." The gunners were viewed as heroes by the infantry they had supported, and the inquiry found that they had acted with bravery rather then carelessness. Regardless, the event illustrated the effectiveness of mustard gas in quelling artillery fire – or causing high casualties.[32]

Unable to move from their shallow trenches, the infantry were also at the mercy of Yellow Cross shells. They were instructed to don their respirators at any hint of smelling mustard and to wrap themselves in their ground sheets to reduce the risk of blistering. This good advice could not negate all the gas casualties. In a letter to his wife, one Canadian recorded the reaction to the first use of mustard gas against his position: The Germans "opened up with gas and H.E. – a terrific strafe, and we were tight in it ... For a second, I was afraid that there was going to be a stampede. The fellows got a bit rattled with the gas, [but] grabbed for [gas] helmets." Private Wallace Carroll remembered that his introduction to mustard gas was not as frightening, simply because he did not know he was being poisoned: "The gas settled into all the muck and mud in the trenches ... and it was cold enough to freeze it. Well after stand down in the morning ... a certain number of us go into the dugout ... and we have a sleep ... While we were sleeping the sun came out nice and strong, thawed out the mud and the gas rose again. Because it was heavy, it drifted into the dugouts and we got it when we were asleep. Three quarters of our platoon got it."[33]

Most of these men were invalided out, having lost their voices and gone blind. The same thing was occurring in the 46th Battalion at a larger scale, as Private R.D. Roberts recalled: "Two thirds of the battalion was suffering from this gassing. And still they were in the line and no hope of getting any relief." Even with no relief from the gas environment, the Canadians clung to their hard-won position and continued to beat off German attacks. In the midst of the fighting, officers continued to suffer a higher proportion of the blinded casualties as they were often forced to remove their fogged-up SBRs to coordinate the Canadian defensive positions.[34]

In order to prevent the front-line positions from receiving food or ammunition, the Germans deluged the rear areas in gas. Six kilometres from the front, the men of the 7th Battalion were forced to wear their respirators as they marched to the trenches as reinforcements, with all stores and ammunition lugged into the line under such conditions. As one infantryman wrote, "it was probably the most difficult [relief] ever carried out by any troops."[35] The gassing of reserve trenches remained a problem, and commanders had to factor in extra time for units to get into the line when wearing respirators.[36] It was a difficult lesson to learn, and at Passchendaele, British and Canadian soldiers often arrived late to their trenches due to the weariness imposed by marching in gas masks and either narrowly made the deadline or missed their creeping barrage, often with terrible consequences.

Although other areas of logistics were disrupted, many of the Canadians realized the need to support the infantry in the front lines and pushed on. While bringing up food and ammunition, William Green suffered terrible mustard burns as he struggled through the mud. Mustard gas affected areas on the human body that were moist – armpits, back, knees, and groin: "I got burned pretty bad ... I got blisters the size of fifty cent pieces all over my back from my neck to my buttocks." Fear works in complex ways in battle. For example, soldiers were more terrified about having their genital area wounded than any other part of their body. To the men in the trenches it must have seemed like the German barbarity would never stop as soldiers were threatened with having their private parts burned and blistered. The educational messages from the Canadian Gas Services did little to relieve their stress: "Touching and scratching of these parts should be carefully avoided ... Scratching with hands that have been exposed to the gas causes great irritation, and swelling of the penis and scrotum."[37]

As the Canadians grimly held on to the hill, suffering from mustard-gas burns and blindness, there were no feelings of sympathy for those German prisoners who were in the Canadian lines and had thrown away their masks when captured. Some of the men of the 4th Battalion goaded their crying prisoners, "Serves you right, serves you right," when they asked for masks to protect themselves against the gas.[38] Although receiving the worst of the chemical attacks, the Canadians responded to the mustard gas with phosgene shells, and one German prisoner reported that "Your gas shells descend on us by the ton, and life in the underground defences of Lens is simply Hell."[39]

The battle for Hill 70 was bloody and vicious, where the Canadians and Germans attacked for three days without rest in the new, deadlier gas environment. Between 15 and 18 August, the Germans launched twenty-one counter-attacks on the Canadian lines. In the words of the German official history, "Even though we soon succeeded in sealing off the local penetrations of Lens, the Canadians had attained their ends. The fighting at Lens had cost us a considerable number of troops which had to be replaced. The entire preconceived plan for relieving the troops in Flanders had been upset." The Canadians had achieved both of their objectives: the taking of Hill 70 and the "chewing up" of German divisions slated to assist in the defence of Passchendaele. General Currie wrote in his diary that "It was the hardest battle in which the Corps had participated ... and G.H.Q. regard it as one of the finest performances of the war." As a result of the battle, one French war correspondent wrote that the Canadians "at the present time completely hold the limelight in the theatre of war" and that there is a saying among Allied troops that "one Canadian is worth three Germans."[40]

Although the Germans suffered an estimated 30,000 casualties, the Canadian victory also came at a heavy price. From 15 to 18 August, the Canadians lost 449 killed, 1,378 wounded from fire, and another 487 to gas. As the fighting continued to consolidate the victory, the Canadians suffered a total of 7,136 casualties, of which 1,122 were gas victims. In a letter home, one Canadian noted that Hill 70 and the battle of Lens "is not another Vimy; this is no walk-over, it is a pitched battle." It was a deadly affair, and it illustrated among other things, that the gas war had taken another step toward rendering the trenches even more uninhabitable.[41]

TACTICAL EMPLOYMENT OF GAS SHELLS

The German shells at Hill 70 were not only effective in harassing the infantry and gunners, but they also wreaked havoc with the transportation system. Canadian Richard Adamson, a transport driver bringing ammunition to the front, remembered with revulsion the effect of German gas shells on his horses. He could do nothing as he sat with his respirator attached and listened to his horses make screaming sounds as they were being poisoned.[42] Although horses were able to stand greater concentrations of gas than humans were, they were finally equipped with chemically treated nose bags that fit over the face after it was noticed that they were, as historian Basil Liddell Hart noted, being "killed off like flies." The first horse respirators were issued to the Canadian Corps in May 1917. Unfortunately, such an apparatus made the animals stop moving due to the great strain and annoyance produced by having a bag placed over their heads. "According to the Army manual to place a gas mask on a horse was only to take thirty seconds," slyly remarked Adamson, "but the officer that was to show us how to do it was still working at it forty-five minutes later." Horses had to be equipped with crude gas masks if food and ammunition were to get to the front, but with broad bombardments of mustard gas, whole areas – especially known roads and trench lines – were contaminated. Not only could the animals not graze in chemically infected zones, but through secondary contact with mustard on their flanks and heels, horses and mules caught within the gas environment for extended periods of time began to take on nightmarish appearances: animals lost clumps of hair to pink scar tissue, developed a sickly yellowish-brown pigment to their coats, and finally went blind and lame as the effects of gas and disease set in. The gas environment played a sad part in the estimated low life expectancy of a horse, which was, as one officer in the Canadian Army Veterinary Corps (CAVC) noted, approximately six days. Gas was an effective killer of transport animals and could thereby render logistical systems inoperable for significant periods.[43]

Along with the harassment of logistics, gas interfered with communication between the front and the rear. Passing information from the front was a problem for all armies during the First World War, and, as already seen through the chaos at St. Eloi, the Canadian Corps was no exception.[44] During a battle, the telephone lines that were dug into the ground were consistently severed from artillery barrages, and it became the responsibility of runners to get messages from the front to the rear, and vice versa. The bravery of such runners, darting from shell hole to shell hole, as shells rained down, is sometimes forgotten. Their perilous job became even more trying during a gas barrage. Due to the failure of respirators to allow enough oxygen to pass through the filter, the runners simply could not move quickly in gas. Thus messages that were slow at the best of times became outdated and even useless or misleading by the time they reached commanders in the rear. Private Arthur Brown of the 116th Battalion remembered that bombardments of HE and gas cut telephone wires and blocked the use of lamps by signalmen, adding more strain on the communication system so that additional runners had to be sent to from headquarters to ascertain the position of the front.[45] Clutching their messages, many never re-emerged from the chemical clouds, further casualties of the hidden gas war.

To help combat this confusion, pigeons were also sometimes used by trench soldiers to carry messages to the rear. Owing to the birds' importance, by October 1917 Canadian battalions were issued with anti-gas pigeon baskets. At Verdun one French pigeon, who succumbed to gas after it delivered a desperate message calling for reinforcements, was even awarded the French Légion d'Honneur for its "bravery." But most often pigeons became disorientated and unable to deliver their messages before they died from the poisonous vapours.[46]

The tactical application of gas was slowly being mastered by both sides, especially as it was used to increase the inherent friction on and behind the battlefield. To this end, the Germans introduced another war gas, the primary function of which was to cause confusion and disorder. The Germans developed their Blue Cross shell in July 1917, although it was not used on the Western Front until mid-August. The properties of this new gas, which was actually a fine dust, caused violent sneezing, vomiting, delusions, and general weariness in the victim. The gassed men were, as one report noted, the "picture of utter dejection" and in extreme cases were temporarily "driven mad by their pain and misery" as the chemical attacked the nervous system and resulted in violent convulsions and the loss of motor control. The exhausted aching feeling induced by the gas usually took twenty-four hours to wear off and was yet another burden shouldered by the Great War soldier. An added problem was that the Blue Cross shell was almost impossible to recognize – its burst was the same as an ordinary shell, and there was no appearance of a cloud of gas.[47]

The Germans devised the Blue Cross shells to be fired before Green Crosses and thus affect the defenders in that crucial period before alarms and sentries could give warning. During the lethal gas attack that followed, the soldiers would be sneezing and vomiting in their SBRs. Canadian infantryman Victor Wheeler depicted the serious repercussions of this Blue Cross effect: "A gas respirator 'objected' violently to being splattered within by the wearer's up-chucking. On the first belch, off flew the mask, exposing its owner to severe blistering and poison." One captured German document remarked, "If Blue Cross gas has been breathed, the wearing of the mask becomes impossible owing to the coughing and sneezing effect as well as the difficulty of breathing." At least, that was the hope based on controlled test environments, but it was far less successful on the Western Front. Its effects, other than psychological, were limited, and the faith that Blue Cross gases would force all soldiers to remove their gas masks underrated the common soldier's capacity for endurance.[48]

Soldiers had been thoroughly warned through lectures and good gas discipline that to remove their masks meant a slow and painful death, so those
exposed to the poison gas could sit through an assortment of tortures – sneezing, coughing, and even vomiting in their respirators – if the alternative meant
death.[49] The chemical adviser to the British V Corps summarized the effects of
Blue Cross as a "negligible menace so far as causing serious and prolonged casualties; but it is a very real factor in a battle, particularly in a retreat, where both
its moral and physical effects may greatly influence the issue during a limited
number of hours."[50] As a long-term, debilitating, casualty-causing agent, Blue
Cross gas was generally viewed as a failure by the Allies, but it continued to be
used up to the last day of the war because of the mental and physical burden it
placed on the trench soldier.

Bloody Passchendaele: October-November 1917

The Canadian diversionary attack at Lens had achieved its goals, but due to the
terrible weather conditions and a vigorous defence by the Germans the breakthrough in the Passchendaele campaign (as the 3rd Battle of Ypres was commonly known) had not materialized. Millions of shells and constant rain had
churned the ground into viscous mud that devoured matériel, men, and horses.
The main goal of the infantry was to survive under such conditions, rather than
launching successful attacks to break the German lines. The hoped-for advance,
during which Passchendaele Ridge was to be overrun on the first day, had long
been replaced by attritional grinding in unspeakable conditions. The strategic
objectives had dissolved like the ground to be fought over, and the capture of
Passchendaele Ridge became an end in itself. "When we get the Ridge, we've
won the war," was Haig's assessment of the importance of Passchendaele, and
everything was thrown into garnering it.[51] Passchendaele became Haig's obses-
sion, and of sixty British and dominion divisions on the Western Front at the
end of October 1917, all but nine were sooner or later engaged in the Flanders
offensive. The Canadians, who had twice recently proved that they could
achieve their operational objectives, were ordered to the area when the British
attack bogged down.

On 3 October, General Currie was curtly informed that he was to be ready to
move to Passchendaele; after the Canadians' ordeal at Hill 70, he was less than
pleased. Currie made a personal appeal to Haig, stating that the losses in the
recent fighting had been heavy and could not be adequately replaced with new
recruits. He hoped that this appeal, along with the possibility that the Canadian
Corps would be reunited under General Byng, commander of the Third British
Army, who asked for them in his upcoming tank attack at Cambrai, would sway
Haig, but he was to be disappointed: Haig's plan for them remained unchanged.
The abrupt move to the Flanders front was a shock to the Canadians, who had

already done their bit in the fighting. The rankers had settled in to lick their wounds, and there were even some like Private C.E. Barnes who, with some of his mates, had lifted two jugs of rum shortly after the battle of Hill 70 and had hidden them for a belated celebration. Much to their chagrin they were forced to pack up and move before they could reclaim their "treasure." The trench soldiers' lives were made more bearable through the pleasures of smoking, grousing, and drinking, but there would be no escape from the horror of Passchendaele or of gas.[52]

After sending out officers to view the battlefield, and even taking a personal reconnaissance himself, Currie had his worst fears realized: he found a muddy wasteland through which it would be almost impossible to bring up guns to adequately protect his men in the trenches.[53] Following the operational successes at Vimy and Hill 70, Currie had realized that victory depended on close interaction between the artillery and infantry. Notwithstanding their reputation as shock troops, the Canadians would be ground up if they tried to cross the firezone without a thorough artillery barrage. Thus, the most important preparation for the first phase of the battle was to build roads and gun pits close to the jumping-off point to assist in counter-battery work and to ensure that the artillery would be able to create an effective creeping barrage.

One advantage of the clogging mud, which had dragged the battle to a standstill, was that it cushioned and dispersed the blast from the tons of high explosives that continually pulverized the battlefield. Canadian infantryman Will Bird remembered that "the mud saved a lot of men," who became splattered with sludge but not blown to bits. Nonetheless, mere survival in the sea of goo was exhausting: one soldier of the 10th Battalion who staggered out of the wasteland found that his muddy great coat alone weighed forty-seven pounds.[54]

Gas was once again an essential component of the Canadians' counter-battery work as their lines were in view of the Germans located on the Passchendaele Ridge. In a memorandum, Brigadier General Foulkes, the director of Gas Services, admonished Allied artillery to continually press the enemy guns with gas shells. Anything to create uneasiness or misunderstanding was promoted: gunners were to fire intensely for three minutes, hold off for ten, and then resume; other pieces were to move from one battery to the next and then back again so that enemy gunners could never be sure when – or from where – gas would be creeping up on them.[55] Terrain was also utilized, with valleys and forests targeted so that defenders would be under heavy gas clouds and meterological conditions would be less likely to dissipate the fumes. Ultimately, the Canadian gunners aimed to disrupt and damage the morale of the enemy with poison gas, so that when the actual time of battle came they would be slow or apprehensive in responding.

During the four days before the attack on 26 October, two daily preparatory barrages were designed to throw off the Germans. Although in a relatively defenceless position, the artillery was not short of ammunition. General E.W.B. Morrison remarked after the war that the Canadians fired so many shells in support of the infantry that if loaded on railway trucks they "would make a train 17 1/2 miles long." The daily barrages were used to soften up the German defences, which had their focal points around concrete pillboxes within the muddy wasteland. The Canadian artillery had been issued special orders to focus on those areas because men huddled there not only for safety but also to escape the all-encompassing mud for a few hours. Using HE, shrapnel, and gas, the Canadian artillery worked in preparation of the infantry advance by thoroughly "de-lousing" the enemy's defences. With the fury of each barrage, the German defenders learned to dig deeper into their dissolving trenches.[56]

On the day of the attack there was no preparatory barrage, only the infantry following a creeping barrage in hope of surprising the Germans in their trenches. To augment the moving wall of explosives, at zero hour all known German batteries and roads bringing ammunition and reinforcements to the front were hit with a fireplan – 75 percent of which consisted of chemical shells – involving HE and gas. "The gas shell provided the most valuable means of obtaining that reduction of hostile artillery fire at critical periods," was how one Canadian order described the gas operations. With the German counter-barrage momentarily paralyzed, the infantry of the 3rd and 4th Canadian Divisions, floundering in knee-deep mud, waded to their objectives.[57]

The next phase of the battle, the seventh phase in the campaign, was made easier because field pieces could be moved forward and spread out into more stable and protected positions. During the offensive launched on 26 October, the artillery had been extremely vulnerable. Confidential Canadian reports admitted that "our own Artillery was distributed in two large groups ... and situated so far back that only the near German Batteries could be reached"; fortunately, "the German Higher Command does not appear to have realized to the full their element of advantage in the situation ... It should have been possible by proper use of enfilade [fire] to have increased our losses many fold."[58]

The Germans were not to let the Canadian successes go unanswered, and chemical molestation was added to the quagmire of mud, unburied corpses, and stagnant water. The exhaustion of fighting in and holding onto such deplorable positions made poison gas all the more exhausting. Gas masks invoked new frightfulness as men blindly stumbled in the clinging mud. From the success of their mustard-gas tactics against the British, the Germans had realized the importance of shelling forward areas to make them uninhabitable, especially, as one Canadian Corps report indicated, "during the night before an expected attack." Moreover, when an entire German division had to be pulled out of the line in September, after being forced to wear their respirators for seven and a half hours, the Germans had clear evidence of the debilitating effects of fighting in gas masks. By late October, their gunners were instructed to employ Yellow, Blue, and Green Cross shells not only to inflict casualties but, more important, to force the Canadians to wear their respirators constantly and thus erode their fighting efficiency.[59]

If the "face of battle" is ravaged by blemishes, then that of Passchendaele was corrupted by smallpox. In that wasteland of destruction, one could not look anywhere without seeing shell holes, millions of which, as Canadian trench soldier H.A. Searle remembered, were filled or half-filled with water.[60] Soldiers counted with a mixture of horror and disbelief the duckboards, called track, that joined the battlefield. Greasy from slime, the series of wooden planks built over the quagmire of mud, equipment, and corpses, were precarious at the best of times. As well, because German artillery occupied the higher ground, all troops had to be brought up at night so they would be hidden from German gunners. Absolute darkness was necessary and soldiers could see almost nothing, for even lighting a match could draw shells or a sniper's bullet.

In October 1917 the Canadian Corps was issued with anti-dimming solution to prevent gas masks from fogging up. Gunners, signallers, and other units that needed to see exact details were given the concoction. In most cases, though, the paste failed to allow an adequate view (and was no help for a heavily perspiring man), and respirators often had to be removed. The infantry appear never to have been given the anti-dimming solution; they continued to go about their business almost blind until the end of the war. With the Germans firing gas shells into the Canadian lines day and night, the added blindness of a respirator made it exceedingly difficult to move over the narrow, slippery planks in complete darkness. One soldier recounted how the Germans pocketed the area with gas while his unit was travelling over duckboards to the front:

> Gas shells were bursting over me and I couldn't see where I was going. All of a sudden, my foot slipped on the slippery plank and I went right into a muddy hole. I was up to the neck in mud and couldn't get out and tore my nails trying to get a hold [of the track]. Other fellows came across, but, they ran and took no notice as I shouted to them. At last, two fellows came with a rope and hauled me up and lay me on the muddy ground. Then, I got three buckets of water thrown on me and was left there. I was choking with gas and couldn't see.

Equally chilling were the memories of C.J. Albon of the 25th Battalion. He remembered that there were always men who had fallen off the boards and were pleading for help; but in the dark there was little a man could do, and with HE and gas shells falling all around "somebody would push you off the board walk" if you stopped to help. The abomination of the battlefield was only multiplied by gas: a man wearing a mask was effectively blinded, could barely hear his mates, and felt only the frightening whistle of his own intake and exhale of breath.[61]

For the soldiers squatting in the front-line trenches, in some areas with water up to their waists, mustard-gas shelling of their positions was terribly effective. Although Private Russell Tubman was aware of the German proclivity for retaliation with gas, he fell victim without even noticing: "I wondered what was the matter and I was unable to eat my dinner. My eyes started to water and I could feel a burning sensation on my tender spots ... I coughed until I could not get my breath." With gas infecting everything, soldiers, and especially those of the kilted regiments, suffered a multitude of burns and sores on their legs from brushing against diluted areas of gas pollution. Besides the annoyance of blisters and open sores there was the very real danger of such wounds being infected by the filth of the battlefield and expanding into serious infections. Soldiers in the front line, effectively cut off from the rear, were cold and miserable. Ironically, they were also plagued by thirst as they stood up to their waists in water. With lines of communication flooded, and with most of the surrounding water poisoned by mustard gas, it was not uncommon for soldiers to receive burns on legs and faces from the infected water. Standing sentry or even partaking in the daily ritual of shaving could result in a stream of gas casualties.[62]

Along with the infantry, the valiant stretcher-bearers, who repeatedly made the arduous six-hour trip through the mud as they carried wounded and dying men to the rear, were plagued by gas. A wounded man became the charge of the stretcher-bearer. If gas shells were sent over while a casualty was being transported back to the rear, the stretcher-bearer had to adjust the victim's SBR and constantly be aware of the possibility of the man vomiting into his mask and thereby choking to death. Ernest Black described his brief stint as a stretcher-bearer as his most trying time of the war, especially when the Germans bombarded the area with gas: the stretcher-bearers had to go "half a mile ... At every step we went knee-deep in mud ... As we struggled through trying to make time, with a comrade on our shoulders bleeding to death, we were nearly frantic. As soon as we delivered our burden to the doctor I opened my tunic and stripped off my gas mask in an attempt to get my breath back ... [My mask] was completely soaked with perspiration from my face. It would hardly have been wetter if it had been dipped in a pail of water."[63]

For mustard-gas victims who were not stretcher cases, the slow trek out of the wasteland was made with eyes slowly closing and going blind. One can only imagine the terror as the light became dimmer and dimmer until the blinded soldier was left in the middle of wasteland, where a step in any wrong direction meant being swallowed in the voracious mud. While the use of gas seriously hindered all forms of logistics, it was most trying when it prevented or slowed the movement to the rear. Casualties who might have been saved by doctors lost precious hours as they were forced to wait for exhausted stretcher-bearers or dissipating gas clouds.

Enduring the gas environment as well were the gunners whose positions were hit with mustard gas almost every day . In the words of Canadian artillery-man Gordon Howard, "the whole area was a mess of shell holes filled with water contaminated with gas . . . We were under intermittent shell fire and gas every night." "Gas was Fritz's most effective weapon against the artillery," claimed the regimental history of the 55th Canadian Field Battery.[64] Poison gas was an effective agent against the opposite gunners for it caused casualties, reduced the rate of fire, and generally wore down the troops. A British gunner described the effects of one German chemical bombardment:

> Surely the God of Battles has deserted a spot where only devils can reign. Think what it means, weeks of it, weeks which are eternities, when the days are terrible but the nights beyond belief. Through it all the horror of continual shell fire, rain and mud. Gas is one of the most potent components of this particular inferno. Nights are absolutely without rest, and gas last night is the crowning limit of horrors. The Battery that occupied the position before we came was practically wiped out by it, and had to be relieved at short notice, and the battery that relieved them lost 37 men on the way in. You can imagine how bucked I was when they handed me out these spicy bits of gossip on the way up. I daren't risk more than three men per gun up here at the same time and only 2 officers besides myself, at the moment they are rather sorry for themselves after last night's gas stunt, and doing unhelpful things to their eyes with various drops and washes. I've got a throat like raw beef and a voice like a cow.[65]

Brigadier-General J.S. Stewart, who temporarily took control of the 4th Division's Field Artillery, aptly remarked that "No gunner without experience of Passchendaele really knew the horrors of war." It was the "devil's own instrument of death – poison gas" that added to the apocalyptic nature of the fighting.[66]

The Canadians, like other soldiers before them, learned to survive in the brutal battlefield conditions. Survival was one thing; carrying out successful operations was another. That required battle-hardened troops, trained in over-coming the chemical quagmire. Private Andrew Munro of the 50th Battalion, who was known as "bomb-proof" within the unit because he was one of the few originals who was still living by the time of Passchendaele, wrote with a hint of swagger about the Canadian advance and the German retaliation: "Am in a recently captured 'Fritz' dugout, so if there are occasionally misspelt words or if there are a few scratches you will know that 'he' has lobbed one fairly close. 'He' is quite sore at losing his formidable strongholds, and deeply resents us occu-pying them, and consequently he 'pounds' away, shoots over his gas and liquid fire, all to no avail, for the Canadians have a nasty habit of hanging on to what they have taken, regardless of Prussian Guards, Bavarians or anybody else." But hanging on was not without its cost. During the capture of their two objectives the 3rd and 4th Divisions suffered 3,802 casualties, of which 432 were recorded as from gas. Throughout the battle of Passchendaele all soldiers were engulfed in an intense gas environment, but the Canadians were about to end all of that as they launched two more offensives to capture the ruined town of Passchendaele.[67]

With the success of the first two offensives on 26 and 30 October, the depleted 3rd and 4th Divisions were replaced with the rested 1st and 2nd Divisions for the final push to take the pounded and barren ridge. The soldiers coughed and hacked as they trudged exhausted to the rear, and Private John Mackenzie of the 72nd Battalion recounted after the war that "a lot of us got gas that was never reported."[68] It was hoped that rest would cure many of the men. While this worked for some, others became diseased and wasted away. Into this contaminated wasteland strode fresh troops, past the stench of unburied bodies, in order to undertake General Currie's two-staged attack on what was left of Passchendaele.

Once again, for the attack to succeed, a close liaison between the artillery and infantry was needed to stun the Germans and allow the infantry to cross the firezone without being massacred. Yet unlike Vimy or Hill 70, the German artillery from the start continued to harass the trenches at the front, especially billets and forming-up locations, with gas shoots. R.J. Manion, a Canadian medical officer, remembered the effects of the German gas: "Misery? Never elsewhere had we experienced anything akin to it – the inflamed eyes; the suffocation in our lungs; the knowledge that inhalation of sufficient gas would put us into Kingdom Come." Another Canadian machine gun officer concurred when he remarked that "the toughest at Passchendaele was the gas." Although tormenting the Canadians, the Germans failed to capitalize on their overwhelming advantage over the dominion troops who were floundering in the mud below them. On the morning of 6 November, following a creeping barrage, which accounted for the slow movement of troops advancing through muck, the attacking Canadians took the ruins of Passchendaele before most Germans were able to man their machine guns. On the 10th, the Canadians cleared the area north of Passchendaele and once again had proved that they were the BEF's elite force, capable of finishing the job Haig had started four months earlier.[69]

During the period of battle, the 1st and 2nd Division suffered 3,332 casualties, of which 401 were from gas. The greatest proportion of gas casualties fell on 2-3 November, just as the new troops were entering what passed for the Canadian front line and beginning to hunker down into the mustard gas-infested slime. The relatively large number of gas casualties on those two days was indicative of the effectiveness of concentrated shots of mustard gas in welcoming unprepared troops to the front. As well, the difficulty in taking over any new position meant that standard protection, such as gas curtains, was always late in arriving at the front, leaving the infantry more vulnerable to enemy gas. For some, the added strain of chemical bombardments was enough to break a man's morale, as one soldier indicated: "By dawn we were all gassed. I had to send the rest of the HQ officers down, and face another night of it alone. As a result, I was rather bad. Passchendaele broke me. When I got out again in April [from his gas wound], I lasted only three months, as I simply couldn't stand it any longer."[70]

In addition to the psychological strain, men were pushed to their physical limits. "I was in pretty poor shape, what with a touch of gas and the wet and the cold because of the wretched living conditions. I could hardly speak and my eyes were red, also I was in need of a good sleep," was how Gordon Howard described himself. H.A. Searle of the 18th Battalion remarked with clarity that the only way he and his companions survived the horrors of the battlefield was "the limitless supply of rum." But no amount of rum could erase the memory, as one soldier's seared recollection of the wounded makes clear: "From the darkness on all sides came the groans and wails of wounded men; faint, long, sobbing moans of agony, and despairing shrieks. It was too obvious to me that dozens of men with serious wounds must have crawled for safety into shell holes, and now the water was rising above them and, powerless to move, they were slowly drowning." The gurgles and moans of the wounded carried over the battlefield, interspersed with the harsh coughing by those unable to don their respirators within the gas environment.[71]

All soldiers who spent any time at the front were gassed to varying degrees. The tactical use of gas by the Germans amplified the utter exhaustion of simply surviving in the semi-aquatic world of Passchendaele. Mustard gas added to the misery of the soldiers, and it was also an effective casualty-causing agent. The British Official History placed the total casualties for the BEF during the 3rd Battle of Ypres at 244,897. The total number of recorded gas casualties, not counting those that simply died on the battlefield and vanished beneath its muddy surface, was almost 40,000. The gas environment of Passchendaele took its toll on the Canadian Corps as well. While the Canadians moved away from the soupy battlefield, final tallies showed that 1,015 of their 15,654 casualties had been from gas. The gas war continued to evolve in intensity and certainly earned its part in Private Bill Walkinshaw's description of Passchendaele as a "useless waste of life."[72]

Following the increasing potency of gas at Vimy and Hill 70, the enterprising Brigadier Victor Odlum of the 11th Canadian Infantry Brigade suggested in an 18 October 1917 letter to the Canadian General Staff that Special Gas Units, like the British ones, be set up in the Canadian Corps. "Gas has reached a position of great importance in stationary and semi-open warfare" and, as Passchendaele illustrated, "is still developing with ever increasing rapidity." Odlum suggested that four Special Companies and one stokes battery be set up, consisting altogether of almost nine hundred men, in order to provide ready available gas discharges for the Canadian divisions. It was an attractive suggestion, and there was much discussion at the Canadian General Staff Headquarters on how to establish the units. Seeing a way to get involved in attack operations, the Canadian Gas Services argued for the creation of two gas companies for releasing canisters and employing projectiles. Being the logical organization to implement this, the Gas Services based their argument on the grounds of the ever-increasing importance of gas in all operations and the role the gas companies would play in enabling the Canadian Corps to become a more self-contained unit. They also alluded to the long-term effects for the Canadian military: "unless the proposed companies for offensive warfare are formed, Canada will have after the war no personnel ... trained in this fighting." Despite the favourable letters by senior Canadian officers, including Currie, the Canadian Overseas Ministry in London eventually refused to endorse the plan. Interestingly, the formation of the Special Companies may have been a casualty of the Overseas Ministry's angry reaction to Currie's refusal to split the Canadian Corps into two corps after the addition of the 5th Division. Following the Passchendaele fighting and unwilling to weaken his tempered fighting force, Currie decided to break up the 5th Division for use as reinforcements. It was a move that ultimately strengthened the corps when other British units were strangling for lack of men, but having won his victory against the powerful partisan forces in London and Ottawa, Currie apparently sacrificed the gas companies and cut his losses after achieving his larger success.[73]

The fourth year of fighting – 1917 – had proved a hard one for the Allies. With the French Armies in mutiny after Nivelle's failed offensive on the Aisne, the continuous bloodletting by Italians on the Isonzo front, the failed British tank battles at Cambrai and in the mud of Passchendaele, and the collapse of the Russian Army, some wondered if the Allies would ever be able to bring the German war machine to its knees. The few successes by the British Expeditionary Force came with the Canadian Corps spearheading attacks. But the costly Canadian operations at Vimy, Hill 70, and Passchendaele had resulted in losses of more than 50,000 men. All the while, the battle-hardened dominion troops had fought through an ever-thickening gas environment. The corps had been subjected to Yellow, Blue, and Green Cross shells as the Germans combined them in a deadly concoction to lower morale, inflict casualties, and induce friction on the battlefield. Still, the gas war was expected to evolve continuously, as one 1st Divisional order warned: "The use of gas shells by the enemy has steadily increased, and further developments may be expected in the future." The only solution to the gas war was the implementation of strict gas discipline. While this could not eliminate all casualties, it kept losses at an acceptable level. The year 1918 would once again show a marked escalation in the use of gas. Soldiers, having been forced to confront chemical agents more and more during the battles of 1917, were to be living, fighting, and attempting to survive in a continuous gas environment.[74]

CHAPTER SIX

Combatting the Chemical Plague

THE CANADIAN MEDICAL ARMY CORPS AND GAS WARFARE

"Gas shells have been used against the Canadian Corps front on many occasions – almost daily since April 9th, 1917," was the frank appraisal of a Gas Services' report in late 1917 on the expanding use of poison gas. The nature of living in a continuous gas environment necessitated even more rigid gas discipline. On the night of 4 September 1917, the 4th Canadian Mounted Rifles were bombarded with high explosive and chemical shells and by the next morning had lost 133 to the effects of mustard gas. Recognizing the potential for crippling casualty rates, the Canadian Corps instructed its medical authorities to investigate the handling of gas casualties and, in particular, to recommend what could be done to hasten their return to the line.[1]

With a prewar strength of 23 permanent-force officers, the Canadian Army Medical Corps (CAMC) eventually ballooned, by the end of the war, to 1,525 medical officers, 1,901 nursing sisters, and 15,624 other ranks. Almost all had been civilians prior to the war. Flocking to support the flag and the Canadians in the field, these doctors and nurses experienced conditions drastically different from any they had previously encountered. Nothing in their civilian practices could prepare them for the trials of battlefield medicine. For the first time in a major war, death by enemy action overshadowed death by disease. Doctors and nurses were confronted by a dizzying array of horrific casualties: jagged wounds caused by tumbling bullets and shrapnel; heads, chests, and abdomens crushed, flayed, and ripped to pieces. Soldiers arrived at dressing stations held together only by strings of flesh. One surgeon noted that some bullets were so destructive that flesh was reduced to pulp and could be wiped off with a swab. Multiple wounds were common: a machine gun could leave a man with half a dozen or more holes. In addition to this charnel-house atmosphere was the constant threat of open cuts becoming infected from the Flanders soil, which for centuries had been enriched by animal and human manure. Having bits of clothing, leather, or metal driven into the wound by the force of impact also left victims susceptible to infections. The subsequent gas gangrene (not related to poison gas) exploded the surrounding cells and spawned an anaerobic gas that produced a revolting smell and an equally grotesque swelling as the body was slowly and painfully consumed by it. These sickening sights left doctors and surgeons grappling for ways to save their patients.[2]

Throughout the extended conflict, the CAMC continually struggled against the mounting wounds induced by modern warfare. The efficient honing of the skills of Medical Corps members required a long learning process. The frustration and strain of working on a man for hours, only to watch him die during the recovery process forced doctors to instigate new procedures that helped to minimize the damaging effects of some battlefield wounds that had previously left them baffled. Once gas gangrene was identified as a killer, precautions were taken to have all injuries thoroughly cleaned. When that was not completely effective, lesions were enlarged, with the surrounding skin trimmed away and holes often cut all the way through the body, so that the oxygen from the air would kill the infection. Although the resulting hole was often large enough to admit a clenched fist, and required constant draining and attention, fewer soldiers swelled up and died a hideous death. Earlier in the war, abdominal wounds killed almost all who received them, due to infection caused by the intestines emptying their waste into the body. The survival rate was later greatly increased after doctors made close study of such wounds. Even blood transfusion was introduced and almost perfected.[3] Within this abnormal learning environment, the CAMC worked toward saving soldiers. Some of the most baffling wounds, however, remained those caused by gas warfare.

A Canadian historian has suggested that "if the army doctors could do little about the ravages of poison gas, they could prevent them."[4] Yet it was not the CAMC but the Gas Services that had the mandate to prevent gas casualties. And although some historians have argued that the doctors were relatively impotent in counteracting the effects of gas, that is misleading. Despite failing to triumph over the imposed wastage, doctors efficiently reduced the casualty-causing effectiveness of chemical agents. Without proper treatment, gas put men out of the line for several months and even the whole war; with new medical procedures this chemical attrition was reduced and soldiers were returned to the line within two months. The CAMC was less successful in combatting phosgene than mustard gas, but the constant diligence of the medical officers helped reduce the effectiveness of all poison gas. It was a long and difficult process that relied on intense study, shared observations, and a willingness to practise new techniques.

LUNG GASES

Before the introduction of gas shells, it had been relatively easy to diagnose gassed men: if soldiers had not been able to get their gas helmets on in time or if officers had been forced to lift them to give orders or to see over the parapet, a doctor could be reasonably certain that they had been affected by a chlorine cloud. The immediate effects – laborious breathing, burning eyes and throat, and even brass buttons turning green – were all evidence. With the unleashing of phosgene, however, things became more difficult for medical officers. Even when aware of a cloud attack, they could not immediately ascertain if men had been severely gassed, as the effects could take hours to manifest themselves. Soldiers often did not know themselves; one British front-line medical officer remembered "a number of officers and men in a highly hysterical condition" because they were under the false impression that they had been gassed. However, a mistake in sending a truly gassed soldier back into the line could cost him his life. As one gas officer noted, because of the complex and deadly effects of untreated gas "anyone who claimed to be gassed was immediately sent to the rear." Except for the "tobacco method" (in which tobacco tasted acrid to a man poisoned with gas), there remained no immediate method of telling if a soldier had been poisoned until he began to feel weak from fluids filling his lungs. At that point it was often too late.[5]

Phosgene made all gassed soldiers – suspect or not – into stretcher cases, since it could be fatal to allow them to walk to the rear. In February 1916, on orders from the Royal Medical Services, a pamphlet was issued to all front-line commanding officers stating that "No man suffering from the effects of gas should be allowed to walk to the dressing stations." Unfortunately, the "phosgene-rule," as one British colonel noticed, resulted in "trenches packed with men who considered themselves gassed and thought that further movement would be fatal." The evacuation from the front was slow at the best of times, and fighting units generally passed their soldiers through a regimental aid post. Soldiers who were wounded in the field either walked to the aid posts or waited for plucky but under-strength stretcher bearers to ferry them back.[6]

When the patients arrived at the battalion aid posts, the medical officer did his best to treat any wounds that could prove immediately fatal and then sent the soldier to the next link in the chain of medical units, the advanced dressing stations, usually a mile or two in the rear. Stretcher-bearers from one of three field ambulances in each division went forward to gather the wounded and deposit them at the division's casualty clearing station.[7] The system produced wounded soldiers in trickles and floods depending on whether it was the normal wastage of the trenches or a big push was on. When thousands of men were being sent to the rear, relying on exhausted stretcher-bearers when unable to walk, many were mired in No Man's Land or the front trenches as they waited their turn. Moreover, the "body-snatchers," as they called themselves, practised their own form of triage. A man with a deep leg wound, for example, was more likely to be brought back than a soldier who had been gassed and was suffering no visible effects. Depending on the length of the delay, the result was more severe burns and blisters for mustard-gassed men. Even more seriously, those gassed with phosgene generally engaged in various forms of activity in the trenches – actions that quickened the filling up of their lungs. As the British Official Medical History noted with regard to chlorine and phosgene cases, "almost half the total number of deaths took place in the trenches or in the regimental aid posts before the casualties could be evacuated to a medical unit."[8]

A doctor did not begin to examine and work on soldiers until they arrived at the advanced dressing stations or sometimes the casualty clearing stations. Gassed men came in literally smelling of death and exhibiting symptoms of varying degrees of severity. Some were blue in colour and suffered hacking coughs in between their struggling breaths; others outwardly looked healthy. All were scared and unsure of what was in store for them. One British soldier wrote in his diary while convalescing in a rear hospital that both he and his friend had been surprised by gas shells and "were feeling the effects of them badly. We tried a cigarette to see if it would help. It did not."[9] The average soldier was unclear on how to save himself, and if the all-purpose cigarette did not work then he must have really begun to worry. The medical officers knew a little more, but they too took some time to understand the effects of chlorine and phosgene gassing and how to properly attend to their patients.

In the Directorate of Gas Services at the British General Headquarters there was a special medical and physiological advisory committee that facilitated studies on gassed patients and disseminated the information to the medical officers and surgeons within the British Expeditionary Force. During the war the committee published three important memoranda (in June 1915, July 1916, and April 1918) to highlight successful approaches and techniques for combatting gas poisoning. Still, treatment was largely a process of trial and error; much of the information sent out was contradictory, and the gassed soldiers often became living experimental subjects. For example, initially some unit medical officers and even the chemical advisor of the Third Army observed that phosgene cases began to "feel ill soon after breakfast and it appears likely that the effects of the gas are accentuated during the process of digestion." It was thus decided that men exposed to phosgene should not be given any solid food for twenty-four hours. What was not realized was that the gassed men had usually been on working parties and the march back before sunset was the reason why they were feeling sluggish, as their lungs filled up with fluids they could not cough up. (It is worth noting that soldiers did not begin to cough up liquid until hours after the initial poisoning.) The learning process was slow, but through a constant re-evaluation of their methods and observations the Canadian Army Medical Corps, much like the Gas Services itself, was able to discount incorrect theories and focus on the true problems.[10]

Unclear about how to save gassed men, Major G.B. Peat of the CAMC described his ward filled with recent phosgene-gassed soldiers: "The agony suffered by this group of cases was intense and the scene was the most gruesome one could imagine, whilst the sounds of the suffering were horrible, and the evidently hopeless outlook for so many of them made it most discouraging for us. One would be at the one end of the ward, give some orders about a patient, go to the other end of the ward, then get back to the first patient, and get there in time to see a gush of froth and serum followed by death in a moment or two." It was an additional strain for doctors and other patients to watch gassed men struggle as they lay "coughing, gasping and fighting for breath" like "fish on land." The most healthy were pale in colour, those that were more ill were cyanotic, and the worst cases had skin the colour of mahogany and lips that looked like they had "been marked in blue crayon." On an equally macabre note, doctors and nurses were warned to keep sharp objects away from thrashing, suffocating men after a British Tommy cut his own throat while in his death throes and choking for breath.[11]

For the burning and raw throats of gassed soldiers, various emetics of salt and water were administered to help ease the pain and induce vomiting. Dangerously ill patients were given ammonia capsules, rum to "allay fright," caffeine stimulants to keep their hearts beating, and, if possible, oxygen inhalations, orally as well as through the rectum. The oxygen was deemed useful, especially by patients for whom it acted as a psychological stimulant, but as there were generally few tanks, and with all men begging for them in between "grunty catches of breaths," there were hard decisions to make. Generally, it was up to doctors to perform the traumatic but necessary task of triage – deciding who would receive treatment first and who would be left to expire. In some of the worst cases gassed men were given high doses of morphine to ease their pain. Generally they did not survive very long; yet, tragically, they were often conscious until minutes before their last agonizing breath.[12]

If a soldier survived the first day of gassing, during which a typical phosgene victim might cough up four pints of liquid an hour from his lungs, then he was moved into a hospital in the rear.[13] Cough and dyspnoea were prevalent in all victims of the lung gases. The chlorine or phosgene, drawn into the respiratory passages, also damaged the bronchial mucous membrane and alveoli, causing acute pulmonary oedemas and tracheal haemorrhages. The resulting discharges blocked the respiratory tract, making breathing more and more laborious. Although there were a few drugs to stimulate the patient, ease his pain, or reduce his movement, there remained no antidote capable of reversing the effects of the gas.[14] Ensuring that patients remained motionless was the most important aspect of the recovery process for lung gases.

Simply prescribing rest left doctors feeling helpless, and many in the CAMC hoped to quicken the recovery process. One of the earliest attempts to treat the gassed men followed the French medical practice of bleeding victims. It was done in hope of relieving pressure on the heart, which was found to be enlarged in men who had died from gas. Sounding frighteningly reminiscent of medieval medical care, one report dated 28 June 1917 remarked how it was advisable to bleed all but the slightest cases and "that those cases which were bled early tend to progress much more favourably than those bled for the first time after a delayed period." "It often improved a patient's appearance," Canadian historian Desmond Morton has remarked, "while accelerating death." This approach was fortunately phased out after December 1917, when a group of doctors at No. 1 Canadian General Hospital issued a report indicating that "Bleeding [was] considered a useless measure." Other attempts to purify the lungs included the method used on Wallace Carroll of the 15th Battalion, who was gassed at Hill 70 in August 1917. He remembered having a teapot filled with sulphurous fumes, which he had "to inhale through the spout" every day. Despite these "cures," palliative measures and exposure to fresh air was found to be the best policy for phosgene-poisoned cases after the initial treatments. Because the weakened state of the lungs was increased by activity, it was not unknown for soldiers to be strapped to their beds if they had a tendency to ignore the doctor's advice. A patient of Major Peat's, an officer who thought he felt better, got up to walk around and promptly collapsed, his lungs filling with fluid until he died. The use of restraints had to be tempered, however: the French Army had several gassed men die of shock when they were strapped to their beds and left outside in the cool air in their fragile states. Despite the fresh air, recovering victims were susceptible to a host of lung problems, most notably pneumonia and chronic bronchitis. Even if phosgene victims survived the initial poisoning, in the words of one veteran, "many men were condemned to months of lingering illness and early death as a result of gas poisoning."[15]

MUSTARD GAS

A secret British assessment of gas casualties in 1919 observed that mustard gas was "in a class by itself so far as casualty producing power is concerned." Although gas masks could negate most of the fatal effects of mustard gas, it still caused hundreds of thousands of casualties by burning exposed skin in a way that chlorine and phosgene did not. In fact, captured German artillery plans indicated that one of the main uses for mustard gas was against "infantry strong points and billets to cause large numbers of slight casualties." Such losses weakened the fighting efficiency of units and put a strain on the already overtaxed medical corps. From 21 July 1917 to 23 November 1918, British clearing stations admitted 160,970 gas casualties, of whom 1,859 died; 77 percent of the casualties were victims of mustard gas. General Amos Fries, head of the United States Chemical Warfare Service, wrote after the war that even if gas did not kill many men, "the reduction in physical vigour, and therefore, in efficiency of an army forced at all times to wear masks, would amount to at least 25 percent, equivalent to disabling a quarter of a million men out of an army of a million." Although Fries employed a questionable leap of logic, there is no doubt that mustard gas was devastatingly effective in crippling the fighting efficiency and morale of all troops. Interestingly, within the first weeks of its use, the British initially failed to comprehend the casualty-causing potency of mustard gas. Historian Denis Winter has even suggested that the British went so far as to wipe the War Diaries clean of reports of its devastating effects. Certainly the high casualties induced by mustard gas created a desperate need to devise methods to ease the effects of the gas and to return soldiers quickly to the front.[16]

Mustard gas worked like a disease in its ability to jump from victim to victim or to be transmitted from contact with infected clothing or equipment. Quickly identified as such, this chemical plague required new precautions at the front. Those in the rear were equally susceptible, and there were numerous cases of field doctors who were burned by their patients as they attempted to alleviate their suffering. One doctor was even affected by mustard gas after examining a British soldier who had been dead for ten days.[17] Nurses were often victimized by the secondary effects, as they tended to be the ones who initially dealt with the infected men. The following account by Staff Nurse C. Macfie of No. 11 Casualty Clearing Station, Godwaersveldt (which the troops called "Gert wears velvet"), indicates the conditions under which nurses worked:

> I just arrived with another nurse from the south, because they needed as many staff as they could get with the big stand coming, and it was just a couple of nights later that the mustard gas cases started to come in. It was terrible to see them. I was in the post-operative tent so I didn't come in contact with them, but the nurses in the reception tent had a bad time. The poor boys were helpless and the nurses had to take off their uniforms, all soaked with gas, and do the best they could for the boys. Next day all the nurses had chest trouble and streaming eyes from the gassing. They were all yellow and dazed. Even their hair turned yellow and they were nearly as bad as the men, just from the fumes from their clothing. And all the time, of course, the bombs were falling, night after night.[18]

Learning from their mistakes, surgeons working on mustard-gassed patients soon began to wear respirators and oiled leather gloves to save themselves from falling victim – unfortunately not the most ideal conditions under which to perform surgery.[19]

Initially, there was no cure for the shiny faced mustard-gas victims who arrived at the clearing stations with their steady nasal discharges and bulging eyelids streaming tears. With a quick onset of infection, ears and genitalia quickly became enormously swollen. As patients waited for help, they were racked with harsh coughing; burns and lesions began to appear all over their bodies, but most notably around the armpits, neck, back, and groin. They took on the aroma of decaying fruit, particularly trying for men and doctors who realized they were rotting both from the outside and from within. Once symptoms began to manifest themselves, they quickly escalated. Doctors could leave a patient coughing slightly with reddish-hued sputum and return after their rounds to find him hacking blood-streaked phlegm and covered in suppurating blisters.

After witnessing the first patients going through these terrible stages, the medical services found that the immediate removal of infected clothing and the bathing of the body in a mild alkaline solution would reduce the spread of blisters. Without these measures, sores began to appear on the skin in small blobs and quickly coalesced to form extremely painful and extensive blisters, sometimes a foot in length, weeping pus. To combat the spread of the abscesses, the prevention of gas moved forward; trench medical officers and field ambulances were, in early 1918, equipped with stores of bicarbonate of soda to apply quickly to the gassed man to neutralize the mustard gas as soon as possible. Soldiers were even ordered to snort the soda through their nose and mouth in order to relieve the burning – an unpleasant task but better than the alternative. Still, the main treatment remained at the dressing stations, where eyes were washed with warm water and sodium bicarbonate before being treated with sterile oil, followed by an eye-shade or bandage to protect them from the light. Recording in his diary, Canadian Ansan Donaldson, an officer in No. 3 Field Ambulance, who was gassed at Hill 70 with almost 70 percent of his men, wrote: "I certainly suffered the fortune of the damned and it was only because I got under treatment immediately and had such good nursing ... that I was not Blighty." The cleaning of mustard-gassed men generally fell to orderlies and nurses, who assumed more responsibility for gassed patients as the war progressed. Nothing could be done for the crushing headache, chills, and vomiting, but immediate reaction at the advanced dressing or casualty clearing stations saved thousands of Canadians from being horribly burned and maimed.[20]

The effects of poison gas were trying for most doctors and nurses, but they were positively terrifying for soldiers. Perhaps one of the reasons for this fear was that, after chlorine had been superseded, poison gas was not an immediate weapon. A bullet or shrapnel caused immediate damage; gas took longer. It slowly built to a crescendo of agony, and in some cases death. British serviceman Harold Clegg of the Liverpool Rifles was gassed on the night of 27-8 July

1917 at Armentières after an officer ordered his company to take billets in a cellar polluted by gas. His recorded account describes the effects of the gas:

> A large school house served as a Dressing Station ... Outside ... was strewn all over the road a seething mass of humanity, civilians, and military. Women and children wailing and groaning in their agony; everyone vomiting; some dead and many unconscious ...
>
> ... Drops were injected into the eyes of everyone in turn ... and by 11 a.m. I was totally blind ... A high fever also set in ...
>
> ... I spent my time sleeping and coughing. The marquee was full of gas cases, and there was a steady stream of shuffling feet which denoted stretchers being brought in and carried out; some ... to the mortuary.[21]

Clegg was invalided back to England and spent the rest of the war recovering in a hospital. Almost all mustard-gassed men suffered the same fate: coughing, blindness, and blisters, not to mention the usually unrecorded psychological strain. Although most mild cases recovered physically within months, it took five years for Clegg's health to return to normal.

The injuries to about two-thirds of the mustard-gas victims were minor, and the men returned to their units within eight weeks. But there were always reports – like this one by a British nurse – of more serious instances:

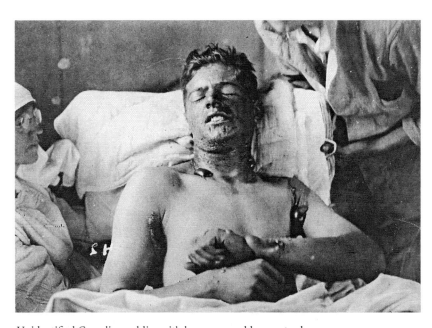

Unidentified Canadian soldier with burns caused by mustard gas.

Gas cases are terrible. They cannot breathe lying down or sitting up. They just struggle for breath, but nothing can be done. Their lungs are gone – literally burnt out. Some have their eyes and faces entirely eaten away by gas and their bodies covered with first-degree burns. We must try to relieve them by pouring oil on them. They cannot be bandaged or touched. We cover them with a tent of propped-up sheets. Gas burns must be agonizing because usually the other cases do not complain even with the worst wounds but gas cases are invariably beyond endurance and they cannot help crying out. One boy today, screaming to die, the entire top layer of his skin burnt from face and body.[22]

Another British soldier vomited daily for three years before he regained control of his body. Canadian poet and padre F.G. Scott, not a stranger to the horrors of war after having eased and comforted countless dying and wounded soldiers, remembered that "there was nothing more horrible than to see men dying from gas. Nothing could be done to relieve their suffering. The body, as well as the throat and lungs, were burned and blistered with poison." Despite these ghastly cases, the last year of the war produced mustard-gas victims who were usually only temporarily blinded and lightly burned; however, men were still susceptible to "chemical pneumonia" and secondary lung infections, which killed many after the war.[23]

The number of soldiers suffering from the inhalation of mustard gas remained a problem throughout the war, and only a constantly enforced anti-gas doctrine could keep it under control. The mustard gas attacked the bronchial tubes and stripped off the mucous membrane, literally leaving men coughing and hacking up pieces of their lungs. It was a horrible way to die, but most bronchial ingestion cases became less severe as the war progressed because much of the gas came off other infected men or from the polluted ground and was less concentrated than mustard-gas vapour directly released from shells. Still, the unlucky man who had a Yellow Cross shell explode near him would be burned externally and internally with terrible consequences: one Australian soldier suffered for five years before he died, permanently soaking in a warm water bath after having had all of his skin burned off.[24] These gruesome cases were mercifully limited in number; more debilitating to the armies were the thousands of minor wounds that degenerated into chronic, war-ending casualties.

Secondary infection among gas victims remained a constant worry for doctors and patients. Those soldiers who had been slow in receiving attention or were still wearing their dirty, vermin-infested clothing were prime victims. One medical report noted that with mild burns a boracic ointment could be used, but that deep burns were "practically always infected." Painful and difficult to heal, the burns required hours of care and treatment in hot alkaline baths. The danger of sepsis festering in wounds required a treatment process that was slower and more painful than conventional burns, with the lesion having to be continually lanced, drained, and rebandaged. Secondary lung infections also remained a very real fear. Their severity depended on the degree of damage to the tissue as well as the previous general health of the patient. Almost all phosgene- and mustard-gassed men suffered, in varying degrees, patches of necrosis – or dead cells – in their respiratory tracts. One CAMC study documented that 30 percent of mustard-gas patients developed serious bronchial rales, and phosgene-gassed men were even worse off. "The bronchitis often goes on to a broncho-pneumonia and this is the commonest cause of death," wrote Major G.S. Strathy, an experienced Canadian medical officer. Despite these grim forecasts, if a patient survived the initial period, after several months most men recovered.[25]

COMPLEMENTING THE GAS SERVICES

Certainly one of the most striking scenes of the First World War were the lines of mustard-gas victims, eyes burned and blinded, lined up with a hand on the shoulders of the man in front, being led from the battlefield.[26] The loss of entire platoons to blindness following a mustard-gas bombardment was immediately recognized as a serious problem for commanders. In conjunction with the call for more stringent gas discipline, the medical services complemented the Gas Services by attempting to get soldiers back into the line as quickly as possible.

Major S.G. Ross and Captain A.T. Henderson of the Canadian Army Medical Corps carried out an investigation using 275 Canadian mustard-gas cases between 2 and 13 November 1917 in order to gain some understanding of how soldiers became gas casualties and their resulting symptoms. Of the cases, 151 occurred in the infantry, 74 in the artillery, and 50 in other services. Most were gassed for three main reasons: insufficient warning, wherein shells burst near them or poisoned them while they were asleep; lack of recognition that they were being poisoned, because Yellow Cross was mixed with HE bombardments; and lack of gas discipline, which ranged from orders being given to remove masks too soon, the inability to work while wearing masks, and simple neglect, where individual soldiers did not think there was a high enough concentration of gas. In a majority of cases, symptoms appeared from one to three hours after exposure and ranged from irritation of the eyes and burning sensations in the throat and chest to violent sneezing and vomiting. It was also discovered that soldiers who had been burned once with mustard gas were much more suscep-tible for wounds to flare up into ugly, long skin lesions if they encountered the gas again. From various reports it was clear that mustard gas was a new factor that could strike anyone on the battlefield. What still remained unclear was its effectiveness as a battlefield weapon.[27]

The lethality rate of mustard gas, while 19.5 percent among serious cases, fell to a low of approximately 3 percent of the total number of gas casualties throughout the war.[28] Most of these deaths were due to damage suffered by the respiratory organs from subsequent bronchial infections two or three weeks after the initial gassing. Table 6.1 shows the results of a study in which the Canadian Medical Corps was able to estimate how long all mustard-gas cases admitted between 1 July and 31 October 1918 were in convalescence. It is worth noting that the time would have been much longer, or even indefinite, in late 1917, when the medical corps was still learning to reduce the effects of the gas. Generally, those who had been blinded and suffered from sub-acute conjunctivitis – swelling and closing – of the eyes had their sight return by the third or fourth week. The problem of the chemically wounded, however, remained an issue throughout the war. The length of time required for the recovery of even mild cases resulted in congestion at casualty-clearing stations and corps rest stations.

The most severe gas cases, between 10 and 20 percent of the total, were sent to hospitals in England after their conditions were stabilized. They generally did not return to their units, as many developed secondary pulmonary infections or were posted to home defence or training units in the United Kingdom. The policy of the CAMC was to rush the lightly gassed out of medical centres and quickly get them back into the rhythm of army discipline for, as one report noted, "prolonged stays in hospitals, either primary or auxiliary, is particularly apt, in these cases, to exaggerate the neurotic conditions, which are difficult to overcome." The CAMC feared that the psychological effects of gas would lead to further mental problems and perhaps even to shell shock. Major H.G. Nyblett of the CAMC argued that wounded soldiers had to be shaken out of their mental state; thus, even after having been wounded and "done their bit," they were to be returned to the front. This was not always an easy task. Gassed at Hill 70,

TABLE 6.1

Recovery from exposure to gas

Time after exposure	Percentage who returned to full duty
First two weeks	0.3
Third week	13.4
Fourth week	12.5
Fifth week	12.9
Sixth week	9.6
Seventh week	6.5
Eighth week	9.5
Out for war	35.3

Source: NAC, RG 9, vol. 3975, folder 1, file 16, "Chemical Advisor, First Army – 3 December 1917."

Private G. Wright of the 1st Canadian Mounted Rifles, for example, had lost sixty-five pounds in the three weeks after the battle as he vomited up everything the doctors prescribed for him. Although a patient's recovery was not always so difficult, wounded men had to be healed physically and mentally in order to be effective.[29]

To reduce possible "neurotic conditions" in mustard-gas cases, eye shades were removed within two or three days, even when it was painful for the patient. All men were forced to get out of their beds and move about in increasing bouts of physical activity. Other doctors included "cold douching" in the recovery process under which patients were to have their heads dunked in cold water so they were made aware that they could not simply sit back and wait for their eyesight to return. Doctors "encouraged" patients to take an active part in quickening the process of returning to the unit, and it was hoped that lethargy and passivity could be avoided or driven out of the gassed men. The goal was to reduce the psychological fears of gas as well as any psychosis that tended to develop after a patient was gassed. It was also a reflection of the known fact that the longer a patient was away from the front the more difficult it was to return him to his unit. Depending on the severity of their exposure, mustard-gas cases had better results at recovery than did phosgene victims, who continued to sporadically suffer from chronic fatigue, shallow breath, and intense chest pains. This long process was often trying for senior commanders, who had shortages among front-line units and potential fighting men "lounging" about in the rear waiting for their "breath" to return. As a consequence, many soldiers were returned to the front not fully healed mentally – and sometimes not physically. This was especially the case during the German March Offensive in 1918, when any gassed man who could hold a gun was sent to stem the German tide.[30]

The dual and sometimes conflicting responsibility of doctors to their patients and the army forced the CAMC to work toward hastening the return of soldiers to their units.[31] Some men were caught aggravating their condition by wilfully rubbing their eyes in order to stay out of the trenches longer, but generally the soldiers were compliant. Unfortunately, this also made them easy objects for experimentation. One of the most sadistic "cures" was devised by a British medical officer commanding No. 39 Stationary Hospital, who injected calcium chloride into soldiers' eyes. The results must have been excruciating, for even in the clinical language of military doctors, the patients suffered "painful swellings and haemorrhages in their eyes." The experiment was not tried again. With the varying degrees of blindness, the best solution was to wash the eyes gently with a weak alkaline solution. For a time a mixture of cocaine and castor oil was used for patients in severe pain, but it was discontinued by 7 August 1917, for it tended to "loosen the Epithelium of the Cornea and therefore encourage exfoliation and ulceration." Canadian doctors reverted back to a warm saline solution and continued to apply it as quickly and frequently as possible in order to reduce the length of hospitalization. Nonetheless, at best soldiers went through days of agony, at worst, perpetual blindness.[32]

Gas remained a constant problem for the CAMC throughout the war. The growing gas environment continued to plague not only the soldiers in the trenches but also the doctors in the rear. The learning curve for the CAMC in combatting chemical warfare mirrored that of the Gas Services, and the Medical Corps went through numerous trial-and-error methods in the hope of alleviating the pain of their patients as well as following the army's mandate of hurrying these men back into the line. Like the Gas Services, the Medical Corps were not entirely successful, but through perseverance and applied learning they were able to reduce the atrophying effects of gas on the Canadian Corps.

A Way Out?

By the end of November 1917, the Canadian Corps had been relieved from Flanders and had resumed control over the Lens-Vimy front. The familiar pattern of retraining the new recruits, who were to fill the gaping holes in the battalions, began to recur. Following the fighting in the gas environment, the experiences were analyzed and then codified into doctrines. Subsequently, the chemical advisor declared that the protection of dugouts was unsatisfactory and would no longer be left to the discretion of individual battalions but controlled by the division.[33] Double chemically treated curtains were issued for every dugout, shelter, cellar, and dressing station near the front. The importance of having a gas-free sanctuary was recognized as a necessary precaution after the extensive use of gas during the battles of Hill 70 and Passchendaele.

Gas discipline, although acknowledged by most soldiers as necessary and useful, was not always carried out in drill-parade fashion. Battalion and brigade gas officers continued to impress upon their men that it was important to remove tunics, greatcoats, and equipment that could be infected with mustard gas before they entered the dugout, but that was often impossible for soldiers at the front.[34] It was not like politely taking off your shoes before entering a study; soldiers did not have the luxury of kicking off their boots before going down into a dugout. More often, and especially during the winter months, soldiers rarely removed their clothing, choosing to forgo sanitary conditions in favour of surviving against the cold. Also, as soldiers were used to scrounging anything and everything to make their lives more bearable at the front, there was an epidemic of stolen anti-gas blankets – despite their chemical treatment. The 2nd Canadian Infantry Brigade suffered some unnecessary gas casualties during the winter months of 1917 when freezing soldiers pilfered anti-gas blankets "for sleeping purposes."[35] Although some of the finer points of gas discipline were not always rigidly followed at the front, Canadian soldiers continually received lectures and were forced to practise anti-gas doctrine in an attempt to make it second nature. When freezing in the front line, the infantry could be somewhat casual regarding the use of contaminated blankets, but as the chemical advisor's War Diary for November 1917 illustrated, the gas discipline was generally successful: the Canadian Corps suffered only one-third of the casualties of the British Corps previously occupying the area in the same battle conditions.[36]

On 21 November 1917 the British received warning from a captured prisoner that the Germans had perfected a gas projector that was similar to the British Livens projector. The Canadian Corps was indeed hit with four projector attacks during December, but it had trained its gas sentries in the importance of recognizing any metallic pounding noise coming from the German lines (indicating the setting up of projectors) and the necessity for quick reaction to alert the unit when they heard the tell-tale loud explosion and saw a sheet of flame projecting from the German lines. The last of the projector attacks was carried out by the Germans on 30 December against the 52nd Battalion. At 5:00 a.m. the Germans projected between 500 and 600 gas cylinders into the Canadian lines and caused seventeen casualties – five serious, ten slight, and two deaths. Nearly all casualties were due to the slowness of some soldiers in adjusting their SBRs. Once again the chemical advisor emphasized the need for rigid discipline in response to the introduction of projectors as well as the "development and increase in number, calibre and kind of enemy gas."[37]

The continuous use of gas against the Canadians during the last two months of 1917 left Canadian Army Medical Corps doctors with ample cases to study. In one examination of twenty-two patients passing through a special clearing station designated for gas casualties, Canadian doctors attempted to ascertain how they were exposed to gas and the severity of their case:

1.	Took off mask – shell lit 20′ off	Mild Case
2.	Took off mask	Mild Case
3.	Gassed in pill-box	Mild Case
4.	Delay in adjusting SBR	Mild Case
5.	? Insidious	Mild Case
6.	During sleep – mask off	Mild Case
7.	Gas shell burst very near	Mild Case
8.	Mask not worn	Mild Case
9.	Without eyepiece mask worn	Mild Case
10.	Delay adjusting mask	Mild Case
11.	Faulty respirator	Mild Now
12.	Answering SOS no time to adjust SBR	Mild Case
13.	Did not notice gas shells	Mild Case
14.	Giving Orders – took off SBR	Mild Case
15.	Did not notice gas in pill-box	Mild Case
16.	Delay in adjusting SBR	Medium Case

17.	Sleeping when gas put over	Mild Case
18.	Burned by shell	Mild Case
19.	Packing ammunition left off eyepiece	Mild Case
20.	Surprised by gas shell	Mild except eyes
21.	Straps of water bottle over SBR	Mild Case
22.	Gas remained in gunpit	Mild Case[38]

The report is informative in many regards. All but four of the cases had been exposed to mustard gas, and their wounds illustrated the nature of mustard gas in injuring rather than killing, although it is also important to keep in mind that the more severe cases of phosgene poisoning would have resulted in death rather than a trip to a hospital in the rear to be classified in a report. The statistics further illustrated the need for strict gas discipline in order to keep casualties low, especially since both the Germans and the Allies continued to employ gas more often and in greater intensity. But within such figures lurked a menace to High Command: self-inflicted wounds.

The unnatural situation of trench warfare was a physical and mental abuse to men who had left Canada to fight in a quick, patriotic struggle. More debilitating than any other weapon, the tons of high-explosive shells dropped on the trenches day after day and night after night drove some men to the edge of insanity. There was no escape from the constant psychological erosion imposed by living in such conditions, as one Canadian who was under heavy fire for longer than a week noted in a letter home: "A man arrives at the stage after being in for a time where he'd welcome a bullet whether it kills him or not. When you are dead tired ... it seems preferable to get knocked out and be at peace."[39] The soldiers at the front, bone-weary, sometimes disillusioned and looking for any method to escape the horrors of the war, often embraced wounds as their ticket back home – a safe passage to Blighty (the name for England or a rest area in the rear).

With the introduction of the gas war, the chance for a Blighty and the problem of self-inflicted wounds (SIWs) became more prevalent. The soldiers' antipathy to gas was combined with genuine fear and augmented the already present dilemma of malingering. George Bell described the effect of morale after the Passchendaele campaign: "Malingering was becoming too common, not only among those who were naturally shirkers, but among those who had been good soldiers. They had seen so much death, bloodshed and suffering that they were sick of it all." One Canadian who was gassed at Passchendaele remarked after the fact from his hospital that his wound was a "nice soft Blighty." Scooping up some chemically infected soil to wipe in the eyes was certainly preferable to the earlier method of putting a bullet through the leg or hand, and the result was the same – a quick exit from the trenches. Gas-induced SIWs were hard to identify; there was no close gunshot wound with its distinctive gun

Attacking under smoke.

Training with respirators on.

powder residue. Commanders feared that their soldiers might eventually give up and deliberately burn or blind themselves with gas in order to escape the intolerable world of trench warfare.[40]

The Canadian Gas Services had always been aware of the potential for malingering from mustard gas; they were simply unable to do anything about it. In desperation, the Gas Services, while continuing to establish and maintain good gas discipline, turned to the CAMC. It was the medical officer (MO) in the trenches, usually one per battalion or regiment, who became responsible for distinguishing legitimate wounds from those that were self-inflicted. As the war progressed, unit and senior commanders looked to the MO to play a greater role in maintaining morale. The "croaker," as he was sometimes called by the soldiers, carried out his mandate by enforcing discipline and examining the men during the daily ritual of the sick parade. The search for malingerers – skrimshankers or lead swingers, in trench soldier parlance – fell to him. It was sometimes a difficult task as the MO weighed his natural feelings of empathy for the "poor bloody" soldier in the trenches and the greater need of the army to ensure discipline.[41]

Fearful predictions that whole armies could be invalided out with gas poisoning required strict anti-gas precautions. After the introduction of the respirator, soldiers were punished for becoming gassed; the blame was put on them for failing in their gas discipline. Casualties were forced to wear a special "wound stripe" to indicate that they had allowed themselves to be gassed. This practice was abolished when mustard gas was introduced. Not only were there too many casualties, but MOs recognized that it was not the fault of all gassed men that they had become victims.[42]

From the first chemical death clouds, the alien nature of poison gas attacking both the body and mind caused many soldiers to flee from the great rolling walls of gas. Early in the war, the British High Command issued an order stating that "It has been clearly proved that men who remain in their trenches during gas attacks do not suffer so severely as men who leave them … It has been decided by the G.O.C. that all men who leave their trenches during gas attacks will be tried by Field General Court Martial." The records do not distinguish between gas-induced court martial and simply fleeing from the front, but the punishment was severe, including death by firing squad. If soldiers did not want to be caught by the military or found out by their comrades that they had shirked their duty, they sometimes came down with what one specialist called "gas fright. Soldiers, hearing a report that gas was in the area, would acquire [or pretend to have] all the symptoms of gas poisoning although they had not been gassed." Sometimes it was a case like that of a gunner from the 1st Battery, Canadian Field Artillery, who had helped to lead blinded men from the rear area during the Hill 70 fighting and at the end simply lay down with the rest of the men to be sent to the rear. Other times soldiers who had seen too much of battle viewed a slight gas wound as a final ticket away from the front before mental collapse occurred.[43]

MOs were to label gassed soldiers as one of the following: drift gas wounded; shell gas wounded; or mine gas wounded. Soldiers who claimed to be gassed but showed no symptoms were kept under observation. Men were offered food and closely watched; any who started to eat were immediately labelled frauds, as gas poisoning caused a loss of appetite. Another trick was to give the suspected man a cigarette laced with diphosgene – a bout of gagging meant that he was faking. If the soldier began to develop symptoms, he was sent to a Special Medical Unit in the rear and labelled NYD (Not Yet Diagnosed) Gas – or Not Yet Dead, as some cynics mumbled under their breaths. Those who failed to manifest gas wounds were returned to their units, with a stiff warning and punishment ranging from the degrading field punishment number I to a court martial.[44]

A report by Chemical Advisor W.E. Harris, dated 27 September 1917, lamented SIWs involving poison gas: "Since the introduction by the enemy of Yellow Cross gas, there are indications of men purposely exposing their eyes to the gas, and becoming casualties. They know now that the effects on the eyes is [sic] only temporary and purposely expose them in order to have three or four weeks in hospital that this brings with it." Although Harris and his gas officers had "no definite evidence of any particular case," they assumed it must be happening due to the high and rising gas losses. Although further reports attempted to appeal to the soldier's honour and discipline, Harris also used fear and uncertainty. He ordered his gas officers, the gas experts to whom the men had been listening for almost two years, to "spread the statement that a small number of those affected become permanently blind." Mustard-gas casualties continued to rise in the Canadian Corps, and High Command had no clear method of curtailing these casualties that were atrophying their units.[45]

Better respirators and training, when combined with more frequent encounters with chemical agents through the proliferation of gas shells, meant that poison gas was increasingly seen less as an immoral, terrifying weapon by the trench soldiers. However, gas remained a fearful weapon, one viewed with antipathy and caution. The doctors had a role in this change of perception through their ability to save most of the gassed men who came through their clearing stations and hospitals. The earlier inability to help the gassed had been replaced with proven techniques and approaches. In a way similar to the Gas Services, the CAMC learned through a process of trial and error. There was no way to defeat the gas environment and what it did to men caught within it, but an effective medical program was essential to partially restore the fighting efficiency of units, bolster morale, and combat the spectre of self-inflicted wounds.

CHAPTER SEVEN

It's Got Your Number

JANUARY 1918–AUGUST 1918

The Calm before the Storm

The winter of 1918 in France, the fourth for the few veterans of the 1st Contingent who had survived from the beginning, was one of the coldest in fifty years. With the Canadian Corps not involved in any major military engagements, keeping warm became a preoccupation for the infantry. On the other side of No Man's Land, General Erich Ludendorff, following the collapse of the Russian Army, began transporting battle-hardened German veterans from the Eastern Front for his upcoming offensive in the West in early 1918.

Mustard gas remained a problem for Canadian soldiers in this cold weather, as it lay dormant on the ground for weeks in freezing temperatures, clinging to boots and clothing. Soldiers had to stand their miserable hour or two in the cold mud of the trenches as sentries while their comrades snatched whatever sleep they could in their fetid yet warm dugouts. After their stint, relieved sentries headed for the dugouts to thaw out. What they brought with them was akin to a plague: one infected man could spread mustard gas to everyone in a dugout, especially as the warmth of the fire vaporized any frozen mustard gas clinging to boots or clothing. Sam Hewit, a gas NCO of the 15th Battalion, remembered being "in a fix" when he reported that there were no gas casualties from a gas bombardment during a cold night, only to find that by noon the next day the sun had warmed the gas on the ground, resulting in several dozen gas casualties within his unit. For the last year of the war the majority of Canadian gas casualties were a result of mustard gas vaporizing on the ground – in trenches, shell holes, or dugouts – and affecting unaware soldiers as they went about their daily business. The transformation in gas casualties alluded to the vast importance in gas discipline: the Canadians had learned their gas lessons, sometimes through the pain of failure. Despite the revolutionary nature of mustard gas in causing casualties, the Canadians had a good base of anti-gas discipline on which to fashion a coherent defence.[1]

Monitoring the gas war and protecting the trench soldiers required constant attention. In addition to the problems posed by the persistent nature of the gas, in several cases Canadian troops in the winter of 1918 fell victim to gas while wearing their SBRs. To guard against the severe cold, soldiers tended to wear woollen balaclavas under their steel helmets; numerous men were gassed when they failed to remove the woollen hats and thus allowed gas to enter their unsealed masks. Gas officers continued to work with and give lectures to senior officers, brigade and divisional staff, as well as all commanding officers of all units, on the need for greater cooperation and enforcement of gas discipline. Dull repetition and persistence were the key to success, but, to paraphrase Clausewitz, although everything in war is simple, the simplest things are difficult. The Gas Services were once again forced to adapt to a new variation in the gas war: the effects of winter and mustard gas in complicating gas discipline.[2]

On New Year's Eve and the first day of 1918, the 10th Infantry Brigade was the object of three gas shoots involving several tons of lethal diphosgene. With good gas discipline, sentries keeping accurate watch, and the men responding quickly, only three light casualties were sustained. Direct gas assaults were actually easier to defend against than was the persistent gas that lingered, affecting both the unsuspecting and the careful. From the last day in 1917 to the first week of 1918 the Canadian Corps suffered forty-three gas casualties, almost all from mustard gas lurking on the ground. Although good gas training had generally prevented large groups of men from being killed off, Canadians, as with all soldiers of the BEF, regularly lost men to mustard gas. As a consequence, the gas officers used these and other gas figures to preach to their men about the need for rigid gas discipline. The strict adherence to gas training remained a high priority among the Canadian Corps, and its eventual success was partly due to battalion commanding officers being threatened with punishment as they were "responsible for any gas casualties occurring in their Units which are proven to be a result of lack of training in Defensive Gas measures." A combination of the Gas Services vigorously pressing the issue and intimidating orders to commanding officers resulted in a continuous policy of refining gas discipline within the Canadian Corps.[3]

Displaying the constant cycle of training and learning, the men of the 2nd

Division, who were out of the line and in "rest" for January, were forced to carry out a series of exhausting long-distance night marches while wearing their SBRs. The infantry embarked on their blind march, stumbling and falling into holes and ditches, and although they gained some experience, one officer noted that "on very dark nights, marching with Box Respirators is practically impossible." Another soldier described the drill as a "most torturous thing." Such tasks had to be carried out, despite their difficulty and the loathing of officers and ranks, for it was suspected that during upcoming battles soldiers might have to wear their masks for hours or days and struggle against their paralyzing effects on logistics and movement. Even so, the friction imposed by gas on the Canadian Corps, despite two years of actively carrying out trial-and-error reforms on the battlefield, was nothing compared to the chaos within the newly arriving American troops.[4]

The United States had great difficulty getting troops trained, equipped, and shipped to France in a timely fashion after it declared war on Germany in April 1917. The French armies, suffering from high and needless casualties during the Nivelle offensive, had mutinied in May and June 1917. General Nivelle had been replaced by Philippe Pétain, who was known for his cautious nature. Pétain had been able to convince the French soldiers to follow orders only by telling them there would be no more campaigns until the American Expeditionary Force (AEF) arrived – and by executing the ringleaders of the mutiny. Despite the anticipation that surrounded his arrival, the American doughboy, who had had all his training in the United States, would have little concept of how to survive on the Western Front.

A few Canadian soldiers had a hand in training the AEF in an area they knew very well: establishing a coherent anti-gas doctrine. The Americans were woefully unprepared for all aspects of trench warfare but particularly with regard to the pervasive gas environment of the Western Front, which the Secretary of War in his 1917 Annual Report derided as a "scientific novelty." When the Americans declared war they had no experience with gas; more detrimentally, as one historian has noted, they "had no idea of how to conduct defensive training." To help prepare the AEF, the Canadian Corps contributed two of its most experienced gas officers, Lieutenant A.A. McQueen, DGO of the 1st Division, and Captain A.B. Campbell, DGO of the 2nd Division, to train the Americans in anti-gas protection and discipline. The delegation of British and colonial instructors was led by Major S.J.M. Auld, an offensive gas expert in the Special Brigade, and set about creating several workbooks on gas in the hope of filling the doctrinal void. Unfortunately, protecting against gas involved both theory and practice. Although the Americans were warned and trained in a rudimentary anti-gas doctrine, it would not be until they encountered gas on the battlefield that they would comprehend the deadly nature of the gas environment. The Americans, unlike the Canadians, did not have a gradual acclimatization to the spiralling gas war; they were immediately immersed in it. Although the AEF would not become a military threat to the Germans until the end of the war, the psychological impact of a quarter of a million men arriving every month in France compelled Ludendorff to launch his offensive in hope of ending the war before the AEF could influence the strategic outcome.[5]

By mid-January, while the Canadian Corps was combatting the unpredictable factor of mustard gas and preparing for the ever-increasing gas environment, the first in a series of tougher orders to commanding officers demanded that "all ranks should look upon Anti-Gas measures as routine of defence, rather than a special branch of Military procedure." Anti-gas training was taught to new soldiers in the same way they were to be trained in marching or the handling of rifles. Gas officers were given full control over what they thought necessary to strengthen gas discipline among their soldiers, and they monitored the gas war to ensure that the Canadian defence was never far behind, and preferably was ahead of, the offensive employment of war gases. The continued application of education was a necessary precaution as the Germans in the Canadian sector began to instigate large-scale raids and gas bombardments on the Canadian lines.[6]

During the first three months of 1918, after Germany had foisted peace terms on Russia and before it launched the offensive that it hoped would end the war, the morale of the German Army was very high. General Currie described in his report for the Overseas Ministry that the "enemy assumed early in February a very aggressive attitude, raiding our lines very frequently, using for the purpose specially trained troops. His destructive shoots and intense gas shelling were also of frequent occurrence." The Corps War Diary noted that "there was a marked increase in the [enemy's] use of gas shells." The Canadians in turn, following the code of the Western Front, retaliated just as vigorously. In this world of "tit for tat," the Canadian artillery continued to refine its attack gas doctrine and, with advice from the chemical advisor, "special stress [was] to be laid on the employment of gas shells" in retaliatory bombardments. Most important, gas was increasingly being used as a pre-emptive strike against enemy infantry, and the firing of a "decisive concentration of gas shells" into suspected forming-up points became one of the first lines of defence. Gas was an integral part of the Canadian operational defensive doctrine, just as it was an essential aspect of the combined-arms German offensive doctrine. The result was that the Western Front was increasingly becoming submerged in a sea of gas.[7]

From 1 January to the first week in March, the Canadian Corps suffered 519 gas casualties: almost one out of every seven casualties came from gas. But even with thousands of gas shells and projector canisters falling on their lines, the Canadian Corps suffered fewer casualties than the British Corps flanking the Canadians. The Canadians were at a constant gas alert with SBRs worn on the chest in the ready position and all soldiers wary of possible gas shells falling at any time, day or night. At the end of February, after 2,000 gas shells and 300 projectors were fired into the Canadian-held area around Lens, Sir Henry Horne, commander of the First British Army, congratulated the Canadian Corps on this "proof of the high state of discipline and of the efficiency of the gas training of the troops" after suffering almost no casualties. The Canadian Corps had trained hard to improve its gas discipline, and those skills would be tested throughout the year in the new gas environment of the Western Front.[8]

The increased activity on the German front and the massive build-up of shells and men clearly indicated to the British and Canadians that the Germans were massing for a large-scale attack. Canadian batteries were warned as early as 4 March that "counter-battery work will probably commence with an intense surprise gas bombardment, and it may be continued at a slower rate of fire for a number of hours." To prepare for the German gas assault, artillery gas officers such as Lieutenant G.J. Culham of the 3rd Division ordered that extra SBRs be moved to forward areas for artillerymen, increased the amount of available washing soda and baking soda to help any man who was exposed to mustard gas, and created a separate dugout for mustard-gas cases so that the rest of the unit would not be exposed to the secondary effects of the gas. There were many cases like the one used as an example by the brigadier-general of the General Staff, P. de B. Radcliffe, to all gas officers on 19 March 1918: three gunners were gassed by a Yellow Cross shell, took refuge in the communal dugout, and infected nine more men due to their contaminated clothing. In addition to the continued diligence against peripheral mustard-gas poisoning, gas officers worked with the commanders of the infantry and artillery to adopt more flexible defences. Notwithstanding these precautions, there was no escape from the German gas. Brooke Claxton, a future Canadian minister of national defence, noted in his memoirs the "extreme discomfort" of keeping up the rate of fire "while wearing gas masks." Yet those gunners who were not warned about or prepared for the gas would be rendered ineffective in the chemical environment.[9]

When areas of the front had become permeated with mustard gas, soldiers were forced to wear their SBRs all day and change their clothes so as to avoid burns. In early March, line gas officers, under orders from DGOs, began to implement a policy of first avoiding all work parties in trenches that had been gassed and later of simply moving out of trenches that had been saturated and leaving behind a skeleton force. This precaution went against everything the Allies had believed about the "sanctity of ground," but it also reflected the changing perception and active learning that went on in the trenches. Yet holding on to ground had become an end in itself, and trading ground for time or space was a difficult concept to adopt. It took some units longer than others to accept the new reality imposed by the gas war, and gas officers continually fought with infantry officers, especially new ones, who viewed this as a reflection of their "ability as fighters." Some units learned faster than others;

F.G. Thompson of the 78th Battalion remembered needless casualties to men in his battalion because the officers refused to move out of contaminated trenches. Despite the resistance, these temporary retreats were necessary: during the two weeks prior to the March Offensive, the Canadian front was gassed forty-four different times. The worst case was a projector attack against the front of the 43rd Battalion on the night of 6 March 1918. The gas sentries mistook the crimson flame of the projector as a flamethrower and failed to give adequate gas warning. The 43rd suffered heavy casualties with fifty-eight gassed, of whom eleven died. Again it proved that the gas war could be curbed only with constant vigilance, education, and training. Yet equally important, gas caused officers to be aware of and react to the limitations imposed by gas on their men. Victor Lefebure, in his post as liaison officer between the French and British Gas Services, noted that by 1918 gas had become "a serious factor in Staff consideration of losses."[10]

German Gas Tactics and the March Offensive

Fritz Haber remarked after the war that "as soon as you had a Box Respirator, I knew it [gas warfare] was a waste of time."[11] Haber was right in assuming that gas was not a war-winning weapon; he was wrong, however, in his assessment of gas shells, which became important as harassing agents and finally as a weapon for numerous tactical functions. Few weapons are utterly decisive on their own – not bombers, not tanks, not even high-explosive shells – and it is wrong to assume the poison gas should have been any different. Poison gas worked most effectively as part of a system of weapons. Infantry commanders were initially openly hostile toward gas for its suspect offensive capabilities but also because of their perception that it was more harmful to themselves than to the enemy. Yet with the introduction of gas shells and the general acceptance by the artillery of their uses, gas became a constant factor on the Western Front. Although there were no repeats of the panic of April 1915, gas was a valued weapon within the attack doctrine of all armies.

By 1917, under Lieutenant Colonel George Bruchmueller's guiding judgment, the Germans had further refined a new attack gas doctrine. After the success of the German artillery fireplan using gas shells in September 1917 at Riga on the Eastern Front, "Breakthrough-Mueller" coordinated attack plans with severe gas shelling to attain different results. The tactics involved the combination of high explosives and gas shells in "crash" bombardments. Delivering a combination of gas and high explosives in a short period not only hid gas shells in the ear-shattering explosion of conventional weapons, but also forced soldiers to go to ground, to take shelter in the dugouts and shell holes where gas most readily collected. Officers became so worried about being able to identify the gas hidden within HE bombardments that units with poor gas discipline often forced men to wear their masks during any bombardment, thereby further augmenting the debilitating aspect of gas. Recognizing the drain on the fighting efficiency of men having to operate with respirators attached for long periods of time, Bruchmueller "nourished" a target or area, slowly but constantly firing gas over several hours, saturating an area with 21,000 shells per square kilometre for six hours. Such "Gas Squares," as Bruchmueller called them, could deposit a death cloud over large concentrations of troops. Moreover, if mustard gas were employed, it would make parts of the front uninhabitable as well. Bruch-mueller's sophisticated attack gas doctrine was codified in the December 1917 manual for employment of chemical shells and permeated throughout the German artillery. These new battle tactics were incorporated into all future German operations and employed to full effect in the upcoming offensive.[12]

The German March Offensive in 1918 was launched behind an enormous barrage of high explosives, whirling metal, and poison gas. Gas shells made up 25 to 50 percent of the total number of shells and were generally employed up to a depth of three miles from the front. Ludendorff acknowledged that gas made a vital contribution to the offensive: powerful artillery bombardments, relying upon gas for effect, had served tactically to "paralyse the enemy's artillery and keep the infantry in their dug-outs." As well, gas effectively severed the forward position from the commanders in the rear and induced a "temporary paralysis of the defence." Soldiers were cut off from the command structure and then abandoned, forced to fight on their own and faced with the constant threat of a neighbouring unit retreating and leaving them to be surrounded by the enemy. The effects of the gas decimated morale just as the Germans had hoped, and whole battalions and brigades retreated from the front lines in a disorganized rout. As soldiers fled from the chemical and conventional onslaught, they threw away whatever would lighten their load – rifles, helmets, food. Attesting to the absolute necessity of protection against gas, one sample of 10,000 panic-stricken soldiers noted that 6,000 were without rifles, 4,000 were without helmets, but only 800 were without respirators. "At half-past four in the morning I thought the world was coming to an end," was how one British artillery officer remembered the start of the German bombardment.[13]

The Germans, ever the forerunners in the gas war, used their four main types of gas in different combinations in order to create an effective bombardment. Using a strategy known as *Buntkreuz* (coloured cross), the Germans differentiated between Yellow Cross, Green Cross, Blue Cross, and lachrymators to achieve specific results. For instance, after Yellow Cross was fired, the affected area could not be occupied by the infantry for days; Green Cross-infected trenches could be occupied within two hours; and areas gassed with Blue Cross or tear gases could be occupied as soon as the cloud dissipated. Lieutenant-Colonel Harold Hartley of the British Gas Services noted in a conference of chemical advisors during the later stages of the offensive that one-third of the casualties of the March Offensive were from gas and that some units suffered 100 percent casualty rates from gas. The British had 33,000 casualties from mustard gas alone, a bleak record that Charles Foulkes, British Director of Gas Services, noted as a "source of serious embarrassment to us." Gas was not a war-winning weapon, but employing it allowed commanders to accomplish the set goals of causing casualties and inducing friction and chaos within the enemy lines – an action that complemented the German storm-trooper tactics that attempted to do the same thing.[14]

With such tactics the Germans believed they had found a way to break the "riddle of the trenches." No longer would the infantry batter itself against the enemy's static defences, for once they found a break in a line they flowed through it around areas of stronger resistance to attack the soft underbelly of the enemy. As Ludendorff remarked, "we hack a hole. The rest comes on its own." Gas became one of the tools through which the Germans were able to negate areas of defence and move around strong pockets of resistance without worrying about flank attacks. With infiltration tactics, the farther the attacking groups penetrated into the rear of the defence, the more threat there was to the unguarded flanks. The Germans solved the problem by using gas, especially mustard gas, as a protective device to provide a chemical buffer zone. So effective were the mustard-gas tactics, that "even in open warfare," a German officer wrote, "the troops soon were asking for gas."[15]

Mustard gas could be used tactically, much like a box barrage, to create barriers against the enemy and isolate whole areas of the battlefield. Enemy strong points, key terrain, supply routes, batteries, and forming-up points for counterattacks all became targets. The German operation "Georgette," a renewed thrust of the March Offensive, was preceded by an intense gas bombardment on Armentières on the night of 7-8 April. An estimated 30,000 mustard gas shells fell on the town, inflicting more than 900 gas casualties on the defending troops of the 34th Division and extensive losses to the civilian population. At the operational level, it allowed the Germans to move around defended positions, avoid the costly fighting of a city battle, and, finally, take the city with minimal casualties to themselves when the British were forced to pull back to cover their exposed flank. After extensive observations by gas officers, the British eventually realized that areas saturated by mustard gas would not be attacked. In this way, they were able to predict where the German attack was aimed. Yet this knowledge came too late, was difficult to transmit to senior officers, and did little to help slow the tide of gassed victims being sent to the hospitals.[16]

The March Offensive eventually collapsed because of a breakdown in logistics, the failure to reinforce success, and a strong Allied fighting retreat that blunted the devastating break-in just as it was painfully close to crashing through the trench system and rolling up the British and French Armies. The gas tactics had proved effective in protecting the flanks, but the simple fact that the Germans outpaced their artillery often meant that the later stages of their advance pitted infantry against the fixed defences of the Allies. Although the results were often impressive, they were won with appalling costs to the German troops. The British and French artillery responded by laying heavy gas bombardments behind the lead storm-trooper units, deluging the German reinforcements and slower-moving artillery in a swamp of gas. Unable to continue such deep thrusts due to lack of men, matériel, and support, the Germans had played their "last card," as some German officers referred to the operation. The "Peace Offensive" left the German Army bereft of its best soldiers; moreover, its general loss of manpower simply could not be replaced. The German Official History estimated that from March to mid-July the Germans lost almost a million men. As shock trooper Rudolf Binding lamented, "One cannot go on victoriously forever without ammunition or any sort of reinforcements." During this thrust, however, the British Fifth Army was nearly annihilated, with the British and French suffering hundreds of thousands of casualties as they "fought with their backs against the wall."[17]

When Do We Get at Them: Spring 1918

During the offensive, the Germans avoided the Canadian-held sector with its commanding heights of Vimy and Lens. Nonetheless, the dominion troops were still harassed, and Private Albert West detailed in his illegal diary that "the enemy seems to have inaugurated a 'reign of terror' ... Every day and all night shelling goes on some where near."[18] The rank and file knew that the Germans were launching a major offensive but, as one remarked, "Many conflicting rumours are coming down the line just now but we don't pay much attention to them, but if they were all true the British Army is wiped off the earth."[19] General Currie, perhaps hearing reports that the Canadians were feeling uneasy about stories of the Fifth Army's defeat, sent out a Special Order of the Day on 27 March 1918 to be read to all men:

> In an endeavour to reach an immediate decision the enemy has gathered all his forces and struck a mighty blow at the British Army. Overwhelmed by sheer weight of numbers the British Divisions in the line between the SCARPE and the OISE have fallen back fighting hard, steady and undismayed.
>
> Looking back with pride on the unbroken record of your glorious achievements, asking you to realize that today the fate of the British Empire hangs in the balance, I place my trust in the Canadian Corps, knowing that where the Canadians are engaged there can be no giving way.[20]

Despite Currie's "stiff upper lip" message, he believed otherwise. Two days earlier he had written in his diary: "Nurses and staff of hospital running away.

Everything very windy down there [in the British Fifth Army rear], gale increasing the further back you went."[21] The British Fifth and Third Armies may have been retreating in disarray, but the Canadians were resolved to stand fast and refused to relinquish the hard-won heights of Vimy and the surrounding area without a fight.

Although not in the direct line of attack, the Canadian trenches were continually strafed with HE and gas shells. As an officer of the 50th Battalion indicated in a correspondence book, between 27 March and 30 April every time the 50th entered the front line, their position was inundated with gas. The forward and secondary lines of the Canadian Corps were gassed at least sixty-five separate times during this period, but the veterans of the corps, who had been through the recent chemical saturations at Hill 70, Passchendaele, and the constant drilling by the Gas Services, suffered only forty-five recorded gas casualties. The low casualties did not mean that the Canadians did not suffer from the gas, however. Arthur Lapointe remembered the terrible days of April: "For two days now the enemy has been firing gas shells," he lamented. "The air is heavy with fumes, and we have masks on a great deal of the time. For two days we have suffered from thirst ... having no water, have been able to swallow little food, and I am weak as a result." Among the gas projections and shells, Canadians were "attacked" by German airplanes dropping rubber balloons filled, it was believed, with mustard gas. In the end, the fear of a new German delivery system was unwarranted: the balloons were for meteorological surveillance. Yet the threat of gas continued to weigh heavily on all in the trenches.[22]

During the first days of April, the Germans continued to plague the Canadian lines with gas shells. H.A. Searle of the 18th Battalion bitterly remembered how the Germans had gassed their lines. No one was safe, not even the generous padres and men who staffed a nearby YMCA canteen that supplied the men with coffee: all were invalided out of the line as gas casualties. Other reports noted that the Germans were using higher calibre guns, with the result that gas shells could be fired up to 20,000 yards into the rear. In response, on 5 April, the Canadian counter-battery officer unleashed a twenty-four-hour gas bombardment to silence the German batteries. The plan called for a barrage of HE to disrupt the German positions and force the men to take shelter away from their dugouts, which would then be followed by lethal two-minute bursts of phosgene shells. In a flurry of firing, howitzers were to deluge 100-yard grids with fifty shells. And, to exhaust the enemy gunners, prolonged lachrymatory and HE shell bombardments, mixed with lightning strikes of lethal gas, were fired to continue harassing the enemy throughout the night. The high-explosive and chemical blitz provided a needed respite for the Canadians, and Maurice Pope of the Royal Canadian Engineers probably spoke for all when he found out the Special Companies planned to return some of the gas that the Germans had thrown at them: "Pour sa ration ce soir nous allons projeter sur le sale Boche cinquante tonnes de gas liquide cela lui fera du bien." More important than the Special Companies to the overall attack doctrine of the corps, the Canadian counter-battery role continued to evolve, and the use of gas during these weeks helped to prepare the artillery for its integral role in the Last Hundred Days.[23]

Although the Canadians were not in any of the main battles in early 1918, they were defending an extensive part of the British line. General Currie noted in his diary that his corps was "holding 10-mile front with two divisions, altogether too much but owing to lack of men in British Army cannot be helped. I am told we have 430,000 men in Mesopotamia." As he received reports of the British Armies being ground out of existence by the German war machine he added, "What a splendid place for a reserve." The Canadian-held line was at the time the only major BEF sector that was not attacked by the enemy. Colonel Dan Ormond of the 10th Battalion argued that the Canadian reputation had a lot to do with it: "The Boche was quite aware of who was holding it and he deliberately stayed away." Field Marshall Haig would have preferred to have it otherwise, by breaking up the Canadian Corps' divisions to shore up the crumbling British positions, but Currie resisted for both military and nationalistic reasons, causing Haig to snipishly remark in his diary that "I could not help feeling that some people in Canada regarded themselves rather as 'allies' than fellow citizens of the Empire." As the Germans drove the British and French back, the Canadians were left in a dangerous salient. Although at least one Canadian infantryman wondered why the corps' shock troops were being used as "Block Troops," rumours were passed around by some Canadian wags that the Germans were trying to isolate the Canadians in order to make a separate peace with them. The Canadians certainly saw themselves as elite troops, and while the Germans often acknowledged this, they were also not interested in attacking up the well-fortified defences of the ridge when they had weakly held and poorly defended open ground to either flank.[24]

The Canadian divisions disguised their weakness with heavy raiding, intensive patrolling, and elaborate programs of harassing fire using generous portions of gas.[25] Private Claude C. Craig wrote in his diary on the predatory nature of the Canadian Corps:

> From now on for the next few months every time that a fresh Bn. [Battalion] went into the line the first thing that they would do was to make a raid and find out what the enemy was doing. Sometimes there were two or three raids a night and never less than one a night. The result was that all we had to do was to fire a few shots from our Machine Guns and down would come a counter barrage of the heavies and when we really did go over he didn't have enough ammunition to do us very much harm. He got so nervous that the lines in front of us was [sic] as light as day from the rockets that he kept firing off. We did all this so as to relieve pressure of his big drive down the south.[26]

Accompanying the raids was extensive use of gas and smoke. Employing their gas shells, Canadian artillery focused on firing several short bursts of lethal agents during the night in the hope of attaining a surprise killing effect. Even if the surprise element failed, the Germans would still have to wear their respirators for longer periods. Moreover, as the directions in one fireplan noted, such bombardments would increase the attrition of German morale so that "men did not acquire the habit of assuming they were safe after they had one dose." To cause further damage, during the period of the March Offensive up until 20 April, the British Special Companies launched five projector attacks from Canadian lines against the Germans in order to harass them and keep them off guard.[27]

The projector attacks still contained only phosgene, for the Allied scientists had not been able to manufacture mustard gas in quantities that could be used as a battlefield weapon. Canadian soldiers, aware that mustard gas made living in the trenches almost intolerable, sent a series of requests to General Headquarters through their officers asking for its quick introduction. The commander of the concerned soldiers received a memo in return stating that delays in the research and manufacture of the gas itself was slowing down the production of mustard gas shells, but that they would soon be available for use against the Germans.[28] Such was not the case, and it was not until the final weeks of the war that Canadian gunners would be issued mustard gas shells.

As already noted, the British had serious shortcomings in their chemical production and research facilities. With the introduction of Yellow Cross shells by the Germans in July 1917, there began a frenzy of work by the British to try to reproduce large quantities of the persistent gas. Between August and December 1917, a group of British scientists examining the production and implementation of mustard gas as a battlefield weapon wrote seventy reports without finding a solution on how to manufacture the gas efficiently. It took months to develop the theory behind the creation of the gas, something that German scientists had examined before the war, and when it was finally achieved in April 1918, the resulting gas was 30 percent weaker then the German variety. The scientific name for the British mustard gas was BB dichlorethyl sulphide, and the shells were later labelled BB. The substance itself was referred to by Canadians as HS – Hun Stuff. The subsequent failure to produce large quantities of the gas meant that the Germans encountered their own creation only very late in the war.[29]

Because the British were unable to master the process of manufacturing mustard gas in 1917, they were forced to rely on heavy doses of phosgene to penetrate the inferior German leather gas mask. In what was a fortuitous find, British intelligence units translated captured German documents that illustrated the success of the naval blockade and its effects on gas defence. The German report frankly noted that "leather masks arose by reasons of economy of raw materials ... [, have] been manufactured since 1st July 1917 ... [, and do] not adequately protect against Green Cross and Blue Cross shells."[30] Not only did the filter on the respirator wear out more quickly than those on the Allied SBRs, but the mask failed in high concentrations of gas; as a result, the British Special Companies added a new method of delivering gas in dense concentrations.

On 12 July, the British carried out a "beam" gas attack from the Canadian front. Train tracks were laid at night into No Man's Land by Canadian Railway Troops, and light trains containing hundreds of gas cylinders were furtively pushed up to the front by unhappy groups of infantry, the noise masked by artillery fire. The soldiers in the front lines were withdrawn and forced to follow "alert" procedures in case of a reversal in the wind. With their jobs done, the infantrymen fled back to the safety of their lines and allowed the men of the Special Companies to carry out their business.[31]

At zero hour, 879 canisters were electrically detonated. The gas cloud quickly expanded and "beamed" over the German lines, lethal to a depth of 9,000 yards. Once the gas had been released, the Special Company men and railway troops desperately pulled on the forty-foot ropes to get the trams and canisters back into their lines before the German artillery opened up with retaliatory fire. Such attacks, along with the use of projectors, were greatly feared by the German infantry; one report indicated that each "surprise" attack caused "100-200 gas cases ... about 10% fatal." The attack was believed to be a success. However, a Canadian listening post had not been notified of the gas discharge, and all three Canadians within it died a horrible death from their own gas.[32]

Between March and July both the British and Germans continued to harass each other with projector gas attacks. The British carried out close to one hundred projector attacks and the Germans responded with sixty of their own, although on average, the Germans released less tonnage of gas per operation. The British chose to rely on projector attacks more than did the Germans, but by 1918 an analysis of the chemical armaments in all countries noted that 94 percent of all gas used was being delivered by the artillery, with an overall total for the war of sixty-six million gas shells. The constant attacks at irregular intervals, even in relatively "quiet" sectors, kept soldiers, who were otherwise recuperating from the fierce battles of the March Offensive, relentlessly tense and on the edge.[33]

THE IMAGINATION FEEDS

One perceptive German infantryman remarked about the battle of Verdun that "the Germans created the battle of material, but they had unfortunately forgotten to reserve exclusive rights to it." Such was also the case with the gas war. When the initial technological lead was closed – or at least when the Allies could respond with similar force – the individual German soldier, just like the Allied soldiers who had suffered first, began to feel the sting of a reciprocated gas war. German Pioneer Georg Zobel described the ghastly effects of poison gas: "Here and there were men from other units who had been surprised by the gas. They sat or lay and vomited pieces of their corroded lungs. Horrible, this death! And, much as they implored us, nobody dared give them the coup de grace. We were badly shaken by it." The British, aware of the psychological effects of gas, incorporated that knowledge into their offensive gas doctrine. With the prevailing winds in their favour, the British continually harassed the German lines with canister, projector, mortar, shell, and beam gas attacks.[34]

Enemy units that were known to have been badly affected by gas were tracked by intelligence and became targets. On at least one occasion, a canister attack was postponed to await the rotation of a division that had only recently been hit by a series of gas assaults. As a result of this strategy, the 1st Bavarian Reserve Regiment was gassed fifteen times in a period of six months in 1917. The Canadian artillery was instructed to impede the enemy by causing him to wear his mask, "and thus decrease his movements, especially at night, owing to the serious interference with vision and the increased difficulty of breathing." Equally important, the infantry was to be harassed by gas "day after day," which would "rapidly reduce their efficiency." Exhausted soldiers attempting to recuperate from lost sleep were to be targeted by "short bursts of lethal gas" in order to catch them before respirators could be attached. These gassings would have been an exhausting experience for anyone, but for the soldiers at the front, bone-weary from weeks of battle, they were crushing to morale. As war-weariness set in, gas continued to erode the soldiers until they were little more than husks of their former selves. As a captured German diary recorded, "We have again had many casualties through gas poisoning. I can't think of anything worse; wherever one goes one must take one's gas mask with one, and it will soon be more necessary than a rifle. Things are dreadful here." The Germans, leery of the anxiety caused by British gas attacks, passed an order that all prisoners refrain from discussing gas casualties and that all men killed by gas be secretly buried at night.[35]

Gas became the ultimate symbol of the trench war in which it was conceived: it was a tactical weapon of attrition, used to wear down the enemy physically and mentally. One German prisoner remarked "that if an offensive were conducted only with gas, half the Germans would be put out of action and [the] other half would malinger." While gas failed to have that effect, its use as a psychological weapon was a very powerful factor in destroying the morale of soldiers at the front who were already tottering on the edge of a breakdown. Even slightly gassed soldiers tended to take on a weariness and lassitude that, when combined with their already heightened levels of stress, made it very difficult to restore them to their units without periods of rest and recuperation. Like water rotting wood, gas was not often immediately deadly, but it was constant, insidious, and demoralizing to the soldiers in the trenches.[36]

Two doctors, Lieutenant-Colonel J.C. Meakins, CAMC, and Captain J.G. Priestly, MC, RAMC, wrote that the effects of gas were "both of a physical and mental character. The unusual and uncanny appearance of ... gas made a great impression on the soldiers' minds. This was further accentuated by the distress and agony produced in those who were severely gassed." Lord Moran, author of one of the most famous books on battle stress and psychology, *The Anatomy of Courage,* also believed that gas was a major cause of psychiatric casualties. Drawing on his experiences as a regimental medical officer in the trenches, Lord Moran made the following analogy: "A man's courage is his capital and he is always spending. The call on the bank may be only the daily drain of the front line or it may be a sudden draft which threatens to close the account." In the trenches soldiers became careless: days and months of living with poor food, too much rum, lack of sleep, and constant inundation with horrible sights caused some soldiers to become numb to the horror. The numbness could transform itself into recklessness or negligence. Forgetting to duck in low trenches or simply taking too many dangerous chances were symptoms of a soldier on the edge. Such actions were just as dangerous in the gas environment, especially where strict attention and alertness were needed not only to identify but also to avoid chemical agents. Even when soldiers were able to react to the present or forthcoming danger, gas remained one of those "cheques" that continually drained a man's "courage account."[37]

Fear in war is not always rational. Gas, like the terrible artillery barrages, failed to give the soldier a fighting chance against the enemy. Canadian medical officer R.J. Manion described the powerful psychological effects of gas: "As a result of this gas attack many of our men had to go to the hospital, and those of us who escaped that were depressed for several days. Gassing weakens the morale of troops. Men do not fear to stand up and face an enemy whom they have a chance of overcoming, but they do hate dying like so many rats in a trap, when death is due to a gas against which they cannot contend." Echoing Captain Manion, the eminent British doctor W.H.R. Rivers, who treated countless shell-shocked soldiers throughout the war, was convinced that "his patients' sense of helplessness contributed far more to their condition than the routine horrors of combat." Discipline, training, and esprit de corps all helped to give the soldier a chance of coping with the stresses of battlefield, but as one Canadian padre who worked closely with soldiers noted, "the hardest battles for the individual men were not always fought in No Man's Land of France, but in the No Man's Land of the mind." Covering the Western Front, poison gas continued to eat away at bodies and also at minds.[38]

With the introduction of mustard gas, the trenches and shell holes – formerly areas of physical and psychological safety – could become poison traps that burned eyes and genitals. Soldiers lived in a world where they had no control over what was lurking in the shadows. It was not a fight against an enemy, nor was it even taking shelter in a dugout against a heavy shelling. Gas could be anywhere: in the air, on the ground, trekked into dugouts, on food, or in contaminated water. As one doctor writing about the causes of shell shock recorded: "A man awoke to his danger by seeing his comrades stricken down and by the sight of their wounds, and any further desire he felt of probing the action of modern projectiles was soon dissipated by his imagination, which conjured in his mind the view of himself as a casualty."[39] This comment was equally applicable to gas. As an agent of attrition, gas played on the psychology and willpower of the soldiers. It must be remembered, however, that by almost all accounts drum-fire artillery barrages were a far more terrifying experience. This has been identified in many other sources, but, unlike artillery, the effects of gas on the soldiers have remained unnoticed.

By 1918 gas was a weapon that was continually present at the front. Although artillery was the great killer of the war, soldiers who had been in the trenches for any time had an amazing ability to tune out all but the heaviest bombardments.[40] Gas alarms were impossible to ignore. Old hands could not sleep through a gas attack, as everyone in the sector would be killed unless they quickly donned their masks. As well, with companions falling to the right and left of a soldier from the regular attrition of battle, most men, to save their sanity, fatalistically chalked survival up to chance.[41] Arthur Hickson, a New Brunswicker and Lewis gunner with the 26th Battalion, remarked before he was invalided out of the army with pneumonia that in "combat [a] man would be a nervous wreck if his imagination were given free rein. Perhaps it was all summed up in the lines of a popular soldiers' song: 'The bells of hell ring ting-a-ling, a-ling, a-ling / For you but not for me.'"[42] Gas destroyed the idea of chance, and that was why it was so terrifying. There is a subtle difference between crawling on a trench floor or advancing under fire and praying that a shell or bullet does not get you, and simply waiting for a death cloud to pass over you. Soldiers could fatalistically write off the fear of shells or bullets with the grim trench phrase "you'll get it when your number's up," but gas potentially had everybody's number.

Hysterical soldiers who forgot their gas discipline were prime victims. Rapid heartbeat, sweating, blurred vision, and shortness of breath were all signs of gas poisoning; yet they were also normal signs of stress in battle. Symptoms of gas poisoning were often misinterpreted. A common occurrence among gassed soldiers was that they smelled gas, became frightened, and believed that their SBRs had a leak.[43] By ripping off their helmets to get their replacement masks, they were truly gassed. It was a deadly self-fulfilling prophecy. Other soldiers suffering from the very real terrors of the battlefield became isolated from their mates within their claustrophobic respirators. No longer was there a helpful word or smile; voices were garbled and eye contact was impossible. Human interaction was blunted and quickly disintegrated within the gas environment. Soldiers were left to their own devices, and that was often not enough in the maelstrom of the Western Front. Such soldiers could freeze or panic. Thus, the nature of gas was just one more factor pushing men toward shell shock. With constant drill and education, the Gas Services attempted to reduce the very real and deadly results of gas hysteria, which could lead to casualties, mental break-down, or the attrition of fighting efficiency. It did not always work.

Those wounded by conventional weapons were among the most susceptible to being gassed. George Bell described his injuries from an HE shell: "Both my ankles had been badly wrenched, my collar bone had been dislocated, and I was badly dosed with gas, while buried unconscious beneath the earth." Daniel Ormond, commanding officer of the 10th Battalion, remarked how one of his privates became a casualty through shellfire and was then gassed: "It was most difficult to keep his respirator in place. It is not known if he died from gas or his wounds." Men were also known to try and rip off their helmets when wounded, and reports warned, "that they should be watched to prevent this." Despite such knowledge, in the chaos of battle, few men could keep an eye on their mates; infantryman William Woods remembered with shock when his comrade screamed he had been "hit" and pulled off his mask during a gas attack. Although Woods forced his respirator back on his head, his mate spent three months in a hospital with burned-out lungs. Soldiers had a love/hate relation-ship with their respirators. They hated to wear them, for they felt suffocated and blinded, but they needed them to survive in the deadly environment on the Western Front. The fine balance was sometimes lost when soldiers gave in to their psychological anxieties or their wounds forced them to remove their res-pirators. Soldiers who were buried, mad with pain, or incapable of adjusting their SBRs might wake up to find they had been gassed. Or they might never regain consciousness.[44]

One Canadian infantryman wrote that "war is a great ager. Young men grow old quickly here."[45] That was true, if they survived the first couple of weeks at the front. New recruits quickly learned to keep their heads down and find shel-ter behind an eighteen-inch mound or to stand stark still when a Very light was fired over the battlefield, illuminating everything in a ghostly glow. Such tricks of survival were necessary, but even if a soldier ended up cowering or crying during an artillery barrage it made no real difference except to his own ego or psychology. In the end it did not matter if a shell landing in a trench hit near a man who was in control of himself or petrified with fear. Both would be dead.

Gas was a different story. Those men who were educated and drilled so that they could identify gas and don respirators quickly were generally safe from the effects of lethal gas, so long as a shell did not land right next to them. Mustard gas could affect anyone, but those with efficient gas discipline at least knew what areas were dangerous by the smell or by the discolouration of the ground, and they knew when it was necessary and to wear an SBR and when it was not. Green troops had less idea of how to defend themselves against unconventional weapons like gas. Erich Maria Remarque described how five to ten recruits fell for every old hand, especially during gas attacks: "We found one dug-out full of them, with blue heads and black lips. Some of them in a shell hole took off their masks too soon; they did not know that the gas lies longest in the hollows; when they saw others on top without masks they pulled theirs off too and swallowed enough to scorch their lungs. Their condition is hopeless, they choke to death with haemorrhages and suffocation." Reinforcing Remarque's testimony, a 22 May 1918 Canadian Corps report warned that "the majority of gas casualties lately have occurred amongst recently arrived reinforcements." Although the fear of gas was greatest for soldiers who were new to the front, poison gas continued to harass all soldiers, who knew that at any moment they might have to reach for their mask or risk having their lungs burned out.[46]

Most gas casualties were not fatal. Did this make them unimportant, as most historians have indicated? Huestis H. Reeves, who served in both the 26th and 78th Battalion, was one of the many non-fatal gas casualties of the war. Toward the end of the war a Yellow Cross shell exploded near him and some of the viscous fluid landed in his hair. Within days not only had his hair begun to fall out in clumps but his scalp was badly burned. When he returned home to see his loved ones, his "grand, thick, curly hair" had been replaced by scarred baldness.[47] Such a minor wound – compared, for example, to having a jaw shot away or a sucking chest wound – might not even be registered as a casualty and would certainly fall within the notion that gas was simply another annoying factor for the poor bloody infantry. But it was obviously more than that for Reeves, and the countless other Canadians who suffered under the strain of gas.

One of the most interesting demonstrations of the fear of battlefield gases by First World War soldiers was the spontaneous rumour mills that sprang up. "The prevailing opinion in the trenches," one soldier remarked, "was that anything might be true, except what was printed." News was notoriously hard to come by, and rumours were rampant among all soldiers, who craved information. The times spent idle, picking at lice or grousing, were breeding grounds for surmises. A fascinating report issued by the French Direction des Services Chimiques de Guerre in January 1918 examined the claims of soldiers who were subjected to new or extraordinary gases. Soldiers reported that they had been affected by everything from gas shells that shot out "electric waves destroying everything" in their path, to Blue Cross shells "killing everything in a radius of 200 metres." Over 50 percent of all reports came at the beginning of each year, during the period of waiting before active operations. The French attempted to lay the blame for such wild reports not on their own soldiers, but on German spies. German High Command had allegedly ordered its spies to influence

Allied soldiers and reduce their morale. More likely, the High Command of all armies did not fully understand the psychological fear their soldiers had of gas. The manifestation of such fears were the reports of new varieties of non-existent killer gases.[48]

The men at the front had varied reactions to gas: soldiers who were level headed and well trained may have viewed it simply as one more discomfort of the battlefield, but for those who were exhausted, on the edge of a breakdown, or untrained, poison gas was a constant bugbear. It seemed to suck the life out of a man's lungs. To fear it was normal, especially for anyone who had ever had the experience of choking. It must also be remembered that respiratory diseases like pneumonia and tuberculosis were great killers before the war, wiping out men, women, and children with a seemingly random selection. Unlike other weapons, gas killed in unconventional ways, and, as one historian noted, it could be that "the sensation of choking and slow suffocation releases fears which are stronger than the anticipation of pain from bullets and shell splinters. Who can say?"[49] Only the soldiers who lived through it and recorded it in their private letters and diaries. An analysis of those sources makes it clear that poison gas lurked in the trenches and in the hidden places in the mind, exposing itself at various times for different men, but always ready to pounce.

PREPARATION FOR BATTLE: SUMMER 1918

Fulfilling its role as an advisory and defensive organization, the Canadian Corps Gas Services in France had grown to twenty-seven officers and eighty-six other ranks by July 1918.[50] The Canadian Gas Services continued to be directed by Major W.E. Harris, who was responsible to the chemical advisor of the Army and through him to the newly appointed director of Gas Services for the whole BEF, Colonel C.H. Foulkes. Accountable to Harris as chemical advisor of the Canadian Corps were the other principal gas officers of the corps: the commandant of the Canadian Corps Gas School; the gas officer, corps troops, who was in charge of troops in the corps area other than those soldiers under the control of the divisional gas officers; gas officer, Canadian Corps Reinforcement Camp, who organized initial gas training and the supply of equipment for new recruits in France; and finally, the four divisional gas officers in France and their direct subordinates, the brigade, battery, and battalion gas officers and gas NCOs.[51]

The Gas Services were divided into two separate parts: those in the rear and those at the front. The DGOs and the chemical advisor had the important role of implementing policy and sharing information with other chemical advisors. But it was the gas officers at the front who earned the men's trust, as they laboured to make the front-line soldiers safe from gas. The examination of dugouts, the checking of respirators to make sure they worked effectively, the constant practice, even if viewed with annoyance, and even sometimes the sending of gas casualties to the rear, all fell to the gas officers in the trenches. The greatest respect from the soldiers was won by these front-line gas officers and sergeants living and suffering with the men – not by some faceless chemical advisor forcing them to comply with orders from the rear. Yet both the front and rear gas officers were necessary for the implementation of anti-gas doctrine.[52]

The constant burns and minor infections from stray traces of mustard gas forced the soldiers in the trenches to find methods to decontaminate their clothing. Hot water, exposure to air, and bleaching powder were used to remove gas from clothing. These methods were partially successful, but it was not until the development of chlorine stations that clothes could be fully decontaminated. Shell holes containing gas remained a problem, and although buckets of chloride of lime were issued as part of front-line stores, the smell from the lime masked any other gas that was present at the front. Gas-protected dugouts remained an important sanctuary from the pervasive gas environment, and with good gas discipline the infectious nature of mustard-gas casualties was contained.[53]

By July 1918, the British had firmly established that chlorine effectively neutralized the effects of mustard gas. It must have seemed ironic to those Canadians who had survived the first gas attack at 2nd Ypres that they were now forced to walk through chlorine chambers (with respirators on) in order to protect themselves from a more pervasive and frightening gas. Unfortunately, it was not until 10 September that chlorinating stations would be established for each brigade in the line. As a result, soldiers continued to suffer from contaminated clothing as it burned and blistered them.[54]

Although the total number of mustard-gas casualties continued to rise, the effects of the poisoning were distinctly milder than those that occurred in the autumn of 1917. Mustard-gas victims still suffered from bronchial infections and blindness, but doctors were now more aware of these effects. As a result of this forced education, the horrible blisters that were characteristic of the first mustard-gas victims were very much reduced by the immediate cutting off of all infected clothing and bathing of the body in mild solutions of soda to dilute the effects of the gas. Although soldiers had much stricter gas discipline, they continued to fall victim to mustard gas for several reasons: the Germans "camouflaged" it within HE bombardments; it was tracked into dugouts on the boots or clothing of companions; or, most important, it caused no immediate painful reaction and thus deceived soldiers into thinking they were not being gassed. Like all units in the BEF, the Canadian Corps continued to lose a steady trickle of men to mustard gas, and so the Gas Services turned to even stricter gas discipline to protect the troops.[55]

Through the creation of a rigid gas discipline the Gas Services could hope to minimize the damage of the gas war, but never to stop it completely. Although stiff leather suits of heavy oilcloth and asbestos were introduced to front-line troops in the hope of stopping the effects of mustard gas, their use was not continued, for soldiers could barely move in such clothing, which also acted as ovens in hot weather. More useful to the soldiers was the provision of bicarbonate of soda to the front lines by the end of May 1918 for soldiers to wash their eyes or skin if they were mildly exposed to mustard gas. Less effective was a Vaseline-like paste issued to front-line soldiers to prevent and treat mustard burns. Soldiers were to smear their bodies with the salve, and although it tended to reduce the serious nature of the burns, it was understandably uncomfortable to be slathered in the ointment for any length of time. If the salve were uncomfortable before contact with gas, it was downright dangerous after contact: the paste absorbed the mustard without neutralizing it and thereby drew the agent to the flesh. It is unclear how frequently the Vaseline was used, but it may have been widely asked for by soldiers because it had the welcome effect of eliminating lice for a period of time. Despite such notable failures, precautions reduced the wastage of soldiers forced to the rear and the time they spent out of the line recovering from mild burns or irritations.[56]

Leather suits and anti-gas paste were just some of the suggestions that made it to the front. Patriotic citizens, caught up in the fervour of trying to "do their bit" for the war effort, periodically sent letters suggesting "helpful" hints for the gas war. Two of the most bizarre letters, illustrating the complete disassociation of the home front from what was happening to soldiers living in a maelstrom of destruction on the Western Front, revolved around offensive gas shells and cures for poisoned men.[57]

A would-be scientist, Mr. Murphy, suggested to the director of Medical Services (DMS) of the 2nd Division that the CEF should open its eyes to the possibility of a powerful irritant that was prolific in Canada. "Vast quantities of poison ivy throughout the United States and Canada," could be used in gas shells and fired at the enemy, who would presumably scratch themselves into submission.[58] Notwithstanding the impossibility of turning poison ivy into a battlefield weapon, soldiers were already subjected to the much more potent Blue Cross shells, which provoked violent itching, burning, sneezing, and vomiting.

Even less connected with reality was a letter by Mrs. L. Davies of Seaford, England. Mrs. Davies suggested an "antidote for soldiers suffering from the effects of Poison Gas": "Get a two lbs can of black molasses and in it put a small tea cupful of boiling water and then squeeze two lemons and mix it up well. Then give the patient one tablespoon every morning half an hour before breakfast, and same at night. It may make the patient sick for one or two mornings but that will pass away. It is only bringing up the bad stuff."[59] Such letters indicated the gulf between the home front and the soldiers suffering daily encounters with gases that could blind and burn their lungs out. Mrs. Davies's "antidote," sounding more like a home cure for an upset stomach, was rejected by the DMS as useless and dangerous to already suffering patients. To survive the gas war was a slow, arduous task that required learning from the mistakes of those who had not succumbed, and could only be garnered from soldiers who were at the sharp end or the doctors who studied them.

Rather than turn to poison ivy or molasses, the Gas Services continued to drill Canadians in carrying out their duties while wearing their SBRs. With the trickle of mustard-gas casualties from front-line battalions, the Canadian Gas Services decreed that the training of soldiers and new recruits was insufficient. Artillery officers understood that new gunners had to be able to survive in the gas environment and an urgent report, originated by the Third Army but passed to the Canadians, strove to warn against the enemy's propensity to employ gas shells in their counter-battery attacks: "Every possible form of ingenuity must now be considered and practised in order that our batteries may live through the bombardment, and may be available for crushing the attack." Under such counter-battery-induced gas conditions only constant and vigorous gas training could succeed in preventing whole batteries from being wiped out. In the past, infantrymen were required to wear their masks for only an hour a day, but new regulations required that they wear them marching, when practising musketry fire, and even while playing soccer games to grow accustomed and to accept the feeling of wearing the respirators. The primary aim of gas discipline was to get a soldier to do anything with his SBR on that he could do without it. Such was seldom the case, but constant training and practice were the only ways to attain that goal.[60]

In May 1918, Colonel Amos Fries, head of the United States Chemical Warfare units, stated in a letter to General John J. Pershing, Commander of the American Expeditionary Force, that the "war will be won by gas." That was certainly overstating its role, as all gas officers were wont to do, but it was a truism that the war would have been lost if an anti-gas doctrine had not been created and implemented. Gas drill and discipline were a continuous cycle and had to become second nature to the soldiers at the front. Actually encountering gas in the field was the best experience, however. One report remarked that some men "who could adjust respirators in good time on a gas parade [became] muddled when an unexpected alarm goes off," with the realization that a mistake meant a horrible death. Most were able to react because of the ingrained gas discipline they had learned; the few who could not paid the highest price. Generally it was the new recruits who continued to fall victim to gas. Although they were now proficient in adjusting their respirators, as they had been taught in England, many were poorly equipped to identify and take action against the various insidious poison gases.[61]

Along with constant drill, the importance of being alert was still a necessary precaution at the front. Standing for a few hours each night during an alert period, gas sentries were imperative in giving the warning to don respirators.

The sentries still relied on klaxon horns (now increased to twenty-six per mile of front), bells, and anything that they could beat to arouse the unit, which would then warn all formations in the rear through a telephone call or visible warning rockets. Due to the frequency of gas attacks, such warnings were only to be given during intense gas shelling. Military police in the rear areas had the dual role of passing along the gas alarm by strombos horns and making sure that front-line soldiers did not move to the rear to escape the gas shelling. Although this had rarely been a problem in the Canadian Corps, it became an epidemic in the American Expeditionary Force, where gas discipline was unsound. One analysis of the American forces noted that "An important cause of the low morale was the mounting fear of the enemy's use of gas ... It was largely responsible for creating so great a straggler problem that ... a solid line of MPs back of the fighting front had become necessary to keep the men in the line. The basis for that fear was the gas atmosphere that the enemy maintained over much of the front by his regulated gas fire each day."[62]

The nature of gas shelling and the small gas cloud created by such action (compared to a Livens or canister cloud attack) forced alarms to be kept local – otherwise a whole brigade or division could be awakened several times a night. Individual battalions relied on their gas officers to judge the severity and type of gas assault and whether to withdraw the troops to a predetermined safe area or wait until the Green or Blue Cross gas dissipated. By 1918, such gas assaults occurred on a daily basis in some areas. As gas shells silently dropped around them, disrupting their sleep or work, trench soldiers were forced to sit in miserable silence, taking their respirators off and then putting them on again in a maddening cycle.

After analyzing the retaliatory gas barrages by both enemy and friendly fire during the March Offensive, the Canadian artillery gas-shell doctrine had been further refined. As Colonel L.V. Cosgrave remembered, "we were learning by experience, and pretty bitter experience, but we learned." Gas had become more accepted by artillerymen: not just its questionable morality, but the very necessary difficulties of employing new range tables, staggered firing rates, and the different tactics demanded by gas-shell fireplans. The weapons technology – although never acknowledged in such words during the war – had moved from a very select group of specialists to a broader general application. No longer were artillerymen reliant on the chemical advisor for advice on when to use gas shells; this was now established by the counter-battery staff officers. Such procedure was finally codified in an order from the Canadian Corps General Staff dated 14 June 1918, which stated that the employment of gas in tactical situations was to be organized by the artillery. Although the Gas Services relinquished their control over the last facet of offensive use, they were still mandated to develop the anti-gas doctrine among the troops. In certain instances, the decentralization of attack gas moved from the corps to the divisional artillery. In the set-piece battle, gas delivered by the artillery was still under the control of the general officer commander, but during the break-in period, which required greater flexibility, the use of gas shells to achieve tactical objectives fell to the divisional artillery staffs. The employment of gas was becoming more pervasive, requiring that larger numbers of officers master its role on the battlefield.[63]

In the summer of 1918, the Canadians were pulled out of the line for a rest, but as one Canadian machine gunner remarked, "while they called it a rest, it was really a reconstruction period getting ready for the next offensive." General Currie subscribed to a similar philosophy as Ivor Maxse, the finest trainer of British troops in the war: "80 percent of the work we do in battle is carried out in training before the battle. That battle is won or lost by arrangements made beforehand. We have learnt that from personal experience." New troops and old veterans were thus continually drilled in gas discipline, and part of that training required men to practise small-unit tactics with their SBRs on to overcome the confusion of advancing under fire nearly blind. Officers were further ordered to stop valiantly leading their men, respirators unworn. The friction and loosening of control induced by the gas had to be weighed against squandering good officers to foolhardy bravery and almost sure gas-induced casualties. British officers seem to have been more susceptible to this type of leadership, and a report by senior corps gas officers in the British services noted that many British officers "did not receive special anti-gas courses and that the Canadian actions is [sic] much ahead in this matter." Such reprimands were important and proved that the soldiers were actively attempting to learn in the unmerciful classroom of the Western Front. The blood curve continued to be high, and careful gas discipline was the only cure. As one July 1918 Canadian training order starkly put it, "when the amount of time available [for training] is limited, [gas training] will be given precedence before other branches of instruction." Soldiers were being instructed to not only survive in the gas environment, but to overcome it.[64]

CHAPTER EIGHT

The Gas Environment

THE LAST HUNDRED DAYS

By June 1918 the German Offensive had finally been repulsed, with heavy casualties to both sides. But it was the Allies, with the injection of 250,000 Americans a month, who now enjoyed material and troop superiority. The French had launched a series of counter-attacks against the Germans and, since June, had been employing their new mustard gas shells. The mustard gas, called "Ace of Trumps" by General Foch, appointed overall Allied commander during the dark days of the German Offensive, was a terrible shock to the German infantry, who seem to have not been informed by their officers that they would surely encounter mustard gas at some point. It caused panic among the troops, much as the German forerunner had done to the Allies a year earlier. Herbert Sulzbach, a lieutenant commanding a battery in the German artillery – and who, incidentally, worked as a translator for the British in the Second World War – wrote in his diary that the French launched a terrible artillery barrage of gas and HE: "I pull my gas-mask over my face, and it works, but his damned new gas held on for days; it lies on the ground, you don't know it's there, you can't see it or smell it, it clings to the grass like dew, and does its dreadful work. We have a very large number of casualties, and the poor chaps suffer from temporary blindness and continuous vomiting."[1]

Rumours abounded in the German Army that a British officer had disguised himself as a German gas officer and had stolen the formula for the mustard gas from a gas school.[2] Such stories were simply the product of trench rumours: the British were still months away from producing enough mustard gas to be used in a tactical operation. The Germans, however, were culpable in not fully impressing upon their soldiers the necessity of protection against the effects of mustard gas. That the Allies had not retaliated with the gas for more than year after it was first used had probably eroded whatever drill the German Gas Services had initially attempted to instigate. Whatever the case, the Germans reeled from its unexpected use; in conjunction, General Foch ordered a series of small operations to secure communication lines. The culmination of these, a much larger attack, was to be launched on 8 August.

The Canadian Corps (minus the 2nd Division) was pulled out of the line in the first week of May and relieved by five British divisions. The Canadians had remained relatively unscathed during the March Offensive, compared to many British divisions that had desperately fought with "their backs against the wall." Due to his loss of faith in Field Marshall Haig's ability to deliver victory without further senseless slaughter, Prime Minister Lloyd George drastically reduced reinforcements, causing British units to slowly strangle. Many divisions could mount only brigade-strength roll calls, and all were eventually forced to reduce their battalions from twelve to nine per division. While the British were reducing their divisions, the Canadians had a surplus of men as a result of conscription in Canada and the breakup of the 5th Division. With their dwindling reserves, which reduced the fighting strength of the British Expeditionary Force, the British continued to press the Canadians to reform the existing force into two corps. General Currie, acting like a backroom political brawler, successfully fought such a move, playing the British off against Canadian nationalism. Currie forcefully claimed that "the Canadian Corps in the existing formation had proved itself a smooth-running machine of tremendous striking power, and any radical alteration in its constitution might have resulted in a reduction of such power without any compensating advantage." The Canadian Corps thus remained a coherent fighting body, with significantly more men who were able to fight at the sharp end of battle: approximately 12,000 in a Canadian Division in contrast to an average of 8,100 in a British Division. The Canadian Corps was, in effect, almost as strong as a small British Army. During the last days of July, Currie informed his divisional commanders that the Canadian Corps would be secretly moved to a concentration area west of Amiens.[3]

It was a monumental task to move the Canadian Corps secretly, with over a hundred thousand men, corresponding military equipment, and stores. In addition, the dominion troops needed to deceive the Germans into thinking that they were moving away from rather than toward Amiens. This deception was necessitated by the reputation of the corps. As Liddell Hart observed, "regarding them [Canadians and Australians] as storm troops, the Germans tended to greet their appearance as an omen of a coming attack." Such German assumptions would only be reinforced by the corps having survived the March Offensive relatively unscathed and therefore ready for battle. To add to the secrecy, in each Canadian soldier's paybook was posted a note that read "Keep Your Mouth Shut." More ingenious was sending wireless operators and small groups of infantry to Flanders at the end of July to send messages in that area and conduct raids against the German lines, where Canadian badges were "conveniently" dropped. Such actions resulted in the Germans thinking that all the Canadians were heading to Flanders.[4]

As the Canadian troops began to form up in the area around Villers-Bretonneux, west of Amiens, a 2nd Canadian Division report indicated that the commander feared the Germans would find out about the large groups of men and begin shelling the area. The report argued that, "the Bois l'Abbé and Bois d'Aqueene were capable of concealing a large number of troops, but as those woods had been frequently subjected to gas shelling, it was considered advisable to forbid to use of them for assembly purposes." R.H. Camp of the 18th Battalion had the same apprehension as a soldier in the line, observing that "If the Germans had ever got wise as to how the troops were massed down there, it would have been a terrible slaughter." Mustard-gas shelling would have forced tens of thousands of men to move from their positions, thereby revealing their locations and destroying the secrecy of the operation. The fear of gas ruining the carefully laid plans was very real, and a final artillery report indicated that the "source of greatest danger will be counter pre-paration [sic] by the enemy with gas shells"; it was a fear that left thousands of Canadians straining their ears for the soft thump of gas shells as their synchronized watches slowly ticked down to zero-hour.[5]

The spearhead of the thrust into German lines was to be carried out by three Canadian Divisions (the 3rd, 1st, and 2nd, from right to left) and two Australian Divisions to the north of the Canadians (the 5th and 4th). As was the case with past victories, the Canadian infantry was to work in close conjunction with the artillery in a set-piece battle. General Currie had 646 pieces of artillery under his command, which he organized into different tasks. The most important factor in the attack was the creeping barrage, but the counter-battery work, for which the Canadian Corps were famous, was also necessary in neutralizing German guns. Employing aeroplane and reconnaissance reports, forward observers, and sound-ranging equipment, the Canadian guns silently registered on the enemy batteries; no shells were fired before the barrage that would allow the Germans to realize the danger they were in. In the words of Colonel Harry Crerar, then an officer in the counter-battery section: "The primary object of all Counter Battery work is the reduction of enemy fire at critical periods ... [This] is obtained by previous destruction of guns and prepared positions, by previous destruction of personnel and lowering morale, or by surprise effect."[6]

A necessary component in the counter-battery work was the use of gas shells to hamper the enemy gunners and screen artillery pieces that were difficult to hit by conventional fire. Command centres, assembly trenches, observation points, and lines of communication were also targets to maximize friction in the German defence. The Canadian artillery thought so highly of poison gas that 20 percent of its counter-battery fire was made up of it.[7] Still, there were worries about Canadian soldiers having to advance through their own gas, so the substance was used sparingly except against the enemy artillery pieces or on the flanks. It was during the consolidation phase of battle that gas would be used to saturate enemy guns and disrupt counter-attacks by placing heavy gas bombardments between the new Canadian and German lines.

Amiens: The Black Day of the German Army

The first wave of Canadians to advance were eager to get at the Germans – the operation was known informally as the "Llandovery Castle Operations," after the hospital ship that had recently been sunk by a German submarine. J.R. Cartwright of the 3rd Battalion remembered the experience of almost complete silence before zero-hour and "then one gun went off, [followed] by all the other guns at once." Each known hostile battery was engaged by two or more Canadian batteries, and when the infantry "went over the top" at 4:20 a.m. there "was very little retaliation." The counter-battery work, aided by an integrated attack gas doctrine, had done its job.[8]

Canadians wearing gas masks bringing in wounded.

The infantry, carrying only the barest of equipment, advanced in waves, leaving behind all but those few tanks that did not become bogged down in the shell-pocked ground. The enemy lines were overrun, and one German report indicated the "loss of the entire artillery position and the virtual destruction of all the front line and support battalions." Although the British and French assaults were not as successful as that of the Canadians and Australians, overall the German Army had suffered its greatest defeat since the beginning of the war.[9]

The decisive victory by the Allied Armies cost the Germans 28,000 casualties, more than two-thirds prisoners. Accordingly, General Erich Ludendorff labelled 8 August 1918 as the "black day of the German Army in the history of this war."[10] The terrible setback was all the more painful for the German general, who had proclaimed to his soldiers just four days earlier that "I have a feeling that there is much concern felt by many people over enemy attacks. This is not justified ... We should be pleased if the enemy does attack, since he will expend his strength all the quicker by doing so."[11]

Although the dominion shock troops had proved Ludendorff wrong in his soldiers' eyes, it had still been a costly advance. The Canadians had suffered 3,868 casualties – 1,036 killed, 2,803 wounded – but captured 5,033 German prisoners and 161 guns. The casualties were grim, but acceptable, considering the advance was measured in miles, rather then yards as had earlier been done on the Western Front. As one Canadian remarked, "for the first time we felt that we were winning the war and that feeling permeated through all ranks and of course it was a tremendous morale lifter." Echoing his "ground pounders," General Arthur Currie wrote to Prime Minister Sir Robert Borden that "the Canadian and Australian success at Amiens did a very great deal to raise not only the morale of the British Army, but the morale of the British nation."[12]

The Canadians' advance, with their reputation preceding them, had one captured German brigadier remarking that he knew that the Canadians had "at least 11 divisions in France." To counter the deep thrust, the Germans rushed seven infantry divisions and numerous machine-gun companies to the area to strengthen the German lines. Along with the reinforcements, what remained of the German artillery fired thousands of Yellow, Green, and Blue Cross shells into the Allied lines in attempts to create impenetrable zones of gas. The Canadian battalion gas officers attempted to use dirt and lime to fill in gas-polluted shell holes, but moving above the trenches left one susceptible to the traditional dangers of warfare, shells and bullets. The cold and hungry Canadians, having left all but the most necessary equipment behind, dug into hastily transformed trenches as the Germans saturated the front and lines of communication with HE and gas.[13]

As the Canadians searched for cover among the ruins of the towns they had liberated, they encountered traps set by the Germans. The retreating Germans had exploded a series of Yellow Cross shells in dugouts, exactly where the

Canadians would be taking shelter. Several cases of gas casualties were reported before gas officers had been able to examine all the dugouts. Along with such traps, the Germans polluted water wells in the area with mustard gas in order to further tax the weary Canadian troops.[14]

Constant subjection to small-arms and artillery fire and the strain of action began to tell at all levels. The friction caused by conventional weapons was only exacerbated by gas. The man in the trench had to fight with respirator attached, which led to overheating and to greatly reduced vision and breathing, compounding the effects of normal exhaustion incurred in battle. In the isolation imposed by his mask, he was reduced to confusion. For commanders in the rear, gas added to the chaos of modern war by not only obscuring the battlefield, but, more important, by slowing and disrupting communication from the front. Signallers and radio operators were hampered by the gas, and since their success was precarious at the best of times, commanders received late or outdated information when they received anything at all. The friction of battle was drastically increased on the chemical battlefield, and although the employment of poison gas was initially intended to bring about open warfare, it was finally used on the defensive to grind it to a stop.

While leading several platoons seeking to make contact with forward German lines, W.M. Marshall, an officer of the 46th Battalion, had to abort the operation when his men were forced to advance through dense German gas pockets. Losing several men to the "fiendish" effects of the gas, he noted that "about every third shell turned out to be a gas shell." Thomas W. Gossford of the 1st Canadian Mounted Rifles clearly remembered their position being bombarded after their deep advance with "only gas shells, no heavy shells ... We had to wear our masks, as all that night filthy mustard gas rained down." The constant pollution of the battlefield by mustard gas, sometimes in small doses but often in pools of dangerous oily liquid, eventually deadened the olfactory sense that many soldiers used to distinguish between safe and dangerous areas. In many cases casualties resulted because soldiers could no longer smell the gas and recognized the danger only after the damage had been done. Within this gas environment the "law of diminishing returns" began to assert itself, and the combined effects of German reinforcements, the exhaustion of the Canadian infantry, the inherent friction of capturing new positions, along with the breakdown in communication, the loss of surprise, and the difficulty in bringing up the guns, made the further advances of the next three days less fruitful and more costly than the initial one. Equally important was the use of gas to deny ground and slow the Canadian advance, an aspect of the fighting at Amiens ignored up to now. The corps' thrust was still a remarkable feat, and by the end of the battle on 11 August, they had driven a full eight miles into the German lines, pushing the Germans back as far as their old 1916 trenches.[15]

During the last days of the battle, the Germans continued to saturate all areas of the Canadian front with Yellow Cross shells, as one captured document illustrated, to "compel the enemy to wear his mask." Private A.E. MacFarlane, only nineteen at the time, remembered gas shells blanketing the battlefield and forcing an end to his reconnaissance mission. Even after filling his respirator with vomit, he kept it on until getting the orders to pull out of the gassed area. As the fighting dragged on, the constant stress of gas all day and every night drained the combat efficiency of the Canadian troops. Another soldier recounted: "With men trained to believe that a light sniff of gas might mean death, and with nerves strung by being shelled for long periods and with the presence of not a few who really had been gassed, it is no wonder that a gas alarm went beyond all bounds. It was remarked as a joke that if someone yelled 'gas,' everyone in France would put on a mask ... Two or three alarms a night was common. Gas shock was as frequent as shellshock." "After 1917," wrote Lord Moran, "gas partly usurped the role of high explosives in bringing to a head a natural unfitness for war. The gassed men were an expression of trench fatigue, a menace when the manhood of the nation had been picked over." Lord Moran, echoing earlier fears by the High Command, saw gas as a weapon that could seriously undermine the Allied armies, for it allowed a way out for inferior soldiers, who, despite their shortcomings, were needed for the final victory push.[16]

In attempting to slow the Canadian advance and disorganize soldiers who had only recently begun to carry out open-warfare tactics, all forward areas were gassed, especially woods and the remains of the recently retaken villages where the Canadians might be entrenched. The defenders grimly determined that if the Canadians were going to advance, they would do so through a gas environment and over polluted ground. To augment this, the Germans also introduced a new 17 cm Minnenwerfer shell filled with mustard gas, fitted with timed fuses to detonate in the air. These new shells were more efficient at spraying the mustard gas over the battlefield and thus made it impossible to neutralize infected shell holes with chlorine and lime. The Germans also introduced a new mustard gas shell that contained a higher quantity of high explosives and therefore had the same effect of spreading the gas over a larger area. An added complication was that these innovations had changed the sound of the gas shell in flight and exploding, and sentries could no longer tell a mustard gas shell from a high explosive. Soldiers were warned to expect any HE bombardment to contain within it a corresponding amount of gas shells. Such tactics were successful in tormenting the front-line soldiers, and there was little that the Gas Services could do to protect them. Each had to survive the onslaught on his own.[17]

Once again, the wounded were most susceptible to the assortment of German gas bombardments. Hundreds of Canadians lay where they had fallen on the recent battleground. It was the natural instinct of wounded soldiers to pull themselves in shell holes to escape the shrapnel flying on the battlefield as well as for the psychological safety of being partially protected. Of course, the insidious tendency of gas to collect in such "safety-holes" made them potential death traps. The fact that some of the wounded were too weak to adjust gas masks, or had their senses dulled from the pain and loss of blood, would have made them prime victims of the gas. Those infected by severe doses of Yellow or Green Cross gas would never leave their holes, while those who inhaled Blue Cross gas simply endured more agony. It is hard to imagine what the violent sneezing and relentless vomiting would do to a wounded man suffering from a gaping stomach wound.

Canadian staff officers were aware that the infantry, plagued by gas shells or forced to advance over mustard-gassed ground, would as a result suffer high gas casualties. At the Headquarters of the Canadian Red Cross Advanced Stores, a centre was established for gas patients, men with suspected self-inflicted wounds, and the sick. Grouping the gassed victims alongside those men who were viewed as having suspect wounds, commanders clearly wished to stigmatize gas wounds as "inferior" to conventional ones in a hope of discouraging their growing frequency. The gas casualty figures for 8-14 August are missing, but the number of cases admitted to the Canadian Corps Field Ambulance for 15-24 August was 229. The figures for the previous week would have been at least as high, especially as the Germans relied heavily on gas to slow the Canadian initial advance. Anne E. Ross, a nurse at one of the medical tents, remembered the "overflow of patients in the tents." One night during the offensive, Ross had to take care of 700 patients, many of whom were victims of gas attacks. Gas, although only infrequently fatal, forced the Canadians to use limited supplies, personnel, and medical space to care for the growing number of casualties.[18]

The period for training was over, and there was little the Gas Services could do to help their men; the Services did, however, marvel at the splendid information obtained during the Canadian advance regarding the German Gas Organization, its equipment, method of supply, and papers on the tactical uses of shells. Vast stores of equipment, including 30,000 respirators, and over 20,000 rounds of Blue, Green, and Yellow Cross shells, were also taken. The captured shells were fired back at the Germans, and the valuable information, papers, and German equipment were exceptionally important in defending against the gas warfare that was expected to increase in 1919.[19]

As the officers of the Gas Services picked over the battlefield for German gas appliances, the battle slowly trickled to an end. Between 8 and 13 August the Canadian Corps had met and defeated elements of fifteen German divisions, completely routing four. By the 14th of the month, General Currie had sent a letter to Field Marshal Haig suggesting that any renewal of the operation would result in high casualties without obtaining any more results and advising that a new front to be opened against the Germans. Haig accepted his victorious corps commander's suggestion, and on the night of 19-20 August the 2nd Division began moving to the Arras sector, followed the next night by the 3rd Division. Although the battle had been called off at a strategic level, raiding parties, snipers, shelling, and gas took their toll on both the Canadians and Germans still in the front lines. When the Canadians were pulled out of the area, they could be proud of their record: a penetration of fourteen miles and the liberation twenty-seven villages. Nonetheless, it was accomplished at the cost of 11,822 well-trained Canadians. Although the Canadian rapier had found flesh, it was losing its edge in the ferocious fighting. Notwithstanding the blunting of the corps, Amiens marked the beginning of the end for the German Army.[20]

The Battle of the Scarpe and Drocourt-Quéant Line, 26 August-2 September 1918

Sensing the weakness in the German Army, the Allies continued to hammer away. An attack by the French Tenth Army south of Amiens, a drive by the Third British Army north of Albert, and the success of the Fourth British Army astride the Somme kept the pressure on the Germans, forcing them to commit their dwindling reserves to stem the relentless offensives. In this battle to the finish, the period of rest for veterans and acclimatization for new recruits was denied to the Canadians: the Canadian divisions were thrown back into battle toward the end of August to break the "hinge" of the heavily fortified Hindenburg Line. General Foch, aware of the difficulty, remarked, "I think that the Canadians are the force on which I can rely to clean up between Arras and the Hindenburg Line ... [They are] the ram with which we will break up the last line of the resistance of the German Army."[21] The sector given to the Canadians was well defended and absolutely imperative to the whole German defensive system. It would not be relinquished lightly.

Assaulting over shell-pocked battlefields, lost British trenches, barbed-wire entrenchments, old German trenches (prior to the March Offensive), and the Fresnes-Rouvroy Line, the Canadians would finally have to break the strongest position of all, the Drocourt-Quéant (D-Q) Line. Staff Sergeant Howard Graham, who would later rise to a lieutenant-general during the Second World War, remembered looking across the area the Canadians would have to transverse "on a sunny afternoon and noting what appeared to be fields of ripened buckwheat as far as one could see."[22] Instead of buckwheat, it was roll upon roll of rusted barbed wire. Behind the razor defences the Germans were aware that an attack was imminent; thus the Canadians would be frontally assaulting a strongly fortified position. It was a recipe for disaster, but General Currie, although recognizing the monumental task given to the Canadians, had faith in his corps. Yet that faith was not based on naïveté; before the battle, the general wrote that with only three days notice, the corps was to undertake "the hardest battle in its history."[23]

Due to the German awareness of an impending operation, Currie ordered a risky night attack in hope of gaining some surprise. The 2nd and 3rd Canadian Divisions attacked at 3:00 a.m. on 26 August behind fighter-bombers and the all-important artillery and machine-gun barrage. Stumbling over broken ground, with respirators attached to protect against the German counter-barrage of gas, the Canadians made deep advances into the German line.[24] "The din of the battle was furious, artillery ... [machine guns], vickers, tanks, men, aeroplanes," remarked Albert West as his machine-gun company went forward, "and all aided in filling the air with hideous sounds." Amid that horrible din, at day's end, the Canadians had advanced to the Fresnes-Rouvroy Line by defeating some of the best German units, most notably the Prussian Guards, in vicious hand-to-hand and bayonet fighting. Haig was ecstatic and claimed that the Canadian attack, along with the British successes, "was the greatest victory which a British Army has ever achieved."[25]

The Canadians continued to press the Germans back, overrunning trenches and machine-gun posts through sacrifice and dogged determination. The desperate defenders showered the battlefield with poison gas while in retreat, thereby forcing the Canadians to wear their respirators or suffer the consequences. Lieutenant Ralph W. Donaldson, the DGO of the 2nd Division, was rebuked by the commander of a Canadian battalion when he inquired about its forty-four gas casualties after a night of gas bombardments. He was told that "even though the men were in gas, owing to the stress of very severe fighting combined with periods of vigorous digging in ... the close proximity of the enemy and the very great strain endured by all ranks men could not be expected to adjust respirators unless they were in overpowering concentrations of gas." The difficulty of the infantry advancing with respirators worn meant that in all but the densest gas clouds the Canadians grittily ignored their weeping eyes and burning lungs to clear the enemy trenches. Yet in many areas the need to advance through heavy concentrations forced the Canadians to attach their respirators, either on command from officers or through their own knowledge. Notwithstanding the terrible conditions, most soldiers made it to their objectives.[26]

Once again, though, the initial deep advances were slowed by fierce German counter-attacks, the friction of war, and heavy dosages of gas; and, like at Amiens, the assault became increasingly costly. The friction on the battlefield rose dramatically as Canadian infantry units made deep thrusts into the German lines and moved out of range of their own artillery. As well, confusion developed among the forward divisions, who became uncoordinated and attacked separately. Lastly, communication, temperamental at the best of times, was lost for hours on end, thereby leaving commanders in the rear isolated from their soldiers at the front. After three days of exhausting fighting, the two Canadian divisions were relieved after suffering 5,801 casualties, of which at least 332 were from gas.[27]

As the 1st and 4th Divisions secured the newly won lines and the Canadian artillery blasted lanes through the German wire, the new relieving battalions carried out a series of minor operations to gain better jumping-off trenches. In retaliation the Germans once again deluged the Canadian forward positions with gas. Even the usually laconic War Diarist for the 10th Battalion remarked that "considerable hostile shelling and much inconvenience was experienced from Gas shelling which at times was quite heavy." The effects of the gas environment were amplified by the lack of anti-gas blankets for dugouts and shelters. Luckily though, during the break-in attacks, the weather turned and rain soaked the battlefield. To the "poor bloody infantry" it was just one more obstacle, but an unintended advantage was that the overpowering German gas bombardments, which had been fired in the hope of saturating the front and No Man's Land between the two forces, were reduced in potency. Despite the natural dispersal, the gas still hung in sporadic deadly pockets, and the conventional defences remained a powerful deterrent. In addition to the machine guns and rows of barbed wire, the German front-line troops were to put up a fanatical defence. One captured prisoner informed his captors that "they had do-or-die orders" to keep the Canadians away from the D-Q Line.[28]

The focus of the assault, the D-Q Line was a strongly fortified double trench of concrete shelters and entrenched machine-gun nests surrounded by open fields of fire to cut down any attackers. The attack was pushed back from 1 to 2 September as roads had to be fixed, artillery brought up, and shells stockpiled. Both General Currie and General Henry Horne of the First British Army realized that the D-Q Line was the backbone of the enemy's resistance. It would be folly for the Canadians to attack before all preparations could be carried out. Field Marshall Haig also acknowledged the importance of the Canadian attack, having received an ominous letter from Sir Henry Wilson, chief of the Imperial General Staff, which indicated that the War Cabinet would probably relieve the field marshall of his command if the BEF suffered high casualties at the Hindenburg Line.[29]

On 2 September the battle-hardened but severely depleted infantry stormed the D-Q Line. Once again, there would be no surprise attack. The Canadians relied on their artillery to paralyze the defenders so that the assault groups could close with the enemy without being slaughtered. The Canadians advanced behind a devastating barrage of 762 field pieces. Although they broke through the D-Q Line, they were unable to cross the Canal du Nord behind it due to intense artillery, small-arms fire, and concentrated gas attacks by the Germans on the other side of the canal. Canadian Roy McNaught, whose brother had been killed at Lens in August 1917, proudly wrote to his father after the battle: "We were given the hardest part of the line to take ... We captured all kinds of prisoners, guns and machine guns. General Haig came in person and congratulated the 1st Division of Canadians, which is the division I am in, but the praise I think should be given to the artillery. They put up a barrage of smoke, gas and shrapnel which was hard to beat and they sure played havoc with Fritz."[30]

During the attack the Germans once again resorted to "extensive gas shelling," and some Canadians became disorientated and slowed down when forced to wear their SBRs. While advancing across the Canal du Nord, Gordon Hamilton of the 58th Battalion became "hung up on wire" and was gassed when he could not reach his respirator in time. Others, like Lieutenant J. Chambers of the 7th Battalion and his platoon, fell victim to the chemical agents when a gas sentry got "a full dose of it himself and didn't warn the rest of us." Although all of the men in the unit suffered from wracking coughs, periodic vomiting, and had lost their voices, they continued to stay in the line and keep fighting – technically never considered gas casualties by the bean-counters in the rear. As the infantry overran the enemy positions, the exhausted and gassed Canadians could take some delight in the continuing Canadian Corps policy that "all captured gas shells shall be returned to the enemy." Through dogged determination, the Canadians had once again taken an almost impregnable position and continued to advance through the German defences – machine-gun nests, barbed wire, trench barriers, and pervasive mustard-gas zones.[31]

At the same time that the Canadians applied such intense pressure to the German positions at the front, the Brigade Gas Officers continued to operate gas stations to the rear of the fighting. Units out of the front line in reserve were paraded to the gas stations to have their rusted or defective SBRs replaced. Some undoubtedly cursed the extra fatigue, but most, like Victor Wheeler, overlooked the marching to the rear in return for having their well-used respirators in perfect shape: "Our lives depended on our gas masks being in tiptop shape when needed. Mud, grime, wetness, and the wear and tear of trench conditions shortened their effectiveness sometimes to a very few weeks. It was of paramount importance, therefore, to have our 'life-savers' examined as often as practicable and, when necessary, replaced with new respirators."[32]

SBRs had to have their charcoal canisters replaced after forty hours of wearing, and battalion gas officers and gas NCOs initially tried to record how long soldiers wore their SBRs during gas attacks. Such recordings became almost impossible in the pervasive gas environment of 1918. As one front-line gas officer sarcastically remarked, "any man who in the hell of battle can keep a record [of the amount of time wearing a mask] should be at once awarded a Distinguished Services Medal."[33] As a result, soldiers were repeatedly being sent to the gas stations to have their SBRs replaced. The Canadian Gas Services, unlike the Germans, enjoyed a surplus of respirators and followed a policy of careful inspection and rotation.

The battle continued as fresh troops were rotated into the line. German units flanked by the break-in on the D-Q Line pulled back behind the canal on the night of 2-3 September and left the Canadians in control of the once-powerful German fixed positions. Once again though, the cost had been high: the 1st and 4th Divisions suffered 5,622 casualties. Units at the sharp end of battle were decimated. Albert West of the 43rd Battalion confided in his diary that "he was not anxious for a trip 'over the top' now for we are in poor shape, nearly 75% of [the] batt[alio]n are new men." In writing to a friend back home shortly after the war had ended, General Currie noted that "high French and British officers think that our smashing of the Quéant-Drocourt line was the turning point in the campaign." The taking of the D-Q Line was a pulverizing battle, and as historian Denis Winter has remarked, it "remains the British Army's single greatest achievement on the Western Front."[34]

While spearheading the BEF's assaults on the German lines, the Canadian Corps had suffered over 20,000 casualties since Amiens. Some Canadians began to grumble about why they were doing all the fighting and dying. R.H. Camp of the 18th Battalion remembered the Last Hundred Days "as the worst part of the war, because you were just going ahead, all day, every day." Gas added to the burden on the individual soldier as he was forced to live, work, and fight with his respirator attached in the gas environment. One Canadian infantryman described the gas environment as "very demoralizing" while another soldier remarked: "We gaze at one another like goggle-eyed, imbecile frogs. The mask makes you feel only half a man. You can't think. The air you breathe has been filtered of all save a few chemical substances. A man doesn't live on what passes through the filter – he merely exists. He gets the mentality of a wide-awake vegetable."[35]

The costly toll on the Canadian Corps required that new recruits, barely trained, be added to the decimated battalions. With the influx of recruits from England – in the military reports they were known as men whose "training has been accelerated" – Colonel Ox Webber of the Canadian Corps General Staff and future chief of the Imperial General Staff of the British Army, warned the receiving units that "particular attention [be] paid to anti-gas training" because new men "must necessarily be weak" in it. Along this line, gas officers at Etaples issued a damning report in August 1918 regarding the poor gas training of the new recruits. It was difficult to keep the Canadian Corps as an effective fighting unit when twenty thousand of its best soldiers – and almost all infantry – had been killed or wounded, and were replaced by poorly trained new recruits. Notwithstanding the losses, the difficult task of crossing the formidable Canal du Nord was still left to the battered corps.[36]

The Canal du Nord was another daunting obstacle to assault. Bristling with machine guns and barbed wire, the fortifications on the other side of the canal were protected not only by the forty-foot-wide canal but also by swampy marshes that funnelled any attack into a natural killing-ground. Behind the position lay Cambrai, the centre of the German logistic system in the Flanders theatre. Such an assault would require extensive planning, stockpiling of guns, and time for the corps to rest and recuperate. After the breakthrough of the D-Q Line, and except for the occasional clash of patrols, the Canadian front was "quiet" until 27 September. The term is only relative; there were few days when the casualties fell below 100.[37]

General Foch ordered that a general offensive be launched from the Meuse to the English Channel to keep pressure on the Germans. The British were to attack toward Cambrai and St. Quentin; the French centre would continue pushing the Germans beyond the Aisne; the Americans would reduce the St. Mihiel salient; on the northern flank the Belgian forces would drive on Ghent and Bruges. The Germans were unable to withstand such pressures and relied heavily on their machine gunners and mustard gas to slow the pressure by the Allied soldiers. Most historians give credit, and rightly so, to the brave pockets of German gunners who often sacrificed themselves so that their comrades could retreat to the next line of defence; but the tactical use of gas was an important, and largely ignored, aspect of the tenacious German defence.

To hamper the Allied advance the German gunners simply blocked out map grids and fired shells to saturate the whole sector, thereby eliminating that area from the front. The Allies could advance through the gassed areas only if they were willing to take collateral casualties. The inexperienced Americans unfortunately made a practice of this in their attack on the St. Mihiel salient in September 1918, where they suffered disturbingly high gas casualties. Throughout their involvement in the war, gas accounted for 70,752 (27.4 percent) of the 258,338 casualties in the American Expeditionary Force.[38] The Americans severely lacked good gas discipline, and their near-crippling gas casualties once again illustrated the need for an encompassing anti-gas doctrine if fighting forces were to remain effective on the Western Front.

This operational use of gas against the Allies by the retreating Germans created a continuously miserable experience for the pursuers, who had to deal not only with the German fixed defensive positions and machine-gun nests but with entire areas of infected ground. In their fighting retreat and when they abruptly turned and attacked, the German gunners blanketed areas with gas in order to disperse troop concentrations, harass supply lines, and generally make life difficult for the exhausted attackers before pulling back to another fortified line and organizing another flexible defensive. As the historian of the American 316th Regiment wrote:

> The woods were soaked all the time with a light concentration [of gas] and everyone was breathing it. It was only when a gas shell burst near at hand, spreading heavy concentrations, that gas masks were used, however, for one cannot work all

the time in a gas mask. It was the gas at night that was the most wicked – being wakened out of a deep sleep, or even a half doze, by a muffled cry of "Gas!" from one's comrade who was already struggling into his mask … In spite of casualties from gas and high explosives, the routine work of the sector went on.[39]

The Allied troops were never free from the gas environment, and those without training suffered harshly from its effects. The importance placed on the gas shells by the Germans can be seen by the composition of their artillery dumps, which by the last year in the war sometimes contained 50 percent gas shells.[40] However, by this time the Allies were equipped with extensive stocks of chemical shells, almost rivalling the German numbers. Consequently, the Allies relied heavily on crash poison-gas bombardments as retaliatory attacks against the German artillery and front lines. It was chemical "live and let live" – the Allies would not use their gas if the Germans did not use theirs – but since the Germans relied on gas to slow the overwhelming Allied forces, they could not desist from using it.[41] The result was the pervasive gas environment that plagued all soldiers on the Western Front.

While holding the ground west of the canal, the Germans continuously shelled the Canadian positions with gas, inflicting casualties among the en-trenched and immobile troops. As the 2nd Infantry Division's commander General Burstall recorded in his 1918 Narrative of Operations, the German tac-tic of laying mustard gas at night meant that "a large portion of the forward area of my Division became thoroughly impregnated with gas which it was very difficult to detect." Claude Craig, a signaller with the 28th Battalion, remem-bered his unit's period in the front line at that time as very trying: "Gas and H.E. started at 6 A.M. and lasted till noon and off and on during the after-noon. On account of the poor trench we had no protection against the stuff and had to have our gas helmets on all that day and nearly all that night and most of the next day. One whole platoon out of the Company I was with were sent out of the line gassed. We moved 1000 yards over to another trench that night." As Craig's unit was being relieved after a six-day stint in the front lines, he wrote in his diary that 75 percent of the casualties suffered by the unit had been gassed.[42]

The weekly reports on gassing during the month of September clinically noted the vast increase in German gas shelling of Canadian infantry and artillery units. With the high ground on the German side of the canal overlook-ing the Canadian-held area, the Canadians found it impossible to move up any supplies except during the night. As a result, little anti-gas equipment could be brought to the front and the infantry were able to find scarce protection against the mustard-gas shelling. Although General Currie attempted to alleviate the pressure on his infantry and lines of communication by undertaking numerous gas bombardments across the canal, in the second week alone the Canadian Corps suffered a near-crippling 553 gas casualties. The Canadian soldiers had been taught to protect themselves while fighting in the gas environment, but with no escape from the pervasive mustard-gas shelling, which polluted the villages, trenches, and a good portion of the dugouts, gas promised to be an additional factor in the already steady atrophy of the Canadian Corps.[43]

Toward the middle of the month the Germans, suspecting another Canadian advance, shifted their salvoes of gas against batteries and routes of approach to the front. During the third week in September, the Germans fired mustard-gas shoots every night, regardless of the atmospheric conditions, which greatly reduced the potency of the gas. This failure to maximize the effectiveness of gas shells reflected the desperate nature of the Germans, who were anxious to disrupt any Canadian plans for attack. Nonetheless, the Canadian artillerymen were lashed with continuous chemical bombardments, and of their 2,389 total casualties for September, 344 were attributed to gas. The area was so polluted that Canadians soldiers entering the alert zone were warned by their gas officers that they must be prepared to wear their respirators for up to eight hours straight and that the Germans fired gas during the night so as to catch un-masked soldiers the next day when the sun rose and heated the semi-dormant mustard gas. As the Canadians attempted to survive in the gas environment, a report by the 1st Division finished with the ominous phrase, "Gas is a very effec-tive weapon and the most difficult to combat."[44]

In a secret report, Colonel Wight, the assistant director of Medical Services, noted that of the 2nd Canadian Division's casualties for September, over 50 per-cent were a result of mustard gas.[45] Soldiers suspected of being mustard gassed were to be marched to the rear, where they would pass through the new chlori-nation stations to neutralize any gas. Within the constant gas environment most soldiers could not be withdrawn from the front, and high gas casualties left some commanders suspecting that some soldiers were once again exposing themselves to gas to get out of the line.

The new commanding officer of the 3rd Division, Major-General F.O.W. Loomis, ordered on 16 September that soldiers be continually reminded that mustard gas could be fatal. A 1st Division order followed suit, proclaiming that all troops "realize that Yellow Cross ... is often lethal. The current impression that this gas only produces slight casualties ... is erroneous and should be checked." The tone and wording of the orders reflected the commanding officer's belief that some of the mustard-gassed soldiers were deliberately becoming gassed in attempts to get a Blighty. As the Canadian gas casualties lowered toward the end of the month, there were no more letters "warning of the danger of gas" and implying malingering, but it remained a constant threat to all commanders as the soldiers of the Canadian Corps wearily spearheaded battle after battle.[46]

Breaking the Canal du Nord, 27 September-1 October 1918

If anybody can do it, the Canadians can.
—GENERAL JULIAN BYNG, Commander of the Third British Army

The difficulty in crossing the canal with dug-in defenders on the other side was compounded by the narrow gap of dry land through which the Canadians had to attack. General Currie planned to mass his artillery on a small area of the German line, push through the lead battalions, and then expand the break-in like a rushing torrent. The danger of attacking from a restricted front was that the Germans could focus their artillery solely on the small staging ground. The similar vulnerability of the troops to gas shelling could disrupt the whole operation and remained "the Corps' worst nightmare as it awaited Z hour."[47] Even if the dominion storm troopers could break through without a Somme-like slaughter in No Man's Land, they would still have to cross bayonets with determined defenders, for the loss of the canal and Cambrai would render untenable the last German line of prepared defence.

In the weeks leading up to the attack, the Canadian artillery shelled the enemy front with high doses of poison gas. Constant chemical harassment, day and night, was employed to lower enemy morale, disrupt communications and logistics, cut off front-line units, and inflict casualties. To achieve victory, both the Canadian artillery and infantry would once again have to work closely, which one historian has described as being "not glamorous, but effective."[48] The one advantage the Canadians had was that the Germans, being assured of their superior defensive and geographical position, did not expect an attack in that area. They were wrong.

Following a rolling barrage on the morning of 27 September, which moved forward and backward to obliterate the enemy's position, the 4th Division punched through the Canal du Nord defence line and relentlessly drove into the German rear to allow the second wave of units to follow and pass through the forward, but now weakened, battalions.[49] Upon crossing the canal, units of the 11th Brigade attempted to outflank and capture the 230 German artillery pieces in Bourlon Wood (ground vital to the protection of the main attack on the Hindenburg Line by the Third and Fourth British Armies), which had bombarded and tormented the Canadian lines for the last month.[50]

The failure of British troops (on the right of the Canadians) to advance alongside the Canadians forced the 102nd Canadian Battalion to form a defensive flank facing south and ended the chance to flank Bourlon Wood. In the hard fighting, the advancing Canadians were flooded with area gas shoots of Blue Cross and forced to attack with SBRs on, but there was almost no Yellow Cross shells fired in the defensive barrages. Several officers were surprised at the lack of mustard gas and later wrote that on some occasions advances could not have been made had Yellow Cross replaced much of the Blue Cross that was used. During the last two months of the war, the Germans fired an estimated two million rounds of mustard gas against the advancing BEF alone; the lack of mustard gas on the battlefield was due to the Germans using up their supply and the Canadian attack catching the Germans before they could replace their munitions. Because of a breakdown in logistics and a lack of railway men and cars, large stockpiles of German gas shells never made it to the front, where they were desperately needed. The German artillery was instead forced to marinate the Canadian advancing parties with Blue Cross, which although successful in slowing the advance was not deadly. Still, the DGO for the 4th Division reported that by having to travel great distances with SBRs attached, the soldiers reached "their objectives in more or less exhausted condition through resistance to breathing." More telling about the gas war was a final observation of the gas officer: "The repugnance of men to approach the enemy with masks adjusted, partly due to restricted visions and discomfort in wearing, has on previous occasions caused casualties, and had the enemy mixed Green Cross and Yellow Cross in his fire, the presence of so much high explosive in conjunction with smoke screens used would I feel sure have been productive of casualties." Lieutenant C.E. Barnes of the 8th Battalion remembered advancing over shell-holed ground wearing his SBR and having to "take the damn thing off" because he could not see anything. Nonetheless, enough Canadians reached the enemy lines and tenaciously drove the defenders from their fortified positions.[51]

The need to capture the Bourlon Wood and secure the flanks was accomplished largely through a blitz of gas over the whole area. The Canadians, preparing almost a month for the operation, were well-stocked with gas shells and used them in a comprehensive tactical bombardment. For fifteen days prior to the assault, the Canadian artillery had fired over 17,000 gas shells into the woods to chloroform the German guns. On the morning of the attack, the artillery sent an additional 7,600 lethal and lachrymatory shells into the woods to sow confusion and hinder the German gunners and defenders. Additional gas shells were used in "back barrages" to compel the enemy's reserve and reinforcing troops to wear their respirators and thus impede their advance and exhaust them before they even went into battle. As one Canadian Corps artillery report noted, "Gas concentrations will be freely employed" to harass and wear down morale. The Canadian and British gunners had learned their gas lessons well – from 1 January to 30 September 1918 the German Army suffered 58,000 recorded cases of gas poisoning.[52]

With the 102nd Battalion guarding their flank in the south, both the 54th and 87th Battalions quickly cleared Bourlon Wood. As Lieutenant Bud O'Neill of the 2nd Division's Mortar Battalion remembered, the artillery "filled the woods full of gas," and the troops were able to easily mop up the remaining Germans. One German prisoner stated that "all batteries in and near the wood sustained gas casualties, the most serious being those within his battery which sustained 45 casualties." The unfortunate gunner also remarked that their gas protection was ineffective and unless he and his unit were in the open they dreaded a gas bombardment more than high explosives. German artillerymen were under orders to temporarily evacuate batteries that fell under gas bombardments for a "relatively long period." Having their entire area saturated in both HE and gas often gave some faint-hearted gunners a way out of the enemy-induced Armageddon. The employment of gas had played an important role in the capture of Bourlon Wood and the establishment of a secure flank from which to launch further offensives into the German interior. Despite the Canadians' having to attack, in many cases, with respirators attached, they had achieved their objectives. The superior Canadian gas training was truly paying off.[53]

The fighting raged four more bitter days until 2 October as the Germans strongly contested every inch of ground. Once again the Germans defended against the pressing Canadians by gassing artillery positions and suspected jumping-off points. Gunner W.J. O'Brien remembered that during the night of 29 September he "lay awake in an old brewery all night under the most awful bombing, shelling and gassing I have ever had." Still, the Canadians had broken through and they would not be driven back.[54]

Taking into account the exhaustion of the Canadians at the sharp end, General Currie continually pressured the Germans in order to give them no chance to counter-attack and throw back the Canadian attackers. The Canadians were repeatedly gassed as they progressed through the German lines, sneezing and vomiting, but were not prohibited from advancing through the infected areas as the Germans had hoped. Although the gas reduced fighting efficiency, Captain Arnold Allcott, the chemical advisor of the British First Army, noted that the Canadians had only fifteen serious gas casualties reporting to casualty clearing stations during the crossing of the Canal du Nord and subsequent fighting up to 5 October. In contrast, the two British Corps – VIII Corps and XXII Corps – had 115 and 148 gas casualties during the same period. Once again the Gas Services were vindicated – Canadian soldiers obviously knew when their SBRs had to be worn, and when they could be safely removed.[55]

The loss of yet another "impregnable" defensive position to the Canadians was shocking to the German High Command, as its soldiers had been well-prepared and had the advantage of natural obstacles. Sound planning, constant training, superior coordination between the infantry and artillery, and the ample use of gas underpinned another Canadian success. In the six days of hammer blows inflicted on the German lines, the Canadian Corps had advanced twenty-three miles and had captured 18,585 prisoners and 371 guns. Such impressive gains had been won at a high price in Canadian lives: the Canadian Corps casualty rate was nearly ten times that of the British XXII Corps on its flank. One captured German staff officer frankly admitted that his headquarters realized that the end was near "when the Canadians broke through the Hindenburg line." Such a sentiment was not limited to disillusioned staff officers, for the Allied advance had propelled Ludendorff to lose faith in a fighting retreat, and he informed the kaiser that the war would have to be ended as quickly as possible. The taking of the D-Q Line and the crossing of the Canal du Nord were the most difficult operations of the Canadian Corps in the First World War. Although overshadowed by Amiens and Vimy in history and popular mythology, they remain the Corps greatest battles – battles fought within a gas environment.[56]

The Final Push

During the period of 2-8 October, the Canadian sector was relatively quiet. The colonial storm troopers continued to follow an aggressive policy of patrolling, for as one order declared, "there is no reason why the enemy should not be made most uncomfortable." Canadian artillery, using mustard gas shells for the first time, initiated a fireplan of harassing the German lines in order to reduce the defences around Cambrai, but gas shells were not used farther back due to the presence of French civilians. The Germans had no such qualms and responded to the aggressive Canadian raiding parties by gassing the Canadian front. Even though he, like all soldiers, was aware of the constant German chemical bombardments, Driver A.N. Davis of the 47th Battalion fell victim to a Yellow Cross shell when it "lit alongside" him and gassed him before he could adjust his respirator; he spent the next six weeks recovering in a hospital and was even too weak to raise himself to cheer when the Armistice was declared. Davis was not alone: during the second week of October there were 144 recorded cases of Canadians gassed on the chemical battlefield. The nature of casualties, however, had changed; because of instilled gas discipline, soldiers generally fell victim only when gas shells burst near them or from the secondary effects of mustard gas. Gassed men died less frequently and their wounds healed faster; nonetheless, for almost all of the soldiers gassed during the Last Hundred Days, this was their ticket to Blighty.[57]

Despite being forced to travel through the chemical battlefield, the Canadians advanced onward. As the lead battalions passed through captured towns they were shocked at the devastation wrought by the Germans and by their own guns. More difficult to accept were innocent civilians who had been gassed to death. Major Edgar MacNutt, originally of the 105th Battalion and then posted as town major with V Corps of the BEF, recorded the effects of the German gas: "Thousands of refugees are flocking back through here the past few days ... Many of them are ill with influenza and very large numbers gassed to various degrees. I remember one woman with her baby only two or three days old in her arms. The mother was ill and the baby was dying from the effects of gas."[58] Gas continued to render its evil effects indiscriminately on all caught within the gas environment of the Western Front.

Following their artillery policy of area denial, the Germans smothered the Canadian front with gas. Ever reliant on effective respirators, the Canadian Gas Services took it upon themselves to supply French civilians not only with their extra gas masks but also with an effective alarm system. Civilians were organized and trained to look for the first signs of gas, whereupon bells and whistles were to be blown and everyone was to head for their houses, closing doors and windows. John Lynch, an American who served with the Princess Patricias and won the Military Medal for bravery under fire, remembered how odd it was to "see small children playing in the street with their gas masks slung on their backs." Despite these precautions, the indiscriminate gassing of civilians was viewed with disgust, and more than one Canadian called it a "terrible crime." Such anger certainly did not bode well for the next German soldier attempting to surrender.[59]

Spearheading attack after attack had taken its toll; Canadian units were ragged from their hard-fought successes. Albert West summed up the feelings of many troops with his private tirade in his diary: "To-day we received warning to be ready to move up at an hour's notice. In Heaven's name, surely we handful of men ... are not to be put thro' the mill without more reinforcements. We need 400-500 men at once. If such a disorganized mob is sent 'over' now I shall call it a crime."[60] Luckily for West and what was left of his companions, the Germans began to pull out of Cambrai the next night, and on 9 October the Canadians occupied the ruins of the town.

The record of the Canadian Corps from 26 August to 11 October was as impressive as it was costly. Since Amiens the four divisions of the Canadian Corps had encountered and smashed an incredible thirty-one German divisions. The corps suffered 30,806 casualties from 22 August to 11 October, but the Canadians had succeeded in breaking some of the most fortified of the German defences and had precipitated the end of the German Army. Despite the cost in Canadian dead and wounded soldiers, which were much higher than the Somme or Passchendaele campaigns, the Last Hundred Days was viewed by most of the participants as a great success due to the discernable gains. In all these actions, gas had played an important role in both the attack and defence.[61]

With the German Army collapsing on all fronts, its continued pursuit by the Allies was only lightly opposed. General Currie, aware of the fighting retreat by the Germans, asked his artillery on 9 October for "more gas concentrations to take place on the enemy's front." While the German war machine crumbled, poison gas was employed to further reduce the enemy morale. A 13 October counter-battery instruction called for any SOS calls from the front to be responded to with intense bombardments made up of 50 percent high-explosive shells and 50 percent phosgene gas shells to surprise the enemy. The German infantry were not the only targets, and a steady stream of NC shells with lethal and lachrymatory qualities was also to be fired to harass the gunners, lines of communications, and forming-up points. All belligerents, not just the Canadians, understood the tactical advantage of gas. As one historian has remarked, by the spring of 1918 "commanders called for gas shells constantly, and the number of rounds fired was limited only by the availability of such shells." Currie and his officers regarded gas as a valuable weapon to slow the enemy withdrawal or weaken counter-attacks before they were launched, and it had been fully incorporated into the Canadian artillery attack doctrine.[62]

The BEF had received its first shipments of mustard gas shells in late September, and although "causing a great jubilee" it was little compared to the output of the German chemical industry. Mustard gas shells were used sparingly by the Canadians – because the Germans were constantly retreating, the pursuing units would have to travel over the polluted ground. Within the Canadian Corps the employment of mustard gas in artillery bombardments had to be first cleared on orders from Corps Headquarters, as their indiscriminate use could be a hazard to all. Perhaps the most important footnote with regard to the Allied use of mustard gas in the war was the British bombardment of Werwick on 14 October, where among the casualties in the 16th Bavarian Reserve Infantry was an angry and blinded corporal, Adolf Hitler.[63]

During the second week in October, the Canadian Corps was sent back into the line at the centre of General Horne's First Army. The battle-hardened dominion troops, used to years of gritty fighting, were elevated into the role of liberators of French villages.[64] On the Canadian front, the German retreat stopped at Valenciennes, where the Germans held a superior defensive position that anchored their new line. On 28 October the 51st British Highland Division attacked Mont Houy, but were driven off the hill by a spirited counter-attack by the Germans determined on holding their ground. It fell to the Canadians, the experts of the set-piece battle, to capture the village and Mont Houy, where the Germans had a commanding view of the countryside.

Sensing the end was in sight, General Currie ordered that nothing be spared in the bombardment. The Canadian Corps artillery report for the battles noted: "Owing to the fact that the German Army was approaching a defeat ... it was the proper time to neglect economy and to exert every possible effort by means of supporting mechanical weapons to break down the enemy's resistance and thus, as far as possible, minimize the infantry casualties." Although the Canadian artillery had been issued the new BB (mustard gas) shell less than a week earlier, they refrained from using it, not wanting to contaminate the German trenches Canadian troops would soon be occupying. The Canadian artillery were able instead to bombard the German position in a combination of frontal, enfilade, and reverse fire. This strategy not only devastated the German defences, but also made it seem to the German infantry that they were being attacked from all sides and from their own guns.[65]

The 10th Canadian Brigade, attacking behind the devastating rolling barrage and a smoke screen, quickly overran the demoralized defenders and pushed on to the city of Valenciennes. Richard Adamson remarked that the Germans used gas against the attacking Canadians. It was not well-received by the weary warriors, who had tired of the fighting, particularly in their stifling respirators: "The enemy poison gas barrage of missiles is getting our men mightily mad. They feel that the enemy cause to fight the war has long since been gone. The way our men feel I am sure that there will be far fewer prisoners taken." The Canadians suffered 501 casualties and only 60 killed in the assault. Pulverized by the barrage, the Germans had 800 soldiers killed and another 1,554 captured.[66]

The Canadians fired a punishing 88,090 artillery rounds or 2,149 tons of shells on the German lines during the pre-battle barrage. For some notion of the firepower, the entire weight of fire at Waterloo was 37 tons. One captured German snickered contemptuously that "You Canadians did not win this war, you just had more guns and ammunition." Although that was partly true during the Last Hundred Days, it was ultimately the skilful combination of both artillery and infantry along with superb training and discipline that brought victory to the Canadian Corps in a continuous string of operational successes. With respect to the Allies' artillery doctrine, the continuous use of poison gas during the Last Hundred Days in order to wear down the enemy's morale and strength left the German gas expert Fritz Haber to remark: "If the war had gone on until 1919 you would have won by gas alone." Gas helped the Canadians during all of the battles, and after losing the strategic position of Mont Houy, the Germans pulled out of Valenciennes the next morning. There were no other set-piece battles fought by the Canadian Corps until the occupation of Mons on 11 November 1918.[67]

The Germans, always retreating in front of the Canadian onslaught, relied on their isolated groups of machine gunners, demolition teams, poor roads, and the tactical use of mustard gas to interrupt the Canadian advance. The pursuing Canadians were continually harassed and slowed by the coherent tactical defensive gas barrages and more than one Canadian remembered that "a terrible amount of mustard was thrown around in that time." Others like Colonel Ian Sinclair of the 13th Battalion noted that the "Hun showered us like hell with everything he had ... We lost quite a number of men to blindness from gas." On 7 November, dozens of soldiers from the 50th Battalion were evacuated back to hospitals. The War Diary stated that "the casualties from gas are regretted, but I do not know how they could have been avoided. The gas was scarcely perceptible to the senses, and in many cases the effect seemed to take hours to develop – then coming on quite suddenly." Even with only hours left in the fighting on 11 November, Colonel P.P. Hutchinson of the 42nd Battalion noted that the Germans continued to saturate their positions with gas. In the last eleven days of the war the Canadians suffered 270 gas casualties – almost all from mustard gas delivered in shells.[68]

When the Armistice was declared on 11 November most soldiers could scarcely believe that the war was over. Private Guy Mills remembered that he and his mates stood in shocked silence – "to us, the war seemed to be a permanent way of life." To others like Private Roy Henley of the 42nd Battalion, the Armistice was to be remembered for other reasons. Henley had the misfortune of squatting in a shell hole of phosgene, and he was invalided back to a hospital. He spent months recovering from gas-induced tuberculosis while his unit returned home.[69]

The Last Hundred Days had been marked by a new form of open warfare, with the use of tanks and aeroplanes to help the infantry cross the killing ground of No Man's Land and to push through the enemy's mutual supporting lines of defence. Few formations practised this open warfare successfully, and most Allied forces, the Canadian Corps included, still relied on the close interaction between infantry and artillery. As it turned out, though, in a neglected aspect of tactical analysis, both the offensive and defensive role of gas has remained greatly undervalued. The integration of gas into the operational way of war became an essential component by which the Germans attempted to slow the Allied advance. Throughout the Last Hundred Days it took a fearful toll, both physically and mentally, on the weary attackers. At least 2,500 gas casualties were suffered by the Canadians in the Last Hundred Days; it was a number that would have been significantly higher had it not been for the intense gas doctrine drilled into the men of the Canadian Corps by the Canadian Gas Services.[70]

Major W.E. Harris continued his role as chemical advisor during the initial occupation of Germany, and he continued to issue orders – his last being on 20 December 1918 that all men were to carry their SBRs until ordered otherwise. With the end of the fighting the Gas Services became a superfluous organization and was formally disbanded on 20 January 1919. Although gas officers returned to their original units with little fanfare, they could look back on their important role in helping to solidify the Canadian Corps' reputation as shock troops. Some British soldiers and generals, especially the British official historian James Edmonds, believed the complaint of Sir Henry Horne that the "Canadian Corps is rather apt to take all the credit it can for everything and to consider that the BEF consists of the Canadian Corps and some other troops." Yet on examining the corps' string of victories it is clear that not only were the Canadians an elite force but were very probably among a handful of the best British formations on the Western Front.[71]

Such statements are notoriously hard to quantify, but it is difficult to name any unit that could come up with even half of the successes garnered by the Canadian Corps. The much publicized last stand at 2nd Ypres; the learning battles of 1915 and 1916, culminating in the bloody Somme; capturing Vimy Ridge, deemed almost impregnable by the French, who had failed twice, and by the German defenders; the brilliant set-piece battle of Hill 70, which annihilated so many German soldiers who desperately attacked across the Canadian killing ground; overrunning Passchendaele after so many other units had failed; inflicting the "black day of the German army" with the Australians at Amiens; and the neglected but hardest fighting of the war with the breaking of the D-Q line and Canal du Nord. Its continuous flow of reinforcements, its homogeneity, and its semi-autonomous nature were all important factors in making the Canadian Corps a formidable force.[72] These factors were coupled with an ability and a desire to evolve to new levels of proficiency, as exemplified through its corps commanders, Sir Julian Byng and Sir Arthur Currie, and their insistence on the close liaison between the infantry and artillery. Yet a lesser unquantifiable factor must surely be the role of the Gas Services.

The Canadian way of war was steeped in poison gas. The Canadian Corps Gas Services, initially suffering from lack of recognition and supplies when it was created with the introduction of the DGOs, grew in importance and stature as the gas war progressed in deadliness, intensity, and frequency. Combining education and drill, the Gas Services played a crucial role in forcing the troops of the Canadian Corps to follow strict anti-gas guidelines that saved thousands of lives and strengthened the corps' fighting efficiency. Although at times the Canadian Gas Services turned to gas discipline out of desperation at not being able to do anything else to combat the effects of gas, the resultant demystifying of gas allowed individual soldiers to cope with their dread. The greatest accomplishment of the gas officers was in alleviating the fear of the unknown and teaching soldiers that poison gas could be defeated with proper training. Thus, the Gas Services, omitted in the annals of Canadian military history, played an integral psychological role in transforming the soldiers of the Canadian Corps into one of the finest fighting forces on the Western Front.

Conclusion

IT TAKES MORE THAN GAS TO STOP
A CANADIAN

As the firepower of modern weapons was unleashed on First World War battlefields, soldiers were forced to take cover beneath the earth to escape their killing effects. In the first two years of the war, with defenders in these entrenched positions, surrounded by barbed wire and protected by machine guns, waves of attackers, regardless of their bravery and élan, were invariably annihilated. After the surprising effect of chlorine at the 2nd Battle of Ypres in April 1915, gas clouds were envisioned as a method by which to root the enemy out from his entrenchment and break the stalemate that confounded all. But it soon became apparent that gas alone would not have this war-winning effect. Consequently, gas went through a period of decline in 1916, when it was sustained only by the will of the chemical specialists, until it was reborn and transformed with the development of new delivery systems into an effective harassing agent and, finally, a tactical weapon. On the Eastern Front, the Russians were killed in the tens of thousands until they were equipped with British gas masks; in the East, gas indeed for a time worked as it had first been envisioned. In the Austrian, Italian (except at Caporetto), and Turkish theatres, gas was limited in scope due to geographical considerations. Still, when it was used, the often poorly gas-disciplined troops suffered high casualties. As well, American use of gas in an attack doctrine was limited in comparison to the nations that had been fighting since 1914; the Americans relied almost entirely on

British experience and equipment until the last couple of months. If the war had continued into 1919, then the Americans would have played a much larger role. But as it did not, their impact on the gas war was negligible, except in suffering high gas casualties. In the end, gas came into its own on the Western Front, and remained a key weapon in that central theatre of operations.[1]

The initial abhorrence toward gas as an unnatural and unchivalrous weapon was prevalent on all sides, due to its impersonal killing nature, alien qualities, and, initially, the defencelessness of its victims. By the 2nd Battle of Ypres, over a million of Europe's young men had been slaughtered or maimed by bullet and shell, yet gas was seen as beyond the pale. The abdication of the soldier's code of war to scientific mass murder, the uncontrollable and unstoppable nature of released gas, and the ghastly act of suffocating a man to death with chemical agents, left most participants viewing gas as an immoral weapon. After the costly failures of the battles of 1914, the introduction of poison gas pushed the conflict further into the realm of total warfare. Gas was envisioned as a weapon of extinction; those caught in its grasp would be asphyxiated without chance of survival. Perhaps surprising then, that in the face of mounting casualties the commanders on both sides had within a year pushed aside their earlier objections to the immorality of gas warfare and were frantic to break through the enemy line – using any method available. The trench soldiers' perception of poison gas also changed during the war: by 1917 very few of them still saw it

Fighting in the gas environment of the Western Front.

as a depraved weapon. Nonetheless, soldiers actually facing the death clouds were always wary and viewed gas with apprehension.

With the chemical industries on both sides producing more and deadlier substances, gas became a valuable auxiliary weapon to commanders of both Allied and German troops. But it was not until the development of a coherent doctrine with reliable delivery systems that gas could be used to fulfil a number of tactical roles or be applied in combined operations. By 1917, gas was employed in an attack doctrine to paralyze soldiers in their trenches, neutralize enemy batteries, disrupt communication from front to rear and laterally, and render attacking units' flanks safe during deep penetrations. Defensively, gas was used to cover withdrawals and retreats, deny areas for troop concentration, and harass enemy soldiers and logistical systems. Initially gas was employed by the Germans to break the stalemate of the trench warfare; ironically, it was finally employed as a protective weapon by those same Germans attempting to grind down the movement phase of the war.

Although the last chemical clouds dissipated from the Western Front on 11 November 1918, the image and perception of gas warfare continued to linger in open debates and the inner subconscious of soldiers who had survived its horrors. Historian Edward Spiers has estimated that 124,200 tons of poison gas were deployed in battle, compared with 2 million tons of high-explosive shells and 50,000 million rounds of small-arms ammunition. While gas was used in relatively minuscule proportions in comparison to conventional armaments, there was a steady progression of employment throughout the war. In 1915, 3,870 tons of gas were dispersed; in 1916, 16,535 tons; in 1917, 38,635 tons; and finally, in 1918, 65,160 tons. At the same time, the Germans had continually introduced deadlier battlefield gases, forcing the Allies to play the role of adapting and catching up: chlorine and phosgene in 1915, deadlier phosgene and diphosgene in 1916, mustard and Blue Cross in 1917, and a deadly mixture of all these in 1918. As a result of this evolution, gas became an integral component of the artillery; by 1918 it made up an incredible 20-40 percent of all shells within the artillery dumps for all armies. By the Armistice chemical shells made up 35 percent of French and German ammunition supplies, 25 percent of British, and 20 percent of American supplies (and a 25 percent ratio was planned for 1919). Although there are no compiled Canadian statistics, McNaughton's and Currie's preference for gas would certainly have made their stocks equal to if not greater than the quota used by the British in 1918. The important and varied tactical roles of gas were recognized by all armies and helped to make the Western Front a gas-plagued battlefield unique in the history of warfare.[2]

Despite these impressive figures, several recent re-evaluations of the role of poison gas on the battlefield have concluded that it was, in short, a failure. This is certainly true when considering its initial incarnation as a war-winning weapon. However, as has been pointed out throughout this book, poison gas was a much more complicated and nuanced weapon. The best weapons are those that remove fighting men and leave fear and unrest among the survivors. Years after the war one man who lived through the gas environment wrote that "it is a hateful and terrible sensation to be choked and suffocated and unable to get breath: a casualty from gun fire may be dying from his wounds, but they don't give him the sensation that his life is being strangled out of him."[3]

The qualities of poison gas affected men in unique ways that conventional weapons did not. First, gas was a weapon of fear that blanketed everyone in a large area. There was no escape from gas – one simply had to survive using respirators, discipline, and an iron will. Gas worked as a psychological weapon on many levels. Although the historian L.F. Haber has written, and rightly so, that gas was a "chancy" weapon that struck each soldier differently, he fails to come to grips with the true calamity of the chemical battlefield.[4] Even if a soldier were not affected by poison gas, his guard could never entirely be let down. The spectre of gas could be as debilitating as the real thing. Everyone was forced to react during gas alerts. There was no way to tell if one was out of reach of the gas cloud, was already enveloped in unseen, lethal gas, or was waiting for hours in a sweltering respirator because a trench sentry mistook night fog for a phosgene cloud. The habitual apprehension toward gas produced an environment where no one was safe: there was no escaping the very real physical and psychological effects of the chemical plague.

Second, poison gas – despite the connotations of its name – was primarily a casualty-causing agent rather than a killer. One of the misconceptions of the gas war was that all gas was lethal. The offspring of that tenet meant that once the respirator was introduced, chemical weapons were rendered impotent. The respirator indeed could provide almost total protection, but it did not negate the fact that gas continued to cause thousands upon thousands of casualties. During 1918, when mustard gas was the most successful of the poison gases employed by the Germans, the British gas casualties, which had been 7.2 percent of the total battlefield casualties in 1917, rose to 15 percent of the total; yet, only 2.4 percent of those gassed died, as compared with 3.4 percent in 1917. The old military maxim from the Duke of Wellington, that on the battlefield it takes one ton of lead to kill a man, could also apply to gas. However, as one Gas Services' report indicated, pound-for-pound, gas was more effective in causing casualties than was HE. Acknowledging this fact, an American report prepared after the war candidly noted that "In the last two months gas warfare began to approximate the pattern of HE fire – continuous gas shelling punctuated by bombardments ... And it was then that gas proved its extraordinary superiority over HE in producing mental as well as physical casualties." Thus if one were looking to produce casualties, poison gas was an ideal weapon. Of course, it remains that many of those gas casualties would not have occurred had soldiers not been preoccupied with the traditional terrors of conventional weapons. Nonetheless, one has to look beyond the images of soldiers gasping for breath through corrupted lungs or sitting in trenches with respirators attached. A more reflective analysis reveals the intricate underpinnings of the gas war.[5]

Throughout the major battle sites of the First World War – Verdun, the Somme, Ypres – there are massive graveyards and sites of commemoration for thousands of unknown soldiers who died on the battlefield and dissolved into the earth. It is clear from the analysis in this work that many of these men would have fallen victim to gas as they struggled back to their trenches or waited in shell holes for aid. The deluge of gas on the battlefield in 1917 and 1918 claimed countless casualties who were unconscious, befogged, or too weak from loss of blood to attach their gas masks. Others were, as the British Official Medical History recorded, "rendered ... useless [by gas] for fighting and equally incapable of taking precautions for their own protection from gunfire." Although countless numbers died on the battlefields – a combination of injuries from conventional and chemical weapons – a much larger proportion of soldiers were "for Blighty." However, it is then, as John Keegan has ironically observed, that in most histories the "wounded apparently dematerialize as soon as struck down." But in battle the wounded and maimed do not disappear like pawns silently removed from a chess game; they moan and scream, beg for help, or gurgle in their death throes. Gas required that hundreds be carried to the rear. While a wounded man required aid, as one postwar writer callously but accurately put it, "a corpse need only be buried." These "dematerialized" men clogged supply lines that were bringing up food, ammunition, and water and created congestion in the rear, where they had to be housed and cared for. Another noted military theorist observed that a wounded man will "spread the wildest of rumours, will exaggerate dangers, [and] foster panic," and inadvertently reduce the morale of the survivors. Reflecting this burden, the long lines of gassed victims were not only lost to their units but were also a drain on the whole army as they siphoned resources, unnerved their mates, and demanded attention from an overtaxed medical corps.[6]

As in most attempts to quantify destruction in war, there are discrepancies in the total number of gas casualties. Notwithstanding such difficulties, the figure is considered to be between 1 million and 1.3 million. Of these, 91,000 were recorded as killed by gas. Whatever the recorded casualties, they contain some significant omissions. British gas figures do not include any of the men injured or killed by gas in 1915 or any gas victims who became prisoners of war. German gas statistics terminated on 31 July 1918, just when they began to suffer from Allied mustard gas and intricate artillery gas bombardments. The documentation of gas casualties on the Eastern Front was filled with inherent inaccuracies due to lacklustre record-keeping practices. In many cases and for all nations, casualties from a variety of sources (gas, high explosives, bullets) were simply lumped together under conventional wounds. Finally, all nations failed to keep records of soldiers who died from gas through illness or disease in the postwar period. The intricate nature of gas itself suggests that many of the soldiers recorded as "missing" – those who were incapacitated and often simply dissolved into the churned earth – and any wounded men killed by gas in No Man's Land after they were unable to don their respirators, would be among the hidden statistics. As one historian has quipped, "becoming an official gas casualty required roughly the same amount of verification as winning a medal."[7]

There is a more subtle flaw behind the statistics. The Official Histories of the war are very good at describing the broad panorama of battles – how they developed and their final outcomes – but they often fail to take into account the human factor of the soldiers fighting in these battles. If the Germans let off 600 chlorine canisters and only a dozen soldiers were gassed, it would be listed as a failure or simply ignored in most histories. But 600 canisters of gas covered a mile of trench, and all the men in that area would be affected one way or another. The repeated disruption of sleep, the fear of having one's respirator fail, in addition to the very real discomfort of wearing a respirator and the difficulty of breathing while carrying out any work, were all factors that, to borrow Lord Moran's analogy, withdrew funds from the soldier's "courage account." In their memoirs and first-hand observations of what gas did to them and to their companions, front-line soldiers readily acknowledged their deep fear of gas, a factor rarely recognized by commanders in the rear. "More life," Thomas Hardy wrote, "may trickle out of men through thought than through a gaping wound." Acknowledging this debilitating role of gas, one postwar analysis of two American divisions fighting in July and September 1918 noted that "battle fatigue quickly followed intensive gas shelling." Although such circumstances are not always recorded in reports of action, it is clear that, when combined with communications and warnings from the Gas Services, gas played an important role in producing lassitude and reducing morale in all troops caught within its real and imagined sphere.[8]

Poison gas never lost its ability to inspire dread and apprehension in the soldiers who encountered it. Such wariness was not the panic of 2nd Ypres, but it was still a fear that was based on experience, education, and a healthy respect for this uncontrollable weapon. Although gas was an effective casualty-causing agent, artillery shells and small-arms fire were the true killers of the war, indiscriminately massacring millions as they crouched terrified in the trenches or vainly attempted to advance through the muck of No Man's Land.[9] But to suggest that gas was simply a peripheral or negligible weapon because it killed only 91,000 men is to miss the whole psychological and tactical aspects of gas warfare and their effects on the soldiers who have to survive in the chaos of battle. Certainly poison gas requires more historical examination and analysis. Too many historians still view gas in a way similar to the American official who dismissed it as a "scientific novelty." The conclusions of rigorous examinations of gas by historians such as Ludwig Fritz Haber and Donald Richter have still been that poison gas was a failure. Yet after a thorough examination of all facets of battle, one wonders how this weapon could be labelled as such given the unique and devastating role it played on the battlefield. It can be classified as a disappointment only if one fails to understand the enormous impact it had on the soldiers at the sharp end of battle. It is a fundamentally flawed argument that gas was not effective after the respirator. The notion that having a flimsy layer of chemically impregnated cloth and charcoal between lung-ravaging gas or, worse, blistering agents, would completely counter the physical and psychological effects of gas is a superficial observation that misrepresents the true nature of warfare and the men who must take part in it.

The Never-Ending War

Throughout the war, eminent doctors in England were noting in medical reports that returned gas casualties were usually afflicted with acute bronchopneumonia in their convalescence. Gassed soldiers with ravaged lungs, who were diagnosed as unsalvageable in terms of a return to active duty, were sent back to Canada and discharged. Noting the doctors' observations, what happened to these men? Hundreds or thousands of Canadian men lurched and wheezed their way through their remaining years, physically and mentally scarred by their war experiences with gas. Little could be done for them, and veterans' coughing fits were often explained away with a "tap on the chest and an apologetic, 'gas you know.'"[10]

The postwar negligence toward gas victims requires more attention than that. As doctors noted, Canadian veterans invalided out of the army with gas poisoning were dying at home even before the war was over. One report on the aftermath of gas on soldiers noted that gassed soldiers continued to develop active tuberculosis for some years after their initial gassing. Others had the "upper part of the chest fixed as in an old emphysema, and this is remarkable when one considers that most of the men are under thirty years of age."[11] This was not occurring only to the men of the Canadian Corps. In 1927 one British medical report noted the examination of a group of eighteen veterans:

> In the summer time these patients are not so bad, but with early winter, their symptoms are aggravated. These patients seldom improve, but gradually get worse ... It is only a matter of time until a cardiac condition develops in addition ... It should be mentioned, also, that such patients have a very poor prognosis should pneumonia or other severe pulmonary conditions supervene ... Some of these have chests like men of over sixty ... definitely and permanently damaged. The

evidence suggesting that Mustard is the cause appears to be conclusive. These pensioners, young and fit before the war, have a definite history of having spent some weeks or months in hospitals with conjunctivitis, laryngitis, bronchitis and in some cases skin burns.[12]

If some men could not be cured of the physical infirmities resulting from exposure to gas, others continued to be tortured mentally. Pitiful accounts of men overcome by the horrors of war, who sat in their hospital beds all night, "crying out for their gas masks, which they could not find," shook even the heartiest observers. Both medical reports and the Gas Services throughout the war continued to warn against the psychological effects of poison gas, and many afterward even went so far as to suggest that gas had a very prominent role in worsening or even creating shell shock victims. Despite the occasional medical report, most soldiers slipped through the cracks of the system, and the true numbers of deaths from gas after the war are impossible to quantify. Although often "anecdotal, ambiguous and fragmentary," the evidence of chronic physical debilitation in many gassed men was certainly present. As one veteran recounted, those soldiers who spent any time in France during the last two years of the war "were bound to absorb a certain amount of gas because there was a bit of it around all the time." The question remained as to the severity of these ceaseless minor gassings. Following the war there developed a fierce controversy between advocates of veterans who were gassed and afflicted with long-term disabilities and those who believed that the real number of truly incapacitated gassed ex-soldiers was very small.[13]

The British Official Medical History notes that approximately 12 percent of gassed soldiers received pensions after the war; that number would presumably have been similar for the Canadians. Yet trench soldiers found it exceptionally hard to prove that their postwar health problems were the result of gas. A letter from a major-general at the Director-General Medical Services in Ottawa to the surgeon-general of the United States in August 1918, responding to his inquiry regarding gassed soldiers who had been invalided, frankly noted "that it is regretted that the number of gas cases returning to Canada, although records were kept of them for some months, was so small and their condition so usually complicated by Tuberculosis, Asthma, Chronic Bronchitis, etc., that special observation of them and provision for them has been discontinued." Strangely, such observations seem to overlook the connection between gas and respiratory diseases. As one historian has noted, "Cases involving loss of limbs were usually straightforward, but others, such as those concerning respiratory diseases or mental disability, were open to wide, often unfair, interpretation." The medical profession in Canada viewed many of the gas cases as suspect, and some celebrated cases of soldiers concealing the existence of tuberculosis that was not attributable to the gas and then claiming to be gas casualties caused many gassed men to be viewed with a jaundiced eye by professionals.[14]

Just as damaging, simply to be released from the army after being away from their loved ones for years, many men had signed themselves "A-1" in health when they were in fact suffering from the effects of gas poisoning. Others were pressured. A.A. Galbraith of the 44th Battalion remembered the medical boards strongly urging him to sign "A-1" during demobilization and reinforcing this by informing him that "there was nothing wrong with [him]" even though he had lost one eye during the war. When their medical problems began to surface years later, the former trench warriors had an upward battle to prove that they were not, as in the trenches, malingering from gas. Was it poison gas or living in dank ditches for four years that caused lung disease at age thirty? Insurance companies and pension boards were particularly interested in finding out, and it fell to gassed men to prove that their handicaps were attributable to specific gassings during the war. This near-impossible task forced many men to live with their disabilities for the rest of their lives without adequate compensation.[15]

Immediately following the war, many veterans and those speaking on their behalf argued that soldiers deserved higher pensions for the hidden or future debilitating effects of gas. One example occurred in Hamilton, Ontario, where Reverend R.W. Dickey organized a series of letter-writing campaigns to the minister of soldiers' civil re-establishment, the Honourable Sir James Lougheed, in which he argued that "the intervening years has [sic] demonstrated that the gas so weakened the lungs' powers of resistance that its victims fell an easy prey to pneumonia and tuberculosis." In conjunction with burned-out lungs, pulmonary haemorrhages and cancer were prophesied as the fate of gassed men. Others, such as Dr. J.B. Hawes of Boston, argued at the Canadian Association for the Prevention of Tuberculosis meeting in 1921 that "there are very definite and sometimes malignant after-effects of gas poisoning, received by soldiers in Hun gas attacks." Because of the interrelated symptoms and similar ravages to the body through the lungs, pneumonia, tuberculosis, and poison gas were usually discussed in tandem.[16]

Tuberculosis, the great killer of the nineteenth and early twentieth century, provoked enormous fear among veterans and civilians alike. In 1919, soldiers with tuberculosis outnumbered their civilian counterparts in the same age group by three to one.[17] The higher levels of soldiers returning with the "white death" were attributed to unsanitary conditions, close living, poor diet, lack of sleep, and the assortment of horrors surrounding the fighting on the Western Front. Tuberculosis was an airborne disease spread through coughing and sneezing. Much like mustard gas, it retained its deadly nature even after the moisture it was carried on evaporated, whereafter it could be passed on to unsuspecting victims through the inhalation of spores. Of every hundred men killed while in uniform, six died of tuberculosis. Even larger numbers were disabled for a long period of time, and for every hundred men who received a pension, one-quarter were labelled as tubercular.[18]

On return to Canada, tubercular soldiers were sent to sanatoriums, where they were forced to rest and were exposed to fresh air – the same prescribed cures for advanced gas victims. Although federal government studies and doctors claimed that only 6 percent of soldiers with tuberculosis had been exposed to gas, other doctors and specialists claimed that such exposure was a contributing factor in a much greater number of cases. The full role of gas as a catalyst for TB remains unknown; as one historian, who has conducted a detailed study of soldiers and tuberculosis, observed, "the subject was explored frequently by physicians in the postwar literature and the majority of them could not determine precisely what role gassing played in the later development of tuberculosis."[19] It must be observed, though, that with the effects of gas resembling influenza and resulting in chronic fatigue, shortness of breath, and marked psycho-neurosis, the gassed soldier was often misdiagnosed back home.[20] The simple observance of young men wheezing and clutching their chests as they walked down the streets of all Canadian cities, provoked further outrage and apprehension by all toward the aftermath of gas.

In both Canada and the United States there was a heightened level of fear among returned soldiers, almost all of whom would have been exposed to some level of gas, that they too would suffer the lingering and debilitating fate of their more severely gassed companions. As one federal government sessional paper commenting on disabled soldiers observed, "During the latter half of the war, nearly all soldiers in the field are said to have been exposed in some degree to different kinds of gas. Exposure to gas enters, therefore, into the clinical histories of a large number of cases." Despite a series of reports by doctors, of which a large majority argued that there were no serious health issues for mildly gassed soldiers, the apprehension remained.[21]

The lingering effects of gas were, if not neglected following the war, shunted to the periphery because of their complicated nature. Although many soldiers blamed their lung diseases on their terrifying and damaging experiences with poison gas, chemical agents were not always a factor. The problem remained, as with any disease, in trying to figure out how it was contracted. Tuberculosis, like poison gas, was a silent killer. Tracing the point of entry or exposure was not always possible. For men coughing up bloody sputum as they lay isolated in sanatoriums, the chemical clouds were sometimes the easiest thing to blame. Moreover, the acknowledged effects of poison gas on the lungs were undoubtedly factors in the early deaths of some soldiers.[22] How many more veterans were confined to hospitals or their houses in perpetual agony for the remaining years of their lives due to the creeping effects of gas? The numbers remain unknown; what is known, however, is the fear that lingered in the minds of soldiers long after the gas had dissipated from the battlefield.

The Legacy: Gas Warfare after 1918

This protracted fear had a profound impact not only on how poison gas was remembered, but on how it was envisioned as a future weapon of mass destruction. In the aftermath of the Great War, survivors attempted to put their lives back together and find meaning in the conflict. Given the millions of casualties, it is not surprising that many began to question the unfettered slaughter of the war, where machines and technology were pitted against men. The monumental losses in trench warfare eventually led to a large anti-war movement in the 1920s, as citizens hoped to prevent a similar horrific recurrence. War, it seemed, had become an inhuman event of mass slaughter, where bravery, chivalry, and strength were superseded by technology, mass production, and munitions. Poison gas became one of the principal foci of this new crusade. Despite the gradual and grudging acceptance of gas by commanders and soldiers during the war, the civilians on the home front had continued to view it as an infernal weapon. Poison gas seemed to encompass the most terrible aspects of the worst war in history, and it was conceived as the prime example of scientific barbarity. Against such perceptions, there were few professional soldiers – except for those who served directly with gas during the war – who wished to jeopardize their careers by publicly contradicting this view and supporting the future use of poison gas.

There were scattered groups of pro-gas theorists, however. In the hope of restoring gas to its wartime importance, the gas specialists from all countries strove for some balance in the debate over chemical weapons and attempted to convince the public and military about the relatively humane nature of gas. Most often, ex-gas officers such as Charles Foulkes, Victor Lefebure, and Amos Fries focused on the low kill rate of gas in comparison to conventional weapons. Chemical warfare, it was argued, was the most humane of all battlefield weapons. Statistics clearly showed the low death rate of gas (approximately 3-5 percent) in comparison to conventional weapons (approximately 25 percent), but the weight of public opinion was against them. Influential military theorists such as Basil Liddell Hart and J.F.C. Fuller also supported chemical weapons but they were in the minority. Other survivors were more ambivalent. "If you are a combat soldier, there is not a great deal of difference between being gassed, having a bayonet through the chest, an incendiary bullet through the lungs, a belly ripping hunk of shell casing or a squirt of napalm. The quickest way to get it over with is the most humane," was how one soldier explained his feelings about the stigma associated with certain weapons. In contrast, other studies and interviews with veterans have clearly shown that certain weapons like the flame-thrower, Stuka dive bomber in the Second World War, and mines that explode at groin-level, inspire a fear – no matter how rational or irrational – that reached beyond the possibility of death from the bullet or shell.

As indicated by the personal accounts of survivors throughout this book, gas, it seems, fell into the category of these unique weapons. As a result, and despite the work of the pro-gas lobbyists, in the 1920s, poison gas remained tainted. Although there were tank enthusiasts and air-power proponents, few serving professionals wished to be known as chemical commanders.[23]

Added to the cacophony of voices demanding the ban of gas were theorists and soothsayers who began to predict future military aspects of chemical warfare; most important, these people increasingly associated the evolution of gas as a weapon with air power. Attack from the air appealed to politicians and air theorists who saw the potential to escape a war of attrition on the ground and to deliver victory over great distances. Of course, with this new ability to attack over rivers, oceans, and static trenches came the troubling realization that an enemy could now do the same. In his influential 1921 treatise *The Next War: An Appeal to Common Sense,* Will Irwin, a former war correspondent, wrote about the dangers of future weapons: "Here is a projectile – the bomb carrying aeroplane – of unprecedented size and almost unlimited range, here is a killing instrument – gas – of power beyond the dream of a madman."[24] Two years later, respected military theorist J.F.C. Fuller concluded,

> I believe that, in future warfare, great cities, such as London, will be attacked from the air, and that a fleet of 500 aeroplanes each carrying 500 ten-pound bombs of, let us suppose, mustard gas, might cause 200,000 minor casualties and throw the whole city into panic within half an hour of their arrival. Picture, if you can, what the result will be: London for several days will be one raving Bedlam, the hospitals will be stormed, traffic will cease, the homeless will shriek for help, the city will be in pandemonium. What of the government at Westminster? It will be swept away by an avalanche of terror. Then will the enemy dictate his terms.[25]

These analysts and others began to predict massive aerochemical bombardments against defenceless cities; in effect, the chemical battlefield would seep back to the home front. Not only was there the ever-present spectre of gassed veterans, who continued to lurch through life, blinded or surviving with cancerous lungs, but now the citizens of all nations feared they might join them once the chemical bombers did their nasty work.

In accordance with the warnings by "experts," it was not uncommon to see newspaper articles like the following published in the *New York Herald*: "Ordinary killing is bad enough, but that a man should treat his fellow as he treats a rat or cockroach is inherently repugnant to all men for whom decent instincts have not fled." Another editorial condemned the "gas men" for arguing about the humane nature of gas when its evolution as a weapon was likely to produce far deadlier agents: "It has become commonplace of prediction that chemists would kill their millions in another war between great nations. If this be a chemist's idea of humane warfare, God deliver the world from its chemists." Despite the gas proponents speaking to the foolhardiness of not preparing for gas in the next war, the public was vehemently against all aspects of chemical warfare.[26]

Heeding this widespread indignation, the United States called for a general disarmament conference in 1922. Although the conference was organized to limit the great powers' naval arms race, which many thought could bring on another war, the debate on chemical weapons was highly politicized, partisan, and emotional. Large groups of civilians, politicians, and veterans were pitted against a much smaller but influential group of pro-gas proponents. In addition to its arguments that gas was a more humane weapon than conventional armaments, the pro-gas lobby lectured that the danger of poison gas meant that to prepare for peace, one must prepare for war. Those wishing to ban chemical weapons countered with emotional arguments decreeing their reprehensible and morally illegitimate nature. One report signed by General Pershing stated that "chemical weapons should be abolished among nations, as abhorrent to civilization. It is a cruel, unfair and improper use of science. It is fraught with the gravest danger to noncombatants and demoralizes the better instincts of humanity." With the conflicting views and interest groups, it was impossible to get a consensus from the numerous national representatives. The conference failed to ban chemical weapons and another Hague Convention in 1925 also produced ambivalent results. Nations agreed not to use gas in a first-strike capability, but without the United States or Japan ratifying the accord, few thought it would stand up in the face of future hostilities.[27]

Despite their slashed budgets and an emasculated military, the Canadian forces were keeping an eye on the proceedings of the conferences. For instance, as Canadian Brigadier-General Andrew McNaughton wrote in a 1922 intelligence report, "this Convention has had little or any effect on the authorities of the various countries who are all reliably reported to be preparing plans for and carrying out the experimental work preliminary to chemical warfare." McNaughton was undoubtedly correct but, unfortunately, as acknowledged by the chief of staff for the Canadian Forces, J.H. MacBrien, Canada had no resources or men available to begin retraining its forces in anti-gas measures.[28] The expertise that had been developed through such hard work in the war had been lost due to fiscal and political neglect. While Canadians struggled to deal with the obvious continued threat of poison gas, their geographical seclusion from aerochemical bombardment, when combined with the civilian distaste for all things military, meant that gas was once again pushed to the periphery.

Around that time, J.B.S. Haldane, a famous chemist closely associated with the British gas program during the war, wrote a widely read article, "Chemistry and Peace," published in the *Atlantic Monthly*. In it he blamed the efficient propaganda of the First World War for perverting the image of gas. "People still think about it as they were told to think by the newspapers during the Great War," he lamented. Despite delivering a scolding on the gas issue, he acknowledged that the extremely lethal lewisite gas, called the "Dew of Death," which was never used on the Great War battlefield and was only tested by the American military against its soldiers, was likely to be employed in the next war. Lewisite had caused some victims to attempt suicide, while others, he noted, "went temporarily raving mad and tried to burrow into the ground to escape the gas." Civilians could imagine and conceptualize great fleets of naval vessels or mechanized armies, but a city of men, women, and children driven mad by gas and burrowing into their gardens did little to rejuvenate the image of gas warfare.[29]

The prospect of aerochemical warfare was terrifying: in one night, it could transform, in the words of a supposed expert, a "metropolis to a necropolis." Such warnings were not issued only in obscure books; in British Parliament in July 1927, one debate escalated to near-hysteria, with a member of Parliament exclaiming that "our cities will not merely be decimated but rendered uninhabitable by chemical bombs ... It is not war in the ordinary sense ... We are faced with the wiping out of civilization." There was little to rehabilitate the reputation of gas; in 1929 a committee made up of American private citizens conducted a poll asking the public if they agreed in principle to the abolishment of chemical weapons: an incredible 366,795 were for with only 19 against. Not surprisingly, chemical warfare remained an important issue in the interwar period as interest groups continually strove have it banned.[30]

Canadian Defence Quarterly, Canada's military journal, also voiced its opinion, noting that poison gas was an effective tactical weapon and predicting that it would surely be used in upcoming wars.[31] In the 1920s, the fear of aerochemicals was only strengthened by air theorists such as Italian Guilio Douhet, who predicted and advocated that future war would entail bombers raining explosives, incendiaries, and poison gas on cities to break the will of those on the home front; and, as was acknowledged at the time, by none other than the British prime minister, Stanley Baldwin, the bomber would always get through.

The public's apprehension of gas bombers was made all the more real by the conflicting reports that circulated. Quasi-scientists and military analysts were continually predicting and challenging each other's numbers on the damage caused by chemical bombs. One infamous assertion in 1933 by Lord Halsbury, former chief of the Wartime Explosives Department, was that a single gas bomb, "if dropped on Piccadilly Circus, would kill everybody in an area from Regent's Park to the Thames" – about a million people at that time. Others, such as Thomas Edison, whose fame caused his predictions to be repeatedly cited in newspapers and in Parliament, postulated that a gas bombardment could kill the entire population of London in three hours. New delivery systems and new gases were also foreseen, all of which would rain down with murderous consequences. One Canadian colonel excitedly wrote that the "most poisonous gases used in the last war are but as a lady's perfume, in comparison." Gas experts hooted with derision at such claims and wrote articles that stressed the lack of technology, the low death rate of gas, its unlawful nature as expressed in the Geneva Conventions, its reliance on the weather, and even the unproven quality of aerochemical warfare. Nonetheless, their arguments rang hollow with much of the public, which was living on chemical ground zero.[32]

Because of the fantastic and fearful imagery of gas in the First World War and the 1920s, it was not surprising that science-fiction writers began to work gas into their novels and film scripts in apocalyptic terms. Their texts usually centred on urging the nation to disarm or rearm in order to ensure future survival in light of gas armadas suffocating civilians in their beds and pantries. Futuristic novels with such titles as *The Gas War of 1940*, *The Black Death*, and *The Poison War*, appeared regularly in the 1930s, and all focused on aerial gas attacks. The most famous and far-reaching work was by the doyen of science-fiction writers, H.G. Wells. In 1933 he published *The Shape of Things to Come*, describing a civilization out of control and moving blithely to the brink of destruction, where great air fleets eventually bomb cities with high explosives and "peace gas bombs." Three years later the book was transformed into a film, *Things to Come*, with a powerful musical score and scenes that left viewers startled and uneasy for the future. The shock of the film cannot be attributed only to poison gas, but the stark images of civilians who are unprepared and lulled into passivity by their politicians, of gas hissing from planes to blanket the citizens of Everytown, of scenes of panic as officials unsuccessfully attempted to hand out gas masks, and of close-up views of poison gas pouring in windows and down chimneys, all served to stir further anxiety among civilians about the use of aerial gas attacks in the next war. While the Great War soldier, enured to the horrors of war, had not been broken by gas, the same was not thought possible for civilians on the home front.[33]

Just as *Things to Come* opened on screens to frighten audiences, the Italians were using aerially dispersed mustard gas against the ill-equipped Abyssinians in their war of conquest. The devastation of mustard gas in denying ground, protecting their own lines of communication, and causing casualties against the tribesmen clearly showed that gas was still a powerful weapon. It appeared that life was imitating fiction, or vice versa. Some nations drew conclusions that the effective use of gas against the Abyssinians was simply another indication that it would be employed in future wars.[34]

With civilians receiving messages of aerochemical bombardments from novels and films, journalists, sensing an audience, also made it an important and topical issue. Kim Beattie, a regimental historian and writer on the Great War, published a 1936 article in *Maclean's* magazine, in which he described the unheeded warnings from intelligence and prisoners' reports foretelling the first use of gas against Canadians at Ypres in April 1915. There were probably few who did not see the parallels to a surprise gas attack in the next war. Other periodicals followed suit. The *Canadian Magazine* had a November 1937 article on poison gas and depicted dozens of faceless students wearing respirators. The question asked – "Is our world to look like this?" From the chilling photographs and phrases like "manufacture ... for murder," and "it is inevitable that poison gas will play a major role in the next war," many readers must have feared the answer and what the future held.[35]

As war seemed to loom on the horizon, the threat of gas pervaded all aspects of European cities and living: cigarette cards gave tips on air-raid precautions and how to gas-proof cellars; the flat tops of sign posts and mailboxes were treated with chemicals to turn a bright warning colour to indicate when invisible gas was deployed in the area; retailers advertised that budgie birds would warn families of gas long before members heard the sirens; there were even sets of toy soldiers equipped with respirators.[36] When future war was envisioned, it was to be a full chemical one; it was not a question of if gas would be used, but how and when.

Poison gas struck a nerve in the national psychosis, and the level of apprehension rose with each newspaper story read or film viewed. The imagery of gas asphyxiating whole cities was pounced on by "gas experts," who attempted to alleviate fears by pointing out the absurdity of most of these statements. But why, citizens would have muttered, were they going to be handed respirators if this catastrophe was all fiction? Gas proponents and apologists continually waged an uphill battle against the perceived immoral nature of poison gas. It can be said with certainty that they ultimately failed to convince the public. As one gas authority noted, the mystery and fear of gas, starting with its use in the Great War, had "stimulated the growth of fantastic horror speculation." Not only was there evidence of gassed men from the last war, but the push to ban chemical weapons had ultimately failed, and both Italy and Japan had employed poison gases during their wars in the 1930s. It seemed that "things to come" would involve air assaults on cities in an armageddon of chemical fury.[37]

The legacy of the Great War was very real, and with the declaration of the Second World War in 1939, everyone expected gas to be used. The Treaty of Versailles had forbidden the manufacture of or experimentation with poison gas in Germany, so when the advanced German scientists began to study chemical warfare again in the 1930s they simply assumed that they were ten years behind the Allies. Despite quickly developing nerve gases – a much more lethal chemical agent than those used in the Great War – the Germans were sure the British and French must have the same chemical-warfare stockpiles. They did not. A German search of American and British scientific periodicals in the early part of the war revealed no trace of nerve gases. In a classic example of self-intimidation, the Germans assumed that censorship was in place and that the

Allies must therefore have perfected their manufacture. That assumption revealed one of the key factors in why chemical weapons were not used in the Second World War. Given the inability to gather good intelligence on the enemy's gas arsenals, both sides assumed that the other possessed ample supplies. This was generally not the case, but both the Allies and Axis were reluctant to instigate a gas war in case the other had a new, more powerful chemical agent. There was a delicate system of checks and balances, some open and some implied, some real and some imagined. In the end, gas was never instigated as a battlefield weapon. Several factors contributed to an uneasy gas truce, where each nation waited for the other to strike first: the desire not to break international conventions and treaties unnecessarily; technological inferiority and obsolescence of delivery systems that did not seem to live up to the science-fiction literature; a continued mistrust of chemical weapons by senior generals, who knew well the added burden of poison gas in hindering the command and control of armies; the memory of gas in 1918 causing stagnation on the battlefield (the exact antithesis of the *Blitzkrieg* or lightning war hoped for by most armies); and the fear of massive aerochemical bombing reprisals against civilians.[38]

Caught unprepared in the First World War, Canada refused to suffer that fate a second time and actively pursued the production of chemical and biological weapons during the Second World War. Not only did the Canadians develop chemical weapons, but they tested them on Canadian soldiers, burning and maiming some for life. The Canadian government and military were also worried about German and Japanese bombers launching aerochemical sorties against coastal cities. An interdepartmental committee for Air-Raid Precaution was struck in March 1938 to prepare Canadians for defence against air raids. One of the prime concerns was to protect against poison gas, and during the war provincial training centres were organized to teach anti-gas discipline to civilian volunteers. The volunteers, in turn, were to go back to their communities to further disseminate the gas warnings. The nature of the various chemical agents, expected German gas tactics, the handling of gas casualties and decontamination procedures, along with various methods of collective and individual protection, were all taught in short courses. Notwithstanding the good intentions of the committee, this was a most difficult and cumbersome process, especially since there was no coordinated effort to hand out respirators to the Canadian public. Had the gas been released, it would surely have wreaked terrible havoc on the alerted but totally unprepared Canadian population.[39]

Despite the impediments to the use of poison gas, it was always at the ready and might easily have been unleashed during the Second World War. Although the Allies never used their chemical shells, Churchill had several squadrons loaded with mustard gas bombs to drop on any amphibious landing by German troops on Great Britain. Hitler was also against starting a gas war, but with

German cities smoldering in the last weeks of the war, he began to question his generals as to how they could employ the 70,000 tons of chemical agents they had amassed. It is interesting to note that although the Allies continued to view gas as a punitive second-strike weapon, Churchill would certainly have unleashed his gas in a last-ditch effort to save his homeland in a desperate defensive stand.[40]

Battlefield chemical agents are known to have been used numerous times since the First World War: Italy's employment of mustard gas against the Abyssinians, Japan's use of various chemical agents against the Chinese before and during the Second World War, Egypt's unconfirmed use of chemical weapons against Yemen in the 1960s, the United States' employment of chemicals and defoliants in Vietnam, allegations of chemical weapons by the Soviet military in the decade-long battle in Afghanistan, and Iraq's use of mustard and nerve gases against Iran during their war in the 1980s. Although initially banned weapons have been accepted over time, chemical agents have continually been denigrated by most countries and typically classed with biological and nuclear weapons as "retaliation weapons" only. In many of the arsenals of the world, chemical agents continue to be a threat, as the Gulf War illustrated. They are seen as the poor man's answer to nuclear weapons and continue to be held in reserve for massive and deadly retaliation.

In an attempt to control these weapons of mass destruction, on 29 April 1997 the Chemical Weapons Convention (CWC) went into force, with 160 nations signing the agreement. The CWC reinforced the abhorrent nature of chemical weapons, and many of the nations agreed to abstain from a first-use chemical policy. However, many rogue states like Iraq and Libya have not recognized the convention and believe it is a ploy by the great powers to attempt to limit other states by banning chemical weapons even though many of the First World countries have far deadlier nuclear weapons. Despite these recent efforts, the gas war started on a sunny day over eighty-five years ago. Like Pandora's Box, once opened, it will never go away.

CANADIAN CORPS GAS SERVICES

Having noted the importance of gas among veterans and the popular culture of the 1920s and '30s, it is worth returning to the Canadian Corps. The question of how effective the Canadian Gas Services were remains. It is always difficult to quantify the impact of training on soldiers. Yet it seems clear that the Gas Services played a significant role in keeping Canadian gas casualties under control, especially when, by the last year of the war, chemical agents were being used every day and soldiers at the front were forced to survive in a gas environment. Canada's Official History noted that the Canadian Corps suffered 11,572 non-fatal gas casualties during the war.[41] If one compares that with the total killed and wounded – 232,494 – then approximately 5 percent of all battlefield casualties were from gas.[42] However, if one examines the ratio of poison gas casualties to non-fatal battlefield casualties – 11,572 to 138,166 – then we get a much more startling figure. Almost 12 percent of all non-fatal casualties among Canadian soldiers were attributed to gas. Although the final gas figures are not broken down into fatal and non-fatal casualties, it is assumed that with an approximate 3 percent death rate for gas over the war, there were about 350 deaths from gas. Because of the initial gassing at 2nd Ypres, where many men were killed by gas and left behind, a Canadian Corps final figure would be higher than the average. The additional problems of accounting for gas casualties, as indicated throughout this work, must also be taken into account. Regardless of their limitations, surely these figures prove the inaccuracy of assuming that poison gas was simply a nuisance. Without an effective organization like the Canadian Corps Gas Services, the casualties might very well have risen closer to the crippling 25 percent suffered by the Americans. While I am wary of counter-factual speculation, it is clear that without proper anti-gas training the Canadian Corps would have had its spearhead units more quickly dulled and its fighting efficiency degraded during the constant battles in the gas environment of the last two years of the war. The Gas Services were not established to negate all gas casualties; their role was a defensive one of education, prevention, and damage control. They succeeded in carrying out that mandate in the gas environment.

With the release of chlorine at 2nd Ypres, the 1st Canadian Division was involved from the start in the gas war. As one Canadian infantryman remarked, while his company was rushed to the front on 22 April 1915, "gas or no gas ... it takes more than gas to stop a Canadian."[43] That it did, and most Canadians were able to stand their ground against the initial use of gas. They did not break and run, but just as the gas burned Canadian lungs, it was also branded on Canadian minds. How was one to defend against a gaseous cloud that relentlessly rolled over all in its path, where there was no place to find shelter and no place to run?

More frequent use of deadlier gases by the Germans necessitated the creation of divisional gas officers to help coordinate the protection against chemical agents. There was no precedent for the role of gas officers, but their purpose remained constant: to overcome fear and ignorance with education and training. The evolution of the Gas Services mirrored the intensity with which gas was employed on the battlefield. By the summer of 1916 lethal gas was being delivered in both canisters and shells and was no longer something rarely encountered in the trenches. To combat this, the Canadian Gas Services were forced to increase the drill and education of Canadian officers (who were then to instruct their men) in order to protect them and the rank and file in the evolving gas war. "You want something to help you over your fears and, if you can get control over your fears as you do in drill, it helps drive the man forward in war," was how Lord Gort, winner of the Victoria Cross in the First World War and Chief of

Imperial General Staff (CIGS) of the British Expeditionary Force in 1939-40, described the importance of training in war.[44] As the gas environment became increasingly deadly, the anti-gas training kept pace in order to provide physical as well as psychological safeguards.

Up until the battle of Vimy Ridge, the role of the Gas Services was entirely based on creating an effective anti-gas doctrine so that the common soldier would know how to react to gas when it was encountered, how to overcome it, and how to fight through it. With the introduction of British lethal gas shells in early 1917, the role of the newly appointed chemical advisor included instructing the artillery – most importantly, the senior counter-battery officer – on how to incorporate gas shells into an attack doctrine. The conception of gas as simply a terror weapon fails to acknowledge the essential role eventually designated for it in Canadian and belligerent artillery tactical fireplans. From Vimy onward, the Canadian artillery took an interest in incorporating gas shells into their engagements. The attack gas doctrine was honed battle after battle until it became an integral part of counter-battery work, in the harassment and denial of jumping-off points for enemy infantry, in the disruption of the lines of communication, and as a continuous weapon of attrition against both morale and the physical ability to fight. "Gas was Fritz's most effective weapon against the artillery," was how the Regimental History of the 55th Battery, Canadian Field Artillery, described the importance of chemical counter-battery work.[45] The Canadian artillery responded with equal force and determination in employing chemical shells. The British Special Companies continued to be attached to the Canadian Corps to carry out gas-release operations; yet they were not well liked by the infantry, who could not rely on them to deliver their gas effectively when required. Such animosity was only increased with the bloody failure of the 4th Division's raid on 1 March 1917. Thus, gas delivered by artillery was a logical transition, and as a steady flow of chemical shells became available the Canadian Corps began to use gas more often to assist set-piece battles.

In 1917, the use of gas, employed during all major operations, vastly increased from the preceding year. The Canadian Corps' successes at Hill 70 and Passchendaele were greatly assisted by the use of gas in counter-battery work and in harassing enemy counter-attack forming-up points. And on the defensive, the Gas Services continued to strengthen their pedagogical methods through the introduction of a Corps Gas School and mandatory gas instruction for all Canadian officers, especially the artillerymen and soldiers involved in the lines of communication, as these were now, along with the infantry, equal targets for gas shells.

The surprise introduction of mustard gas by the Germans in July 1917 once again necessitated a new role for the Gas Services. All soldiers, not just officers and NCOs, were taught to avoid becoming casualties of the persistent gas. The trend of removing individual responsibility for gas discipline was slowed, and all soldiers were forced to become accountable for their own safety through a combination of imposed gas discipline and individual intuition. The use of mustard gas changed the tactical nature of gas warfare and made it imperative for the Gas Services to train soldiers to operate in a total gas environment. Persistent gas also forced new medical practices, like the removal of infected clothes and the use of chemical solutions to ease the blisters and burns, which helped to reduce the potential for a debilitating flow of casualties from the German gas. The Medical Corps, like the Gas Services, learned from its own mistakes and eventually was able to instigate procedures that helped to save lives, reduce the severity of gas burns, and return men more quickly to their units. An essential component in defending against the gas war, the Medical Corps was successful in many areas, more so when dealing with mustard gas patients than those saturated with heavy doses of phosgene. The interaction of doctors and Gas Services, usually in the form of orders and pamphlets, regarding changes in the gas war, successful and unsuccessful treatments, and the reinterpretation of the roles of doctors, all helped to control and reduce the potential epidemic of chemical warfare casualties.

Despite all these precautions, not all gas casualties could be avoided. Soldiers often unwittingly fell victim through the camouflage of gas shells within HE or, more often, from persistent mustard gas in the mud and shell holes in which soldiers lived and in the water with which they washed. These circumstances gave soldiers, suffering from the overwhelming strain of the front, a chance to administer a self-inflicted gas wound and head to Blighty for a month or two of recuperation in a warm, clean hospital. Some commanders must have worried that their whole army would melt away. This fear of "malingering" was partly quelled by the Gas Services and the CAMC, which developed sound practices in administering gas discipline and a hyper-critical awareness of malingerers, but it never truly came to grips with the trickle of self-inflicted gas wounds.

The most valued role of the Gas Services was its ability to absorb and circulate information on new gases, delivery systems, evolving enemy tactics, defensive measures and equipment, and an assortment of other intelligence reports from other Gas Services in the BEF and then form a coherent anti-gas doctrine for the officers and rankers of the Canadian Corps. Without the Canadian Gas Services, there would have been no consistent method through which to disseminate these vital messages to the troops. Most senior officers were liable to view the use of gas haphazardly because of the stigma attached to it, an approach that would have left the Canadian Corps without an adequate doctrine and susceptible to the steady attrition of the gas environment. As one trench soldier remembered, it was "a nibble here and a nibble there," which continually threatened to reduce good battalions to mediocre, or mediocre to poor. The Gas Services did their job in keeping the gas nibbles at a non-crippling rate. On several occasions, during some of the heaviest gas attacks of the war, the corps was commended by the director of Gas Services, GHQ, for its excellent gas discipline. This defensive doctrine was reflected in the relatively low Canadian gas casualties in proportion to other attacking units, even though the corps often spearheaded attacks during the Last Hundred Days and thus was more susceptible to the German tactics of area gas denial in hopes of slowing the advancing units.[46]

Finally, gas, in the words of Charles Foulkes, "changed the whole character of warfare." Those who did not grasp these changes faced harsh consequences. According to a report by the First British Army, many nuances of the gas war simply "did not seem to be understood" by the American Expeditionary Force. The inability to come to grips with the intricacies of attacking through the gas environment manifested itself in continual devastation of American front-line units. Not only was one in every four American casualties a result of gas, but the fighting efficiency of the survivors was nearly destroyed. The Canadians, on the other hand, not only understood but also had mastered the complexities of the gas environment. Soldiers had no hope of survival on the chemical battlefield without proper respirators, but they would have suffered prohibitive gas casualties even with those devices had they not had faith in their efficacy and advanced training in their use. The creation of a faith in both respirators and anti-gas training was the most important legacy of the Canadian Corps Gas Services.[47]

RE-EVALUATING THE GAS ENVIRONMENT

The constant use of gas, especially by the Germans in their Peace Offensive or their defensive gas barrages, meant that all soldiers, not just those of the Canadian Corps, were forced to survive in this gas environment. However, the regimental history of the 85th Battalion of the Canadian Expeditionary Force is a not uncommon example of how historians have generally disregarded or downplayed the role of gas on the battlefield. Two Canadians who, in this unit, exhibited great bravery also illustrate the failure in writing about poison gas in the war. A guide at Passchendaele, Sergeant Piper James MacIntosh, although gassed, refused to leave the line until he helped to evacuate the wounded; Sergeant Albert S. Ward exhibited great courage in leading "C" Company when all the officers were killed or wounded during the strenuous fighting around Bourlon Wood in October 1918, or also refused to leave the front lines even though he was seriously gassed. The point is not the bravery of the two soldiers, as commendable as that is, but rather that except for the references in these citations the regimental historian makes no mention of the use of gas in the battle.[48] The regimental histories are not alone in this oversight; one has only to turn to the official history and even academic postwar histories to find that the role of gas has been neglected.

That leads to the inevitable question of why poison gas has been ignored. As described in this book, poison gas went through a cycle of acceptance: initial horror and disbelief; a shunting to the periphery once it was clear that it would not deliver the answer to the riddle of the trench warfare stalemate; a gradual acceptance among the artillery and commanders, who began to conceptualize new uses for gas; the development of integrated chemical attack and defence doctrines; and, finally, a new cycle of mistrust and hatred toward chemical weapons in the interwar period. During the collective grieving of nations following the war and within the many peace movements that developed in reaction to the slaughter, the technological and inhumane nature of modern warfare were singled out. Poison gas became a scapegoat for outraged survivors and citizens. During this time, while historians and generals were writing their official works and memoirs, the true role of gas continued to fade from view. Although one could still glean shadows of the gas war through memoirs and fictional accounts written by lower ranks, it remained the grand histories of the war and the memoirs of famous generals that commanded most attention from the public. And in these histories gas was almost completely written out of the war. More damaging to our understanding of the role of gas, with the closing of archival documents until the 1960s it was nearly impossible to contradict the official view of the war.

When those documents became available and historians began to once again explore the Great War, it became apparent that many of the wartime reports had downplayed or had simply excluded the use of poison gas. Gas remained a perplexing ingredient – one, like the constant problem of shell shock among soldiers at the front, that many commanders could not deal with or find a successful solution to. Some generals simply refused to believe there was such a thing as shell shock and did not allow medical officers to label patients with such a term. These men did not find cures to their mental break-downs simply because a general would not allow such a "feminine" ailment among his soldiers; they were labelled as something else and sent to the rear. Poison gas casualties were also sometimes viewed with derision, and a high number of chemical casualties in a unit was often equated with a breakdown in discipline. Again, like shell shock, it was not something that many staff officers and generals wanted to publicize, and casualty figures could be generalized or simply grouped under other headings. Sometimes it was not even so conspiratorial, for the compiling of reports and statistics was often left to exhausted junior subalterns or medical officers, neither of whom had the time or the inclination to recount the pressures of poison gas on the rank and file or, in the case of medical officers, to classify men into separate categories of wounded.

Thus with the initial glossing over of gas in the first histories – like Edmonds's official histories of the British Expeditionary Force or Winston Churchill's *World Crisis* – when combined with many of the inaccuracies of reports and accounts prepared by soldiers at the front or staff officers in the rear, the official documents do not always contain full accounts of the true role of poison gas on the Western Front.[49] Like logistics – the very sinew of war and essential to understanding how modern warfare is carried out – poison gas has been over-looked in history for more glamorous accounts of battle. Yet the clues are there among the official military papers. It simply requires a detailed examination of the documents, a diplomatic reading of the texts. The havoc played by poison gas may not be fully detailed in an after-battle report, but junior-ranking offi-cers' accounts, medical reports, casualty lists, and the many other forms of docu-mentation in military archives, when examined together and cross-referenced, give clues to a more accurate portrayal of battle. But those archival documents must be combined with an equally close examination of the participants' letters home, diaries, and memoirs after the war. Until recently, very few historians have examined all three sources with rigour. Only works that combine research through available literature, archival documents, and first-hand accounts will ever cut through the vapours of a long-dead war.

As nineteenth-century novelist Samuel Butler has noted, "Life is the art of drawing sufficient conclusions from insufficient evidence."[50] Although this study has focused only on the Canadian Corps and how it coped with the gas war, it also sets a framework for re-evaluating the whole nature of fighting in 1917 and 1918 with greater examination into a weapon that caused over a million casualties and changed the tactics of all armies. In addition, the book has explored how soldiers fought through and survived in the gas environment at the sharp end. Awareness of historiographical gaps and plain inaccuracies has led to this reappraisal of the gas war. But filling a hole in the historiography has not been the only goal of this work. Throughout there has been an analysis of the learning process employed within the corps. By examining a complicated psychologically and physically debilitating weapon system in depth, a better understanding is gained of how soldiers dealt with the mental strain of war. One gets an in-depth view of how one example of technology affected soldiers and how the soldiers interacted with it in return. Understanding the vast tech-nological changes in weaponry are essential to understanding the war, but they have often been examined out of context. There is more to fighting a war than simply firing off a machine gun or six pounder in the direction of the enemy: men have to be taught how to use their weapons and, more important, how to use them in conjunction with each other. This was the key to success in the Great War, and one the Allies hit upon in the Last Hundred Days. For comman-ders to separate weapons and doctrine resulted in the slaughter without gain, as at 1st and 2nd Ypres, Verdun, the Somme; for historians to do so, is to miscon-strue the complicated nature of trench warfare. This interplay of technology, doctrine, and men has remained a misunderstood subject within the context of the First World War, and the fleshing out of how soldiers actively created attack and defence doctrines and then put them into practice gives greater insight into the real war fought in the trenches.

To grasp how the Canadians survived, one must understand that gas training was a continuous operation of implementation and refinement of the anti-gas doctrine. Great battles become the core of military history, but it was adaptation and training throughout the war that made the Canadian Corps one of the finest fighting forces on the Western Front. The Canadian Gas Services displayed ingenuity in training the men within the context of the overarching British Gas Services. The gas officers helped to quell the fears of all soldiers, not just new recruits, by constantly drilling them and reassuring them that they would be able to survive when the Germans saturated their positions with poison gas.

When a gas shell landed near Private Donald Fraser during the battle of Vimy Ridge, he instinctively did not breathe and adjusted his respirator without thinking. In effect, the Gas Services saved his life, and the lives of countless Canadians like him, as gas discipline became second nature to the men of the Canadian Corps. Gas preyed on the weak and the uninformed, and it was only through constant gas training that soldiers were given a better chance at survival. Gas discipline forced Canadians into acting and reacting against gas on an "informed" trial-and-error basis. Even during the final battles, when the pursuing Canadians were forced to remove their respirators to see and advance over the great distances, their continuing low casualties even in extraordinary gas exposure indicated that collectively they knew when it was necessary to wear their SBRs. Again and again, the gas-wise Canadian Corps spearheaded the BEF's most crucial breakthrough attacks during the Last Hundred Days. In these gas environments, the Canadians were being forced to wear their SBRs while forming up for battle, during the advance as they "went over the top," across wide areas as they overran German defences, and throughout the consolidation period as they apprehensively waited for the inevitable German counter-attacks. As the use of gas became more prolific, the Canadians were forced to adapt or falter. They adapted.

Excepting the exceptionally open-minded or far-sighted, something unpleasant usually has to happen to most people or organizations before they change. The advantage of having two of the best corps commanders in the war, Byng and Currie, made the role of adapting to the realities of warfare easier for the Canadians. But like all armies, the Canadians were still forced to learn from their mistakes and setbacks. The memory of falling victim to the first series of gas attacks was a catalyst for commanders, and especially the Gas Services, to eventually implement an efficient anti-gas doctrine. The unique structure of the Canadian Corps, its open-minded commanders and efficient Gas Services, helped ultimately to force all soldiers to accept the value of anti-gas training – an experience that most nations had to learn in a slower and more painful manner.

"You could never expect another generation to do what we did," asserted a

First World War officer.[51] Such a statement rings absolutely true and fits well into our understanding of the now unearthed role of poison gas on the Western Front. The usual view is that the horror of the gas war failed to break those men because, within the incredible carnage of trench warfare, gas was only an annoyance that added to the apocalyptic scenery. A failure by historians to comprehend the encompassing gas environment of 1918 has produced an inaccurate image of the war. In addition, perhaps, something must be said about the resilience of the front-line soldiers. To be sure, without a proper anti-gas doctrine the soldiers of all nations were consigned to maiming and death, but even with it, they underwent incredible physical hardship and psychological trauma. As the marching song asserted over and over again, "We are the tough guys / We are the tough guys." Surviving on the Great War chemical battlefield proved that beyond a doubt.

Remembering the men who lived on the chemical battlefield, it is interesting to contrast the near hysteria that gripped the Coalition Forces more than seventy years later during the 1991 Gulf War. The simple threat of Saddam Hussein using chemical weapons resulted in doomsday forecasts about the effects on ground troops, including heightened fatigue factors due to the still debilitating chemical-warfare suits and subsequent grievous casualty figures. This book may go some way in alleviating such fears, as it reveals that the Canadians on the First World War chemical battlefield showed that, with good training, soldiers could survive. With the introduction of deadlier gases – especially nerve agents in the 1930s – chemical weapons have been classified for some time now with the other two spectres of war (nuclear and biological agents) as weapons of mass destruction. Yet since the Great War, better protective and warning devices have been introduced to match the increase in chemical lethality; those who continue to view gas warfare (or chemical warfare as it is now referred to) in an apocalyptic light, might best turn back to the Great War and see that soldiers not only survived but struggled through the only war in human history fought on the chemical battlefield.

The Last Word: A Sudden, Strong Scent

"If I had time and anything like your ability to study war," wrote Field-Marshall Lord Wavell to Sir Basil Liddell Hart, "I think I should concentrate almost entirely on the actualities of war – the effects of tiredness, hunger, fear, lack of sleep, weather ... The principles of strategy and tactics, and the logistics of war are really absurdly simple; it is the actualities that make war so complicated and so difficult, and are usually so neglected by historians."[52] This study has embraced the field-marshall's observation, and has delved into the soldiers' perceptions of the poison gas that so deeply affected them.

Although the fear factor was controlled throughout the gas war, it was never entirely exorcized from soldiers' minds. As Talbot Papineau, an officer of

Princess Patricia's Canadian Light Infantry, wrote before his death in 1917, gas is "like a bad boy walking behind you with a hard snowball, always ready to throw, but not throwing."[53] Soldiers' only protections were alertness, battle intuition, early warning, gas masks, anti-gas appliances, and endless drill and practice. Yet the psychological pressure, not only of the stifling respirators, but also of the "friction" induced by gas warfare, never ceased. The personal isolation from comrades; the nagging suspicion that one's gas mask could fail, have a hole in it, or be lost; the near-blindness and the noxious smell; the vomiting and nausea produced by even mild gassings; the poisonous contamination of trenches and dugouts by mustard gas; and the difficulty of carrying out normal tasks like working, shooting, drinking, eating, smoking, and defecating under such conditions weighed on all soldiers of the Western Front enveloped by the gas environment.

The fear of poison gas should not to be underestimated. One soldier remembered how he continued after the war to have nightmares where he "would awaken in the middle of the night, in a cold sweat, dreaming that I heard the clatter and whistle-blowing all along the line which meant that the gas was coming."[54] There was no escaping the gas – no reliance on bravery or fortified trenches – only faith in good gas discipline would keep one alive in the gas environment. The "fear factor" has dimmed from the memory of modern historians like the long lines of mustard-gassed soldiers, each with his hand on the shoulder of the man in front, shuffling off to the rear to fade into the poor memory of Canadian historiography.

Gas never delivered the knock-out blow initially envisioned by those commanders hoping to solve the "riddle of the trenches." The failure of gas to live up to a decisive role has allowed historians to subsequently downplay its nuanced aspects during the Great War. Yet it certainly had much more than the function ascribed to it by the British official historian. "Gas," wrote Sir James Edmonds, "achieved but local success; it made life uncomfortable, to no purpose."[55] Such an assertion simply fails to grasp the subtle layers of the gas war and its psychological impact on the soldier – something that becomes very clear in an examination of personal memoirs and correspondence of those men who served and lived through the gas war.

Appropriately, then, the final word belongs to one of those trench soldiers. Robert Graves, a survivor of the effects of gas, wrote years after the war that, "since 1916, the fear of gas obsessed me: any unusual smell, even a sudden strong scent of flowers in a garden, was enough to send me trembling."[56] Chemical warfare has been continually viewed by historians as a peripheral annoyance; in fact, it was much more. Blanketing the Western Front with lethal gases caused real and imagined terrors, from which there was no place to run. The soldiers in the trenches saw a different aspect of the gas war from that of the staff officers and historians in the rear – perhaps because they breathed different air.

Notes

Introduction: The Gas War Unearthed

1 In Belgium, the same phenomenon also occurs in farmers' fields covering long-forgotten battlefields. For information about French demineurs see Donovan Webster, "The Soldiers Moved On. The War Moved On. The Bombs Stayed." *Smithsonian* (February 1994): 28-9.

2 Harold Hartley, "A General Comparison of British and German Methods of Gas Warfare," *Journal of the Royal Artillery* (February 1920): 492. Hartley's speech is interesting in revealing what the British believed with regard to gas warfare following the war, but it contains many factual errors.

3 Martin van Creveld, *Technology and War* (London: Free Press, 1989), 17.

4 The best works on the Canadian Corps barely notice the gas war: Desmond Morton, *When Your Number's Up* (Toronto: Random House, 1993), has less than a page describing the gas war; Bill Rawling, *Surviving Trench Warfare* (Toronto: University of Toronto Press, 1992) devotes only a little more space even though his masterful work is devoted to how the Canadians adapted and survived on the battlefield; G.W.L. Nicholson's Official History of the Canadian Expeditionary Force (*Canadian Expeditionary Force, 1914-1919* [Ottawa: Roger Duhamel, Queen's Printer and Controller of Stationary, 1962]) is just as sparse and does not even mention the Gas Services. This is just a sample of the best works on the history of the Canadian Corps; even less space is devoted to gas in other works by Canadian historians.

5 Both Shane Shriver, "Orchestra to Victory" (Master of War Studies thesis, Royal Military College, 1995), and Daniel Dancocks, *Spearhead to Victory* (Edmonton: Hurtig, 1987), make strong cases for the quality of the Canadian Corps. See also Tim Travers, *How the War Was Won* (London: Routledge, 1992), 118. See Rawling, *Surviving Trench Warfare*, for an excellent analysis of the development and professionalization of the Canadian Corps. See Morton, *When Your Number's Up*, 24, for the remark about Canadian officers.

6 As quoted in Richard Holmes, *Firing Line* (London: Pimlico, 1985), 9.

7 The last sentence translates as "It is sweet and fitting to die for one's country." As quoted in Martin Gilbert's, *The First World War* (New York: Henry Holt, 1994), 352-3.

8   John Keegan, *The Face of Battle* (London: Pimlico, 1976), 39.

9   Quotation taken from the preface to Sir Ian Hamilton, *A Staff Officer's Scrap Book* (London: Edward Arnold, 1905).

Chapter 1: Trial by Gas

1   Although Canada had a very small professional army, it had a strong militia tradition. By 1914, the Canadian militia had a peacetime strength of 77,000. Desmond Morton, *When Your Number's Up* (Toronto: Random House, 1993), 3.

2   See Ronald Haycock, *Sam Hughes: The Public Career of a Controversial Canadian, 1885-1916* (Waterloo: Wilfrid Laurier University Press, 1986), 9.

3   Daniel G. Dancocks, *Welcome to Flanders Fields* (Toronto: McClelland and Stewart, 1988), 33-78; Stephen Harris, *Canadian Brass* (Toronto: University of Toronto, 1988), 105-13.

4   Quotation from Robert O'Connol, *Of Arms and Men* (Oxford: Oxford University Press, 1989), 242, 246. See A.F. Duguid, *Official History of the Canadian Forces in the Great War, 1914-1919*, vol. 1 (Ottawa: J.O. Patenaude, 1938), 135-6. Duguid, who was to write the official history of the CEF, had made it only to the middle of 1915 after almost twenty years of compiling documents. G.W.L. Nicholson completed a one-volume official history of the CEF in 1962. Morton, *When Your Number's Up*, 32, refers to the Comedian Contingent.

5   Colonel Malcolm Mercer's 1st Brigade trained with the British 6th Division between 17 and 23 February. They were followed by Colonel Richard Turner's 3rd Brigade, who were in the line until 2 March. Concurrently, Colonel Arthur Currie's 2nd Brigade was apprenticed with the British 4th Division from 21 to 28 February. Dancocks, *Welcome to Flanders Fields*, 117-8; National Archives of Canada (NAC), RG 41, vol. 7, 3rd Battalion, Mr. E. Seaman, tape 2/page 3.

6   NAC, RG 41, vol. 8, 5th Battalion, Mr. R.L. Christopherson, 1/20; William Gritchley of the 10th Battalion remembered the same feeling, vol. 8, 10th Battalion, W. Gritchley, 1/1.

7   Sir Max Aitken, *Canada in Flanders*, vol. 1 (London: Hodder and Stoughton, 1916), 31.

8   D.J. Goodspeed, *The Road Past Vimy: The Canadian Corps, 1914-1918* (Toronto: General Paperbacks, 1969, 1987), 19. Quotation from NAC, MG 30, E8, John J. Creelman diary, 32.

9   NAC, RG 41, vol. 8, 5th Battalion, F.C. Bagshaw, 1/10-11; MG 30, E1, William Alexander Alldritt Papers, Diary, 13; RG 41, vol. 8, 5th Battalion, E.N. Copping, 1/8; A.J. Kerry and W.A. McDill, *The History of the Corps of the Royal Canadian Engineers* (Ottawa: Military Engineers Association of Canada, 1962), 89.

10 In the Middle Ages knights sometimes executed or mutilated captured bowmen. A similar practice continued into the First World War, with the execution of snipers or flame throwers. Martin van Creveld, *Technology and War* (London: Free Press, 1989), 71.

11 Samuel Hynes, *A War Imagined* (London: Pimlico, 1990), 43-4, 46-8; John Ellis, *The Social History of the Machine Gun* (New York: Pantheon Books, 1975), 104-6; Denis Winter, *Death's Men* (London: Penguin Books, 1979), 24-7, 32-6; Modris Ekstein, *Rites of Spring* (Toronto: Lester and Orpen Dennys, 1989), chaps. 1 and 2; A.B. McKillop, "Marching as to War: Elements of Ontario Undergraduate Culture, 1880-1914," in *Youth, University, and Canadian Society*, edited by Paul Axelrod and John G. Reid (Montreal: McGill-Queen's University Press, 1989).

12 It was not actually the "riddle of the trenches" that caused such horrific casualties: machine guns, shrapnel, and high-explosive artillery shells and infantry attacking in massed groups over open ground strewn with barbed wire decimated the armies of 1914. But it was the "riddle" of how to overcome such factors that resulted in the re-examination by both sides of how to break the trench stalemate. See Timothy Travers, *The Killing Ground* (Boston: Allen and Unwin, 1987); John A. English, "The Riddle of the Trenches," *Canadian Defence Quarterly* 15, 2 (1985); Michael Howard, "Men against Fire," in *Makers of Modern Strategy*, edited by Peter Paret (Princeton, NJ: Princeton University Press, 1986).

13 Rudolph Hanslian, "Gas Warfare: A German Apologia," *Canadian Defence Quarterly* 6, 1 (1928): 96-9; William Moore, *Gas Attack* (London: Leo Cooper, 1987), 2; van Creveld, *Technology and War*, 61.

14 Charles E. Heller, "The Peril of Unpreparedness: The American Expeditionary Force and Chemical Warfare," *Military Review* 65, 1 (1985): 15; Ludwig Fritz Haber, *The Poisonous Cloud*

(Oxford: Clarendon Press, 1986), 18-25. The British were equally wary of the conventions, and at the 1899 conference their representative, Sir John Fisher, called the "conference itself as a bad joke." Simon Jones, "Under a Green Sea: The British Responses to Gas Warfare, Part 1," *The Great War* 1, 4 (1989): 127.

15 J.B. Poole, "A Sword Undrawn: Chemical Warfare and the Victorian Age, Part II," *Army Quarterly and Defence Journal* 107, 1 (1977): 90.

16 The French developed the first chemical weapon – a non-toxic lachrymatory hand grenade – in 1912, and by August 1914 some 30,000 cartridges weighing approximately half a pound and containing ethyl bromo-acetate had been manufactured and could be launched from special twenty-six-calibre rifles. They were used in August 1914 but quickly dispersed before any harm was done. Charles Heller, *Chemical Warfare in World War I: The American Experience, 1917-1918*, Leavenworth Papers no. 10 (Fort Leavenworth, KS: Combat Studies Institute, 1984), 6; Hanslian, "Gas Warfare," 100-4; Haber, *The Poisonous Cloud*, 19-21; Ulrich Trumpener, "The Road to Ypres," *Journal of Modern History* 51 (June 1979): 462-3.

17 Richard Price, *Chemical Weapons Taboo* (Ithaca, NY: Cornell University Press, 1997), 18-30.

18 Travers, *The Killing Ground*, chaps. 2, 3, and 4; and Howard, "Men against Fire."

19 Not everyone was caught unaware of the progression of weapons in vastly increasing the lethality of war. Among the most important observers, Ivan Bloch, a Polish banker and civilian, wrote in 1897 about the futility of future wars. He envisioned a battlefield that would be uninhabitable due to the firepower of new weapons. Bloch did not believe that war was impossible, but that between two industrialized powers it would result in a terrible human cost, bankrupt the nations financially, and usher in anarchy. See J.F.C. Fuller, *The Conduct of War, 1832-1932* (London: Eyre Methusen, 1972), 128-30; Timothy Travers, "Technology, Tactics, and Morale: Jean de Bloch, the Boer War, and British Military Theory, 1900-1914," *Journal of Modern History* 51 (June 1979).

20 Robert B. Asprey, *The German High Command at War* (New York: William Morrow, 1991), 218.

21 Moore, *Gas Attack*, 11; Trumpener, "Road to Ypres," 464-5; Ian Hogg, *Gas* (New York: Ballantine Books, 1975), 20. The T-shell was also know as T-Stoff and contained xylyl- and benzyl bromide. The shell was named after its discover, Hans Tappen. Stockholm International Peace Research Institute (SIPRI), *The Problem of Chemical and Biological Warfare*, vol. 1, *The Rise of CB Weapons* (Stockholm: Almquist and Wiksell, 1971), 28; T.J. Gander, *Nuclear, Biological, and Chemical Warfare* (London: Ian Allan, 1987), 13.

22 Haber was raised from an NCO in the reserves to a captain, an almost unprecedented event in the German army. Haber, *The Poisonous Cloud*, 27.

23 Jacques J. Bailliu, "Canada and Chemical Warfare" (Master of War Studies thesis, Royal Military College, 1989), 15, 17; SIPRI, *Problem of Chemical and Biological Warfare*, 26. The following table is a relation of countries and their chemical production.
TABLE N.1

Production of chlorine in 1914

Country	Production by pound	Percentage of the world's production
Germany	308,560,000	85.91
Switzerland	22,040,000	6.14
Great Britain	9,111,000	2.54
United States	6,612,000	1.84
Italy	6,222,000	1.73
Japan	4,408,000	1.23
France	2,204,000	0.61

Source: Augustin M. Prentiss, *Chemicals in War* (New York: McGraw-Hill, 1937), 637.

24 Dancocks, *Welcome to Flanders Fields*, 107; Asprey, *German High Command*, 178.

25 For commanders' attitudes toward the use of gas, see Holger H. Herwig, *The First World War: Germany and Austria-Hungary, 1914-1918* (London: Arnold, 1997), 170; Moore, *Gas Attack*, 16;

Trumpener, "Road to Ypres," 470; Heller, *Chemical Warfare*, 7; Lyn Macdonald, *1914-1918: Voices and Images of the Great War* (London: M. Joseph, 1988), 81.

26 Quotation in Thomas Powers and Ruthven Tremain, *Total War* (New York: William Morrow, 1988), 77. See Dancocks, *Welcome to Flanders Fields*, 108-11, 153-5, for an interesting analysis of the information available to both the French and British commanders; Alan Lloyd, *The War in the Trenches* (New York: David McKay, 1976), 54; Sir Basil Liddell Hart, *A History of the World War, 1914-1918* (London: Little, Brown, 1935), 245-9; Kim Beattie, "Unheeded Warning," *Maclean's*, 1 May 1936, 11, 67.

27 Hugh MacIntyre Urquhart, *Arthur Currie: The Biography of a Great Canadian* (Toronto: J.M. Dent and Sons, 1950), 60-1. Quotation in Dancocks, *Welcome to Flanders Fields*, 148.

28 Currie quotation in NAC, MG 30, E100, Arthur Currie Papers, vol. 43, file 194, diary, 15 April 1915. See also G.W.L. Nicholson, *The Gunners of Canada*, vol. 1 (Toronto: McClelland and Stewart, 1967), 223. McNaughton quotation in John Swettenham, *McNaughton*, vol. 1 (Toronto: Ryerson Press, 1968), 43. British commanders' attitudes toward gas are discussed in D.J. Goodspeed, *The Road Past Vimy* (Toronto: Macmillan, 1969), 20. See Norman Dixon, *On the Psychology of Military Incompetence* (New York: Basic Books, 1976), for the study of senior commanders and the psychological defects affecting their ability to absorb new information. For the GHQ report, see Haber, *The Poisonous Cloud*, 33.

29 Trumpener, "Road to Ypres," 471. Peterson was an engineer officer who rose to the rank of major-general in 1917. For German gas casualties see Haber, *The Poisonous Cloud*, 31; Trumpener, "Road to Ypres," 472. At least three men were killed and fifty injured.

30 NAC, RG 41, vol. 9, 13th Battalion, Lt. Colonel T.S. Morrissey, 2/2, and J. Jeffery, 1/2; MG 30, E113, George Bell Papers, Memoirs, 23; RG 24, vol. 20543, file 990.085 (D1).

31 Lyn Macdonald, *1915: The Death of Innocence* (London: Headline Book Publishing, 1993), 192; Alderson quotation from NAC, Department of Militia and Defence (RG 9), vol. 4823, 1st Division's War Diary, Report of Operations 1st Canadian Division from 5 pm 22 April-10am 4 May 1915 (Hereafter Report of Operations); British report quoted in Edward Spiers, *Chemical Warfare* (Chicago: University of Illinois Press, 1986), 16.

32 NAC, RG 41, vol. 9, 13th Battalion, J. Jeffery, 1/2-3; Herbert Rae [George Gibson], *Maple Leaves in Flanders Fields* (Toronto: William Briggs, 1916), 143. See also Ian Sinclair, 1/15; vol. 8, 10th Battalion, W. Gritchley, 1/1A.

33 Quoted in text from Swettenham, *McNaughton*, 44-5. Spiers, *Chemical Warfare*, 17.

34 Donald Richter, *Chemical Soldiers: British Gas Warfare in World War I* (Lawrence, KS: University Press of Kansas, 1992), 10.

35 The Germans had purchased 20,000 gauze masks in Brussels weeks earlier, but they had not yet arrived at the front: Morton, *When Your Number's Up*, 40; Haber, *The Poisonous Cloud*, 32. See also Jones, "Under a Green Sea, Part II," *The Great War* 2, 1 (1989): 16; NAC, MG 30, E318, Notes by A.E. Kirkpatrick for preparation of 3rd Battalion Official History, 2; Erich von Falkenhayn, *General Headquarters, 1914-1916* (London: Hutchinson, 1919), 85.

36 George G. Nasmith, *On the Fringe of the Great Fight* (Toronto: McClelland, Goodchild and Stewart, 1917), 106.

37 NAC, RG 41, vol. 8, 7th Battalion, J.O. Mackie, 1/5; RG 9, vol. 4823, Report of Operations.

38 NAC, RG 41, vol. 7, Vick Lewis, 2/3.

39 As quoted in Macdonald, *1914-1918*, 85.

40 Quote from NAC, RG 41, vol. 8, 10th Battalion, Sid Cox, 1/3.

41 NAC, RG 41, vol. 9, 13th Battalion, W.S.M. Mactier, 1/7.

42 Sir Andrew Macphail, *Official History of the Canadian Forces in the Great War: The Medical Services* (Ottawa: F.A. Acland, 1925), 193.

43 NAC, MG 30, E300, vol. 16, Victor Odlum Papers, File Report of Events of No. 1 Company, Report of Narratives of Events Ypres April 22nd/26th 1915.

44 Haber estimates that the Germans released 15 tons of chlorine, about one-tenth the amount released on 22 April. But the wind was better and the cloud clung to the ground longer, thereby being more effective. Haber, *The Poisonous Cloud*, 35. See H.H. Mathews, "An Account of the Second Battle of Ypres, April 1915," *Canadian Defence Quarterly* 1, 3 (1924): 38; for quotation see NAC, RG 41, vol. 8, 5th Battalion, R.L. Christopherson, 2/5.

45 First quotation in NAC, RG 41, vol. 7, 3rd Battalion, N. Seaman, 2/12. See MG 30, E113, George Bell Papers, Memoirs, 27. Captain F.A.C. Scrimger, a medical officer of the 14th Battalion, told all who would listen to urinate on a cloth to combat the chlorine. He won the Victoria Cross in the course of the battle. RG 41, vol. 8, 10th Battalion, J. Sprostin, 1/3; vol. 20, L.V. Moore Cosgrave, 1/2. See also Armine Norris, *Mainly for Mother* (Toronto: Ryerson Press, 1919), 164, for the use of urine. For Boyd see RG 41, vol. 8, 8th Battalion, Mr. Boyd, 1/7; for Stevens see 8th Battalion, Lester Stevens, 1/6. The Canadians had not been equipped with any form of gas mask in the period between the first and second attacks. The surprise and intensity of the German gas and conventional attack was so great that little food and ammunition made it to the front lines, which were incidentally under heavy fire. The British and French Commands were not prepared for the German gas attack, and they had no form of protection to be issued to the troops. Historians implying otherwise are incorrect. See, for example, Heller, *Chemical Warfare*, 10.

46 NAC, Department of National Defence (RG 24), vol. 1810, GAQ 1-10; G.W.L. Nicholson, *Seventy Years of Service: A History of the Royal Canadian Army Medical Corps* (Toronto: Borealis Press, 1977), 86; Nasmith, *On the Fringe*, 106.

47 A.B. Tucker, *The Battle Glory of Canada* (London: Cassel, 1915), 128-9. An additional factor caused by chlorine and some of the later war gases was the corrosion of metal. Rifles, small arms cartridges, breechblocks, and gun surfaces were all susceptible, and after a gas attack all metal had to be wiped down with oil and cleaned. Perhaps the effects of the chlorine attack on 22 April had eroded some of the Canadian Ross rifles, an up-to-now unexamined reason for their propensity to jam.

48 Nicholson, *Canadian Expeditionary Force*, 73. For Woods see NAC, RG 24, vol. 1831, GAQ 7-45. For Currie and Turner's predicament see Urquhart, *Currie*, 72. The German report is found in RG 24, vol. 1838, GAQ 10-18B, translation of *Der Weltkrieg 1914-1918*, 13. Binding wrote, "The effects of the successful gas attack were horrible. I am not pleased with the idea of poisoning men." Rudolf Binding, *A Fatalist at War* (London: George Allen and Unwin, 1929), 64-5.

49 NAC, MG 30, E46, vol. 1, R.E.W. Turner Papers, file: Ypres, 1915, Diary of Operations – 3rd Canadian Infantry Brigade, 22nd April to 5th May 1915, 3; RG 41, vol. 8, 8th Battalion, Lester Stevens, 2/3; Stewart quoted in J. Clinton Morrison Jr, *Hell upon Earth: A Personal Account of Prince Edward Island Soldiers in the Great War, 1914-1918* (N.p.: Self-published, 1995), 70.

50 NAC, RG 41, vol. 8, 5th Battalion, J.H. Bowyer, 1/1.

51 Ibid., vol. 9, 13th Battalion, W.F. Dodds, 2/5; Morrison, *Hell upon Earth*, 209.

52 Gordon Reid, ed., *Poor Bloody Murder* (Oakville, ON: Mosaic, 1980), 60-1. NAC, RG 41, vol. 8, 10th Battalion, Sid Cox, 1/15.

53 NAC, RG 41, vol. 9, 13th Battalion, T.S. Morrissey, 2/3; Beaton quoted in Morrison, *Hell upon Earth*, 235-6.

54 NAC, RG 41, vol. 8, 8th Battalion, Lester Stevens, 3/4.

55 Ibid., vol. 9, 13th Battalion, W.F. Dodds, 2/5; Dunlap Pearce Penhallow, *Military Surgery* (London: Oxford University Press, 1918), 509. For Charteris's account see Gilbert, *First World War*, 145; Harold Baldwin, *Holding the Line* (Chicago: McClurg, 1918), 168.

56 Morrison, *Hell upon Earth*, 71.

57 J.H. Elliot and Harold Murchinson Tovell, *The Effects of Poisonous Gases as Observed in Returning Soldiers*, British military pamphlet, December 1916, in NAC, RG 9, vol. 3618, file 25-13-6; R. Dujarric de la Rivière, "Lecture on the Effects of the Gases Employed by the Germans," *Canada Lancet* 49, 4 (1915): 157-8. See also RG 41, vol. 8, 8th Battalion, Lester Stevens, 1/18, and R. Fisher, 1/11-12.

58 During a seven-day period, the hospital treated 5,200 casualties, many of whom were gas casualties. NAC, RG 9, vol. 5027, War Diary of No. 3 Canadian Field Ambulance, 22 April 1915; RG 41, vol. 8, 8th Battalion, Lester Stevens, 1/7 and 2/5. Nicholson, *Seventy Years of Service*, 78. One medical officer on staff at No. 2 Canadian Stationary Hospital wrote that "We have treated during the past six weeks many patients suffering from the notorious gas used by the Germans, and in the treatment of these cases the outdoor life gives wonderful result." As quoted in Mary Plummer, *With the First Canadian Contingent* (Toronto: Hodder and Stoughton, 1915), 105.

59 Robert Harris and Jeremy Paxman, *A Higher Form of Killing* (London: Chatto and Windus, 1982), 3.

60 It was estimated that in 1915 the Germans could fire ten shells for every British one. Hubert C. Johnson, *Breakthrough! Tactics, Technology, and the Search for Victory on the Western Front in World War I* (Novato, CA: Presidio Press, 1994), 116.

61 Duguid, Appendix, 541. General Alderson was just as pleased with the performance of the 1st Canadian Division, and on 28 April he issued the following statement to all ranks: "I have never been so proud of anything in my life as I now am of the words '1 CANADIAN' that I wear on my right arm." NAC, MG 30, E300, vol. 16, Victor Odlum Papers, file Orders & Operations, Ypres. RG 9, vol. 4735, folder 146, file 4; RG 41, vol. 8, 7th Battalion, J.R. Mellree, 1/8; Major Odlum remembered how "the effect [of the music] on our weary marching men was marvellous." MG 30, E300, vol. 16, Victor Odlum Papers, file "Sherwood Foresters Band, 6th BN."

62 Case study given in Elliot and Tovell, *Effects of Poisonous Gases.*

63 NAC, RG 41, vol. 9, 13th Battalion, W.S.M. MacTier, 1/6; Private Prichard of the 8th said the same thing, vol. 8, 8th Battalion, Prichard, 1/5. The description of the battle as murder is in H.W. Wilson, ed., *The Great War,* vol. 7, *Splendid Story of the Canadians,* 8. Johnson's remarks are in NAC, MG 30, E321, William Johnson Papers, letter home dated 3 May 1915.

64 Nicholson, *Canadian Expeditionary Force,* 92.

65 Nicholson, *Gunners of Canada,* 1:229.

66 NAC, MG 30, E157, vol. 15, Harry Crerar Papers, diary 6 May 1915. See Paul Dickson's article on Crerar at 2nd Ypres for an excellent account of Crerar's role in the battle: Paul Dickson, "The New Face of War," *The Beaver* 75 (October-November 1995): 5.

67 NAC, MG 30, E505, W.H. Curtis Papers, letter, n.d.; George G. Nasmith, *On the Fringe of the Great Fight* (Toronto: McClelland, Goodchild and Stewart, 1917), 104. See L. Moore Cosgrave, *Afterthoughts of Armageddon* (Toronto: S.B. Gundy, 1919), for a particularly strong denunciation of the German use of gas. See also NAC, RG 41, vol. 8, 5th Battalion, R.L. Christopherson, 2/2, and vol. 9, 13th Battalion, T.S. Morrissey, 2/3; MG 30, E477, Cameron Ross Papers, 11.

68 One case study indicated that over seven hundred gas cases went through the field ambulances of the 1st Canadian Division for April and the first part of May 1915, although these would not necessarily have been all Canadian troops. J.C. Meakins and J.G. Priestly, "The After-Effects of Chlorine Gas Poisoning," *Canadian Medical Association Journal* 9, 11 (1919): 968. One gas expert suggested shortly after the war that at least a third of the gas cases at 2nd Ypres were fatal. Victor Lefebure, *The Riddle of the Rhine* (London: W. Collins Sons, 1921), 182. See the chart in Chapter 3 taken from the British Official Medical History for other death rates. It should be kept in mind that although many of these gas attacks used higher concentrations of gas, the soldiers at 2nd Ypres were without effective gas masks. Sir W.G. Macpherson, *Official History of the War: Medical Services Diseases of the War,* vol. 2 (London: HMSO, 1923), 282 (hereafter BOMH). Quotation from NAC, RG 41, vol. 8, 10th Battalion, William Walkinshaw, 2/8.

69 NAC, RG 9, vol. 3618, file 25-13-6, Medical Report of Pte. Carolan; Haber, *Poisonous Cloud,* 245.

70 Recorded figures are found in Duguid, Appendix, 851; Dancocks, *Welcome to Flanders Fields,* 315. Postwar figures were compiled for the writing of the official history. NAC, RG 24, vol. 1874, file 22(3), Second Ypres 1915 Casualties. See BOMH, 274.

71 NAC, MG 30, E8, Creelman Diary, 20 April 1916, 59. British Brigadier F. Gore-Anley of the 12th Infantry Brigade noted that the gas attack on 2 May 1915 "was absolutely overpowering, the officers and men seemed to lose their senses, most of them getting out of the trenches and reeling about under enemy's rifle fire." Clearly, the killing of some of the soldiers by conventional arms was a direct result of the gas sent against them. Such casualty figures have never been considered before in trying to gauge the effectiveness of poison gas. As quoted in Andy Thomas, *Effects of Chemical Warfare: A Select Bibliography of British State Papers* (London: Taylor and Francis, 1985), 11.

72 For discussion of British gas casualties see Charles H. Foulkes, *Gas: The Story of the Special Brigade* (London: William B. Blackwood and Sons, 1936), 306-8. See the discussion of Dr. Rudolf Hanslian's article "Der deutsche Gasangriff bei Ypren am 22 April, 1915" in the editorial, "The First Gas Attack: A German's Expert's View," *Army Quarterly* 30, 2 (1935): 302. One of the Canadian official historians, A.F. Duguid, wrote that 60 percent of those men rendered ill from gas at 2nd Ypres had to be sent home, with half of those fully disabled at the end of the war.

Cited in Darlene J. Zdunich, "Tuberculosis and the Canadian Veterans of World War One" (MA thesis, University of Calgary, 1984), 53.

73 For Murray see Malcolm Brown, *The Imperial War Museum Book of the Western Front* (London: Sidgwick and Jackson, 1993), 72. Nasmith, *On the Fringe,* 109.

74 NAC, MG 30, E300, vol. 16, Victor Odlum Papers, file Sherwood Foresters Band, 6th BN, The Canadians' Stand at Ypres.

75 Ibid., E157, vol. 15, Harry Crerar Papers, 29 April 1915.

Chapter 2: Rabbits in a Warren

1 Martin van Creveld, *Technology and War* (London: Free Press, 1989), 67.

2 Kitchener is quoted in Charles H. Foulkes, *Gas: The Story of the Special Brigade* (London: William B. Blackwood and Sons, 1936), 19. The infantryman's assessment appears in Donald Richter, *Chemical Soldiers: British Gas Warfare in World War I* (Lawrence, KS: University Press of Kansas, 1992), 10. The Germans were aware of the potential for Allied propaganda with regard to the first use of gas and even went so far as to claim on 17 April, five days before the first gas attack, that the British had been caught using asphyxiating gas in their shells. Sir Henry F. Thuillier, *Gas in the Next War* (London: Geoffrey Bles, 1938), 20-1. After the attack the Germans issued statements that the gas was not lethal but simply "stupefying." Victor Lefebure, *The Riddle of the Rhine* (London: W. Collins Sons, 1921), 33.

3 William Moore, *Gas Attack* (London: Leo Cooper, 1987), 45.

4 Simon Jones, "Under a Green Sea: The British Responses to Gas Warfare, Part 1," *The Great War* 1, 4 (1989): 128.

5 James Morgan Read, *Atrocity Propaganda, 1914-1919* (New Haven, CT: Yale University Press, 1941), 196. See Robert B. Asprey, *The German High Command at War* (New York: William Morrow, 1991), 214-5; Stockholm International Peach Research Institute (SIPRI), *The Problem of Chemical and Biological Warfare,* vol. 1, *The Rise of CB Weapons* (Stockholm: Almquist and Wiksell, 1971), 231-50, for the use of the German gas attack in Allied propaganda. Such atrocity propaganda was also very effective in attempting to bring the United States into the war. H.C. Peterson, *Propaganda for War: The Campaign against American Neutrality, 1914-1917* (Norman: University of Oklahoma Press, 1939), 63. The contentious issue of the Germans being the first to introduce gas still rankled more than twenty years later. After the fall of Belgium and France in 1940, the German Army demanded that the memorial at Steenstraat, to the first French soldiers gassed on 22 April 1915, be covered in cement. When the cement cracked, the Germans forced the Belgians to blow up the monument in 1941. Incidentally, the Canadian memorial at Canadian Corners, commemorating the heroic stand of the Canadians at 2nd Ypres, was left alone. Martin Gilbert, *The First World War* (New York: Henry Holt, 1994), 539.

6 Cartoon cited in H.A. Wilson and J.A. Hammerton, *The Great War,* vol. 12 (London: Amalgamated Press, 1918), 161. Letter quoted in Fredric J. Brown, *Chemical Warfare: A Study in Restraints* (Princeton, NJ: Princeton University Press, 1968), 13.

7 In comparison, the Germans had three chemical plants near the front alone that could produce over forty tons of liquid chlorine a day. Harold Hartley, "A General Comparison of British and German Methods of Gas Warfare," *Journal of the Royal Artillery* (February 1920): 494.

8 Ludwig Fritz Haber, *The Poisonous Cloud* (Oxford: Clarendon Press, 1986), 27, 42, 52.

9 Edward Spiers, *Chemical Warfare* (Chicago: University of Illinois Press, 1986), 18. Albert Palazzo, "Tradition, Innovation, and the Pursuit of the Decisive Battle: Poison Gas and the British Army on the Western Front, 1915-1918" (PhD diss., Ohio State University, 1996), 160.

10 C.R.M.F. Cruttwell, *A History of the Great War,* 2nd ed. (Oxford: Clarendon, 1936), 153-4, as cited in Hew Strachan, "'The Real War': Liddell Hart, Cruttwell, and Falls," in *The First World War and British Military History,* edited by Brian Bond (Oxford: Clarendon Press, 1991), 58.

11 The figures are given in Donald Richter, *Chemical Soldiers: British Gas Warfare in World War I* (Lawrence, KS: University Press of Kansas, 1992), 11; Moore, *Gas Attack,* 47. For a reprint of the appeal from the War Office see National Archives of Canada (NAC), RG 24, vol. 1837, GAQ 9-37, "Murderous Gases." Quote is from Major S.J.M. Auld, "Gassed," *Saturday Evening Post,* 25 May 1918.

12 The chemical solution consisted of sodium carbonate, sodium thiosulphate, and water. Augustin M. Prentiss, *Chemicals in War* (New York: McGraw-Hill, 1937), 534; Moore, *Gas Attack,* 46. Robert Graves, *Goodbye to All That* (London: Penguin Books, 1929), 91.

13 Macready quote from NAC, MG 30, E300, vol. 23, Victor Odlum Papers, File Gas Warfare, D.G. no. 280/2. For lack of training and the mistakes in using masks see Andy Thomas, *Effects of Chemical Warfare: A Select Bibliography of British State Papers* (London: Taylor and Francis, 1985), 12; Moore, *Gas Attack,* 56; Spiers, *Chemical Warfare,* 17.

14 NAC, RG 24, vol. 2528, HQC 1683.

15 Guy Chapman, *Vain Glory* (London: Cassell, 1937, 1968), 170.

16 NAC, RG 41, vol. 8, 10th battalion, Sid Cox, 1/2; Daniel G. Dancocks, *Welcome to Flanders Fields* (Toronto: McClelland and Stewart, 1988), 312.

17 Orders in NAC, RG 24, vol. 1867, folder 41, Routine Orders, 8 May 1915. For memories on testing see Herbert Rae, *Maple Leaves in Flanders Fields* (Toronto: William Briggs, 1916), 224 and 264. Gas veteran quoted in MG 30, E113, George Bell Papers, Memoirs, 31-2.

18 NAC, RG 9, vol. 3981, folder 2, file 3, lecture 2: Notes on Previous Gas Attack and Evolution of Helmet.

19 Auld, "Gassed"; Lefebure, *Riddle of the Rhine,* 121; SIPRI, *Problem of Chemical and Biological Warfare,* 1:53; Robert Harris and Jeremy Paxman, *A Higher Form of Killing* (London: Chatto and Windus, 1982), 17; Haber, *Poisonous Cloud,* 47.

20 Not to confuse the reader, but most reports refer to the soldier's gas helmet as simply a helmet. With the introduction of the small box respirator (SBR) in late 1916, the Canadian reports tend to refer to the soldier's gas apparatus (gas mask) as a respirator. This work will refer to the soldier's gas apparatus as a gas helmet when denoting the use of the Hypo, P-, and PH-helmets, and a respirator or gas mask following the introduction of the SBR.

21 The helmet was treated with hyposulphite of soda. For the assessment of the smell of the helmet, see Peter G. Rogers, ed., *Gunnery Ferguson's Diary* (Hantsport, NS: Lancelot Press, 1985), 31. The British officer's predicament is described in J.C. Dunn, *The War the Infantry Knew* (London: P.S. King and Son, 1938), 197.

22 The order to wear coats is in NAC, RG 9, vol. 4245, folder 5, file 19, G.479. Order to keep helmets clean is in RG 24, vol. 1867, folder 41, 2nd Army Circular No. A/734/74.

23 Irritation mentioned in NAC, RG 24, vol. 1867, folder 41, RO 681; RO 716; RO 710. Quotation in MG 30, E241, D.E. Macintyre Papers, Diary, 29 November 1915. Physiologists' warnings in RG 9, vol. 3981, folder 2, file 6, lecture 2: Notes on Previous Gas Attack and Evolution of Helmet.

24 Graves, *Goodbye to All That,* 165.

25 The P-helmet had an alcohol-based mixture added to it. In addition, sodium phenate, caustic soda, and glycerine were applied to the helmet's protective solution. NAC, RG 9, vol. 3981, folder 2, file 6, lecture 2: Notes on Previous Gas Attack and Evolution of Helmet. Quotation from Richard Adamson, *All for Nothing* (N.p.: Self-published, 1987), 38.

26 NAC, RG 41, vol. 7, 4th Battalion, G.S. Twigg, 5/3.

27 Memo in NAC, RG 9, vol. 4039, folder 10, file 15, untitled document dated 16 June 1915. Wilfred Brenton Kerr, *Shrieks and Crashes: Being Memoirs of Canada's Corps 1917* (Toronto: Hunter Rose, 1929), 130-1.

28 NAC, RG 9, vol. 3751, War Diary of Major G.S. Strathy, CAMC, 25. The twenty-minute figure was told to him by a medical gas officer during an 8 April 1916 gas lecture.

29 Adamson, *All for Nothing,* 42. Erich Maria Remarque described similar feelings of terror from the perspective of a German soldier on the receiving end of a British gas cloud: "These first-minutes with the mask decide between life and death: is it air-tight? I remember the awful sights in the hospital: the gas patients who in day-long suffocation cough up their burnt lungs in clots." *All Quiet on the Western Front* (New York: Fawcett Crest, 1929), 68.

30 Rogers, ed., *Gunnery Ferguson's Diary,* 31. Armine Norris, *Mainly for Mother* (Toronto: Ryerson Press, 1919), 19.

31 The Germans used bromine; the French and English, who lacked the material, were forced to use variations of iodine. The principal lachrymators used during the war were: bromoacetone, bromomethylethylketone, benzyl bromide, ethyl iodoacetate, bromobenzyl cyanide, and phenyl carbylamine chloride. Modern American studies estimate that soldiers in chemical

protection suits have their combat efficiency reduced by 50 to 80 percent and are subject to rapid heat exhaustion. Richard A. Gabriel, *No More Heroes: Madness and Psychiatry in War* (New York: Hill and Wang, 1987), 38.

32 R.J. Manion, *A Surgeon in Arms* (New York: Doran, 1918), 72. On the effect see Dunlap Pearce Penhallow, *Military Surgery* (London: Oxford University Press, 1918), 506.

33 NAC, RG 9, vol. 1346, 2 CD-GS 20.

34 John Keegan, *The Face of Battle* (London: Pimlico, 1976), 71.

35 Tactical expectations discussed in Moore, *Gas Attack*, 87; T.J. Gander, *Nuclear, Biological, and Chemical Warfare* (London: Ian Allan, 1987), 14. Quotation from SIPRI, *Problem of Chemical and Biological Warfare*, 1:31.

36 State of Russian industry discussed in Asprey, *German High Command at War*, 42. Russian saying quoted in Joachim Krause and Charles K. Mallory, *Chemical Weapons in Soviet Military Doctrine* (Boulder, CO: Westview Press, 1992), 19. Figures on gas use from Haber, *Poisonous Cloud*, 39. Casualties given in Gander, *Nuclear, Biological, and Chemical Warfare*, 16.

37 Falkenhayn believed it was the Western Front where the war would be won or lost. When the duo of Hindenburg and Ludendorff took command of the General Staff in 1916, they too concentrated gas against the Allies, and mostly the British, on the Western Front.

38 Asquith's letter in Thomas, *Effects of Chemical Warfare*, 9. For chemical officer's advice, see Haber, *Poisonous Cloud*, 48. Formal instruction discussed in Foulkes, *Gas*, 90-1.

39 Foulkes remembered being interviewed by General Robertson, chief of staff to Sir John French: "'Do you know anything about gas?' he asked, to which I replied quite truthfully, 'Nothing at all.' 'Well, I don't think it matters,' he went on; 'I want you to take charge of our gas reprisals here in France.'" Foulkes, *Gas*, 17. This was juxtaposed with the Germans, who were led by the world-renowned scientist Dr. Fritz Haber. For a good overview of Foulkes and the Special Companies see Richter's *Chemical Soldiers* and Foulkes's *Gas*.

40 Churchill argued with Kitchener that gas should be used on the Gallipoli front as the Turks were without gas masks, but the War Committee believed that it would result in British prisoners of war being murdered for reprisal. General Smuts also requested gas to be used in his South African campaign but declined its use when he found that the canisters were difficult to transport. The minutes from the Dardanelles Committee and the War Committee Papers as quoted in Thomas, *Effects of Chemical Warfare*, 18-20. Churchill was mistaken. Preparing for a British gas attack at Gallipoli the Germans had issued anti-gas instructions to the Turks. NAC, MG 30, E300, vol. 23, Victor Odlum Papers, File Gas Warfare, Translation of a Document Captured from the Enemy in the Dardanelles on the 21st Nov., 1915. Containing Instructions with a View to Guarding against a Gas Attack.

41 For Castner-Kellner production figures, see Thomas, *Effects of Chemical Warfare*, 13. Training is discussed in Guy Hartcup, *The War of Invention* (London: Brassey's Defence Publishers, 1988), 98; Haber, *Poisonous Cloud*, 53.

42 Work of corporals discussed in Malcolm Brown, *The Imperial War Museum Book of the Western Front* (London: Sidgwick and Jackson, 1993), 77. For gas merchant's comment, see NAC, MG 30, E16, W.H. Hewgill Papers, Diary, 19 December 1916.

43 Richter, *Chemical Soldiers*, 21.

44 Richard Holmes, *The Little Field-Marshall: Sir John French* (London: Cape, 1981), 300, refers to British self-deception. Charteris is quoted in Jones, "Under a Green Sea, Part 1," 132.

45 The British would eventually employ six types of canistered gas, but relied heavily on chlorine and phosgene. The six types, and the symbols by which they were identified, were: chlorine (Red Star); a mixture of sulphuretted hydrogen and carbon disulphide (Two Red Star); a mixture of phosgene and chlorine (White Star); a mixture of sulphur chloride and chlorine (Blue Star); a mixture of chloropicrin and chlorine (Yellow Star); a mixture of chloropicrin and sulphuretted hydrogen (Green Star). NAC, RG 9, vol. 3976, folder 5, file 6, DGS A/148, List of Key Names to Chemical Substances.

46 Dunn, *War the Infantry Knew*, 146; for Gough see Richter, *Chemical Soldiers*, 32, 87.

47 For information to officers, see Dunn, *War the Infantry Knew*, 151. Protection offered by helmets in Simon Jones, "Under a Green Sea, Part II," *The Great War* 2, 1 (1989): 14-5. On German lessons see Haber, *Poisonous Cloud*, 38-9; Moore, *Gas Attack*, 89.

48 As quoted from the diary of Sir Douglas Haig, in Lyn Macdonald, *1914-1918: Voices and Images of the Great War* (London: M. Joseph, 1988), 102. On the weather forecast see Denis Winter, *Haig's Command* (New York: Viking, 1991), 39-40. Graves, *Goodbye to All That*, 123.

49 Martin van Creveld, *Technology and War* (London: Free Press, 1989), 223; Shelford Bidwell and Dominick Graham, *Firepower: British Army Weapons and Theories of War, 1904-1945* (London: George Allen and Unwin, 1982), 2-3.

50 The pipes were eventually replaced with flexible rubber pipes in 1916.

51 Jones, "Under a Green Sea, Part II," 17.

52 For Thomas quotation, see Richter, *Chemical Soldiers*, 77. The German response is described in F.A. Hessel, *Chemistry in Warfare* (New York: Hastings House, 1940), 86.

53 Graves, *Goodbye to All That*, 131.

54 Quoted in Malcolm Brown, *The Imperial War Museum Book of the Western Front* (London: Sidgwick and Jackson, 1993), 82.

55 Harris and Paxman, *Higher Form of Killing*, 14-5; Heller, *Chemical Warfare*, 11; Thomas, *Effects of Chemical Warfare*, 16. In addition to the psychological fears of gas, there were 2,632 British gas casualties from their own gas. Many of these were light in nature or subsequently found to be intentional or unintentional malingers. Haber, *Poisonous Cloud*, 57; Foulkes, *Gas*, 93; Jones, "Under a Green Sea, Part II," 16.

56 Moore, *Gas Attack*, 86. The new German drum mask was made of rubberized fabric. A drum filled with neutralizing agents and layers of crushed brick or pumice stone was attached to the lower part of the mask. The gas helmet worked well, except that it relied on an air-tight fit to keep out poison. When soldiers went into the front line, the masks fit well enough, but after any length of time spent in the carnage of the Western Front, with the lack of proper food and sleep, along with the fear and the general stress of shells and bullets, the men lost weight. Thus, some of the gas masks gradually lost their air-tight seal and men became gassed while wearing their respirators.

57 Richter, *Chemical Soldiers*, 50.

58 Ibid., 123. This was seconded by Frederick Manning's anti-hero, Bourne, who found carrying the canisters a miserable job. Frederick Manning, *Her Privates We* (London: Readers Union, 1965), 57.

59 Jones, "Under a Green Sea, Part II," 16.

60 For transportation strategies, see Report of the Ministry, *Overseas Military Forces of Canada, 1918* (London, 1918), 256. Quotation in Richter, *Chemical Soldiers*, 134.

61 "That's what the infantry feared," British gas specialist Edwards-Ker remembered, "that with the gas laid in there might be a shell that would split open a cylinder." Richter, *Chemical Soldiers*, 184.

62 See Tony Ashworth, *Trench Warfare: The Live and Let Live System* (New York: Holmes and Meier, 1980).

63 For mock gas attack, see NAC, RG 24, vol. 1859, file CWM WWF 34, Loos; Hessel, *Chemistry in Warfare*, 97-8. Quotation in RG 9, vol. 4098, folder 42, file 1, Summary of Operations, 2nd Canadian Division.

64 NAC, MG 30, E113, George Bell Papers, Memoirs, 63-4.

65 Ibid., E75, H.M. Urquhart Papers, vol. 2, file 3, Harrington to Kearsley, 27 November 1915. Captured German documents show that they too had begun to see other uses for gas shells. RG 9, vol. 4098, folder 42, file 2, CD-GS 78, Memorandum regarding the Employment of Gas Shells.

66 The Canadian Corps was issued a report on the failure of the gas attack at Loos. NAC, RG 9, vol. 4098, folder 42, file 1, 2 CD-GS 67.

67 For trench foot, see NAC, RG 41, vol. 7, 3rd Battalion, H.S. Cooper, 3/16; Desmond Morton, "Military Medicine: Historical Notes on the Canadian Army Medical Corps in the First World War, 1914-1919," in *Canadian Health Care*, edited by C. David Naylor (Montreal: McGill-Queen's University Press, 1992), 46. Report citing officer responsibility for gassing in RG 9, vol. 4263, folder 12, file 1, CRAC 77464/7 (G).

68 NAC, RG 9, vol. 4043, folder 1, file 18, BM 572. There is a good account of this initial struggle to create a firm anti-gas doctrine in Herbert Rae, *Maple Leaves in Flanders Fields* (Toronto: William Briggs, 1916), 224.

69 Foulkes, *Gas*, 100-2; NAC, RG 9, vol. 3975, folder 1, file 16, "Demonstration with Ayrton Fans"; Moore, *Gas Attack*, 93. On the black boxes, see Auld, "Gassed."

70 Auld, "Gassed." See Gibson for an amusing account of officers being ordered to pick up Vermorel sprayers, and having no clue what they were for or how they were to be used. Gibson, *Maple Leaves*, 261-4.

71 The gas cloud contained 25 percent phosgene and 75 percent chlorine. Phosgene's rate of evaporation was too high for the chemical to be used by itself. Within months the mixture of gas clouds would be 50/50. For casualties, see Harris and Paxman, *Higher Form of Killing*, 17; Moore, *Gas Attack*, 89. NAC, RG 9, vol. 4349, folder 6, file 1, GX 758, and Peter Vansittart, *John Masefield's Letters from the Front, 1915-1917* (New York: Franklin Watts, 1985), 16 April 1917, for describing the difficulty in smelling the phosgene.

72 For failure of warning, see NAC, RG 9, vol. 4115, folder 1, file 15, Secret memo from J.L. Keir dated 20 December 1915. For speed of gas, see Harris and Paxman, *Higher Form of Killing*, 17.

73 NAC, RG 9, vol. 4349, folder 6, file 1, Medical Report on the Recent Gas Attack on 19th December.

74 Although most of the gas victims were killed by phosgene, it was mustard gas that caused hundreds of thousands of casualties. Hessel, *Chemistry in Warfare*, 87; Gander, *Nuclear, Biological, and Chemical Warfare*, 70.

Chapter 3: A Higher Form of Killing

1 The efficiency and effectiveness in the German production of this new gas is indicated by the fact that five future Nobel laureates were involved in the chemical warfare program, including Fritz Haber, whose comments on winning the Nobel Prize for Chemistry open this chapter. Ulrich Trumpener, "The Road to Ypres: The Beginnings of Gas Warfare in World War I," *Journal of Modern History*, 47 (September 1975), 464, 466, 471.

2 National Archives of Canada (NAC), MG 30, E241, D.E. Macintyre Papers, Diary, 19 December 1915.

3 Department of National Defence, Directorate of History and Heritage, Leslie Arthur Catchpole Papers, Diary, 31-2.

4 James Edmonds, *Military Operations, France and Belgium, 1916*, 2 vols., History of the Great War in Public Documents series (London: Macmillan, 1932-8), 161.

5 NAC, RG 9, vol. 4115, folder 1, file 15, Report by J.L. Kerr, 20 December 1915.

6 Ibid., vol. 3618, file 25-13-6, Professor Dr. Rudolf Staehelin, "After-Effects upon the Respiratory Organs of War Gas Poisoning," February 1920, 2.

7 Ibid., vol. 4158, folder 1, file 12, Report on the Gas Attack on December 19th, 1915, 1-2.

8 See ibid., vol. 3751, War Diary of Major G.S. Strathy, 44, for one example.

9 For MacBrien report see ibid., vol. 4158, folder 1, file 12, A.B. 227. HQ orders in vol. 4129, folder 5, file 13, Memo to 27th Battalion, 20 December 1915. NCOs for anti-gas defence in vol. 3831, folder 14, file 16, 2nd Army No. AB 238.

10 For fraternization, see Ekstein, *Rites of Spring* (Toronto: Lester and Orpen Dennys, 1989), 109-28. Quotation from NAC, MG 30, E241, D.E. Macintyre Papers, Diary, 20 October 1915.

11 G.W.L. Nicholson, *Canadian Expeditionary Force, 1914-1919* (Ottawa: Roger Duhamel, Queen's Printer and Controller of Stationary, 1962), 136.

12 NAC, RG 9, vol. 4349, folder 6, file 1, 2 CD-GS 293, 2 CD-GS 266.

13 For klaxon horns, see ibid., vol. 4158, folder 1, file 12, C.655/1. Quotation in Alexander McClintock, *Best o' Luck* (Toronto: McClelland, Goodchild and Stewart, 1917), 48-9.

14 Precautions in NAC, RG 9, vol. 4129, folder 5, file 13, GS-325; vol. 4158, folder 1, file 12, A.41.1; C.655/1; vol. 4032, folder 1, file 14, Amendments to S.S. 193, Standing Orders for Defence against Gas, and SS 534, Defence against Gas, Appendix IV. For sign posts, see Guy Chapman, *Vain Glory* (London: Cassell, 1937, 1968), 436.

15 For alert zone, see NAC, RG 9, vol. 3976, folder 4, file 8, XIX Corps No. G 609/3, Gas Attack Warnings. Letter home quoted in Armine Norris, *Mainly for Mother* (Toronto: Ryerson Press, 1919), 119.

16 G.W.L. Nicholson, *The Fighting Newfoundlanders* (St. John's: Government of Newfoundland, 1964), 296.

17 Montague quoted in Richard Holmes, *Firing Line* (London: Pimlico, 1985), 115.

18 NAC, RG 9, vol. 4182, folder 33, file 1, 8th Canadian Brigade Report; MG 30, E241, D.E. Macintyre Papers, Diary, 18 May 1916.

19 NAC, MG 30, E111, Walter Robert Rigsby Papers, file 1, Diary, 5 March [1918?].

20 For establishment of British Gas Services, see Edmonds, *Military Operations*, 78; Charles H. Foulkes, *Gas: The Story of the Special Brigade* (London: William B. Blackwood and Sons, 1936), 97. Cummins had unofficially been working on anti-gas measures since the first gassing in April 1915. In June 1917, Thuillier was promoted to command of the 15th Division and Foulkes succeeded him as director of Gas Services.

21 Grace Morris Craig, *But This Is Our War* (Toronto: University of Toronto Press, 1981), 54.

22 As quoted in Martin van Creveld, *Technology and War* (London: Free Press, 1989), 225.

23 Haber remarks that it is difficult to ascertain when the French fired their first lethal gas shells, but it is generally accepted to have been on 21 February 1916 in an attempt to slow the German advance. Regardless, there were very few lethal shells, and when they were produced in greater numbers, they were filled with Vincennite (VN), which was not nearly as effective as had been hoped. Foulkes quotes a British report that listed lethal shells in which "VN is a bad last." The French, unable to accept that their VN gas shells were almost useless, used them throughout the war. Ludwig Fritz Haber, *The Poisonous Cloud* (Oxford: Clarendon Press, 1986), 94-5; Foulkes, *Gas*, 107.

24 For Fleury statistics, see Edward Spiers, *Chemical Warfare* (Chicago: University of Illinois Press, 1986), 23; Haber, *Poisonous Cloud*, 96. The sound is described in NAC, RG 9, vol. 4039, folder 10, file 15, OB 492; British trench soldier Edmund Blunden described gas shells as having a "hypocritical tunelessness" in flight and in explosion. Edmund Blunden, *Undertones of War* (London: Cox and Wyman, 1928), 196. Casualties are discussed in Alistar Horne, *The Price of Glory* (London: Penguin Books, 1962), 284.

25 Arnold Zweig, *Education before Verdun* (New York: Viking Press, 1936), 148-9.

26 One estimate of casualties during the First World War declared that shells and mortar bombs caused 58.51 percent of British casualties, bullets 38.98 percent, bombs and grenades 2.19 percent, and bayonets only .32 percent. Conspicuously absent from such figures are the gas casualties. With over 200,000 in the British Army it is clear that they would be higher then bayonets and bombs combined. Holmes, *Firing Line*, 210. Historian John English has also written that in the Great War artillery accounted for more than 60 percent of all casualties. John A. English, *Marching through Chaos: The Descent of Armies in Theory and Practice* (Westport, CT: Praeger, 1996), 56.

27 Robert Graves, *Goodbye to All That* (London: Penguin Books, 1929), 96-7.

28 A poignant passage in Erich Maria Remarque's *All Quiet on the Western Front* (New York: Fawcett Crest, 1929), 68, illustrates the same point.

29 Victor Wheeler, *The 50th Battalion in No Man's Land* (Calgary: Alberta Historical Resources, 1980), 223.

30 Burns quoted in James L. McWilliams and R. James Steel, *The Suicide Battalion* (Edmonton: Hurtig, 1978), 103.

31 For "tobacco reaction," see NAC, RG 9, vol. 3976, folder 5, file 13, "Phosgene (Carbonyl Chloride)"; vol. 4029, folder 10, file 15, Secret memo from Commanding Officer of 3rd Battalion. F. McKelvey Bell, a Canadian orderly, remarked on the Canadian soldier's affection for his cigarette: "To him the cigarette is the panacea for all ills. I have seen men die with a cigarette between their lips – the last favour they had requested on earth. If the soldier is in pain, he smokes for comfort; when he receives good news, he smokes for joy; if the news is bad, he smokes for consolation; if he is well – he smokes; when he is ill – he smokes. But good news or bad, sick or well, he always smokes" F. McKelvey Bell, *The First Canadians in France* (Toronto: McClelland, Goodchild and Stewart, 1917), 127.

32 For Haig's demands, see Edmonds, *Military Operations*, 80; Spiers, *Chemical Warfare*, 23. Gas shell statistics found in Augustin M. Prentiss, *Chemicals in War* (New York: McGraw-Hill, 1937), 656.

33 For a discussion of incompetence at St. Eloi, see Tim Cook, "The Blind Leading the Blind: The Battle of St. Eloi Craters," *Canadian Military History* 5, 2 (1996). For Alderson's replacement, see Nicholson, *Canadian Expeditionary Force*, 144-7; A.M.J. Hyatt, *General Sir Arthur Currie* (Toronto: University of Toronto Press in collaboration with the Canadian War Museum, Canadian Museum of Civilization, and National Museums of Canada, 1987), 54-7; Desmond Morton, *A Peculiar Kind of Politics* (Toronto: University of Toronto Press, 1982), 73-5. "Murder

hole" quotation from Reginald H. Roy, *The Journal of Private Fraser* (Victoria: Sono Nis Press, 1985), 109.

34 The Canadian Corps began to receive their first PH-helmets on 4 February 1916. NAC, RG 24, vol. 1811, GAQ 3-3. The Germans had been refining their gas-cloud tactics and, although moving toward gas shells, they continued to use gas canisters until the end of 1916. For a description of this gas cloud attack see Edmonds, *Military Operations*, 193-8.

35 NAC, RG 9, vol. 4115, folder 1, file 15, Notes on Gas Attacks by Enemy on First Army Front on 27th and 29th April, 1916. Quotation from vol. 4029, folder 10, file 15, G.449; vol. 4182, folder 33, file 1, Secret memo from Lt. Gen. L.E. Kiggell to 6th Infantry Brigade, 2 May 1916.

36 British Headquarters order in NAC, RG 9, vol. 4311, folder 3, file 1, Report by Medical Officer of the 4th CFA Brigade; vol. 4039, folder 10, file 15, No. AB 306. Irritation caused by helmets is in vol. 4029, folder 10, file 15, G.198 and AC 219.

37 Foulkes, *Gas*, 309. Two days later the Germans released a second gas attack, which blew back over their lines when the wind turned. Thuillier estimated that the Germans suffered 1,200 casualties, a figure more than likely gained through his own gas intelligence and probably inflated. Sir Henry F. Thuillier, *Gas in the Next War* (London: Geoffrey Bles, 1938), 35.

38 NAC, RG 9, vol. 4311, folder 3, file 1, OA 836. Major Peat of the CAMC noted that his casualty clearing station received sixty-five gas cases, of which six died in his care. G.B. Peat, "The Effects of Gassing as Seen at a Casualty Clearing Station," *Canadian Medical Association Journal* 8, 1 (1918): 17-22.

39 Green troops quotation from Ernest Black, *I Want One Volunteer* (Toronto: Ryerson, 1965), 85. NAC, RG 41, vol. 11, G.V. Francoeur, 22nd Battalion, 1/5.

40 Veteran's prank in Charles Heller, *Chemical Warfare in World War I: The American Experience, 1917-1918*, Leavenworth Papers no. 10 (Fort Leavenworth, KS: Combat Studies Institute, 1984), 40. NAC, RG 41, vol. 11, G.V. Francoeur, 22nd Battalion, 1/5, for sleeping in gas mask.

41 Sir W.G. Macpherson, *Official History of the War: Medical Services Diseases of the War*, vol. 2 (London: HMSO, 1923), 282 (hereafter BOMH), 330-1. The DGO was to report to the army chemical advisor. NAC, RG 9, vol. 4039, folder 10, file 15, DRO 2099. Quotation from vol. 3979, folder 12, file 3, 705 (G).

42 This publication is the 1916 revision of the 1914 manual. B.C. Battye, *Some Notes on the Minor Tactics of Trench Warfare with Special Reference to the Co-operation of Infantry and Engineers, 1914* (Ottawa: Government Printing Bureau, 1916), 3.

43 For DGO's responsibilities, see NAC, RG 9, vol. 3979, folder 12, file 3, 705 (G). Quotation is from Heller, *Chemical Warfare*, 40. Numbers given in RG 9, vol. 3979, folder 12, file 3, CH 3/81.

44 NAC, RG 24, vol. 20543, file 990.013 (D11), U.S. Army Chemical Corps Historical Studies, Gas Warfare in World War I, The 26th Division East of the Meuse, September 1918, 18.

45 Ibid., vol. 1815, file GAQ 4-40 pt. 2, "Extract from *The Khaki Call*" Winnipeg, Feb. 1928, vol. 12, no. 1, "Lieutenant-General Sir Edwin Alderson, K.G.B.: A Brave Commander Who Was Sacrificed to the Ross Rifle," by Major-General The Honourable W.A. Griesbach. Anthony Kellett, *Combat Motivation: The Behaviour of Soldiers in Battle* (Boston: Kluwer-Nijhoff, 1982), 84, contains psychiatric studies agreeing with Griesbach. On the Colt machine gun see Bill Rawling, "Technology in Search of a Role: The Machine Gun and the CEF in the First World War," *Material History Review* 42 (Fall 1995): 89.

46 For BGOs' responsibilities, see NAC, RG 9, vol. 4098, folder 42, file 3, G.53. NCO training in vol. 4129, G.776.

47 For NCOs' responsibilities, see ibid., vol. 4336, folder 13, file 13, BM 722; vol. 3831, folder 13, file 4, G.903; Alan Brooksbank, an Australian Gas NCO during the war, wrote a book in the mid-1930s describing the need for gas precautions in the next war. There is an interesting section on the duties of gas officers and the importance of smell and sight in distinguishing gases. Alan Brooksbank, *Gas Alert!* (Melbourne: Robertson and Mullens, 1938). Quotation from RG 9, vol. 4129, G.776.

48 NAC, RG 41, vol. 7, 4th Battalion, Wright, 6/15.

49 Ibid., RG 9, vol. 4129, folder 5, file 13, Defensive Measures against Gas.

50 F.A. McKenzie, *Through the Hindenburg Line* (London: Hodder and Stoughton, 1918), 313.

51 For bombardment, see NAC, RG 9, vol. 4947, file 467 (1), War Diary of the 4th CMR, 2 June

1916. Destruction recorded in Nicholson, *Canadian Expeditionary Force,* 148-9. Casualties found in RG 9, vol. 4947, file 467 (1), War Diary of the 4th CMR, 2 June 1916; Nicholson, *Canadian Expeditionary Force,* 149.

52 For use of gas see NAC, RG 41, vol. 15, 52nd Battalion, Morgan, 1/9; Larry Worthington, *Amid the Guns Below* (Toronto: McClelland and Stewart, 1965), 48; Reginald Grant, *S.O.S. – Stand To!* (New York: Appleton, 1918), 112-5; NAC, MG 30, E523, Sprague Family Papers, Melburne Sprague letter to Jim and Eva, 9 November 1916.

53 Caw letter quoted in *Letters from the Front: Being a Record of the Part Played by Officers of the Bank in the Great War,* vol. 1, edited by Charles Lyons Foster (Toronto: Canadian Imperial Bank of Commerce, 1919), 143. NAC, RG 41, vol. 16, 85th Battalion, A.Y. Jackson, 3/2. For Winslow's death, see RG 9, vol. 3618, file 25-13-6, "His Death Due to German Gas," *Toronto Globe,* 31 April 1922.

54 NAC, MG 30, E16, W.H. Hewgill Papers, Memoir, 29; D.J. Goodspeed, "Prelude to the Somme: Mount Sorrel, June, 1916," in *Policy by Other Means,* edited by Michael Cross and Robert Bothwell (Toronto: Clarke Irwin, 1972), 156; NAC, RG 9, vol. 4688, folder 40, file 16, 2nd Canadian Infantry Brigade Describing the Operations in the Ypres Salient from 2nd June to June 14th 1916.

55 By mid-1918 he was still bedridden from his gas poisoning a year and half earlier. NAC, RG 9, vol. 3618, Director of Medical Services, file 25-13-6, Medical Report on Pte. George Wadsworth.

56 NAC, RG 9, vol. 3618, Director of Medical Services, file 25-13-6, 26.

57 Quotation in NAC, MG 30, E31, T.B. Smith Papers, "Clearing: The Tale of the First Canadian Casualty Clearing Station," 114. For gas-proofing, see RG 9, vol. 4098, folder 42, file 1, G.567. Limitations of PH-helmet in MG 30, E300, vol. 23, Victor Odlum Papers, file Gas Warfare, G.382.

58 Most important, the barrage contained too many shrapnel shells, which could not cut the barbed wire, and too few HE shells to cave in the defenders' dugouts. John Keegan has an excellent analysis of why the artillery barrage failed. John Keegan, *The Face of Battle* (London: Pimlico, 1976), 227-37.

59 Nicholson, *Canadian Expeditionary Force,* 163.

60 The British had trouble manufacturing phosgene; its first use against the Germans was in June 1916. Thuillier, *Gas in the Next War,* 32. NAC, RG 9, vol. 3977, folder 8, file 1, OB/308, Some Lessons from the Recent Employment of Gas in the Attack; Haber, *Poisonous Cloud,* 92.

61 Foulkes, *Gas,* 139.

62 Malcolm Brown, *The Imperial War Museum Book of the Western Front* (London: Sidgwick and Jackson, 1993), 117.

63 Smoke was discharged from smoke pots, smoke candles, mortars, and artillery shells. F.A. Hessel, *Chemistry in Warfare* (New York: Hastings House, 1940), 97-9.

64 For soldiers' dislike of gas near the front lines, see Wheeler, *50th Battalion,* 102; statistics in Foulkes, *Gas,* 109.

65 Quotation in NAC, RG 9, vol. 4098, folder 42, file 1, OB 308, Effect of Recent Gas Attacks on the Enemy. Delayed death of German prisoner recounted in Robert Harris and Jeremy Paxman, *A Higher Form of Killing* (London: Chatto and Windus, 1982), 19. For German report, see MG 30, E300, vol. 23, Victor Odlum Papers, File Defence II, Experience of the German 1st Army in the Somme Battle by General Von Below.

66 NAC, RG 9, vol. 3978, folder 9, file 15, SB/IO/51, Monthly Return of Evidence of Effect of Our Gas on the Enemy.

67 Ibid., vol. 3977, folder 7, file 2, CHF/V/38, Report on an Interview with a Repatriated (Dr. Colle) Re the Medical Aspect of German Gas Casualties; by early 1917 the Germans had realized the danger of sending men gassed by phosgene walking to the rear. Vol. 3976, folder 4, file 16, Captured Document: Gas Defence and First Aid for Gas Cases.

68 For gas as psychological weapon, see NAC, RG 9, vol. 4098, folder 42, file 1, OB 308, Effect of Recent Gas Attacks on the Enemy. For the German Army getting worst of gas warfare see vol. 3978, folder 9, file 15, SB/IO/51.

69 NAC, RG 9, vol. 3976, folder 5, file 16, SB/IO/28, Translation of Extracts of German Documents concerning Gas, Offensive and Defensive.

70 NAC, MG 30, E400, C.V. Williams fonds, letter, 12 August 1916.

71 Richard Adamson, *All for Nothing* (N.p.: Self-published, 1987), 41-2.

72 Roy, *Journal of Private Fraser*, 188.

73 The 4th Division was formed from units already in England and from troops arriving from Canada. It was officially established on 26 April 1916. Nicholson, *Canadian Expeditionary Force*, 134. For the training of reinforcements see Report of the Ministry, *Overseas Military Forces of Canada, 1918* (London, 1918), 9-16.

74 For "special" gas instruction, see Nicholson, *Canadian Expeditionary Force*, 155. Gisli P. Norman, *True Experiences in World War I* (Manitoba: Vini Norman, 1988), 15.

75 For Canadian gunner see *Letters from the Front*, 149. Private Pett discussed in NAC, RG 9, vol. 3618, file 25-13-6, Director of Medical Services. Wounded at Mount Sorrel, A. Selwood ran a gas-testing hut for new troops and remembered having to go in and fish out men after "they'd get panicky." NAC, RG 41, 72nd Battalion, A. Selwood, 2/5.

76 For Garrison, see NAC, RG 41, vol. 14, 44th Battalion, Ted Garrison, 2/8. Quotation from RG 9, vol. 4332, folder 4, file 1, G.8-124.

77 NAC, MG 30, E300, vol. 23, Victor Odlum Papers, File "Gas Warfare," G.32; NAC, RG 9, vol. 4329, folder 14, file 4, G.33.

78 TABLE N.2

The lethality of gas clouds, 1915-6

Date	Total gas casualties	Total deaths	Death per 100 casualties
19 December 1915	1,069	120	11.2
27, 29 April 1916	1,260	338	26.8
30 April 1916	512	89	17.4
17 June 1916	562	95	17.0
8 August 1916	804	371	46.2

Source: Sir W.G. Macpherson, *Official History of the War: Medical Services Diseases of the War*, vol. 2 (London: BOMH, 1923), 282.

79 Casualty figures from Foulkes, *Gas*, 310 and BOMH, 283; Byng quotation in NAC, RG 9, vol. 4332, folder 4, file 1, G.10. For trench learning, see NAC, RG 9, vol. 4329, folder 14, file 4, G.33.

80 For training, see Gordon Howard, *Sixty Years of Centennial in Saskatchewan, 1906-1968* (N.p.: Self-published, 1968), 46; NAC, RG 41, vol. 7, 1st Battalion, Colonel Alley, 2/9. For duties and conditions at the front, see vol. 8, 5th Battalion, R.L. Christopherson, 2/10 and F.C. Bagshaw, 3/6.

81 Ian Hogg, *Gas* (New York: Ballantine Books, 1975), 48.

82 NAC, RG 9, vol. 4043, folder 1, file 4, "White Star" Hand Grenade. In the summer of 1917 after a British officer was killed by a grenade he was examining by a fire, all ranks in the BEF were warned about gas grenades. This did little to endear them to the infantry. Ibid., 2-91. Nickname given in Haber, *Poisonous Cloud*, 51.

83 NAC, RG 41, vol. 7, 3rd Battalion, Colonel Mason, 1/10; vol. 7, 4th Battalion, Chas Brown, 1/17; Nicholson, *Canadian Expeditionary Force*, 198. Walker letter quoted in J. Clinton Morrison Jr, *Hell upon Earth: A Personal Account of Prince Edward Island Soldiers in the Great War, 1914-1918* (N.p.: Self-published, 1995), 70.

84 BOMH, 288; Haber, *Poisonous Cloud*, 97; Harold Hartley, "A General Comparison of British and German Methods of Gas Warfare," *Journal of the Royal Artillery* (February 1920): 494. Establishment of schools from German General Schwarte in Foulkes, *Gas*, 321.

85 Herbert W. McBride, *A Rifleman Went to War* (Plantersville, SC: Small-Arms Technical Publishing, 1935), 161-2. Gas casualties from Casualties by Days – France and Belgium – CEF in France, NAC, RG 150, series 9; RG 9, vol. 4215, folder 3, file 11, CRAC77464/7 (G). 1. Quotation about officers from Peter G. Rogers, ed., *Gunnery Ferguson's Diary* (Hantsport, NS: Lancelot Press, 1985), 112.

86 DeGroot makes this point with officers reluctantly accepting the steel helmets for the same

reason. Surely the more dehumanizing effects of the gas mask would be even more critically viewed. Gerard J. DeGroot, *Blighty* (London: Longman, 1996), 166.

87 The PH-helmet was dipped in a chemical solution of alcohol, 45 percent; glycerine, 25 percent; sodium phenate, 15 percent; caustic soda, 10 percent; and hexamine, 5 percent. NAC, RG 9, vol. 3977, folder 6, file 13, "Lecture – P.H. Helmet."

88 Ibid., vol. 3959, folder 15, file 9, G.263.

89 For gassing of horses, see ibid., vol. 3374, G-2-45. Of the 555 casualties, 76 had been gassed. Arnold Warren, *Wait for the Wagon: The Story of the Royal Canadian Army Service Corps* (Toronto: McClelland and Stewart, 1961), 115.

90 BEF warning in NAC, RG 9, vol. 4263, folder 12, file 1, GA 12/1/36. For Hindenburg program, see Victor Lefebure, *The Riddle of the Rhine* (London: W. Collins Sons, 1921), 66.

91 NAC, RG 9, vol. 4688, folder 4, file 18, Summary of Minor Operations: Night 14th/15th December [1916] by 2nd Canadian Infantry Brigade. The raid was not an aberration, as the 8th Battalion carried out an assault on 27 November 1916 to obtain information, cause loss, and "ascertain whether the enemy trench contains gas cylinders." NAC, RG 9, vol. 4065, folder 2, file 17, 8th Canadian Infantry Battalion Preliminary Operation Order No. A. See report entitled, "Canadian Intelligence Service," where it gives six objects for raids, one of which is to "ascertain the presence of gas apparatus [sic]." NAC, RG 24, vol. 6935, file Intelligence.

92 NAC, RG 9, vol. 3618, Director of Medical Services, file 25-13-6, 132.

93 Ibid., vol. 5048, folder 923, file 10, "Canadian Corps Gas Services 12.1.18."

94 Unlike the Canadian Corps, which kept the four Canadian divisions throughout the war (except for a brief period in early 1918), British Corps were constantly having divisions passing in and out of them. Thus, structural changes for the British generally developed at the divisional or army level.

95 The battalion gas officers seem to have been initially officers but later sergeants. Rank depended on the battalion, and there are examples of both filling the position. All the battalion gas officers had to have experience in chemistry or scientific degrees before they could be selected and trained at the divisional gas schools. NAC, RG 9, vol. 4182, folder 33, file 1, no. 1324/77.

96 Quotation in NAC, MG 30, E521, W.J. Wright Papers, letter to a Mr. Martin, n.d. On taking air samples, see RG 9, vol. 3981, folder 15, file 8, Gas Sampling Bulb; RG 24, vol. 22,005, Pamphlet, Anti-Gas Duties within an Infantry Battalion, September 1916.

97 Quotation from Ernst Junger, *Storm of Steel* (London: Chatto and Windus, 1929), 45. See Report of the Ministry, *Overseas Military Forces,* 228, for a list of duties to be carried out by the battalion gas officer. See SS 193, "Standing Orders for Defence against Gas," issued in October 1917 for the revised roles of gas NCOs. NAC, RG 9, vol. 3983, folder 2, file 16. For date of instigating battalion gas officers, see vol. 5048, folder 923, file 10, "Canadian Corps Gas Services 12.1.18."

98 The British went through seven gas masks and produced a total of fifty million masks throughout the war. Prentiss, *Chemicals in War,* 534. Hogg is wrong in asserting that the SBR was "produced for general issue in April 1916." Hogg, *Gas,* 73. The SBR was developed by Lieutenant-Colonel E.F. Harrison, an eminent chemist before the war, who died in 1918 from multiple prolonged exposures to gas. He had a memorial erected at the examination hall of the Pharmaceutical Society, Bloomsbury Square, following the war. NAC, RG 24, vol. 1837, GAQ 9-37, "Gas Mask Inventor," *Daily Mail,* 28 October 1921.

99 Donald Richter, *Chemical Soldiers: British Gas Warfare in World War I* (Lawrence, KS: University Press of Kansas, 1992), 141.

100 In Nicholson's Official History he writes that the SBR was issued in August 1916. This was true for some units in the British Army, but not for the Canadian Corps. Nicholson, *Canadian Expeditionary Force,* 71; NAC, RG 9, vol. 4129, folder 5, file 13, G.444; vol. 4080, folder 2, file 6, G.6-9. For example, the 10th Battalion received their SBRs on 22 November 1916. Daniel Dancocks, *Gallant Canadians* (Calgary: Calgary Highlanders Regimental Funds Foundation, 1990), 102.

101 NAC, MG 30, E389, W.J. O'Brien Papers, Diary, 11 and 13 December 1916; RG 9, vol. 3981, folder 2, file 6, OB/216.

102 George A. Maxwell, *Swan Song of a Rustic Moralist* (New York: Exposition Press, 1975), 90-1.

103 Heller, *Chemical Warfare,* 62.

104 Brown, *Western Front,* 41.

Chapter 4: Tough Guys

1 National Archives of Canada (NAC), RG 9, vol. 4060, folder 5, file 1, "Provisional Instructions Regarding Precautions against Hostile Gas Shells."

2 On training see Report of the Ministry, *Overseas Military Forces of Canada, 1918* (London, 1918), 11, and for Canadian gas officers, ibid., Appendix IVd, Organisation of the Gas Services, 283. The job of gas officer was left to fifteen gas NCOs supplied by the British. See NAC, RG 9, vol. 3081, file G-13-36 vol. 2, War Office letter no. 121/1/238 for British HE order. For investigation of new recruits see vol. 4129, folder 5, file 13, Letter reference 5927 dated 18 July 1916 and reply 19 July 1916.

3 A.C. Critchley, *Critch!* (London: Hutchinson, 1961), 68, 72; Desmond Morton, *When Your Number's Up* (Toronto: Random House, 1993), 76.

4 T.W.L. MacDermont, *The Seventh* (Montreal: Seventh Canadian Siege Battery Association, 1953), 58.

5 Charles Heller, *Chemical Warfare in World War I: The American Experience, 1917-1918,* Leavenworth Papers no. 10 (Fort Leavenworth, KS: Combat Studies Institute, 1984), 62; John Baynes, *Morale: A Study of Men and Courage* (London: Cassell, 1967), 195-6.

6 NAC, RG 9, vol. 3981, folder 18, file 12, N 4/35612; Denis Winter, *Death's Men* (London: Penguin Books, 1979), 125.

7 Ludwig Fritz Haber, *The Poisonous Cloud* (Oxford: Clarendon Press, 1986), 103-4.

8 NAC, RG 9, vol. 4066, folder 3, file 2, no. 661 (G).

9 Ibid., vol. 4332, folder 4, file 1, G.147.

10 Ibid., vol. 4469, folder 3, file 6, Tw-10-95.

11 For defensive drill and tactics see ibid. For German orders see NAC, RG 9, vol. 3980, folder 16, file 17, CH 206/2/19.

12 NAC, MG 27, III-B-5, vol. 1, Ian Mackenzie Papers, file 1-A, "History of the Canadian Railway Troops," 82.

13 Ibid., MG 30, E32, Albert C. West Papers, Diary, 7 April 1918. The feeling of leaving the safety of the trenches was echoed by Canadian infantryman Louis Keene in *Crumps: The Plain Story of a Canadian Who Went* (Boston: Houghton Mifflin, 1917), 96.

14 Keene, *Crumps,* 83-4.

15 It is interesting to note that both the Battalion and Brigade War Diaries fail to indicate that gas was used in the attack. The omission is more than an oversight; although other documents clearly indicate that gas was used, the Canadians may have been under orders to keep quiet on their use of gas or were otherwise embarrassed.

16 NAC, RG 9, vol. 4182, folder 33, file 1, G.90/8.

17 Donald Richter, *Chemical Soldiers: British Gas Warfare in World War I* (Lawrence, KS: University Press of Kansas, 1992), 201; G.W.L. Nicholson, *The Fighting Newfoundlanders* (St. John's: Government of Newfoundland, 1964), 296; Edmund Blunden, *Undertones of War* (London: Cox and Wyman, 1928), 162.

18 NAC, RG 9, vol. 4182, folder 33, file 1, "Preliminary Instructions for the Gas Discharge on the 8th Canadian Infantry Brigade Front," 1-2.

19 See War Diaries for the 8th Brigade (NAC, RG 9, vol. 4895) and the 4th Canadian Mounted Rifles (vol. 4947).

20 For journalistic accounts see F.A. McKenzie, *Through the Hindenburg Line* (London: Hodder and Stoughton, 1918), 28-9. There is no indication of the raid in the 3rd Division's War Diary. NAC, RG 9, vol. 4852, War Diary of the 3rd Division.

21 NAC, RG 9, vol. 3831, folder 14, file 3, Gas attack made in successive waves, in Champagne, 31 January 1917.

22 G.W.L. Nicholson, *Canadian Expeditionary Force, 1914-1919* (Ottawa: Roger Duhamel, Queen's Printer and Controller of Stationary, 1962), 233-4; NAC, RG 41, vol. 14, W.M. Marshall, 46th Battalion, 1/8.

23 See Pierre Berton, *Vimy* (Toronto: McClelland and Stewart, 1986), 124-35, for a good account of the raid.

24 Joseph Hayes, *The Eighty-Fifth in France and Flanders* (Halifax: Royal Print, 1920), 44. Years

later some soldiers remembered the same claim – "we were going to just simply jump over the top and pick up all these gassed Germans." NAC, RG 41, vol. 15, 50th Battalion, Stephen and MacDonald, 1/12.

25 For the Odlum-Ironside argument see NAC, MG 30, E300, vol. 19, Victor Odlum Papers, File Gas Attack, Vimy Ridge, Odlum to Ironside, 20 February 1917; RG 41, vol. 20, J. Keiller MacKay, 2/11; E.L.M. Burns, *General Mud* (Toronto: Clarke Irwin, 1970), 40. Lt. E.L.M. Burns, then a signal officer in the 4th Division, remarked that Watson's "personality was rather put in the shade by that of his General Staff Officer Grade I – Lieutenant-Colonel E. Ironside. The general opinion was that Ironside was the real commander of the division" (p. 15); see also Humphrey's remarks about Watson's reliance on Ironside in James McGivern Humphrey, *The Golden Bridge of Memoirs* (Don Mills, ON: Thomas Nelson, 1979), 23.

26 For 12th Brigade casualties see NAC, RG 9, vol. 4907, War Diary of the 12th Brigade, 26 February 1917. For the wayward gas cloud see MG 30, E300, vol. 19, Victor Odlum Papers, File Gas Attack, Vimy Ridge, 11th Canadian Infantry Brigade – Report on Damage to Gas Cylinders, 25 February 1917. The sentries were under orders not to raise an alarm. RG 9, vol. 4907, War Diary of the 12th Brigade, 1 March 1917.

27 The code word is given in NAC, RG 9, vol. 3858, folder 83, file 3, Operation Order No. 27. The number of cylinders is listed in Richter, *Chemical Soldiers*, 175. German defensive orders were very similar to the Canadian orders for defending against cloud attacks. RG 9, vol. 4814, "Summary of Operations – German Translation of Extracts." See Richter, *Chemical Soldiers*, 175 for the German counter-barrage.

28 NAC, RG 9, vol. 3858, folder 83, file 4, "Messages," 4:44 a.m. For gassing of the 11th Brigade see vol. 4943, War Diary of the 75th Battalion, 1 March 1917. Maurice Bracewell quoted in Alexander McKee, *Vimy Ridge* (London: Souvenir Press, 1966), 41. See also RG 9, vol. 4943, War Diary of the 73rd Battalion, 1 March 1917.

29 NAC, RG 41, vol. 15, Stephen and MacDonald, 50th Battalion, 1/12. Other Canadian infantryman serving with the 50th Battalion remembered that the small-arms fire was so heavy that "you couldn't stick your hand above the trench." Fred Bagley and Dr. Harvey Daniel Duncan, *A Legacy of Courage: Calgary's Own, 137th Overseas Battalion, CEF* (Calgary: Plug Street, 1993), 174.

30 Other reports indicated that the Germans had mined some of the gaps and detonated them when the Canadians passed through. NAC, RG 9, vol. 4943, War Diary of the 75th Battalion, 1 March 1917; RG 41, vol. 15, Alex W. Jack, 54th Battalion, 1/13. Among those killed were two battalion commanders. Both had objected to the raid in the first place and had refused to allow their men to advance without them at the lead: Kemball of the 54th Battalion was killed as he searched for an opening through the German wire, his body caught on the spooled rolls like some demented scarecrow; while Sam Beckett, at the head of his troops as they scrambled across the killing zone, was shot through the heart by a sniper.

31 NAC, RG 9, vol. 3858, folder 83, file 4, Preliminary Report on 4th Canadian Division Gas Raid, 1-2; "Messages," 5:12 a.m.; RG 41, vol. 16, M. Young, 72nd Battalion, 1/6.

32 NAC, RG 41, vol. 16, M. Young, 72nd Battalion, 1/7.

33 Ibid., vol. 15, Stanley Barker, 54th Battalion, 2/2.

34 Harwood Steele, *The Canadians in France, 1915-1918* (Toronto: Copp Clark, 1920), 96.

35 The Canadian Corps War Diary minimizes the high casualties suffered by the raiders. NAC, RG 9, vol. 4814, "Summary of Intelligence for Week Ending 4 March 1917." For Canadian casualties see Nicholson, *Canadian Expeditionary Force*, 234. Quotation from NAC, RG 9, vol. 4942, War Diary of the 54th Battalion, 1 March 1917.

36 For McBrian see NAC, RG 9, vol. 3858, folder 83, file 4, BM 421; ibid., Report by V.W. Odlum, 13 March 1917. The interrogation of captured German prisoners (of which there were thirty-six) also indicated that "our gas apparently caused practically no casualties to the front companies to which the prisoners belonged." For Watson see NAC, RG 9, vol. 3858, folder 83, file 4, G.52-2.

37 Richter, *Chemical Soldiers*, 176.

38 Bill Rawling, *Surviving Trench Warfare* (Toronto: University of Toronto Press, 1992), 105.

39 NAC, RG 41, vol. 16, A. Selwood, 72nd Battalion, 1/15-6; vol. 15, 54th Battalion, Howard Green, 1/10. Also see Maurice Pope, *Soldiers and Politicians* (Toronto: University of Toronto Press,

1962). Pope was a friend of Victor Odlum, and called the raid a "disastrous gas show" and thought that someone up the chain of command was obviously "of no extensive scope of mind" to force the raid to go on after so many strenuous objections.

40 On the appointment of Harris see NAC, RG 9, vol. 3977, folder 7, file 14, GS 528. To complete the senior structure of the BEF's Gas Services, each army commander had an army chemical advisor, each of the eighteen corps of the BEF were given a corps gas advisor, and each division was assigned a DGO. On the role of the chemical advisor see ibid., and vol. 5048, folder 923, file 1, Chemical Advisor War Diary, 1 April 1917. With his appointment as chemical advisor, Harris was forced to keep an official War Diary. Although it was an inconvenience to him (there is a note commanding him to keep track of his actions daily instead of skipping days and even weeks as he was inclined to), the War Diary provides a valuable source of information on the Canadian Gas Services. Each divisional gas officer was given six NCOs to carry out anti-gas measures: one was to be posted to each Infantry Brigade Headquarters; one sent to the Divisional Artillery Headquarters; one with the DGO to assist in demonstrations and inspections; and the last to be detached to the Corps Gas School in order to instruct the men of that division. Vol. 3979, folder 12, file 2, OB/26.

41 Stockholm International Peace Research Institute (SIPRI), *The Problem of Chemical and Biological Warfare*, vol. 1, *The Rise of CB Weapons* (Stockholm: Almquist and Wiksell, 1971).

42 Robert Harris and Jeremy Paxman, *A Higher Form of Killing* (London: Chatto and Windus, 1982), 21.

43 Haber, *Poisonous Cloud*, 62, 83.

44 The British phosgene shells were given the symbol "CG." The markings on the shell had three bands: red, white, red. Toward the end of 1917 the British also introduced a shell filled with chloropicrin, which was similar to the German Blue Cross shell. Chloropicrin was both lethal and a powerful irritant to the eyes and throat. It was known as "PS," and its shell case was marked with one white band. NAC, RG 9, vol. 3976, folder 5, file 6, "List of Key Names to Chemical Substances Used in the BEF," DGS A/148.

45 Foulkes, *Gas*, 110-1; Richter, *Chemical Soldiers*, 10.

46 The German prisoner quoted in Daniel Dancocks, *Gallant Canadians* (Calgary: Calgary Highlanders Regimental Funds Foundation, 1990), 156; Ian Hogg, *Gas* (New York: Ballantine Books, 1975), 56. The captured German document is quoted in Victor Lefebure, *The Riddle of the Rhine* (London: W. Collins Sons, 1921), 58. During the war Lefebure was the British gas liaison officer to the French in coordinating the gas war between the two Allies. Ernst Junger, *Storm of Steel* (London: Chatto and Windus, 1929), 238.

47 John A. English, *On Infantry* (New York: Praeger, 1981), 14-8.

48 R.G. Kentner, *Some Recollections of the Battles of World War I* (New York: Irene Kentner Lawson, 1995), 24.

49 Desmond Morton, "The Canadian Military Experience in the First World War, 1914-1918," in *The Great War 1914-1918*, edited by R.J.Q. Adams (London: Macmillan, 1990), 88.

50 The divisional gas officers at this time were Lieutenant McQueen for the 1st Division, Lieutenant Campbell for the 2nd Division, Lieutenant Qua for the 3rd Division, and Lieutenant Beaumont of the 4th Division. NAC, RG 9, vol. 5048, folder 923, file 1, War Diary, 2 April 1917.

51 Another report indicated that there were no gas curtains for the German dugouts. NAC, RG 9, vol. 3979, folder 12, file 7, Captured German Document – March 1917, 3; vol. 3976, folder 4, file 16, "German Gas Defence." With respect to the German prisoners, the Canadian Corps War Diary ominously noted that "four turned nasty on [the] way out and were dealt with," vol. 4793, folder 41, Canadian Corps General Staff War Diary, 1 April 1917.

52 For the gas warning see NAC, RG 9, vol. 4076, folder 2, file 12, G. 8-56; For the delivery of shells see vol. 4976, file 582 (1), 1st DAC War Diary, 31 March 1917. The 4th Brigade's regimental history noted that it received a thousand gas shells at the start of the month. J.A. MacDonald, *Gun-Fire: An Historical Narrative of the 4th Bde. C.F.A.* (N.p.: 4th Brigade, CFA Association, 1929), 82.

53 For the advantages of Canadian counter-battery work see Shane Shriver, "Orchestra to Victory" (Master of War Studies thesis, Royal Military College, 1995), 47-8; A.G.L. McNaughton, "Counter Battery Work," *Canadian Defence Quarterly* 3, 4 (1926) and "The Development of Artillery in the Great War," *Canadian Defence Quarterly* 6, 2 (1929). Quotation from Leslie

W.C.S. Barnes, *Canada and the Science of Ballistics, 1914-1945* (Ottawa: Organization of Military Museums of Canada, 1985), 37.

54 The CBSO was responsible to the brigadier general heavy artillery, but generally, the Counter-Battery staff worked very closely within the Canadian Corps and the CBSO could issue orders in his name. NAC, MG 30, E81, vol. 2, E.W.B. Morrison Papers, File "Orders and Instructions 1917 – Oct. 1918," Status and Duties of the Counter Battery Lieut. Colonel in a Corps. The organization of the Counter Battery Office in the Canadian Corps commenced on 10 February 1917. RG 9, vol. 3843, folder 46, file 2, "Notes on Counter Battery Work in Connection with the Capture of the Vimy Ridge by the Canadian Corps on April 9th 1917."

55 For the production of gas see Foulkes, *Gas*, 262. Harris, along with Lieutenant N.C. Qua, was appointed to the position of major in January 1918. NAC, RG 9, vol. 3977, folder 7, file 13, 14/154; vol. 3831, folder 14, file 11-4 GAS, OB26; vol. 5048, folder 923, file 1, War Diary, 7 April 1917. His report can be found in vol. 3977, folder 8, file 2, "Instructions for Firing Gas Shells."

   Gas shells were less reliant on the weather than were canisters, but they were largely ineffective in wind over seven miles per hour; vol. 4039, folder 10, file 15, G. 1296, "Reference SECTION XXII 1st Canadian Division Instructions for Offensive Operations March 1917." For the Special Company see vol. 3843, folder 46, file 7, GO-80-7. The importance of weather when dealing with gas shells necessitated that Harris create an ad hoc weather bureau, and by 24 April 1917 a permanent weather station was established.

56 Each Canadian division (1st to 4th from right to left) was given four lines to which they were to advance.

57 Nicholson mistakenly attributes the German gas attacks as mustard gas. It would be two more months before the Germans used mustard gas for the first time on the Western Front. Such mistakes indicate the unfamiliarity with gas in Canadian historiography – even by the official historian of the CEF. G.W.L. Nicholson, *The Gunners of Canada*, vol. 1 (Toronto: McClelland and Stewart, 1967), 288; Dancocks, *Gallant Canadians*, 113. Quotation from Reginald H. Roy, *The Journal of Private Fraser* (Victoria: Sono Nis Press, 1985), 263.

58 Ordinance Committees eventually decided that it required one gun to cover fifteen yards of front in smoke. Every fifteen yards of front had to receive three rounds of smoke per minute to ensure a continuous barrage. NAC, RG 9, vol. 3925, folder 17, file 1, "Smoke Production." For souvenirs see NAC, MG 30, E241, D.E. Macintyre Papers, Diary, 10 April 1917.

59 Rupprecht quoted in Nicholson, *Canadian Expeditionary Force*, 263, 265.

60 NAC, RG 9, vol. 5048, folder 923, file 1, War Diary, 10 March 1917.

61 Ibid., vol. 3977, folder 8, file 2, "Report on the Use of Gas Shells by Canadian Corps – Vimy Ridge," 2.

62 Ibid., vol. 3826, folder 3, file 13A, "Counter-Battery Work in the Advance." For Crerar's working party see vol. 4682, folder 26, file 12, The Following is a Record for the 11th Battery, C.F.A. of Events for the Period of Preparation for the Attack on Vimy Ridge up to December 7th 1917.

63 NAC, RG 9, vol. 4682, folder 26, file 12, "Report on the Use of Gas Shells by Canadian Corps – Vimy Ridge," 5. Figures for gas shells from vol. 3977, folder 8, file 2, "Report on the Use of Gas Shells by Canadian Corps – Vimy Ridge," 1; vol. 4793, folder 41, Canadian Corps General Staff, War Diary, 14 April 1917; D.J. Goodspeed, *The Road Past Vimy: The Canadian Corps, 1914-1918* (Toronto: General Paperbacks, 1969, 1987), 90.

64 For shelling of German artillery see NAC, RG 9, vol. 3977, folder 8, file 2, no. 4/60; Extract from CB/8, 13 April 1917; John Swettenham, *McNaughton*, vol. 1 (Toronto: Ryerson Press, 1968), 91. German First Army report quotation from file 17, SB/IO/75. McNaughton went so far as to place a request with the chemical advisor that 9.2 inch howitzer shells be filled with gas. In time they were. RG 9, vol. 5048, folder 923, War Diary April 1917.

65 For the failure of the German tactics see Nicholson, *Canadian Expeditionary Force*, 266-8. See *Letters from the Front: Being a Record of the Part Played by Officers of the Bank in the Great War*, vol. 1, edited by Charles Lyons Foster (Toronto: Canadian Imperial Bank of Commerce, 1919), 204 for German praise of Canadians.

66 On the relentless German gas attacks see NAC, MG 30, E351, Claude C. Craig Papers, Diary, 16 April 1917; Nicholson, *The Gunners of Canada*, 289; Desmond Morton, "A Canadian Soldier in the Great War: The Experience of Frank Maheux," *Canadian Military History* 1, 1/2 (1992): 85; Roy, *Journal of Private Fraser*, 276-7; NAC, RG 9, vol. 4814, War Diary, April-May 1917.

67 For reliance on gas shells see NAC, RG 9, vol. 3847, folder 54, file 2, S/430/7 by Brigadier-General Morrison. For the evolution of artillery doctrine see vol. 3980, folder 16, file 2, Notes on the Use of Gas Shells by the French. For the division of command and control see vol. 3831, folder 14, file 11-14 GAS, First Army no. 1 1379 (G), OB/26.

68 NAC, MG 30, E153, 38th Battalion Association, "War Record of the 38th Ottawa Battalion," 26 April 1917.

69 The importance of adequate protection required transferring two medium howitzer batteries to carry out the task of neutralizing enemy batteries. NAC, RG 9, vol. 3847, folder 54, file 2, Artillery Order No. 17 and 19. Years after the war Colonel Cosgrave, commander of the 9th Artillery Brigade, spoke of the importance of breaking up enemy concentrations to protect one's own infantry. RG 41, vol. 20, L.V. Moore Cosgrave, 1/20.

70 NAC, RG 9, vol. 3977, folder 8, file 3, "Gas Shell Bombardments Canadian Corps 29 April 1917-31 May 1917"; vol. 5048, folder 923, file 1, War Diary, 27 April 17; vol. 3847, folder 54, file 2, GS 110; Nicholson, *Canadian Expeditionary Force, 270.*

71 Heller, *Chemical Warfare,* 22.

72 Canadian artillery figures are found in NAC, RG 9, vol. 3826, folder 3, file 31, Artillery Order No. 25. For the effects of the deluge on the 11th Battery see vol. 4682, folder 26, file 12, The Following is a Record for the 11th Battery, C.F.A. of Events for the Period of Preparation for the Attack on Vimy Ridge up to December 7th 1917. Also see MG 30, E249, vol. 1, file World War I – Accounts, "The Diary of the 20th Battery, CFA by J.C.K. Mackay," 28-9.

I wish to thank Marianne Sussex Goodfellow for allowing me to see and use her transcribed notes from Skey's diary. "Going into Action Tomorrow: The Skey Diary, France 1917," 7-9 May 1917. For impassable roads see J.N. Gunn and E.E. Duffon, *Historical Records of Number 8 Canadian Field Ambulance, 1915-1919* (Toronto: Ryerson Press, 1920), 86, 117.

73 German quotation in Hugh MacIntyre Urquhart, *Arthur Currie: The Biography of a Great Canadian* (Toronto: J.M. Dent and Sons, 1950), 157. After the Canadians turned over the position to the British, it was promptly lost to a fresh German division counter-attacking in a heavy rainstorm. NAC, MG 30, E241, D.E. Macintyre Papers, Diary, 8-9 May 1917.

74 NAC, RG 9, vol. 4076, folder 2, file 12, "Provisional Instructions Regarding Precautions against Hostile Gas Shells," May 1917.

75 Ibid., vol. 4060, folder 5, file 1, "Memorandum on a new type of Gas Shell used by the Germans."

76 NAC, MG 31, G30, William Woods Papers, 11.

77 On the goggles issue see NAC, RG 9, vol. 4076, folder 2, file 12, Q/91/47; vol. 3976, folder 3, file 30, G.23-9-198; vol. 5048, folder 923, file 10, "Canadian Corps Gas Services 12.1.18"; MG 31, G 30, William Woods Papers, 7 and Graft [an appendix at the end].

78 NAC, RG 9, vol. 856, file T-56-2, GS 3-4-3.

79 A 10 September 1918 report by Major Harris noted that "since the methods of Gas training of Canadians both in England and within the Corps differ in many respects from those employed by the British, it is recommended that a Cdn. Gas School should be established at Cdn. General Base (England)." NAC, RG 9, vol. 3981, folder 18, file 12, Gas Training at Canadian General Base.

Lieutenant A.B. Mortimer was posted to the position of gas officer, reinforcement camp (France) on 30 November 1917. In this role he delivered a series of condemning reports regarding instruction in England after he had been questioned by the chemical advisor as to why new recruits were so poorly trained in anti-gas measures. Vol. 5048, folder 923, Chemical Advisor War Diary, 30 November 1917. His reports were done in December 1917 and January 1918. Vol. 3082, G-16-32.

The term "canary" is found in Edward Fraser and John Gibbons, *Soldiers and Sailors, Words and Phrases* (London: George Routledge and Sons, 1925), 46.

80 NAC, RG 9, vol. 856, file T-56-2, Tw-10-76.

81 For the medical officers see ibid., G/3-4-3; for the CAVC, see 1329/BM 4-5-1; for a need to improve training, see vol. 3981, folder 18, file 2, GT.799/14-25; vol. 3082, G-16-36, Training in Anti Gas Precautions; vol. 856, file T-56-2, Anti-Gas Training, for a few of the many examples.

82 NAC, RG 9, vol. 856, file T-56-2, Herewith some remarks brought forward at the Conference of Chemical Advisers held recently [26 October 1918].

83 For training officers requesting aid see ibid., vol. 3081, file G-13-36 vol. 3, GHQ/HF/10203/TC.

See vol. 719, file T-116-2, 62-228 for poor instruction. For organization of Gas Services in England see vol. 5048, folder 923, War Diary of Chemical Advisor, 22 December 1917; vol. 941, file E-83-3, Proposed Establishment of Canadian Gas Services.

84 NAC, RG 9, vol. 3981, folder 18, file 12, SS620 box Respirator Drill and Inspection; vol. 4469, folder 3, file 6, "Anti-Gas Training," 4 May 1917; Victor Wheeler, *The 50th Battalion in No Man's Land* (Calgary: Alberta Historical Resources, 1980), 116.

85 NAC, RG 9, vol. 3975, folder 1, file 1, OB/1077/A, Policy Regarding Corps Reinforcement Camp; vol. 3981, folder 18, file 12, Gas Training at Reinforcement Camp.

86 NAC, RG 9, vol. 3981, folder 18, file 12, "Gas Training," 19 July 1918; Heller, *Chemical Warfare*, 58.

87 NAC, RG 9, vol. 3826, folder 3, file 29, OB/2114.

88 Ibid., vol. 3981, folder 2, file 5, "Copy of Gas Lecture by Lieut. E.V. Sherlock," 3.

89 The blankets were sprayed with the same solution as initially used in PH-helmets. NAC, RG 9, vol. 4032, folder 1, file 14, G.602/23-11; vol. 3931, older 15, file 9, G.662/23-11.

90 NAC, RG 9, vol. 4076, folder 2, file 12, G.8-56; Lefebure, *Riddle of the Rhine*, 228.

Chapter 5: Mustard, King of the War Gases

1 That night the British 15th and 55th Divisions suffered 2,000 casualties. Most of the British soldiers did not realize they had been gassed and went to sleep, only to find within hours that they had scorched lungs, blindness, and patches of painful blisters. National Archives of Canada (NAC), RG 9, vol. 4076, folder 2, file 12, no. 1403 (G); Stockholm International Peace Research Institute (SIPRI), *The Problem of Chemical and Biological Warfare*, vol. 1, *The Rise of CB Weapons* (Stockholm: Almquist and Wiksell, 1971), 55.

2 M., *The Story of the Development Division Chemical Warfare Service* (N.p.: General Electric Company, 1920), 175.

3 The Germans were initially unaware of the blinding effects of mustard gas: it came as a surprise to them and to the British. Interestingly, the British considered mustard gas as a battlefield gas at the beginning of 1916 but believed it was less toxic than phosgene and thus discontinued their examination. It would be a folly they would later regret. Ludwig Fritz Haber, *The Poisonous Cloud* (Oxford: Clarendon Press, 1986), 117. See report by the Medical Research Committee, *The Symptoms and Treatment of the Late Effects of Gas Poisoning*, 10 April 1918 in NAC, RG 9, vol. 3618, file 25-13-6. For casualties see SIPRI, *Problem of Chemical and Biological Warfare*, 1:46; Sir W.G. Macpherson, *Official History of the War: Medical Services Diseases of the War*, vol. 2 (London: HMSO, 1923), 282 (hereafter BOMH), 294. Quotation from Robin Glen Keirstead, "The Canadian Military Medical Experience during the Great War, 1914-1918" (Master's thesis, Queen's University, 1982), 244.

4 Albert Palazzo, "Tradition, Innovation, and the Pursuit of the Decisive Battle: Poison Gas and the British Army on the Western Front, 1915-1918" (PhD diss., Ohio State University, 1996), 285.

5 Quotation from Geoff Dyer, *The Missing of the Somme* (London: Penguin Books, 1994), 47-8.

6 The school consisted of a commandant, a quartermaster sergeant, and three sergeant instructors. Added to this were a total of four gas NCOs, one from each division. Generally the school was to be situated at the corps reinforcement camp. NAC, RG 9, vol. 3979, folder 12, file 2, OB/26. For the order on mandatory officer training see vol. 3981, folder 12, file 18, OB/492.

7 NAC, RG 9, vol. 4066, folder 3, file 2, IG 140.

8 Ernest Black, *I Want One Volunteer* (Toronto: Ryerson, 1965), 86; Wilfred Brenton Kerr, *Shrieks and Crashes: Being Memoirs of Canada's Corps 1917* (Toronto: Hunter Rose, 1929), 129-30.

9 Quotations from NAC, RG 9, vol. 4196, folder 1, file 16, OB/492; Gerard J. DeGroot, *Blighty* (London: Longman, 1996), 170; RG 9, vol. 3978, folder 10, file 15, Gas Discipline Lecture, 7.

10 Quotations from NAC, MG 30, E100, Currie Papers, vol. 37, file: Proposed Reorganization of the Canadian Corps, 1918, "Organization of the Canadian Corps in the Field," 3; E.L.M. Burns, *General Mud* (Toronto: Clarke Irwin, 1970), 35; RG 41, vol. 20, L.V. Moore Cosgrave, 2/9. By November 1917, all British corps had followed the Canadian lead and implemented Corps Gas Schools. RG 9, vol. 5048, folder 923, file 4, War Diary, 19 July 1917; Charles H. Foulkes, *Gas: The Story of the Special Brigade* (London: William B. Blackwood and Sons, 1936), 260.

11 The four-day course was taught to a maximum class of fifty officers and a hundred NCOs. NAC, RG 9, vol. 5048, folder 923, file 5, War Diary, 5 August 1917; Appendix II. On the lectures see vol. 3981, folder 2, file 6, Synopsis of Anti-gas Lectures. See James H. Pedley, *Only This*

(Ottawa: Graphic Publisher, 1927), 80-1. George Bell remembered the same restful qualities of the training schools, NAC, MG 30, E113, George Bell Papers, 112. Edmund Blunden, in *Undertones of War* (London: Cox and Wyman, 1928), 40, also remarked that lectures at the gas schools were "leisurely, alarming and useful." See also MG 30, E32, Albert C. West Papers, Diary, 23-8 September 1918.

12 The Germans underwent the same training with their men, as one prisoner of the 413th Regiment indicated: "There is a gas NCO in each company ... [and] a gas officer for each regiment ... When the battalions of the regiment are in rest, he inspects masks, questions each man individually on the use of masks and tests their ability to adjust masks within a given time. 5 or 6 men are placed in a room, the alarm is given, and a few seconds later a gas cartridge is exploded." NAC, RG 9, vol. 4814, Canadian Corps Headquarters War Diary, "Summary of Information," 18 February 1917. Thirty-five courses were given at the Canadian Corps Gas School throughout the war. Vol. 3982, folder 5, file 5.

13 R.A.L., *Letters of a Canadian Stretcher Bearer* (Toronto: Thomas Allen, 1918), 266.

14 NAC, RG 9, vol. 4121, folder 2, file 9, G.27/116.

15 Ibid., vol. 4076, folder 2, file 12, "Organization for Defence against Gas," 1; MG 30, E488, William C. Morgan Papers, Diary, 27 July 1917; RG 9, vol. 4076, folder 2, file 12, "Organization for Defence against Gas," 2.

16 Quotations from John William Lynch, *Princess Patricia's Canadian Light Infantry, 1917-1919* (New York: Exposition Press, 1976), 186; Richard Holmes, *Firing Line* (London: Pimlico, 1985), 212.

17 A.J.M. Hyatt, *General Sir Arthur Currie* (Toronto: University of Toronto Press in collaboration with the Canadian War Museum, Canadian Museum of Civilization, and National Museums of Canada, 1987), 76.

18 Hugh MacIntyre Urquhart, *Arthur Currie: The Biography of a Great Canadian* (Toronto: J.M. Dent and Sons, 1950), 169. Currie had first gone to his commanding officer General Horne of the First British Army and bluntly remarked "If we have to fight at all, let us fight for something worth having." D.J. Goodspeed, *The Road Past Vimy: The Canadian Corps, 1914-1918* (Toronto: General Paperbacks, 1969, 1987), 97.

19 R.G. Kenter, *Some Recollections of the Battles of World War I* (New York: Irene Kentner Lawson, 1995), 75. For the 2 June raid see G.W.L. Nicholson, *Canadian Expeditionary Force, 1914-1919* (Ottawa: Roger Duhamel, Queen's Printer and Controller of Stationary, 1962), 281.

20 Nicholson, *Canadian Expeditionary Force*, 281; NAC, RG 9, vol. 4060, folder 5, file 1, GS631 and BM475, 18 July 1917.

21 Casualties are in Nicholson, *Canadian Expeditionary Force*, 281. The artillery fireplan is in NAC, RG 9, vol. 3978, folder 11, file 17, "Counter Battery Office Canadian Corps Artillery – Order No. 23."

22 NAC, RG 9, vol. 3831, folder 14, file 14, 1378 (G); MG 30, E100, vol. 48, SS 139/4 – Artillery Notes, February 1917, 3; RG 9, vol. 5048, folder 923, War Diary of Chemical Advisor, 28 June 1917, 15, 20 July 1917.

23 In the days before the attack more than 3,500 drums and 900 gas shells had been fired into Lens. Nicholson, *Canadian Expeditionary Force*, 286; see the "Gas and Smoke Fire Plan" in NAC, RG 9, vol. 3850, folder 61, file 4, and vol. 3851, folder 64, file 3, Section IV, Artillery Plan.

24 NAC, RG 24, vol. 20542, file 990.011 (D1); extract from Haig's Diary, 23 July 1917.

25 NAC, MG 30, E488, William C. Morgan Papers, Diary, 3 August 1917. See RG 41, vol. 17, 1 CMR, G. Wright, 2/4-8 and 4 CMR, H.G. McKendrick, 1/1-7, for additional accounts of German gassings. RG 9, vol. 4872, 2nd Canadian Infantry Brigade War Diary, August 1917, Report: "Action of August 15th, 1917, Capture of the Enemy's Positions on Hill 70 and Subsequent Operations," 9 and 27, for German use of gas shells in disrupting the Canadian infantry attack. See also T.W.L. MacDermont, *The Seventh* (Montreal: The Seventh Canadian Siege Battery Association, 1953), 76; Arthur Lapointe, *Soldier of Quebec, 1916-1919* (Montreal: Edition Edouard Garand, 1931), 61-2.

26 Tim Travers, *How the War Was Won* (London: Routledge, 1992), 16.

27 No. 4 Special Company and "B" Special Company discharged the smoke on the Canadian front. NAC, RG 9, vol. 4029, folder 10, file 15, "Special Companies, R.E." The Canadians had one gun to every twenty yards of barrage front. Vol. 3851, folder 64, file 1, Canadian Corps Scheme of Operations – Capture of Hill 70. See Nicholson, *Canadian Expeditionary Force*, 287 for use

of additional firepower. Quotation in MG 30, E488, William C. Morgan Papers, Diary, 15 August 1917.

28 NAC, RG 9, vol. 3907, folder 27, file 8, Artillery Order No. 52: Artillery Plan for the Capture of Hill 70; G.W.L. Nicholson, *The Gunners of Canada,* vol. 1 (Toronto: McClelland and Stewart, 1967), 296; MG 30, E157, Crerar Papers, vol. 22, file 1914-1919, CB 883/1-1, p. 3; MG 30, E100, Currie Papers, vol. 48, SS 139/7, Artillery Notes No. 7, p. 20 and Artillery Notes – No. 3 Counter-Battery Work, SS 139/3.

29 NAC, RG 41, vol. 11, C.B. Holmes and C.J. Albon, 2/10; Gene Dow, ed., *World War One Reminiscences of a New Brunswick Veteran* (New Brunswick: Cummings Typesetting, 1990), 9; Lapointe, *Soldier of Quebec,* 63-5.

30 R.A.L., *Letters,* 271-2.

31 NAC, RG 9, vol. 3977, folder 6, file 17, "Extracts from Captured Documents."

32 Ibid., vol. 3831, folder 14, file 8, "Report on Gas Bombardment." By August 1917, Green Cross shells were available for the entire range of German field artillery, from the small field gun up to the 210 mm heavy howitzer. SIPRI, *Problem of Chemical and Biological Warfare,* 1:35. For the role of the Canadian gunners see NAC, MG 30, E12, vol. 2, A.F. Duguid Papers, "The Canadian as a Soldier," 25; Nicholson, *Canadian Expeditionary Force,* 291; RG 41, vol. 8, 5th Battalion, F.C. Bagshaw, 3/9. At least one infantry brigade noted the valuable service of the Canadian artillerymen, who continued to work under a "most intense gas shelling," for which they should receive the "highest commendation." RG 9, vol. 4872, 2nd Canadian Infantry Brigade War Diary, August 1917, Report: "Action of August 15th, 1917, Capture of the Enemy's Positions on Hill 70 and Subsequent Operations," 28. See Coningsby Dawson, *The Glory of the Trenches* (Toronto: S.B. Gundy, 1918), 133, for another view of an infantryman on the courage of the artillery. Quotations from RG 41, vol. 20, K.B. Jackson, 2/3 and RG 9, vol. 3831, folder 14, file 8, BM4-16, 1.

33 NAC, RG 9, vol. 3831, folder 13, file 4, G.161, Suggestions with regard to the reduction of casualties from Mustard Gas; R.A.L., *Letters,* 269; RG 41, vol. 9, 15th Battalion, Wallace Carroll, 3/3.

34 NAC, RG 41, vol. 14, 46th Battalion, R.D. Roberts, 1/15. For officer casualties see RG 9, vol. 4215, folder 3, file 11, 1403 (G); Daniel Dancocks, *Gallant Canadians* (Calgary: Calgary Highlanders Regimental Funds Foundation, 1990), 136.

35 NAC, MG 30, E300, vol. 23, Victor Odlum Papers, File Casualties, *The Listening Post,* trench newspaper of the 7th Battalion, March 1919.

36 NAC, RG 9, vol. 3831, folder 13, file 5, The Following facts and suggested reorganization of the Gas Defensive Services in Canadian Corps are submitted for the consideration of the G.O.C., Cdn. Corps.

37 NAC, MG 30, E430, William Green Papers, "An Autobiography of World War I," 6. On the pathology of mustard gas, see the review article by A.S. Warthin, "The Pathology of the Skin Lesions Produced by Mustard Gas (Dichlorethysulphide)," *Canadian Medical Association Journal* 8, 8 (1918): 752; Robert Collier Fetherstonaugh, *No. 3 Canadian General Hospital (McGill)* (Montreal: Gazette Printing, 1928), 105. On fear see Holmes, *Firing Line,* 182-3. On warnings see NAC, RG 9, vol. 4121, folder 2, file 9, "Measures to be taken by those affected by the new German Gas."

38 NAC, RG 41, vol. 7, 4th Battalion, Johnson, 1/6.

39 J.A. MacDonald, *Gun-Fire: An Historical Narrative of the 4th Bde. C.F.A.* (N.p.: 4th Brigade, CFA Association, 1929), 106.

40 German official history quoted in Hyatt, *General Sir Arthur Currie,* 77. Currie's diary quoted in Nicholson, *Canadian Expeditionary Force,* 292. War correspondent quoted in NAC, RG 24, vol. 1883, file 5, War Correspondents' Headquarters, France.

41 Dancocks, *Gallant Canadians,* 127; Nicholson, *Canadian Expeditionary Force,* 292; NAC, RG 24, vol. 1844, file GAQ 11-11E, "Casualty Statistics Compiled by the Historical Section of DND." Quotation from R.A.L., *Letters,* 271.

42 Richard Adamson, *All for Nothing* (N.p.: Self-published, 1987), 133.

43 Sir Basil Liddell Hart, *A History of the World War, 1914-1918* (London: Little, Brown, 1935), 319. For the first horse respirators see NAC, RG 9, vol. 4129, folder 5, file 13, A.1741. For lack of movement see William Moore, *Gas Attack* (London: Leo Cooper, 1987), 169. For difficulty getting the respirators on the horses see Adamson, *All for Nothing,* 133. A report by the director of Veterinary Services noted the same thing. RG 9, vol. 4060, folder 5, file 1, "Gas Poisoning during the

Operations of Wytchaete-Messines June 1st to 7th, 1917." Soldiers were eventually ordered to "wear their Box Respirators while grooming and harnessing horses so as to accustom the men to working whilst wearing Box Respirators and also to accustom the horses to the men's appearance with Box Respirators on." Vol. 4524, file 9, Army Book 129, 1st Divisional Train, order 287. For horse life expectancy see Lorraine Jordens, "Veterinarians in World War One," *Alberta History* 41, 2 (1993): 23; D.S. Tamblyn, *The Horse in War* (Kingston, ON: Jackson Press, 1930), 33. See also NAC, MG 30, E14, French Papers, vol. 1, file 4, Revised Copy of History of CAVC, 20.

44 See Bill Rawling, "Communications in the Canadian Corps, 1915-1918: Wartime Technological Progress Revisited," *Canadian Military History* 3, 2 (1994): 6-22.

45 NAC, RG 41, vol. 17, 116th Battalion, Arthur Brown, 1/11; The Adjutant, *The 116th Battalion in France* (Toronto: E.P.S. Allen, 1921), 36.

46 For pigeons see NAC, RG 9, vol. 3981, folder 2, file 3, "Extract from Army Routine Orders dated 23 October 1917 – 1252 Anti-Gas Bags for Pigeon Baskets." As effective as the pigeons were, there was a rumour circulating in the Canadian Corps that the "22nd Battalion had been turning the birds into trench squab on toast until [their] supply became exhausted." NAC, MG 30, E156, Robert W. Clements Papers, "Merry Hell," 109. The awarding of a medal is recounted in Alistar Horne, *The Price of Glory* (London: Penguin Books, 1962), 254.

47 Blue Cross shells contained the chemical diphenylchloroarsine. NAC, RG 9, vol. 3980, folder 17, folder 5, Director of Gas Services, B. No. 412. For its effects see BOMH, 474-5; Moore, *Gas Attack*, 129. For the difficulty in spotting it see RG 9, vol. 4032, folder 1, file 14, "Translation of a German Document, September 26, 1917."

48 Victor Wheeler, *The 50th Battalion in No Man's Land* (Calgary: Alberta Historical Resources, 1980), 281; NAC, RG 9, vol. 4469, folder 3, file 6, TW-11-108. Hartley argued that the Germans tested their Blue Cross gas against captured SBRs in a laboratory under favourable conditions. Within the laboratory it penetrated the mask, but in the field there was generally not a high enough concentration of gas to penetrate the mask and most soldiers remained safe. Harold Hartley, "A General Comparison of British and German Methods of Gas Warfare," *Journal of the Royal Artillery* (February 1920): 499.

49 NAC, RG 9, vol. 4215, folder 3, file 11, O.B./492/T.J.

50 BOMH, 302.

51 Travers, *How the War Was Won*, 17.

52 Hyatt, *General Sir Arthur Currie*, 79. "I carried my protest to the extreme limit," Currie later wrote, "which would have resulted in my being sent home had I been other than the Canadian Corps Commander." Goodspeed, 114. NAC, RG 41, vol. 8, 8th Battalion, C.E. Barnes, 1/9.

53 Nicholson, *CEF*, 312-3; Hyatt, *General Sir Arthur Currie*, 81; Denis Winter, *Haig's Command* (New York: Viking, 1991), 107.

54 Will Bird, *Ghosts Have Warm Hands* (Toronto: Clarke Irwin, 1968), 74. H.A. Searle of the 18th Battalion also remarked on the mud saving men from being killed by the shells. NAC, RG 41, vol. 11, 18th Battalion, H.A. Searle, 2/2. The weight of the coat is found in Dancocks, *Gallant Canadians*, 152.

55 NAC, RG 9, vol. 3975, folder 1, file 12, Director of Gas Services A/96.

56 Ibid., MG 30, E81, vol. 2, E.W.B. Morrison Papers, File Notes and Pamphlets, Speech at Canadian Club in Hamilton, The Canadian Artillery in the Great War, n.d. The "de-lousing" phrase comes from a secret order passed on to the Canadian Artillery by the Royal Artillery, Fifth Army. NAC, RG 9, vol. 3826, folder 3, file 3, "Special Form of Creeping Barrage used against Concreted Buildings and Shelters."

57 NAC, RG 9, vol. 3922, folder 9, file 2, Counter Battery Office. Canadian Corps Artillery, Order No. 49, 1; Table "C," 2; vol. 3922, "Organization and Procedure of Counter-Battery Office, Canadian Corps Artillery," 15 January 1919.

58 NAC, RG 9, vol. 3922, folder 9, file 2, CB20/12, 1; vol. 3852, folder 65, file 1, Canadian Corps Artillery Report on Passchendaele Operations, 17 October to 18 November 1917, 14.

59 NAC, RG 9, vol. 4032, folder 1, file 14, G.941/23-11; vol. 3976, folder 5, file 12, Notes on Enemy Gas in Ypres Area; Haber, *Poisonous Cloud*, 194.

60 NAC, RG 41, vol. 11, 18th Battalion, H.A. Searle, 1/15.

61 Ibid., RG 9, vol. 4119, folder 1, file 20, G.941/23-11; MG 30, E477, Cameron Ross Papers, "Memoirs of Cameron Ross," 16; RG 41, vol. 11, C.J. Albon, 25th Battalion, 3/6.

62 NAC, MG 30, E285, Russell F. Tubman Papers, "Re: Medical Examination of R.F. Tubman."
    For burns and infections see RG 9, vol. 3831, folder 13, file 4, 1st DGO to Chemical Advisor,
    Canadian Corps, 30 July 1917; Arthur O. Hickson, *As It Was Then*, edited by D.G.L. Fraser
    (Wolfville, NS: Acadia University, 1988), 66. See also Goodspeed, *Road Past Vimy*, 117; Howard,
    Sixty Years, 52; Nicholson, *Gunners of Canada*, 304.

63 Ernest Black, *I Want One Volunteer* (Toronto: Ryerson, 1965), 68-9.

64 Gordon Howard, *Sixty Years of Centennial in Saskatchewan, 1906-1968* (N.p.: Self-published,
    1968), 52; D.C. MacArthur, *The History of the Fifty-Fifth Battery, C.F.A.* (Hamilton: H.S.
    Longhurst, 1919), 18.

65 Malcolm Brown, *The Imperial War Museum Book of the Western Front* (London: Sidgwick and
    Jackson, 1993), 199.

66 Stewart quoted in Nicholson, *Gunners of Canada*, 306. See Roy St. George Stubbs, *Men in
    Khaki: Four Regiments of Manitoba* (Toronto: Ryerson Press, 1941), 61.

67 Munro quoted in Brown, *Book of the Western Front*, 142. See also NAC, RG 24, vol. 1822, file
    GAQ 5-30.

68 NAC, RG 41, vol. 16, 72nd Battalion, John MacKenzie, 2/11.

69 Quotations from R.J. Manion, *A Surgeon in Arms* (New York: Doran, 1918), 72-3; NAC, RG 41,
    vol. 20, Logan and Pearce, 2/13. For German failure to capitalize on the situation see RG 9, vol.
    3922, folder 9, file 2, CB20/12, 3.

70 The gas casualties are divided in one report as 148 gas casualties in the 1st Division, 91 in the 2nd
    Division, 62 in the 1st Division's artillery, and 90 in the 2nd Division's artillery. NAC, RG 24,
    vol. 1822, file GAQ 5-30; Nicholson, *Canadian Expeditionary Force*, 325-6, for the non-gas casu-
    alty figures on 6 and 10 November. For gas casualties on 2-3 November see vol. 1822, file GAQ
    5-30. See RG 9, vol. 4032, folder 1, file 14, G.8-1 for the vulnerability of the infantry. Quotation
    from Holmes, *Firing Line*, 218.

71 Howard, *Sixty Years*, 53; NAC, RG 41, vol. 11, 18th Battalion, H.A. Searle, 2/1; Holmes, *Firing
    Line*, 186-7.

72 Moore, *Gas Attack*, 140; NAC, RG 9, vol. 3975, folder 1, file 16, "Summary of Gas Casualties in
    the Canadian Corps from Oct. 21st to Nov. 19th, 1917." Nicholson, *Canadian Expeditionary
    Force*, 327, for the total casualty figures of the Canadian Corps. Walkinshaw quoted in Dan-
    cocks, *Gallant Canadians*, 155.

73 NAC, RG 9, vol. 941, E-83-3, Odlum to General Staff, 18 October 1917; ibid., Proposed Estab-
    lishment of Canadian Gas Services. In one letter to Sir Richard Turner, General Currie thought
    that the Canadians should add both a Canadian Flying Corps as well as Special Gas Companies
    in order to make the "Canadian Corps as self-contained an Institution as possible." Currie to
    Turner, 3 November 1917, NAC, MG 30 E75, H.M. Urquhart fonds, vol. 3, file 6. For Currie's sac-
    rifice of the gas companies see ibid., correspondence from B.B. Cubitt for Commander-in-
    Chief to R. Wallace for CGS, 4 February 1918; P.E. Thacker to the Secretary, War Office, White-
    hall, 27 March 1918.

74 Casualties in Bill Rawling, *Surviving Trench Warfare* (Toronto: University of Toronto Press,
    1992), Appendix B. Quotation from NAC, MG 30, E318, file 130, Gas Training, 5 December 1917.

Chapter 6: Combatting the Chemical Plague

1 The report was a response to a request from Canadian Corps Headquarters. National Archives
    of Canada (NAC), RG 9, vol. 3831, folder 14, file 8, G.272/23-1. For 4th CMR casualties see vol.
    3982, folder 3, file 11, CA 29.

2 Desmond Morton, "Military Medicine and State Medicine: Historical Notes on the Canadian
    Army Medical Corps in the First World War 1914-1919," In *Canadian Health Care*, edited by
    C. David Naylor (Montreal: McGill-Queen's University Press, 1992), 39; Robin Glen Keirstead,
    The Canadian Military Medical Experience during the Great War, 1914-1918 (Kingston, ON:
    Queen's University, 1982), 82.

3 See Edward Archibald, "Abdominal Wounds as Seen at a Casualty Clearing Station," *Canadian
    Medical Association Journal 7*, 7 (1917), 7; Norman Miles Guiou, *Transfusion: A Canadian Sur-
    geon's Story in War and in Peace* (Yarmouth, NS: Stoneycroft, 1985).

4 Morton, "Military Medicine," 45. Keirstead makes the same argument in his impressive mas-
    ter's thesis on military doctors and the First World War. Robin Glen Keirstead, "The Canadian

Military Medical Experience during the Great War, 1914-1918" (Master's thesis, Queen's University, 1982), 234-5.

5 Quotations from Simon Jones, "Under a Green Sea, Part II," *The Great War* 2, 1 (1989):18; Charles Heller, *Chemical Warfare in World War I: The American Experience, 1917-1918*, Leavenworth Papers no. 10 (Fort Leavenworth, KS: Combat Studies Institute, 1984), 83.

6 The edict against walking of course did not apply to mustard gas. NAC, RG 9, vol. 3931, folder 15, file 8, "Lessons from Recent Hostile Gas Attacks, August 1916." Captain (at that time) G.S. Strathy of the 2nd Casualty Clearing Station noted in his diary that the treatment of gas-poisoned men was enhanced by rest and "all except the slightest cases should be transferred to base Hospital lying down." Vol. 3751, War Diary of Major G.S. Strathy, 22. The British colonel's observation is found in Jones, "Under a Green Sea, Part II," 18.

7 Report of the Ministry, *Overseas Military Forces of Canada, 1918*, (London, 1918), 392, for the progress of a casualty from the front. Each Battalion had sixteen reserve stretcher-bearers, a number that was augmented and considerably raised before big pushes. Still, it was never enough for the vast numbers of men who needed to be carried in to the ambulances and clearing stations. Great Britain, *First Army Administrative Report on the Vimy Ridge Operations*, n.d., 81. See Guy Emerson Bowerman, *The Compensations of War: The Diary of an Ambulance Driver during the Great War* (Austin: University of Texas Press, 1983) for an account of ferrying of gas casualties from the dressing stations back to the casualty clearing stations in the rear.

8 Sir W.G. Macpherson, *Official History of the War: Medical Services Diseases of the War*, vol. 2 (London: HMSO, 1923), 284 (hereafter BOMH).

9 Malcolm Brown, *The Imperial War Museum Book of the Western Front* (London: Sidgwick and Jackson, 1993), 174.

10 Victor Lefebure, *The Riddle of the Rhine* (London: W. Collins Sons, 1921), 93. On the three memos see BOMH, 248. On misdiagnosis see NAC, RG 9, vol. 4196, folder 1, file 16, "Report on Hostile Bombardment with Gas T.M. Bombs on the 9th Divisional Front on the Night of June 5th/6th, 1917."

11 All information in the paragraph is taken from G.B. Peat, "The Effects of Gassing as Seen at a Casualty Clearing Station," *Canadian Medical Association Journal* 8, 1 (1918); British soldier cited in BOMH, 394.

12 NAC, RG 9, vol. 3751, war diary of Major G.S. Strathy, CAMC, 22; vol. 4547, folder 1, file 2, "Suggestions regarding the Treatment of Cases Suffering from the New Shell Gas Poisoning"; John Ellis, *Eye Deep in Hell: The Western Front, 1914-1918* (London: Croom Helm, 1975), 66.

13 Captain Gordon argued that "four-fifths of the deaths take place in the first twenty-four hours." NAC, RG 9, vol. 3619, file 25-13-6, Lecture by Captain C.A.R. Gordon, CAMC, on the Medical Aspects of Chemical Warfare, 6; Robert Harris and Jeremy Paxman, *A Higher Form of Killing* (London: Chatto and Windus, 1982), 18.

14 Keirstead, "Canadian Military Medical Experience," 242.

15 On bleeding see Peat, "Effects of Gassing," 20, 21; Robert Collier Fetherstonaugh, *No. 3 Canadian General Hospital (McGill)* (Montreal: Gazette Printing, 1928), 106. Peat believed in bleeding but decided that not more then "ten or twenty ounces should be taken" (p. 21). For 28 June 1917 report see NAC, RG 9, vol. 4551, folder 1, file 9, DG/E/280.87. See also Desmond Morton, *When Your Number's Up* (Toronto: Random House, 1993), 193; "No. 1 Canadian General Hospital Clinical Society," *Canadian Medical Association Journal* 8, 6 (1918): 576; RG 41, vol. 9, 15th Battalion, Wallace Carroll, 3/4. For the importance of palliative care see Dunlap Pearce Penhallow, *Military Surgery* (London: Oxford University Press, 1918), 512. For French army deaths see RG 9, vol. 3751, War Diary of G.S. Strathy, 32. Veteran quoted in MG 30, E156, Robert N. Clements Papers, "Merry Hell. The Way I Saw It," 233.

16 The 1919 British report is quoted in Harris and Paxman, *Higher Form of Killing*, 27. The German artillery plan is in NAC, RG 24, vol. 1837, GAQ 9-37, "Attack Methods." For British casualties see William Moore, *Gas Attack* (London: Leo Cooper, 1987) 193. Fries quoted in Lefebure, *Riddle of the Rhine*, 176. Foulkes also acknowledged the effects of mustard gas and wrote that it caused the loss of the "equivalent of several divisions and ... constitute[d] a serious drain on the strength of the British Army." Charles H. Foulkes, *Gas: The Story of the Special Brigade* (London: William B. Blackwood and Sons, 1936), 264. See Denis Winter, *Haig's Command* (New York: Viking, 1991), 95.

17 NAC, RG 9, vol. 3977, folder 7, file 2, "Suggestions regarding the Treatment of Cases Suffering from the New Shell Gas Poisoning"; Harris and Paxman, *Higher Form of Killing*, 26.

18 Lyn MacDonald, *They Called It Passchendaele* (1978; London: Penguin Books, 1993), 87; see also NAC, RG 9, vol. 3751, Major G.S. Strathy's war diary, 32: "Orderlies have been poisoned by fumes retained in clothing."

19 NAC, MG 30, E31, T.B. Smith Papers, 197; RG 9, vol. 4060, folder 5, file 1, no. 1403 (G); Moore, *Gas Attack*, 149.

20 For removal of clothing see NAC, RG 9, vol. 3977, folder 7, file 2, "Notes for Treatment of Cases of Yellow Cross Gas Poisoning and Suspicious Cases in the Trenches"; vol. 945, file G-5-3 part 1, Report OC, No. 58 Casualty Clearing Station; A.E. Snell, *The CAMC with the Canadian Corps during the Last Hundred Days of the Great War* (Ottawa: F.A. Cland, 1924), 211. For snorting soda see review of A.S. Warthin's "The Pathology of the Skin Lesions Produced by Mustard Gas (Dichlorethysulphide)" in *Canadian Medical Association Journal* 8, 8 (1918): 752. For washing the eyes see NAC, RG 9, vol. 945, file G-5-3 part 1, New German Gas. Donaldson wrote that "I had some 66 of my men gassed and 10 wounded and 3 killed out of about 100 who were clearing the wounded from the front line during the action for Hill 70." MG 30, E566, vol. 1, Ansan Donaldson Papers, letter to his sister Anna Maria 11 October 1917.

Soldiers often referred to England as Blighty, and thus a soldier with a wound was off to Blighty. Not only was Blighty seen as an escape from the horrors of the trenches, it was also a state of mind. Having one's hand shot off or catching a bullet clean through the leg was not met with grief by the victim or his friends, but by cheers of congratulations. John Brophy and Eric Patridge, *The Long Trail: Soldiers' Songs and Slang, 1914-1918* (London: Sphere Books, 1969), 73.

21 Brown, *Book of the Western Front*, 78-9.

22 As quoted in Denis Winter, *Death's Men* (London: Penguin Books, 1979), 123.

23 BOMH, 446; quotation from F.G. Scott, *The Great War as I Saw It* (Vancouver: Clarke and Stuart, 1934), 201. Scott was very popular with the men and was one of the true "celebrities" of the Canadian Corps. See Duff Crerar, *Padres in No Man's Land* (Montreal: McGill-Queen's University Press, 1994), for an excellent account of Scott.

24 Gerard J. DeGroot, *Blighty* (London: Longman, 1996), 280.

25 John C. Meakins and T.W. Walker, *The After-Effects of Irritant Gas Poisoning, 1918*, 8, in NAC RG 9, vol. 3618, file 25-13-6; vol. 3619, file 25-13-6, Lecture by Captain C.A.R. Gordon, CAMC, on the Medical Aspects of Chemical Warfare, 14; vol. 3751, War Diary of G.S. Strathy, 34.

26 The lines of mustard gas victims were immortalized by John Singer Sargent in his painting *Gassed*.

27 NAC, RG 9, vol. 3977, folder 7, file 2, "Report on a Series of Gassed Cases by Major S.G. Ross and Capt. A.T. Henderson." For soldiers burned twice see ibid., "Action of H.S. Vapour on Sores Previously Produced by H.S."; John Bryden, *Deadly Allies* (Toronto: McClelland and Stewart, 1989), 166.

28 NAC, RG 9, vol. 3981, folder 1, file 2, Effects of Gas Shell Bombardments, 17 July 1917; vol. 3975, folder 1, file 16, "Note on the Invaliding Factors amongst Casualties Caused by Dichlorethylsulphide." The chemical advisor of the First Army issued a secret report on 3 December 1917 on the mortality rate of mustard gas victims between the period 13 July and 27 October 1917, as shown in the following table:

TABLE N. 3

Deaths as percentage of total gas casualties, selected periods, 1917

Period	Percentage
13 July-4 August	3.9
5 August-1 September	1.8
2-19 September	3.0
30 September-27 October	3.1
Average	3.2

Source: NAC, RG 9, vol. 3975, folder 1, file 16, "Chemical Advisor, First Army –3 December 1917."

29 For percentage send to the UK see Medical Research Committee, *Report on the Length of Stay in Hospital in the United Kingdom and the Disposal of Gas Casualties*, n.d., 19, located in NAC, RG 9, vol. 3619, file 25-13-6. For the policy on those lightly gassed see vol. 3618, file 25-13-6, *The Symptoms and Treatment of the Late Effects of Gas Poisoning*, 5; RG 41, vol. 17, 1 CMR, G. Wright, 2/10. The question of mental healing is addressed in H.G. Nyblett, "Physical Treatment of Wounded Soldiers," *Canada Lancet* 51, 11 (1918), 500; Richard A. Gabriel. *No More Heroes: Madness and Psychiatry in War* (New York: Hill and Wang, 1987), 52.

30 NAC, RG 9, vol. 3618, file 25-13-6, *The Symptoms and Treatment of the Late Effects of Gas Poisoning*, 5-6. The importance of keeping the patients close to the front and not allowing them to convalesce was an important part of the Canadian Army's method of dealing with battle stress casualties in the Second World War. NAC, RG 24, vol. 4268, file 15-2-35, Campbell Meyers, "The Canadian Soldier and Shell Shock," 5-7; Anthony Kellett, *Combat Motivation: The Behaviour of Soldiers in Battle* (Boston: Kluwer-Nijhoff, 1982), 282. For the faster recovery of the mustard gassed see Meakins and Walker, *After-Effects, 1918*. For the March Offensive see Winter, *Death's Men*, 125.

31 Soldiers returning from any hospital stay (as well as court-martialled men) were forced to undergo a one-day anti-gas course at the Reinforcement Base before joining their units. NAC, RG 9, vol. 3981, folder 12, file 18, *Instructions Concerning Anti-Gas Training and Equipment on the L. of C.*, February 1918; RG 41, 50th Battalion, A.A. Russell and W.J. Gadsden, 1/12.

32 For compliance see Sir Andrew Macphail, *The Official History of the Canadian Forces in the Great War: The Medical Services* (Ottawa: F.A. Acland, 1925), 282. For the "cure" see NAC, RG 9, vol. 4547, folder 1, file 2, DMS No. 830/64. At a meeting of doctors from No. 1 Canadian General Hospital it was remarked that treatment by injection of calcium chloride "had clearly proven to be futile, if not dangerous." "No. 1 Canadian General Hospital Clinical Society," 575-6. The use of cocaine is covered in vol. 4547, folder 1, file 2, "Mustard Gas (Eyes)"; DMS, No. 830/64.

33 NAC, RG 9, vol. 3981, folder 18, file 12, G.809/23-11, 24 November 1917.

34 Ibid., vol. 4032, folder 1, file 14, G.8-80.

35 Ibid., vol. 4060, folder 5, file 1, G.8-26.

36 Ibid., vol. 5048, folder 923, file 8, War Diary, 30 November 1917.

37 For the German projector see ibid., vol. 4060, folder 5, file 1, Memo to All Gas Officers, Canadian Corps, 28 November 1917. The first projector attack against British lines took place on 10 December 1917. Vol. 3982, folder 3, file 11, Ia/46549; vol. 4121, folder 2, file 9, G.27/493. For what gas sentries should do if they saw a projector attack see vol. 4076, folder 2, file 12, C.B. 492. For 52nd Battalion casualties see vol. 5048, folder 923, file 9, "Report on Gas Projector Attack between 4.50 a.m. and 5.00 a.m. This Morning (30.12.17)." The need for rigid discipline is discussed in vol. 5048, folder 923, file 9, War Diary, 9 December 1917; vol. 4076, folder 2, file 12, "Organization for Defence against Gas," 10 August 1917.

38 NAC, RG 9, vol. 4469, folder 3, file 6, Tw-11-122.

39 NAC, MG 30, E321, William Johnson Papers, Letter home dated 3 May 1915.

40 Ernest G. Black described SIWs as "left-hand wounds" because soldiers shot themselves in the hand to escape from the trenches. Ernest Black, *I Want One Volunteer* (Toronto: Ryerson, 1965), 24. NAC, MG 30, E113, George Bell Papers, Memoirs, 113; R.A.L., *Letters of a Canadian Stretcher Bearer* (Toronto: Thomas Allen, 1918), 279.

41 Keirstead, "Canadian Military Medical Experience," 57. Captain Manion remarked on malingerers that "if he is an old soldier and knows the game well, he may get away with the tacit consent of a sympathetic medical officer." R.J. Manion, *A Surgeon in Arms* (New York: Doran, 1918), 105. Others like the famous poet/doctor John McCrae were hard-nosed about discipline and would have let no malingerers pass through. Morton, "Military Medicine," 51.

42 Harris and Paxman, *Higher Form of Killing*, 16; Jeffrey Keshen, *Propaganda and Censorship during Canada's Great War* (Edmonton: University of Alberta Press, 1996), 179. Middlebrook wrote that for a period, becoming "gassed almost became a court-martial offence." Martin Middlebrook, *The First Day on the Somme* (London: Penguin Books, 1971, 1984), 299.

43 The GOC orders are found in Donald Richter, *Chemical Soldiers: British Gas Warfare in World War I* (Lawrence, KS: University Press of Kansas, 1992), 13. For "gas fright" see S.J. Auld, *Gas and Flame in Modern Warfare* (New York: George H. Doran, 1918), 166. Lord Moran made the same observation in his respected work on fear and courage. Lord Moran, *The Anatomy of Courage*

(London: Constable, 1945), 175-7. For malingering see NAC, RG 41, vol. 20, K.B. Jackson, 2/3; BOMH, 496.

44   NAC, RG 9, vol. 4547, folder 1, file 2, "Cases of Gas Poisoning – Disposal of Doubtful Cases." Only a gas casualty from mine poisoning, "which is not in any way due to neglect or disobedience of orders," was to be reported as a "Battle Casualty," without the stigma of gas attached to it. Report of the Ministry, *Overseas Military Forces,* 310-1. See Heller, *Chemical Warfare,* 83; Manion, *Surgeon in Arms,* chap. 10, for how doctors exposed malingering soldiers. See also George Anderson Wells, *The Fighting Bishop* (Toronto: Cardwell House, 1971), 154, for identifying malingers. As well, see NAC, RG 9, vol. 4547, folder 1, file 2, "Cases of Gas Poisoning – Disposal of Doubtful Cases"; vol. 856, file T-56-2, Self-Inflicted Injuries – Gas.

45   The chemical advisor's report is in NAC, RG 9, vol. 5048, folder 923, file 6, War Diary, Appendix 5. A report issued from the Second Army on 14 October 1917 ordered that "It must be impressed on all ranks both by word of mouth and disciplinary action that unnecessary exposure to battle gas is not bravery but criminal folly." Vol. 4215, folder 3, file 11, G.797.

Chapter 7: It's Got Your Number

1   For mustard gas on boots and clothing see National Archives of Canada (NAC), RG 9, vol. 4060, folder 5, file 1, SS184/6, "Monthly Gas Warfare Summary for December." See RG 41, vol. 9, 15th Battalion, Sam Hewit, 1/15. For gas casualties in the dugouts see RG 9, vol. 3975, folder 1, file 16, Secret Report from W. Eric Harris to all Gas Officers, 16 March 1918.

2   NAC, RG 9, vol. 4066, folder 3, file 2, G.811/23-1; vol. 5048, folder 923, Chemical Advisor War Diary, December 1917, Return of Training in Canadian Corps.

3   For the German gas shoot see NAC, RG 9, vol. 4215, folder 3, file 11, GL-34. A Canadian gas report indicated that the large German gas area shoot contained 331 pounds of gas per hectare of front. This was accompanied by a dense barrage of HE to draw attention away from the gas. Vol. 3831, folder 13, file 5, SB/IO/57, Extracts from GHQ Summary of Information dated 23 November 1917. For gas discipline see vol. 5048, folder 923, file 10, "Gas Shell Report Canadian Corps Week Ending 6.1.18." Strict gas discipline was strongly implemented for the German and British (and dominion) troops, but was much less of a concern for the French, Russians, Italians, and Austrians. And although the Russians could not be blamed for their lack of matériel and trained officers, the French seemed curiously uninterested in gas discipline. Their soldiers suffered accordingly when subjected to large German gas attacks. Quotation from vol. 4066, folder 3, file 2, G.8-97; vol. 4187, folder 3, file 10, G. 545.

4   For night marches see NAC, RG 9, vol. 5048, folder 923, file 10, Summary of War Diary January 1918; vol. 4066, folder 3, file 2, G.27/255. The officer's remark is in ibid., Re: B.M. 636. Remarque noted the same thing. Erich Maria Remarque, *All Quiet on the Western Front* (New York: Fawcett Crest, 1929), 114. The soldier's remark is in Charles Heller, *Chemical Warfare in World War I: The American Experience, 1917-1918,* Leavenworth Papers no. 10 (Fort Leavenworth, KS: Combat Studies Institute, 1984), 55.

5   Quotation from Ludwig Fritz Haber, *The Poisonous Cloud* (Oxford: Clarendon Press, 1986) 135. For the AEF's lack of understanding and preparedness for the gas environment of the Western Front, see the very good article by Charles Heller ("The Peril of Unpreparedness: The American Expeditionary Force and Chemical Warfare," *Military Review* 65, 1 [1985]) and chapter 2 in his book, *Chemical Warfare in World War I: The American Experience, 1917-1918,* Leavenworth Papers no. 10 (Fort Leavenworth, KS: Combat Studies Institute, 1984). Secretary of War quoted in "Peril of Unpreparedness," 16-7.

The role of Canadian DGOs can be found in NAC, RG 9, vol. 5048, folder 923, file 10, War Diary, 6 January 1918. The request to send experienced Canadian soldiers to train a portion of the American troops was agreed to by the Canadian prime minister, Robert Borden. Martin Gilbert, *The First World War* (New York: Henry Holt, 1994), 435. Eventually six Canadian gas officers would be sent to the United States to train the "gas and flame" regiment, who would then disseminate the information to their own troops.

For the impact of the AEF see G.W.L. Nicholson, *Canadian Expeditionary Force, 1914-1919* (Ottawa: Roger Duhamel, Queen's Printer and Controller of Stationary, 1962), 362-4; Gilbert, *First World War,* 404.

6 Quotation from NAC, RG 9, vol. 4032, folder 1, file 14, Tw-1-73. For control given to gas officers see vol. 4060, folder 5, file 1, BM 782; BM 880.

7 For German morale see NAC, MG 30, E40, Cyril Woodland, Erlebach Papers, folder 3, "Change in the Discipline and Moral of the German Army," 1. For intensified raiding and gas see Report of the Ministry, *Overseas Military Forces of Canada, 1918*, (London, 1918), 108 and MG 30, E393, A.J. Foster Papers, 7. For Canadian retaliation see RG 24, vol. 1811, GAQ 3-3, Reference – Use of Gas on Canadian front during Winter 1917/1918. Pro and Con. For the Canadian pro-active artillery doctrine see RG 9, vol. 3921, folder 4, file 2, CB268/7-1-1; Report of the Ministry, *Overseas Military Forces*, 108; Daniel Dancocks, *Spearhead to Victory* (Edmonton: Hurtig, 1987), 16; H.M. Jackson, *The Royal Regiment of Artillery, 1855-1952* (Montreal: privately published, 1952), 137. For gas shells versus enemy infantry see RG 24, vol. 1837, GAQ 9-37, "Artillery."

8 For Canadian gas casualties see NAC, RG 9, vol. 3980, folder 17, file 8, Secret Report from Chemical Advisor of the Canadian Corps. The Canadians suffered 3,552 casualties between 1 December 1917 and 21 March 1918, Nicholson, *Canadian Expeditionary Force*, 339. For report on British gas casualties see vol. 3982, folder 3, file 10, G.2/13; vol. 5048, folder 923, file 11, War Diary, Appendix 10, "Gas Shell Report on Canadian Corps for Week Ending February 16th 1918." For Horne's congratulations see vol. 3975, folder 1, File 16, GS 1055.

9 For the German build-up see Denis Winter, *Haig's Command* (New York: Viking, 1991), 171-90. For German counter-battery work see NAC, RG 9, vol. 4335, folder 10, file 15, G.96/23-11. For Canadian precautions see vol. 3976, folder 4, file 16, Notes on Precautions against Gas by 3rd Cdn. Divnl. Artillery Gas Officer. For soldiers contaminating others see vol. 5048, folder 923, War Diary of the Chemical Advisor, March 1918, G.727/23-11. For Claxton memoirs see NAC, MG 32, B5, Brooke Claxton Papers, vol. 220, Memoirs, 142.

10 For orders to avoid gas see NAC, RG 9, vol. 4060, folder 5, file 1, BM 391, 11 March 1918; vol. 4066, folder 3, file 2, IG 10-39. For friction between officers and gas officers see RG 24, vol. 1837, GAQ 9-37, "Attack Methods"; RG 41, 78th Battalion, F.G. Thompson, 1/8. For the number of gas attacks on the Canadian front see RG 9, vol. 3982, folder 3, file 11, "Report of Hostile Gas Shell Bombardments on Corps Front for Week Ending March 16th and March 23rd, 1918." For 43rd Battalion gas casualties see RG 9, vol. 4187, folder 3, file 10, G.31/21; "43rd Canadian Battalion. Cameron Highlanders of Canada. Reference: Gas Projector Attack of This Morning." See also Victor Lefebure, *The Riddle of the Rhine* (London: W. Collins Sons, 1921), 224.

11 Donald Richter, *Chemical Soldiers: British Gas Warfare in World War I* (Lawrence, KS: University Press of Kansas, 1992) 226.

12 For Bruchmueller's tactics and the response see David T. Zabecki, *Steel Wind: Colonel Georg Bruchmueller and the Birth of Modern Artillery* (Westport, CT: Praeger, 1994), 34-6; Bruce Gudmundsson, *Stormtroop Tactics* (New York: Praeger, 1988), 113-20; Heller, *Chemical Warfare*, 24. For "nourishing" a target see NAC, RG 24, vol. 1837, GAQ 9-37, "Application of Gas"; Haber, *Poisonous Cloud*, 97; Ian Hogg, *Gas* (New York: Ballantine Books, 1975), 119-20. For the codification of the gas shell doctrine see Heller, *Chemical Warfare*, 24.

13 A combination of gas and HE shells was fired before every major German operation during the March Offensive. Robert Aspery, *The German High Command at War* (New York: William Morrow, 1991), 338, 347, 381, 393, 414, 429, 436, 447; see Martin Middlebrook, *The Kaiser's Battle* (London: Allen Lane, 1978), chap. 6, for the use and effects of gas on 21 March 1918. For the percentage of gas shells see NAC, RG 9, vol. 3978, folder 11, file 1, No. 1993 (G); Sir W.G. Macpherson, *Official History of the War: Medical Services Diseases of the War*, vol. 2 (London: HMSO, 1923), 282 (hereafter BOMH), 298. Ludendorff quoted in RG 9, vol. 3978, folder 11, file 3, "Notes on Recent Fighting – No. 16"; vol. 3975, folder 1, file 9, "Gas Artillery Tactics in the Offensive Battle in Trench Warfare"; Erich Ludendorff, *My War Memoirs: 1914-1918*, vol. 2 (London: Hutchinson, 1919), 579, 597. The use of gas was so important that Ludendorff nearly postponed the offensive due to unfavourable wind conditions. Lefebure, *Riddle of the Rhine*, 114. For the effects on British troops see RG 24, vol. 1837, GAQ 9-37, "Artillery"; Holger H. Herwig, *The First World War: Germany and Austria-Hungary, 1914-1918* (London: Arnold, 1997), 413. The sample of routed soldiers is found in F.A. Hessel, *Chemistry in Warfare* (New York: Hastings House, 1940), 20. Artillery officer quoted in Trevor Wilson, *The Myriad Faces of War* (London: Polity Press, 1986), 558.

14 See Augustin M. Prentiss, *Chemicals in War* (New York: McGraw-Hill, 1937), 123-8 for how the Germans classified their gases. For use of German battle gases see NAC, RG 9, vol. 4032, folder 1, file 14, "Translation of a German Document," No. 1/136. For Hartley see vol. 3081, file G-13-36 pt. 3, Anti-Gas Conference for Command Chemical Advisors, 22 April 1918, 3. For Foulkes see Charles H. Foulkes, *Gas: The Story of the Special Brigade* (London: William B. Blackwood and Sons, 1936), 323.

15 For German infiltration tactics see John A. English, *On Infantry* (New York: Praeger, 1981), 19-22; Martin Samuels, *Doctrine and Dogma* (New York: Greenwood Press, 1992), 7-97; Bruce Gudmundsson, *Stormtroop Tactics* (New York: Praeger, 1988), 155-71. Ludendorff quoted in Correlli Barnett, *The Swordbearers: Studies in Supreme Command* (London: Eyre and Spottiswoode, 1963), 282. For the use of gas to protect the flanks see Amos A. Fries and Clarence J. West, *Chemical Warfare* (New York: McGraw-Hill, 1921), 176; Lefebure, *Riddle of the Rhine*, 74.

16 For gas at Armentières see NAC, RG 9, vol. 4066, folder 3, file 2, "Report on Hostile Gas Shelling on I Corps Front during the Week 7-13/4/18"; G.W.L. Nicholson, *The Fighting Newfoundlanders* (St. John's: Government of Newfoundland, 1964), 448. The German tactics are found in RG 9, vol. 4187, folder 3, file 10, No. 1089 (G). Foulkes claimed that by 24 February 1918, GHQ issued warnings with regard to mustard gas revealing future German attacks, but it is clear from the actions of the British divisions that they did not receive such information or disseminate it to their officers in the field. Foulkes, *Gas*, 267.

17 German casualties cited in Tim Travers, *How the War Was Won* (London: Routledge, 1992), 108; Gudmundsson, *Stormtroop Tactics*, 166-8. Quotation from Rudolf Binding, *A Fatalist at War* (London: George Allen and Unwin, 1929), 214, 218-9.

18 NAC, MG 30, E32, Albert C. West Papers, Diary, 24 March 1918.

19 Ibid., E351, Claude C. Craig Papers, Diary, 20 March 1918.

20 Ibid., E379, vol. 2, E.W.B. Morrison Papers, File Orders and Instructions 1917 – Oct. 1918, Special Order by Lieutenant General Sir Arthur W. Currie.

21 Travers, *How the War Was Won*, 82.

22 The correspondence was written by an unknown officer and contains valuable information regarding the battalion, life in the trenches, and casualties. NAC, RG 9, vol. 4215, folder 2, Army Book 152, 27 March-29 April 1918. From the beginning of 1918 the Gas Services accurately recorded every gassing (of more than 100 gas shells) on the Canadian lines along with casualties. Such reports were probably used to justify their own existence but, more important, they make it much easier for historians to understand the full role of gas and its effects on the Canadian Corps. vol. 3982, folder 3, file 11, "Weekly Gas Shelling Report Canadian Corps Front." Quotation from Arthur Lapointe, *Soldier of Quebec, 1916-1919* (Montreal: Edition Edouard Garand, 1931), 87-8.

    For the feared German aerial attacks see vol. 856, file T-56-2, Tw-4-62. It is interesting to note that during April 1918, Royal Air Force pilots were equipped with SBRs. If they were forced to down their planes it was decided that they must be equipped to deal with the gas environment on the ground. Lefebure, *Riddle of the Rhine*, 230.

23 NAC, RG 41, vol. 11, 18th Battalion, H.A. Searle, 2/2-3. For German higher calibre guns see RG 9, vol. 3081, file G-13-36 pt. 3, Anti-Gas Conference for Command Chemical Advisors, 22 April 1918, 2. For the Canadian fireplan see vol. 3977, folder 8, file 21, CB 332/20. For Canadian tactics see vol. 3975, folder 1, file 10, XVII Corps Artillery Instructions No. 22 – Chemical Shell Bombardments." See also Maurice Pope, *Letters from the Front, 1914-1919* (Toronto: Pope and Company, 1993), 117.

24 Currie's diary entry is in Nicholson, *Canadian Expeditionary Force*, 382. Ormond quoted in Daniel Dancocks, *Gallant Canadians* (Calgary: Calgary Highlanders Regimental Funds Foundation, 1990), 161. Extract from Haig's diary on 5 May 1918, NAC, RG 24, vol. 20542, file 990.011 (D1). For a brief period the Canadian divisions were removed from the corps, but Currie played his "Canadian card" and the divisions were eventually returned as the British did not wish to offend the dominion government. For block troops see Richard Adamson, *All for Nothing* (N.p.: Self-published, 1987), 157.

25 Dancocks, *Spearhead to Victory*, 16.

26 NAC, MG 30, E351, Claude C. Craig Papers, Diary, 30 April 1918.

27 For fireplan see NAC, RG 9, vol. 3975, folder 1, file 12, A/96, Modifications to Captain Edwards-Ker's Proposal in Standard Gas Bombardments; ibid., XVII Corps Artillery Instructions No. 22. Special Company attacks are listed in vol. 3977, folder 8, file 23, "Projector Attacks, Canadian Corps."

28 NAC, RG 9, vol. 4315, folder 3, file 8, No. 1403 (G).

29 The shortcomings in production were not specifically confined to the chemical industry. Throughout the war the British had problems in the development, manufacture, and processing of war materials. See W.J. Reader, *Imperial Chemical Industries: A History*, vol. 1 (London: Oxford University Press, 1970), 165-317. For British reports on weaker gas and Hun Stuff see Foulkes, *Gas*, 106, 263; Haber, *Poisonous Cloud*, 109, 112.

30 NAC, RG 9, vol. 3976, folder 4, file 28, SB/IO/83, 2-3. Another report noted that "faults, tears and badly fitting parts are frequently met with in new delivered masks." NAC, RG 8, vol. 3831, folder 13, file 5, Extracts from German Documents re: Effects of Our Gas.

31 This was only the second beam attack, the first being on 24 May 1918. Only nine such attacks were carried out in the war. Foulkes, *Gas*, 293; Haber, *Poisonous Cloud*, 221. Ronald Hoff of "O" Special Companies gives an interesting account of the beam attack on 12 July 1918 just north of Arras at Oppy. John Gardam, *Seventy Years after 1914-1984*, foreword by E.L.M. Burns (Stittsville, ON: Canada's Wings, 1983), 63-5.

32 NAC, RG 9, vol. 4060, folder 5, file 1, "Report of Gas Beam Attack Carried out on XVIII Corps Front Night 23rd/24th May, 1918"; RG 24, vol. 1837, GAQ 9-37, "Attack Methods"; RG 9, vol. 4060, folder 5, file 1, "General Remarks on Lessons Learnt," 28 May 1918. For casualties see RG 9, vol. 3976, folder 4, file 28, SB/IO/83, 1. On the death of the Canadian soldiers see Richter, *Chemical Soldiers*, 206; Robert Harris and Jeremy Paxman, *A Higher Form of Killing* (London: Chatto and Windus, 1982), 30.

33 Haber, *Poisonous Cloud*, 221; Harris and Paxman, *Higher Form of Killing*, 24.

34 Arnold Zweig as quoted in Alistar Horne, *The Price of Glory* (London: Penguin Books, 1962), 307. Zobel quoted in Richard Holmes, *Firing Line* (London: Pimlico, 1985), 188.

35 On the selection of units see Heller, *Chemical Warfare*, 22. On the 1st Bavarian see Moore, William Moore, *Gas Attack* (London: Leo Cooper, 1987), 116. Canadian artillery instructions are in Directorate of History, 79/527, Instructions on the Use of Lethal and Lachrymatory Shell, March 1918. For gas eroding morale see Anthony Kellett, *Combat Motivation: The Behaviour of Soldiers in Battle* (Boston: Kluwer-Nijhoff, 1982), 126-9, and BOMH, 258, on this point. German diary entry quoted in Heller, *Chemical Warfare*, 22-3. German order quoted in Foulkes, *Gas*, 296.

36 German prisoner quoted in NAC, RG 9, vol. 3978, folder 9, file 15, "Effect of Our Gas in General." The need for rest is explored in BOMH, 482.

37 J.C. Meakins and J.G. Priestly, "The After-Effects of Chlorine Gas Poisoning," *Canadian Medical Association Journal* 9, 11 (1919): 968. For a more modern context of chemical-induced fear, see Richard A. Gabriel. *No More Heroes: Madness and Psychiatry in War* (New York: Hill and Wang, 1987), 39; Holmes, *Firing Line*, 212. Lord Moran, *The Anatomy of Courage* (London: Constable, 1945), xvi.

38 Holmes makes the argument in his fascinating book on the experience of soldiers on the battlefield that the inability to strike back at an enemy during a bombardment (whether HE or gas) is one of the characteristics that made heavy shelling so damaging to morale. Holmes, *Firing Line*, 29. R.J. Manion, *A Surgeon in Arms* (New York: Doran, 1918), 79. Rivers quoted in John Talbott, "Combat Trauma in the American Civil War," *History Today* 46, 3 (1996): 46. The padre is quoted in David B. Marshall, "Methodism Embattled: A Reconsideration of the Methodist Church and World War I," *Canadian Historical Review* 66, 1 (1985): 56.

39 Chas. G.A. Chislett, "Effects of the Factors Producing Shell Shock," *Canada Lancet* 54, 9 (1921): 394.

40 Ernst Junger, *Storm of Steel* (London: Chatto and Windus, 1929), 61; J. Clinton Morrison Jr, *Hell upon Earth: A Personal Account of Prince Edward Island Soldiers in the Great War, 1914-1918* (N.p.: Self-published, 1995), 237-8; Ex-Quaker, *Not Mentioned in Despatches* (North Vancouver, BC: North Shore Press, 1933), 50.

41 Lord Moran, *Anatomy of Courage*, 48.

42 Arthur O. Hickson, *As It Was Then,* edited by D.G.L. Fraser (Wolfville, NS: Acadia University, 1988), 60. Fred Wingfield, a battalion runner and cyclist, believed the same thing and postulated that those who could not take a fatalistic attitude were "the ones who became shell shocked." NAC, RG 41, vol. 20, Fred Wingfield, 2/8.

43 NAC, RG 9, vol. 3978, folder 11, file 3, "Notes on Recent Fighting – No. 16."; Gabriel, *No More Heroes,* 39.

44 Bell quoted in William D. Mathieson, *My Grandfather's War* (Toronto: Macmillan, 1981), 133. Ormond quoted in Dancocks, *Gallant Canadians,* 153. The warning about ripping off respirators is in NAC, RG 9, vol. 4158, folder 1, file 12, G.8-6. See MG 31, G30, William Woods Papers, 16.

45 Louis Keene in *Crumps: The Plain Story of a Canadian Who Went* (Boston: Houghton Mifflin, 1917), 106.

46 Erich Maria Remarque, *All Quiet on the Western Front* (New York: Fawcett Crest, 1929), 131; NAC, MG 30, E318, file 130, G.717/23-11.

47 Morrison, *Hell upon Earth,* 73.

48 Soldier quoted in Paul Fussell, *The War and Modern Memory* (New York: Oxford University Press, 1975), 115. The comment is attributed to the French soldier/writer Marc Bloch. For French report see NAC, RG 9, vol. 3982, folder 3, file 7, "Report on the Periodical Outbursts of Reports Announcing Extraordinary Discoveries Made by the Enemy," 2. See Lefebure, *Riddle of the Rhine,* 117-9, for another examination of the rumours.

49 Haber, *Poisonous Cloud,* 237.

50 The figure for the Gas Services does not include any unit gas officers below the rank of brigade gas officer who were attached to other units like battalions or batteries. NAC, RG 9, vol. 3976, folder 5, file 20, "Canadian Corps Gas Services," 1.

51 The corps chemical advisors were to report by wire every evening to the Army chemical advisor on details of gas bombardments during the day. NAC, RG 9, vol. 4032, folder 1, file 14, CHB/11/A.60. For Canadian Gas Services see vol. 3976, folder 5, file 20, "Table Showing Organization and Chain of Responsibility of Canadian Corps Gas Services."

52 NAC, RG 9, vol. 3976, folder 5, file 20, "Canadian Corps Gas Services," 2. From Edmund Blunden's choice of words in describing him, it is clear that he respected his gas officer for carrying out his "kindly, [but] deadly work." It was a dangerous job, but a necessary one. Such praise was in direct contrast to his opinions of the corporals in the Special Companies. Edmund Blunden, *Undertones of War* (London: Cox and Wyman, 1928), 220.

53 Methods of decontamination are in NAC, RG 9, vol. 4066, folder 3, file 2, No. 461A. For lime see vol. 3081, file G-13-36 pt. 3, Anti-Gas Conference for Command Chemical Advisors, 22 April 1918, 4.

54 NAC, RG 9, vol. 5048, folder 923, file 18, CH5/5/149; vol. 4043, folder 1, file 18, CHU/14/215-12-9-1918; vol. 5048, folder 923, file 18, G.256/23-11.

55 NAC, RG 9, vol. 3975, folder 1, file 16, "The General Character of the Casualties," 1, 3. For reducing the effectiveness of mustard gas see ibid., 1; G.W.L. Nicholson, *Seventy Years of Service: A History of the Royal Canadian Army Medical Corps* (Toronto: Borealis Press, 1977), 103.

56 For leather suits see NAC, RG 9, vol. 4066, folder 3, file 2, 4004/12 (Q.B.1.); Victor A. Utgoff, *The Challenge of Chemical Weapons* (London: Macmillan, 1990), 25. For the issue of soda see vol. 4129, folder 5, file 13, A/5650. For the paste see Heller, *Chemical Warfare,* 67.

57 See NAC, RG 24, vol. 1158, file HQC 56-12, letter by Mr. E.A. Le Lueur for a suggestion on the use of sulphur trioxide in shells, and vol. 1831, GAQ 8-4, letter from Mr. Pat Foster inquiring on sulphuric ether for treating gassed patients, for other "solutions" to combatting the gas war.

58 NAC, RG 9, vol. 3618, Director of Medical Services, file 25-13-6, Memo: 10 July 1919.

59 Ibid., Memo 236-238.

60 The need for more training is discussed in NAC, RG 9, vol. 4129, folder 5, file 13, A.1283, 1. The Third Army warning is in vol. 4328, folder 11, file 38, Artillery Notes – Defence; folder 12, file 24, Third Army No. GS59/9. Men were required to practise the rapid-fire of ten rounds at 300-yards range while wearing their SBRs. Vol. 3982, folder 5, file 6, Overseas Military Forces of Canada Part IV General Musketry Course, 1 June 1918; vol. 4032, folder 1, file 14, Tw-1-77, "Football in Masks."

61 Fries quoted in Malcolm Brown, *The Imperial War Museum Book of the Western Front*

(London: Sidgwick and Jackson, 1993), 30. The report is found in NAC, RG 9, vol. 3981, folder 18, file 12, GB258/2, 1. For new recruits see ibid., 9/61.

62   For klaxon horns see NAC, MG 30, E6, vol. 4, file 24, Harry Burstall Papers, Appendix 8, "Anti-Gas Defence." For military police see RG 9, vol. 3976, folder 4, file 16, 5/237. Quotation from Cochrane, *The 3rd Division at Chateau Thierry, July 1918,* Study 14 of *Gas Warfare in World War I* (N.p.: Army Chemical Centre, Chemical Corps Historical Office) as cited in Utgoff, *Challenge of Chemical Weapons,* 10.

63   NAC, RG 41, vol. 20, L.V. Moore Cosgrave, 1/22; RG 9, vol. 3976, folder 4, file 26, G.476/1-38; MG 30, E81, vol. 2, E.W.B. Morrison Papers, File: Orders & Instructions, Sept. 1918-Dec. 1918, Policy as to Command of Artillery Units during Offensive Operations; RG 9, vol. 4357, folder 13, file 1, BM 80/712. Divisional artillery still had the right to consult their own DGOs to carry out gas fireplans if they wished. RG 9, vol. 3980, folder 15, file 5, DGS A/151.

64   NAC, RG 41, vol. 20, A. Farmer, 2/10. Maxse quoted in Winter, *Haig's Command,* 145. For the warning to officers see RG 9, vol. 3981, folder 18, file 12, CHG/IV/58. For the British admission see vol. 3018, file G-13-36 pt. 3, Anti-Gas Conference for Command Chemical Advisor, 22 April 1918, 5. For the importance of gas training see vol. 3981, folder 18, file 12, "Gas Training," 19 July 1918.

Chapter 8: The Gas Environment

1   G.W.L. Nicholson, *Canadian Expeditionary Force, 1914-1919* (Ottawa: Roger Duhamel, Queen's Printer and Controller of Stationary, 1962), 386. For Foch's words and German reaction see Denis Winter, *Haig's Command* (New York: Viking, 1991), 210.

2   Herbert Sulzbach, *With the German Guns* (Hamden: Archon Books, 1981), 213, 221.

3   Currie quoted in Report of the Ministry, *Overseas Military Forces of Canada, 1918* (London, 1918), 333-5. In terms of total strength, the average British division mustered approximately 15,000 men. This is compared to a Canadian division of 21,000. Shane Shriver, "Orchestra to Victory" (Master of War Studies thesis, Royal Military College, 1995), 43.

4   For colonial reputations see Sir Basil Liddell Hart, *A History of the World War, 1914-1918* (London: Little, Brown, 1935), 547. Prime Minister Lloyd George agreed with Liddell Hart's statement and later wrote that "Whenever the Germans found the Canadian Corps coming into the line, they prepared for the worst." As quoted in Daniel Dancocks, *Gallant Canadians* (Calgary: Calgary Highlanders Regimental Funds Foundation, 1990), 175. At least one group of British Tommies believed the same thing. When some men of the 4th Battalion walked into a dugout occupied by some Highlanders they recounted the following conversation: "One says, 'Canadians?' I says, 'Yes.' He says, 'Blimey, we're for it. Something's going to happen when the Canadians are around.'" National Archives of Canada (NAC), RG 41, vol. 7, 4th Battalion, 6/9.

For the note in the Canadian soldier's paybook see Nicholson, *Canadian Expeditionary Force,* 389. For deception see Daniel Dancocks, *Spearhead to Victory* (Edmonton: Hurtig, 1987), 29-31; Shriver, "Orchestra to Victory," 72-3.

5   The 2nd Division report is in NAC, RG 9, vol. 4794, folder 52, "Narrative Operations 2nd Canadian Division 13 March-11 November, 1918," 7. See RG 41, vol. 11, 18th Battalion, R.H. Camp, 2/5. Fear of gas shells is cited in MG 30, E81, E.W.B. Morrison Papers, vol. 2, File: Orders & Instructions, 1917-Oct. 1918, R.A. 125/2, 10.

6   On the Australians' left was the 3rd British Corps and to the Canadians right was the French 31st Corps. Currie's artillery cited in Nicholson, *Canadian Expeditionary Force,* 396. Two articles by A.G.L. McNaughton, "The Development of Artillery in the Great War," *Canadian Defence Quarterly* 6, 2 (1929): 160-71, and "Counter Battery Work," *Canadian Defence Quarterly* 3, 4 (1926): 380-91, contain excellent descriptions of the role of counter-battery fire and how it was achieved. See report written by Crerar, "Organization of Corps Counter-Battery Staff Office," quoted in Shriver, "Orchestra to Victory," 48.

7   NAC, RG 9, vol. 3895, folder 2, file 2, 1228/20-15.

8   The *Llandovery Castle* was a British hospital ship sunk by a U-boat on 27 June 1918. Not only were Canadian personnel among the dead, but the U-boat surfaced after the sinking to shoot and ram the survivors in the lifeboats. Joseph Hayes, *The Eighty-Fifth in France and Flanders* (Halifax, NS: Royal Printer, 1920), 124. See NAC, RG 41, vol. 7, 3rd Battalion, J.R. Cartwright,

1/16; RG 9, vol. 3923, folder 10, file 4, CB 872/4-2. General Budworth, general officer comman-der of artillery for the Fourth British Army, signalled out the artillery barrage and counter-battery work of the Canadian artillery as commanding much admiration and appreciation. NAC, MG 30, E81, vol. 2, E.W.B. Morrison Papers, File Notes and Pamphlets, Speech at Cana-dian Club in Hamilton, The Canadian Artillery in the Great War, n.d.

9　Minimal equipment consisted of haversack, 250 rounds of ammunition, gas mask, water bot-tle, "iron rations," entrenching tool, two Mills bombs, and two sandbags. Nicholson, *Canadian Expeditionary Force*, 398n. Quotation from p. 400.

10　A.M.J. Hyatt, *General Sir Arthur Currie*, (Toronto: University of Toronto Press in collaboration with the Canadian War Museum, Canadian Museum of Civilization, and National Museums of Canada, 1987), 114. J.F.C. Fuller also described the battle of Amiens as one of the decisive battles of the Western Front. J.F.C. Fuller, *The Decisive Battles of the Western World* (London: Eyre and Spottiswoode, 1956), 276-99.

11　Roger Parkinson, *Tormented Warrior: Ludendorff and the Supreme Command* (London: Hod-der and Stoughton, 1978), 170; In a more candid statement Ludendorff muttered to Colonel Mertz von Quirnheim on 7 August that "Woe unto us if the Allies should notice our slowdown. We have lost the war if we cannot pull ourselves together." As quoted in Martin Gilbert, *The First World War* (New York: Henry Holt, 1994), 448.

12　Casualty figures cited in Nicholson, *Canadian Expeditionary Force*, 407. Canadian quotation from NAC, RG 41, vol.7, 1st Brigade, W.H. Joliffre, 2/8. Currie to Borden, 26 November 1918, NAC, MG 30, E100, vol. 1, file: Correspondence A to F.

13　The German's mistake was probably a combination of the 2nd Division's shoulder badges, which contained a C and two straight marks beneath it to denote two (but which looked like eleven) along with the fighting reputation of the Canadian Corps. NAC, RG 41, vol. 11, 18th Bat-talion, R.H. Camp, 2/7. Even more extraordinary, James claims that a document issued by the German General Staff, and taken from an officer prisoner, stated that since the war began no less than fifty-two Canadian divisions had been identified in France. Fred James, *Canada's Triumph: From Amiens to Mons* (London: Canadian War Records Office, 1918), 25. The rush of German reinforcements is noted in Nicholson, *Canadian Expeditionary Force*, 408. The use of gas is cited in William Moore, *Gas Attack* (London: Leo Cooper, 1987) 189. For the miserable conditions of Canadian soldiers see NAC, MG 30, E488, William C. Morgan Papers, Diary, 10 and 15 August 1918. See remark in 10th Battalion's War Diary with regard to the heavy use of gas against cavalry units preparing to break into the German lines. NAC, RG 9, vol. 4921, 8 August 1918.

14　NAC, RG 9, vol. 4032, folder 1, file 14, GHQ No. OB/492, G. 604/23-11. For polluted wells see vol. 4335, folder 10, file 15, AQ53/224.

15　NAC, RG 41, vol. 14, W.M. Marshall, 46th Battalion, 1/15 and 2/1; MG 30, E475, Thomas W. Goss-ford Papers, 24. For loss of sense of smell see RG 9, vol. 3081, file G-13-36 pt. 3, Anti-Gas Con-ference for Command Chemical Advisors, 22 April 1918, 4.

16　NAC, RG 9, vol. 3975, folder 1, file 3, no. 9/125, "Preferable Hours for Firing Yellow Cross Shells"; RG 41, vol. 15, 52nd Battalion, A.E. MacFarlane, 4/4. For joke see Denis Winter, *Death's Men* (London: Penguin Books, 1979), 121. Lord Moran, *The Anatomy of Courage*, 126.

17　For gassing forward areas see NAC, RG 9, vol. 4032, folder 1, file 14, G.372-1. For the new Ger-man shell and difficulty in neutralizing gas-infected areas see vol. 4032, folder 1, file 14, OB/492. The warning to soldiers is in vol. 3081, file G-13-36 vol. 2, G.50/23-11.

18　NAC, RG 9, vol. 4810, file Medical, "Medical Arrangements Canadian Corps during Second Battle of Amiens – August 8-20." The same was true during the attack on the D-Q Line. NAC, RG 9, vol. 3855, folder 75, file 1, Medical Arrangements Canadian Corps. Gas casualties can be found in vol. 3975, folder 1, file 16, Gas Cases Reported by A.D.M.S. as Admitted to Fd. Amb. Can. Corps for week ending August 24th 1918. See MG 30, E446, Anne E. Ross Papers, "Narra-tives of World War I Nursing Service," 17.

19　On captured goods see NAC, RG 9, vol. 5048, folder 923, file 17, War Diary, Summary for Month of August. The Canadian Corps was issued a secret report on 16 August 1918 describing how German artillery gas shell fuses could be modified and fired from Canadian guns. NAC, RG 9, vol. 3925, folder 17, file 1, GS11/29. See also H.M. Jackson, *The Royal Regiment of Artillery, 1855-1952* (Montreal: privately published, 1952), 149.

No one suspected the quick collapse of the German Army in 1918. Lloyd George and British politicians were preparing plans for a 1919 or 1920 offensive. The gas war, as in the last three years, was expected to grow in importance.

20 Currie's letter quoted in John Terraine, *Douglas Haig: The Educated Soldier* (London: Hutchinson, 1963), 459. Canadian operational success and casualties listed in Nicholson, *Canadian Expeditionary Force*, 419.

21 Dancocks, *Spearhead to Victory*, 91.

22 Howard Graham, *Citizen and Soldier* (Toronto: McClelland and Stewart, 1987), 65.

23 As quoted in Shriver, "Orchestra to Victory," 140.

24 NAC, RG 9, vol. 5048, folder 923, file 17, War Diary, Summary for Month of August; vol. 4985, War Diary of 2nd Machine Gun Battalion, Action of No. 3 Company, 26-28 August 1918; NAC, MG 30, E32, Alfred C. West Papers, Diary, 27 August 1918.

25 NAC, MG 30, E32, Albert C. West Papers, Diary, 27 August 1918; Gerald De Groot, *Douglas Haig, 1861-1928* (London: Unwin Hyman, 1988), 388.

26 NAC, RG 9, vol. 3923, folder 11, file 2, "Heavy Artillery Support on August 28th," 8. For Donaldson's report see vol. 3978, folder 11, folder 9, "Report on Gas Shell Bombardment for Week Ending Saturday August 31st 1918." The battalion's number is not mentioned in the report.

27 Nicholson, *Canadian Expeditionary Force*, 432; NAC, RG 9, vol. 3975, folder 1, file 16, "Gas Cases Reported by the A.D.M.S. from August 23rd to September 6th, 1918.

28 For minor raids see NAC, RG 9, vol. 3923, folder 11, file 1, "Artillery Notes on Operations of the Canadian Corps August 26th to September 4th, 1918." Quotation from vol. 4921, War Diary of 10th Battalion, "Narrative of Operations Taken Part in by the 10th Canadian Infantry Battalion from 28-8-1918 to 4-9-18," 1. For prisoner's account see A.L. Barry, *Batman to Brigadier* (n.p., 1965), 58-9.

29 Dancocks, *Spearhead to Victory*, 104; Nicholson, *Canadian Expeditionary Force*, 433; John Swettenham, *To Seize the Victory: The Canadian Corps in World War I* (Toronto: Ryerson, 1965), 216.

30 A.G.L. McNaughton, "The Development of Artillery in the Great War," *Canadian Defence Quarterly* 6, 2 (1929): 169. McNaught quoted in J. Clinton Morrison Jr, *Hell upon Earth: A Personal Account of Prince Edward Island Soldiers in the Great War, 1914-1918* (N.p.: Self-published, 1995), 155.

31 For German gas shelling see NAC, RG 9, vol. 3981, folder 1, file 1, G1.197; vol. 4215, folder 2, Army Book 152, 2/9/18; Sir Archibald Macdonell, "The Old Red Patch at the Breaking of the Drocourt-Quéant Line, the Crossing of the Canal du Nord and the Advance on Cambrai, 30th Aug. – 2nd Oct. 1918." *Canadian Defence Quarterly* 6, 1 (October 1928): 11. More than fifty years later Hamilton still suffered from the effects of gas and was incapable of climbing a flight of stairs. NAC, RG 41, 58th Battalion, Gordon Hamilton, 2/7. See also RG 41, vol. 8, 7th Battalion, J.I. Chambers, 1/9. For return of captured gas shells see Shriver, "Orchestra to Victory," 156.

32 Victor Wheeler, *The 50th Battalion in No Man's Land* (Calgary: Alberta Historical Resources, 1980), 115.

33 Heller, *Chemical Warfare*, 63.

34 NAC, MG 30, E32, Albert C. West Papers, Diary, 2/9/18; E100, vol. 1, file: Correspondence A to F, Currie to Alistair, 7 December 1918; Winter, *Haig's Command*, 270.

35 Yvonne S. Burgess, ed., *Who Said War Is Hell!: No. 12895 Private Victor N. Swanston* (Saskatchewan: Modern Press, 1983), 52; NAC, RG 41, vol. 7, 4th Battalion, Trowles, 1/5; vol. 11, 18th Battalion, R.H. Camp, 1/9; and 78th Battalion, F.G. Thompson, 1/8. Final quotation from Winter, *Death's Men*, 124.

36 NAC, RG 9, vol. 3981, folder 18, file 12, G.219/14-25 and "Canadian Anti-gas Equipment." Most infantry battalions stood below 50 percent strength and almost 80 percent of the casualties were suffered by the infantry. Dancocks, *Spearhead to Victory*, 119; Shriver, "Orchestra to Victory," 168.

37 Nicholson, *Canadian Expeditionary Force*, 441.

38 J.F.C. Fuller, *The Conduct of War, 1832-1932* (London: Eyre Methusen, 1972), 174; Edward Spiers, *Chemical Warfare* (Chicago: University of Illinois Press, 1986), 26; Charles Heller "The Peril of Unpreparedness: The American Expeditionary Force and Chemical Warfare," *Military Review* 65, 1 (1985): 22-5.

39 NAC, RG 24, vol. 20543, file 990.013 (D14), U.S. Army Chemical Corps Historical Studies, Gas Warfare in World War I, The 79th Division at Montfaucon, October 1918, 68.

40 Haber estimated that during "Michael," the first German offensive, the Germans used a 50:50 mixture of HE and gas (principally Blue Cross and phosgene) on the enemy infantry and an 80:20 ratio of mustard gas to HE in counter-battery work. Ludwig Fritz Haber, *The Poisonous Cloud* (Oxford: Clarendon Press, 1986), 214. One of the positions overrun by the 2nd Division was a German ammunitions dump. After examining the contents, the DGO found that of the 19,765 gas shells captured, an astounding 88.6 percent were Blue Cross, with 7.5 percent Green, and only 2.5 percent Yellow. Assuming that all types of shell were issued in roughly equal numbers, such a composition illustrated the German predisposition to use up their Yellow Cross and Green Cross and largely ignore the Blue Cross shells unless undertaking an offensive operation. NAC, RG 9, vol. 3975, folder 3, file 10, "Report of DGO, 2nd Canadian Division."

41 NAC, MG 30, E66, Cruickshank Papers, vol. 31, file 84, extracts from the "Summary of Events and Information – RA Can. Corps," 12-4. This document of daily accounts gives a clear indication on the Germans' massive reliance on gas and the Canadian retaliation with like force as punishment.

42 NAC, MG 30, E6, Burstall Papers, vol. 3, file 21, "2nd Canadian Division – Narrative of Operations – From March 13th to Nov. 11th 1918," 39; E351, Claude C. Craig Papers, Diary, 7 and 13 September 1918.

43 The lack of anti-gas materials is noted in NAC, RG 9, vol. 4138, folder 4, file 16, Memo from CO of the 28th Battalion Requesting Gas Fittings, 15 September 1918. Canadian gas casualties are from vol. 3978, folder 9, file 8, BM 50/126-1; folder 11, file 9, "Report on Hostile Gas Shell Bombardment on Canadian Corps Front for Week Ending Saturday September 14th, 1918."

44 NAC, RG 9, vol. 3921, folder 4, file 2, CB 351/7-1; W.H. Anderson, "The Crossing of the Canal du Nord by the First Army, 27th September, 1918," *Canadian Defence Quarterly* 2, 1 (1924): 65; Jackson, *Royal Regiment of Artillery*, 152. For the desperate use of gas see RG 9, vol. 5048, folder 923, file 18, "Enemy Gas Shelling on Canadian Corps Front during Week Ending 21.9.18"; vol. 3923, folder 11, file 4, "Staff College Lecture, 1921: Canal du Nord," 2; Hartley argued that this disorganized gas shelling was occurring all over the Allied front. He gives no reason for this, but clearly it was due to desperation and a hope of forestalling the upcoming offensives. Harold Hartley, "A General Comparison of British and German Methods of Gas Warfare," *Journal of the Royal Artillery* (February 1920): 503. Canadian artillery casualties are found in NAC, MG 30, E66, vol. 31, Cruickshank Papers, file 84, Extract from the War Diary of R.A. Canadian Corps – Casualties [September]. German firing of gas at night is documented in RG 9, vol. 4032, folder 1, file 14, IG 10-34.

45 NAC, RG 9, vol. 4547, folder 1, file 2, GS 7/144.

46 Ibid., vol. 4187, folder 3, file 11, G.429/25-5; vol. 4032, folder 1, file 14, G.429/25-5.

47 David Pierce Beatty, ed., *Memories of the Forgotten War: The World War I Diary of Pte. V.E. Goodwin* (Port Elgin, NB: Baie Verte Editions, 1986), 146, 150; "Corps nightmare" cited in Shane Shriver, "Orchestra to Victory" (Master of War Studies thesis, Royal Military College, 1995), 191-2.

48 See Ian Brown, "Not Glamorous, But Effective: The Canadian Corps and the Set-piece Attack, 1917-1918," *Journal of Military History* 58 (July 1994).

49 NAC, RG 9, vol. 3923, folder 11, file 4, "Staff College Lecture, 1921: Canal du Nord," 13.

50 NAC, RG 9, vol. 3923, folder 11, file 5, CB704/0.82.

51 For Germans' use of Blue Cross see ibid., vol. 3978, folder 11, file 11, CHR/1/119; Hayes, *The Eighty-Fifth*, 156-7. For their use of mustard gas in the final two months see Holger H. Herwig, *The First World War: Germany and Austria-Hungary, 1914-1918* (London: Arnold, 1997), 357. See also Sir Henry F. Thuillier, *Gas in the Next War* (London: Geoffrey Bles, 1938), 74; Sir W.G. Macpherson, *Official History of the War: Medical Services Diseases of the War*, vol. 2 (London: HMSO, 1923), 304. For 4th Canadian Division DGO's report see NAC, RG 9, vol. 3978, folder 11, file 11, HB 95 d/5.9.18. Quotation from ibid. Some officers were forced to remove their respirators because prismatic compasses would be thrown off by 10 degrees if they were viewed through an SBR. The cause of the magnetic disruption was traced to the metal rim of the eyepieces in the SBR. Incidentally, steel helmets did not affect the compasses. Vol. 4187, folder 3, file 11, G.632/23-9; vol. 3983, folder 2, file 16, GHQ QB/215. Quotation in vol. 8, 8th Battalion, C.E. Barnes, 2/2.

52 Currie makes almost no mention of the use of gas in his *Report of the Ministry – Overseas Military Forces of Canada, 1918*. This is not uncommon among reports, war diaries, and official histories of the Canadian Corps, which tend to gloss over the importance of gas and the defence against it. The figure of 17,000 shells is given in NAC, MG 31, G3, "Gas Warfare on the Canadian Front: A Report of Survey by Rexmond C. Cochrane," 22-3. Canadian use of gas given in RG 9, vol. 3978, folder 9, file 9, "Gas Bombardment of Bourlon Wood and Village," 2; vol. 3923, folder 11, file 4, "Lecture ... Canal du Nord," 16; Anderson, "Crossing of the Canal du Nord," 71. The artillery report is found in MG 30, E66, Cruickshank Papers, vol. 31, file 85, RA Canadian Corps 0.907/20/2.
  Although this work focuses on the Canadian Corps, the Germans suffered high gas casualties as well. For German casualties see Rudolph Hanslian, "Gas Warfare: A German Apologia," *Canadian Defence Quarterly* 6, 1 (1928): 100. For an additional view, Stephen Westman records a chilling description of working on mustard-gassed soldiers as a surgeon in the German Army. Stephen Westman, *Surgeon with the Kaiser's Army* (London: William Kimber, 1968), 119-26.
53 NAC, RG 41, vol. 20, Bud O'Neill, 1/14. German prisoner quoted in RG 9, vol. 3925, folder 17, file 1, no. 9/190. The evacuation of guns is described in RG 24, vol. 1837, GAQ 9-37, "Artillery."
54 The slow advance of the British on the left and right flanks forced the Canadians to advance cautiously. Both the 1st and 3rd Canadian Divisions suffered heavy casualties as their attacking battalions suffered enfilade fire from Germans in the British boundaries. The German tactical use of gas was duly noted by Subaltern Robert England, who saw that all jumping off points on 29 September had been "drenched with gas shells." Robert England, MC, *Recollections of a Nonagenarian of Service in the Royal Canadian Regiment, 1916-1919* (N.p.: Self-published, 1983), [12]. NAC, MG 30, E389, W.J. O'Brien Papers, 29 September 1918.
55 For German use of gas see NAC, RG 9, vol. 5048, folder 923, file 19, "Report for Hostile Gas Bombardment for Week Ending October 5th, 1918." The Canadian gas figures include only those who were incapacitated by gas. As already indicated, almost all the Canadians at the sharp end were gassed during the operation but continued fighting regardless of the ordeal. British figures cited in vol. 5048, folder 923, file 19, CHE/1/119.
56 On the Canadian advance see Report of the Ministry, *Overseas Military Forces of Canada, 1918* (London, 1918), 168. During the period of 27 September to 7 October, the Canadian Corps suffered 707 officers and 12,913 other ranks killed, wounded, or missing. Shriver, "Orchestra to Victory," 202-3. German staff officer quoted in NAC, RG 9, vol. 4718, 114/6, When the Germans Knew They Were Beaten. Supplied by the Canadian War Records Office to General Currie, the report also noted that "Generally speaking, Captain Finkel says, it was recognised by everyone on the other side that any strategic opening, no matter how small, was at once recognised and turned to their advantage by the Canadians." See Erich Ludendorff, *My War Memoirs: 1914-1918*, vol. 2 (London: Hutchinson, 1919), 718-22.
57 Quotation in NAC, RG 9, vol. 4138, folder 4, file 16, G. 3/3, "Policy of Patrols." For Canadian use of mustard gas see vol. 3980, folder 15, file 14, CA 150. The first mustard shells were used on 5 October. MG 30, E66, vol. 31, Cruickshank Papers, file 84, Summary of Events and Information for R.A. Canadian Corps. See RG 9, vol. 4794, folder 52, "Narratives Operations 2nd Canadian Division 13 March-11 November 1918," 47-54; RG 41, vol. 14, 47th Battalion, A.N. Davis, 1/11-12; RG 9, vol. 3975, folder 1, file 16, Gas Cases Reported by A.D.M.S. as Admitted to Fd Amb. Can. Corps for week ending 12.10.18.
58 Morrison, *Hell upon Earth*, 159-60.
59 Civilians were to be warned by ringing of church bells: violent ringing of the bell for thirty seconds, followed by a successive series of five strokes on the bell with a ten-second pause between each five strokes. NAC, RG 24, vol. 1847, GAQ 9-37, "Precautionary Measures"; NAC, RG 9, vol. 3975, folder 1, file 11, G.746/23-11, Instructions regarding precautions to be taken against hostile attacks. Quotations from John William Lynch, *Princess Patricia's Canadian Light Infantry, 1917-1919* (New York: Exposition Press, 1976), 47; MG 30, E389, W.J. O'Brien Papers, 21 October 1918.
60 NAC, MG 30, E32, Albert C. West Papers, Diary, 9 October 1918. West also noted that all officers in his Company save one had been wounded or killed.
61 Nicholson, *Canadian Expeditionary Force*, 460.

62 Currie's order is in NAC, RG 9, vol. 4032, folder 1, file 14, B-M.4-861. Targets for Canadian gas bombardments are given in vol. 3923, folder 11, file 6, CB 883/1-1, Counter Battery Instructions. Canadian Corps Artillery. Quotation from Heller, *Chemical Warfare*, 86.

63 Foulkes claims that on the night of 26 September, the British fired 10,000 mustard gas shells. Charles H. Foulkes, *Gas: The Story of the Special Brigade* (London: William B. Blackwood and Sons, 1936), 326. Mustard gas shells were first fired extensively by the French on 16 June 1918; the Americans received their first shipments during the last weeks of the war and used them in a preparatory bombardment on 30 October 1918. Gilbert, *First World War*, 432, 490; Haber, *Poisonous Cloud*, 218-9; Heller, *Chemical Warfare*, 87. For control of mustard-gas shoots see NAC, MG 30, E81, E.W.B. Morrison Papers, vol. 2, File: Orders and Instructions, Sept. 1918-Dec. 1918, O.907/2 0-2. Among the million soldiers who became gas casualties during the war, some of the more famous were Douglas MacArthur, Ford Madox Ford, Sir Basil Liddell Hart, and the British war artist Will Longstaff.

64 From 11 October to 11 November the Canadian Corps advanced 91,500 yards. Report of the Ministry, *Overseas Military Forces*, 183.

65 The artillery report is in NAC, RG 9, vol. 4798, folder 94, "Artillery Report on Mont Houy by Canadian Corps," 5. McNaughton echoed the same sentiments when he wrote that the Canadian Corps commander wished "to pay the price of victory, so far as possible, in shells and not in the lives of men." A.G.L. McNaughton, "The Capture of Valenciennes," *Canadian Defence Quarterly* 10, 3 (1933): 279. The Canadian artillery received its first BB shells on 19 October 1918. RG 9, vol. 4066, folder 3, file 2, G.1093. An order from the First Army describing the effectiveness of gas shells in counter-battery work warned against occupying area gassed by BB shells for six to twelve hours after shelling. Vol. 4032, folder 1, file 14, no. 3007 (G); vol. 4066, folder 3, file 2, G. 1093; McNaughton, "Capture of Valenciennes," 285. The Canadian bombardment is described in vol. 4798, folder 94, "Artillery Report on Mont Houy by Canadian Corps," 5.

66 Richard Adamson, *All for Nothing* (N.p.: Self-published, 1987), 225; NAC, RG 9, vol. 4798, folder 94, "Artillery Report on Mont Houy by Canadian Corps," 15.

67 For comparison to Waterloo see McNaughton, "Capture of Valenciennes," 293. For the captured German's remark see Beatty, *Memories of the Forgotten War*, 195. See also a letter from Haber to Harold Hartley and cited in Albert Palazzo, "Tradition, Innovation, and the Pursuit of the Decisive Battle: Poison Gas and the British Army on the Western Front, 1915-1918" (PhD diss., Ohio State University, 1996), 1.

68 Quotation on the use of mustard gas in NAC, RG 41, vol. 16, 78th Battalion, G.A. Holman and R.D. Hinch, 1/23. Sinclair's remark is in vol. 9, 13th Battalion, Ian Sinclair, 3/2. The 50th Battalion casualties can be found in Wheeler, *50th Battalion*, 374. Between 2 and 5 November 1918 the 50th Battalion suffered forty-one of the sixty total gas casualties in the 4th Division. It seems that the battalion's gas discipline was lacking. RG 9, vol. 3975, folder 1, file 16, "Gassed Cases Admitted to Fd. Ambs. of this Division." Hutchinson's comment is in RG 41, vol. 13, P.P. Hutchinson, 1/1. From mid-October to the end of the war the Canadians suffered 559 gas casualties. This figure was compiled from various weekly gas reports.

69 NAC, RG 41, vol. 7, 1st Brigade, Guy Mills, 1/7; Dancocks, *Spearhead to Victory*, 204.

70 Figure extracted from Casualties by Days – France and Belgium – CEF in France. NAC, RG 150, Series 9. These figures, as noted throughout this work, are certainly much lower then what actually occurred, but they are a good starting point.

71 NAC, RG 9, vol. 5048, folder 923, file 21, War Diary, 20 December 1918. Interestingly, although the Canadian Corps no longer needed the Gas Services there had been a series of memos in October 1918 from Lieutenant-Colonel Brook of the Canadian contingent for the Siberian Expeditionary Force (SEF) with regard to instructing his men in gas discipline and supplying them with SBRs. He suggested that gas officers from the Gas Services would be welcome to enlist in the SEF. Although the SEF received 500 smoke bombs, they were not furnished with the phosgene or chlorine or any of the gas officers they requested. RG 24, vol. 2005, file HQ 762-19-3.

At disbandment the following men were the senior gas officers within the Gas Services: CA, Canadian Corps, Major Walter Eric Harris; Commandant, Major Norman C. Qua, Canadian Corps Gas School; DGO, 1st Division, Capt. George W. Chester; DGO, 2nd Division, Lieut.

Ralph W. Donaldson, MC; DGO, 3rd Division, Capt. Addison C. Clendenning; DGO, 4th Division, Capt. Henry V.L. Beaumont. RG 9, vol. 3975, folder 3, file 5, "Gas Services Canadian Corps."
Quotation from a letter from Sir Henry Horne to Arthur Currie dated 27 March 1919, as quoted by Timothy Travers in *The Great War, 1914-1918,* edited by R.J.Q. Adams (London: Macmillan, 1990), 133.

72 British General Sir Ivor Maxse, commander of the 18th British Corps and later inspector general of the training for the BEF, noted that "he had thirty different divisions pass through his corps in a matter of a few weeks." The homogeneity of the Canadian Corps staying as a coherent unit is not to be underestimated in looking for reasons for its success. Winter, *Haig's Command,* 147.

Conclusion: It Takes More than Gas to Stop a Canadian

1 For gas in other theatres of war see Augustin M. Prentiss, *Chemicals in War* (New York: McGraw-Hill, 1937), 653. Although the role of the American Expeditionary Force in the gas war was very small, many American postwar writers focused on it. This was partly due to the high proportion of American gas casualties to conventional casualties.

2 Edward Spiers, *Chemical Warfare* (Chicago: University of Illinois Press, 1986), 13. For tonnages of gas see Prentiss, *Chemicals in War,* 656. Hartley argued that in July 1918 German ammunition dumps contain 50 percent gas shells. The dumps captured later in the year contained from 30 percent to 40 percent. Harold Hartley, "A General Comparison of British and German Methods of Gas Warfare," *Journal of the Royal Artillery* (February 1920): 498; Victor Lefebure, *The Riddle of the Rhine* (London: W. Collins Sons, 1921), 77-80. Spiers, *Chemical Warfare,* 26; Alden Waitt, *Gas Warfare,* (New York: Chemical Publishing, 1941) 100; American statistics from Charles Heller, *Chemical Warfare in World War I: The American Experience, 1917-1918,* Leavenworth Papers no. 10 (Fort Leavenworth, KS: Combat Studies Institute, 1984), 59; British statistics from Albert Palazzo, "Tradition, Innovation, and the Pursuit of the Decisive Battle: Poison Gas and the British Army on the Western Front, 1915-1918" (PhD diss., Ohio State University, 1996), 430-5.

3 See the publications by Ludwig Fritz Haber, *The Poisonous Cloud* (Oxford: Clarendon Press, 1986), and Donald Richter, *Chemical Soldiers: British Gas Warfare in World War I* (Lawrence, KS: University Press of Kansas, 1992). Quotation from Haber, *Poisonous Cloud,* 292.

4 Haber, *Poisonous Cloud,* 203.

5 British casualties are listed in Waitt, *Gas Warfare,* 5. See National Archives of Canada (NAC), RG 24, vol. 1837, GAQ 9-37, "Amount of Gas per Casualty: 1915-1918." The report indicates that approximately 125,000 tons of gas were used in the war, causing 1,296,853 casualties. Reflecting chemical warfare's more effective role as a casualty-causing weapon, the report gives figures as such: lung injurants, 230 pounds of gas per casualty; mustard gas, 60 pounds; tear gases, 650 pounds; HE, 500 pounds. See vol. 20543, file 990.013 (D11), U.S. Army Chemical Corps report on 26th Division, 69.

6 Quotations from Sir W.G. Macpherson, *Official History of the War: Medical Services Diseases of the War,* vol. 2 (London: HMSO, 1923), 384 (hereafter BOMH); John Keegan, *The Face of Battle* (London: Pimlico, 1976), 40; Donald A. Cameron, *Chemical Warfare* (New York: International Pamphlets, 1930), 17. For wounded men spreading rumours see J.F.C. Fuller, *War and Western Civilization, 1832-1932* (New York: Books for Libraries Press, 1969) 236.

7 See Haber, *Poisonous Cloud,* chap. 10, for an excellent analysis of the gas-casualties controversy. For additional discussion of gas casualties see T.J. Gander, *Nuclear, Biological, and Chemical Warfare* (London: Ian Allan, 1987), 16; Prentiss, *Chemicals in War,* 653. On the failure of record keeping see Spiers, *Chemical Warfare,* 30-2. On verification of gas casualties see Robert Harris and Jeremy Paxman, *A Higher Form of Killing* (London: Chatto and Windus, 1982), 34.

8 The Canadian Gas Services decided not to record any gas bombardments of fewer than a hundred shells. Hardy is quoted in Lord Moran, *The Anatomy of Courage* (London: Constable, 1945), 113. The postwar analysis of two American divisions is in Malcolm Brown, *The Imperial War Museum Book of the Western Front* (London: Sidgwick and Jackson, 1993), 36-7.

9 John Terraine, *The Smoke and the Fire* (London: Sidgwick and Jackson, 1980), 127.

10 Heller, *Chemical Warfare,* 3.

11   J.H. Elliot and Harold Murchinson Tovell, *The Effects of Poisonous Gases as Observed in Return-ing Soldiers*, December 1916, see NAC, RG 9, vol. 3618, file 25-13-6.

12   Quoted in Harris and Paxman, *Higher Form of Killing*, 35.

13   Hospitalized men described in Richard Holmes, *Firing Line* (London: Pimlico, 1985), 269. The report by the Medical Research Committee, *The Symptoms and Treatment of the Late Effects of Gas Poisoning*, 10 April 1918, is riddled with references and accusations that the after-effects of gas poisoning were a result of neurotic and psychological conditions. The report is held in NAC, RG 9, vol. 3618, file 25-13-6. See John Talbott, "Combat Trauma in the American Civil War," *History Today* 46, 3 (1996): 42; RG 41, 58th Battalion, Gordon Hamilton, 2/9.

14   BOMH, 518; NAC, RG 9, vol. 3618, file 25-13-6, HQ 649-1-40, Major-General to Surgeon-General, 9 August 1918. Quotation from Gerard J. DeGroot, *Blighty* (London: Longman, 1996), 259.

15   NAC, RG 41, vol. 13, 44th Battalion, A.A. Galbraith, 2/10. For difficulty at the pension board see "The Disabled Veteran," *Canada Lancet* 59, 5 (1922): 163-4; Spiers, *Chemical Warfare*, 32. See also Desmond Morton and Glenn Wright, *Winning the Second Battle: Canadian Veterans and the Return to Civilian Life, 1915-1930* (Toronto: University of Toronto Press, 1987) 56. This is the seminal work on veterans and their attempts to reintegrate back into Canadian society after the war. See Chapters 3, 7, 8, 10. Robin Glen Keirstead, "The Canadian Military Medical Expe-rience during the Great War, 1914-1918" (Master's thesis, Queen's University, 1982), 248.

16   Dickey quoted in NAC, RG 9, vol. 3618, file 25-13-6, "Pleads for Men Injured by Gas," *Brantford Expositor*, July 1918. For additional problems for gassed veterans see BOMH, 401. Hawes quoted in RG 9, vol. 3618, file 25-13-6, newspaper clipping.

17   C. Stuart Houston, *R.G. Ferguson: Crusader against Tuberculosis* (Toronto: Hannah Institute and Dundurn Press, 1991), 54.

18   See A.F. Miller, "The New Knowledge of Tuberculosis," *Canadian Medical Association Journal* 50 (March 1944).

19   Darlene J. Zdunich, "Tuberculosis and the Canadian Veterans of World War One" (MA Thesis, University of Calgary, 1984), 69-70.

20   "Effects of Gas on Lungs," *Canada Lancet* 55, 2 (1921): 64. See also letter by Dr. David Townsend and lecture by Dr. Rudolf Saehelin believing in the permanent effects in gassed victims, NAC RG 9, vol. 3618, file 25-13-6, David Townsend to E.H. Scammell, 15 May 1922 and "After-Effects upon the Respiratory Organs of War Gas Poisoning," 5.

21   The sessional paper is quoted in Zdunich, "Tuberculosis and the Canadian Veterans," 70. See NAC, RG 9, vol. 3618, file 25-13-6, "Gas After Effects," *Calgary Herald*, July 1918. The most in-depth study found by this author was one carried out by the United States War Department in 1933. It found that although there were indeed cases of long-term permanent effects of gas, they remained a small percentage of the total gassed population. Vol. 3081, file G 25-13-6, Harry Gilchrist and Philip Matz, *The Residual Effects of Warfare Gases* (United States: Government Printing Press, 1933).

22   DeGroot notes that "half a century after the war, war service (and particularly the effects of gas) was still being listed as a contributory cause of death on coroners' reports." *Blighty*, 260.

23   For other pro-gas sources see Alan Brooksbank, *Gas Alert!* (Melbourne: Robertson and Mul-lens, 1938); J.B.S. Haldane, *Callinicus: A Defence of Chemical Warfare* (New York: E.P. Dutton, 1925); Charles H. Foulkes, *Gas: The Story of the Special Brigade* (London: William B. Blackwood and Sons, 1936); Amos A. Fries and Clarence J. West, *Chemical Warfare* (New York: McGraw-Hill, 1921). For Liddell Hart and Fuller see Robin Higham, *The Military Intellectuals in Britain: 1918-1939* (New Brunswick, NJ: Rutgers University Press, 1966), 46, 69-70, 186; Fuller, *War and Western Civilization*, 234-5; Basil Liddell Hart, *Thoughts on War* (London: Faber and Faber, 1943), 174-5. Quotation from Richter, *Chemical Soldiers*, 216.

24   Will Irwin, *The Next War: An Appeal to Common Sense* (New York: E.P. Dutton, 1921), 44.

25   J.F.C. Fuller, *The Reformation of War* (New York: E.P. Dutton, 1923), 150.

26   "Not Poisonous Gas!" *New York Herald*, 7 January 1923; *New York Times* as quoted in Hugh R. Slotten, "Humane Chemistry or Scientific Barbarism? American Responses to World War I Poison Gas, 1915-1930," *Journal of American History* 77, 2 (September 1990): 491.

27   Richard Price, *Chemical Weapons Taboo* (Ithaca, NY: Cornell University Press, 1997), 82. In one of those ironies of history, the United States had pushed hard to abolish gas in 1925, only to

have the Senate refuse to ratify the treaty. The pro-gas lobby unit worked hard to persuade senators that banning gas would leave the United States at a military disadvantage. Despite the pessimism about the treaty, Price makes a good case that it carried some weight and must be considered a factor in why chemical weapons were not employed in the Second World War. See Price, *Chemical Weapons Taboo,* chapters 4 and 5.

28 NAC, RG 24, reel C-5001, file 4354, Memorandum: Chemical Warfare, 5 December 1922. MacBrien wrote his comments on the front cover of the document. See C.P. Stacey, *Arms, Men and Governments: The War Policies of Canada, 1939-1945* (Ottawa: Queen's Printer, 1970) 3, for an examination of the poor condition of the Canadian military in the interwar years.

29 Lewisite was a new chemical compound, named after its discoverer, an American captain, W. Lee Lewis. Lewisite had many of the same properties as mustard gas but afflicted the victim almost immediately. The first shipment of Lewisite (150 tons) was sunk at sea when the Armistice was signed. Quotation from J.B.S. Haldane, "Chemistry and Peace," *Atlantic Monthly,* January 1925, 1-3. Haldane also wrote *Callinicus.*

30 Michael S. Sherry, *The Rise of American Air Power: The Creation of Armageddon* (New Haven, CT: Yale University Press, 1987), 32. July 1927 debate cited in Stockholm International Peace Research Institute (SIPRI), *The Problem of Chemical and Biological Warfare,* vol. 1, *The Rise of CB Weapons* (Stockholm: Almquist and Wiksell, 1971), 101. For American poll see Spiers, *Chemical Warfare,* 41.

31 See editorial in *Canadian Defence Quarterly* 7, 3 (1930): 284-6.

32 Halsbury quoted in Sidney Rogerson, *Propaganda in the Next War* (London: Geoffrey Bles, 1938) 162. Almost every writer attempting either to rehabilitate or condemn gas referred to this statement. Edison quoted in Lieut. R.C. Cooney, "The Air Force – Some General Considerations of Its Functions and Co-operation with the Senior Services," *Canadian Defence Quarterly* 1, 2 (1924): 70. The Canadian colonel was Colonel J.W. Bridges, "Address," *Canadian Defence Quarterly* 1, 3 (1924): 11. In addition to the gas experts of the First World War, see a speech presented by American Lt. Colonel Haig Shekerjian at the Toronto Branch of the Society of Chemical Industry on 7 April 1938. It received wide coverage in the papers, one of which at least reported that "This reporter, who has in his time handled a gas-mask and wondered if it would be any good against the mysterious gases of the bombing planes, felt much better after the interview." NAC, RG 24, reel C-5001, file 4354, Robinson Maclean, "Bullets Better than Gas for Wiping out London Says Practical Colonel," *Evening Telegram* (Toronto), 8 April 1938. A transcript of Shekerjian's talk is also included in the file. See the article, "Gas in Warfare," by "Smoothbore" in the 13 March 1937 issue of *Saturday Night,* for another condemnation of gas fear-mongers.

33 See, for example, the futuristic piece, "A Picture of the Next War," *The New Deal* (1 April 1933). It was penned by Canadian J.R.K. Main, a former pilot in the RAF during the Great War, and depicted a future war where poison gas wiped out all living things in the major industrialized cities and the pilots manning the planes had to deal with the guilt of unleashing such a catastrophe on the world. As the protagonist walks through the silent cities he encounters suffocated mothers and children – nothing was spared from the chemical agents. See I.F.B. Clarke, *Voices Prophesying War* (London: Oxford University Press, 1966) for a fascinating examination of war literature predicting and warning about future war. For H.G. Wells see Jeffrey Richards, *The Age of the Dream Palaces: Cinema and Society in Britain, 1930-1939* (London: Routledge and Kegan Paul, 1984), 280-3; John Batchelor, *H.G. Wells* (Cambridge: Cambridge University Press, 1985), 24; Norman Mackenzie and Jeanne Mackenzie, *The Time Traveller: The Life of H.G. Wells* (London: Weidenfeld and Nicholsons, 1973), 391-2.

34 NAC, RG 24, vol. 652, file 102-2-4, Report from Sir John Hodsoil, U.K. Civil Defence, *Planning and Organisation Experiences (1919-1939) and their Lessons,* not paginated, c. 1939

35 Kim Beattie, "Unheeded Warning: The Tragic Story of Another War Blunder," *Maclean's,* 1 May 1936; "Poison Gas," *Canadian Magazine,* November 1937.

36 R.T. Stean, "The Temper of an Age: H.G. Wells' Message on War, 1914-1936," *The Wellsian,* no. 8 (summer 1985): 16; William Moore, *Gas Attack* (London: Leo Cooper, 1987), 209.

37 Although there were some Canadian prewar plans for issuing respirators, they were never carried out. George Fielding Elliot remarked on how respirators would increase the fear that gas would be used in "Aerial Blackmail at Munich," in *The Impact of Air Power,* edited by Eugene M. Emme (Toronto: D. Van Nostrund, 1959), 65. Quotation from NAC, RG 24, vol. 81,

file 1173-1-8, Lt. Colonel E.A. Flood, "Defence against Gas," lecture given to Canadian Institute of Chemistry in Hamilton, Ontario, on 1 June 1942, p. 1.

38   Clarke, *Voices Prophesying War*, 35. For the failure of Allied intelligence in identifying the production of German nerve gases, see R.V. Jones, *Reflections on Intelligence* (London: Heinemann, 1989), 254-6. For checks and balances see Brown, *The Imperial War Museum Book of the Western Front*, 146-55; Spiers, *Chemical Warfare*, 60-75; Sherry, *Rise of American Air Power*, 170; Joachim Krause and Charles K. Mallory, *Chemical Weapons in Soviet Military Doctrine* (Boulder, CO: Westview Press, 1992), 75-92; SIPRI, *Problem of Chemical and Biological Warfare, 1*: 294-333; Price, *Chemical Weapons Taboo*, 100-27; John Ellis Van Courtland Moon, "U.S. Chemical Warfare Policy in World War II," *Journal of Military History* 60 (July 1996): 495-511.

39   In a superb example of historical revisionism, John Bryden uncovered the secret of both chemical and biological production in Canada. John Bryden, *Deadly Allies* (Toronto: McClelland and Stewart, 1989). See Donald H. Avery, *The Science of War: Canadian Scientists and Allied Military Technology during the Second World War* (Toronto: University of Toronto Press, 1998), for a more scholarly but less readable book on these same issues. For testing on Canadian soldiers see Bryden, *Deadly Allies*, 166-77. For fear of attack on coastal cities see NAC, MG 27, III-B-20, C.D. Howe Papers, vol. 52, file S-14-1, "Forms and Scales of Air Attack on Canadian Seaports and Inland Centres as Assessed by Joint Staff Committee on 6th July, 1938," Committee on Air Raid Precautions, First Report, 30 June 1938, p. 5-10. On the volunteers see MG 30, E211, John Wallace Papers, vol. 5, file 5-13, Civil Defence in Canada, 1936 to 1946, 1-8. On anti-gas training see RG 24, vol. 20323, file 952.003 (D16), Committee of Imperial Defence, Defence of the Civil Population against Gas; vol. 6060, file NSS 1240-5, Part VII of Bombing Committee Paper No. 46 (The Use of Gas from the Air) 1-20; RG 25, vol. 1627, file 485 pt. I, Air Raid Precaution Handbook, 3; RG 25, Handbook of Passive Air Defence, 49-52.

40   For Hitler and gas see Avery, *Science of War*, 149. For Churchill's use of gas see NAC, RG 2, vol. 38, file D-19-A-2, Combined Chiefs of Staff – Allied Chemical Warfare Program, 14 November 1942; RG 24, reel C-5002, file HQS 4354-1-8, Report by Major J.S. Heeman, 4 March 1942, "An Appreciation of the Chemical Warfare Situation in an Attempted invasion of the United Kingdom"; and Martin Gilbert, *Churchill: A Life* (New York: Henry Holt, 1991), 553. As his biographer makes very clear, Churchill was a life-long proponent of gas warfare.

41   The figures come from G.W.L. Nicholson, *Canadian Expeditionary Force, 1914-1919* (Ottawa: Roger Duhamel, Queen's Printer and Controller of Stationary, 1962), 548. Of those casualties, 10,661 were suffered by infantry, artillery, engineer, and machine-gun troops. There is no mention of how many of the gas casualties were fatal. Macphail incorrectly gives the total gas casualties as 11,356. For context, the following table is a rough breakdown of the location of casualties from the Official Medical History by Macphail.

TABLE N.4

Wounds in action

Wounds in action	Officers	Other ranks	Total
Head and neck	907	21,377	22,284
Chest	230	3,550	3,780
Abdomen	78	1,317	1,395
Pelvis	10	43	53
Upper extremities	1,895	49,615	51,510
Lower extremities	1,809	41,843	43,652
Wounded, remained at duty	904	6,698	7,602
Wounds, accidental	107	2,140	2,247
Wounds, self-inflicted	6	723	729
Effects of gas fumes	368	10,988	11,356
Total	6,314	138,294	144,608

Source: Sir Andrew Macphail, *The Medical Services, Official History of the Canadian Forces in the Great War, 1914-1919* (Ottawa: King's Printer, 1925), 396.

42 Total casualties from Nicholson, *Canadian Expeditionary Force*, 535.

43 NAC, MG 30, E113, George Bell Papers, Memoirs, 25.

44 Anthony Kellett, *Combat Motivation: The Behaviour of Soldiers in Battle* (Boston: Kluwer-Nijhoff, 1982), 81.

45 D.C. MacArthur, *The History of the Fifty-Fifth Battery, C.F.A.,* (Hamilton: H.S. Longhurst, 1919), 18.

46 NAC, RG 41, vol. 13, 44th Battalion, D.M. Marshall, 1/10; RG 9, vol. 5048, folder 923, file 15, 6/227; vol. 4066, folder 3, file 2, G.828/23-1.

47 Foulkes, *Gas*, 345. The First British Army report is cited in Charles E. Heller, "The Peril of Unpreparedness: The American Expeditionary Force and Chemical Warfare," *Military Review* 65, 1 (1985): 24. See two studies by the U.S. Army Chemical Corps Historical Office, *The 26th Division East of the Meuse, September 1918* and *The 79th Division at Montfaucon, October 1918,* for examples of two divisions that were crippled by the German use of poison gas against their troops. The reports are held in files 990.013 (D11) and 990.013 (D14), NAC, RG 24, vol. 20543.

48 Joseph Hayes, *The Eighty-Fifth in France and Flanders* (Halifax: Royal Print, 1920), 96,186.

49 See the excellent set of essays that explore some of the issues raised about archival records and the writing of military history in Brian Bond, ed., *The First World War and British Military History* (Oxford: Clarendon Press, 1991).

50 Quoted in a book review by Doug Whyte, "Unravelling the Franklin Mystery," *Archivaria* 33 (1991-2).

51 Holmes, *Firing Line,* 71.

52 Ibid., 7.

53 As quoted in Sandra Gwyn, *Tapestry of War* (Toronto: HarperCollins, 1992), 208.

54 Alexander McClintock, *Best o' Luck* (Toronto: McClelland, Goodchild and Stewart, 1917), 59.

55 J.E. Edmonds and Lt-Col. R. Maxwell-Hyslop, *Military Operations, France and Belgium, 1918,* vol. 5, History of the Great War in Public Documents series (London: Macmillan 1935-47), 606, as quoted in Spiers, *Chemical Warfare*, 33.

56 Robert Graves, *Goodbye to All That* (London: Penguin Books, 1929), 220.

Select Bibliography

Archival Sources

Records from the Directorate of History and Heritage
Records of the Canadian Broadcasting Corporation, RG 41
Records of the Privy Council's Office, RG 2
Records of the Department of Militia and Defence, RG 9
Records of the Department of Defence, RG 24
Records of the Department of External Affairs, RG 25
Records of Veterans Affairs, RG 38
Records of the Overseas Ministry, RG 150

Manuscripts and Private Papers at the National Archives of Canada
E.A.H. Alderson, MG 30, E92
William Alexander Alldritt, MG 30, E1
Frank Baxter, MG 30, E417
George Bell, MG 30, E113
Harry Burstall, MG 30, E6
Brooke Claxton, MG 32, B5
Robert W. Clements, MG 30, E156
Rexmond C. Cochrane, MG 30, G3
Claude C. Craig, MG 30, E351
John J. Creelman, MG 30, E8
Harry Crerar, MG 30, E157
Cruickshank Papers, MG 30, E66
W.H. Curtis, MG 30, E505
Ansan Donaldson, MG 30, E566
George Victor Drew-Brook, MG 30, E478
A.F. Duguid, MG 30, E12

Erlebach Papers, MG 30, E40
A.J. Foster, MG 30, E393
Thomas W. Gossford, MG 30, E475
William Green, MG 30, E430
Aubrey Wyndham Griffiths, MG 30, E442
W.H. Hewgill, MG 30, E16
Charlie Hounsome, MG 30, E476
C.D. Howe, MG 27, III-B-20
William Johnson, MG 30, E321
D.E. Macintyre, MG 30, E241
Ian Mackenzie, MG 27, III-B-5
William C. Morgan, MG 30, E488
H.M. (Tiny) Morrison, MG 30, E379
W.J. O'Brien, MG 30, E389
R.A. Rigsby, MG 30, E111
Anne E. Ross, MG 30, E446
Cameron Ross, MG 30, E477
G. Scott, MG 30, E28
Richard S. Smith, MG 30, E319
T.B. Smith, MG 30, E31
Ernest Jasper Spilett, MG 30, E209
Sprague Family, MG 30, E523
John H. Symons, MG 30, E456
38th Battalion Association, MG 30, E153
Russell F. Tubman, MG 30, E285
John Francis Wallace, MG 30, E211
Albert C. West, MG 30, E32
William Woods, MG 30, G30
W.J. Wright, MG 30, E521

Canadian Published Personal Experiences

Adamson, Richard H. *All for Nothing.* Self-published, 1987.
The Adjutant. *The 116th Battalion in France.* Toronto: E.P.S. Allen, 1921.
Baldwin, Harold. *Holding the Line.* Chicago: A.C. McClurg, 1918.
Barry, A.L. *Batman to Brigadier.* Self-published, 1965.
Beatty, David Pearce. *Memories of the Forgotten War: The World War I Diary of Pte. V.E. Goodwin.* Port Elgin, NB: Baie Verte Editions, 1986.
Bell, F. McKelvey. *The First Canadians in France.* Toronto: McClelland, Goodchild, and Stewart, 1917.
Bird, Will R. *Ghosts Have Warm Hands.* Toronto: Clarke Irwin, 1968.
Black, Ernest Garson. *I Want One Volunteer.* Toronto: Ryerson, 1965.
Burgess, Yvonne S., ed. *Who Said War Is Hell!* Bulyea, SK: Modern Press, 1983.
Burns, E.L.M. *General Mud.* Toronto: Clarke Irwin, 1970.
Canadian Bank of Commerce. *Letters from the Front, 1914-1919: Being a Record of the Part Played by Officers of the Bank in the Great War.* Toronto: Canadian Bank of Commerce, 1920.
Cosgrave, L. Moore. *Afterthoughts of Armageddon.* Toronto: S.B. Gundy, 1919.
Craig, Grace Morris, ed. *But This Is Our War.* Toronto: University of Toronto Press, 1981.
Critchley, A.C. *Critch!* London: Hutchinson, 1961.
Dawson, Coningsby. *The Glory of the Trenches.* Toronto: S.B. Gundy, 1918.
Dow, Gene, ed. *World War One Reminiscences of a New Brunswick Veteran.* Hartland, NB: Cummings Typesetting, 1990.
England, Robert. *Recollections of a Nonagenarian of Service in the Royal Canadian Regiment 1916-1919.* Self-published, 1983.
Ex-Quaker. *Not Mentioned in Despatches.* North Vancouver, BC: North Shore Press, 1933.
Gibson, [George] Herbert Rae. *Maple Leaves in Flanders Fields.* Toronto: William Briggs, 1916.

Grafton, C.S. *The Canadian Emma Gees*. London: Hunter Printing Company, 1938.

Graham, Howard. *Citizen and Soldier*. Toronto: McClelland and Stewart, 1987.

Grant, Reginald. *S.O.S. — Stand To!* New York: Appleton and Company, 1918.

Hickson, Arthur O. *As It Was Then*. Edited by D.G.L. Fraser. Wolfville, NS: Acadia University, 1988.

Horrocks, William. *In Their Own Words*. Gloucester: Rideau Veterans Home Residents Council, 1993.

Howard, Gordon. *Sixty Years of Centennial in Saskatchewan 1906-1968*. Self-published, 1968.

Humphrey, James McGivern. *The Golden Bridge of Memoirs*. Don Mills, ON: Thomas Nelson, 1979.

Keene, Louis. *Crumps: The Plain Story of a Canadian Who Went*. Boston: Houghton Mifflin Company, 1917.

Kenter, R.G. *Some Recollections of the Battles of World War I*, New York: Irene Kentner Lawson, 1995.

Kerr, Wilfred Brenton. *Shrieks and Crashes: Being Memoirs of Canada's Corps 1917*. Toronto: The Hunter Rose Company, 1929.

Lapointe, Arthur. *Soldier of Quebec 1916-1919*. Translated by R.C. Fetherstonaugh. Montreal: Edouard Garrand, 1931.

Lynch, John William. *Princess Patricia's Canadian Light Infantry, 1917-1919*. New York: Exposition Press, 1976.

McBride, Herbert W. *A Rifleman Went to War*. Plantersville, SC: Small-Arms Technical Publishing Company, 1935.

McClintock, Alexander. *Best o' Luck*. Toronto: McClelland, Goodchild and Stewart, 1917.

McKenzie, F.A. *Through the Hindenburg Line*. London: Hodder and Stoughton, 1918.

Manion, R.J. *A Surgeon in Arms*. New York: Doran, 1918.

Mathieson, William D. *My Grandfather's War*. Toronto: Macmillan of Canada, 1981.

Maxwell, George A. *Swan Song of a Rustic Moralist*. New York: Exposition Press, 1975.

Morrison Jr., J. Clinton. *Hell upon Earth: A Personal Account of Prince Edward Island Soldiers in the Great War, 1914-1918*. Self-published, 1995.

Morton, Desmond. "A Canadian Soldier in the Great War." *Canadian Military History* 1, 1 and 2 (1992): 79-89.

Nasmith, George. *On the Fringe of the Great Fight*. Toronto: McClelland, Goodchild and Stewart, 1917.

Norman, Gisli P. *True Experiences of World War I*. Manitoba: Vini Norman, 1988.

Norris, Armine. *Mainly for Mother*. Toronto: The Ryerson Press, 1919.

Pedley, James H. *Only This*. Ottawa: The Graphics Publisher, 1927.

Pope, Maurice. *Letters from the Front 1914-1919*. Toronto: Pope and Company, 1993.

R.A.L. *Letters of a Canadian Stretcher Bearer*. Toronto: Thomas Allen, 1918.

Reid, Gordon. *Poor Bloody Murder*. Oakville, ON: Mosaic Press, 1980.

Rogers, Peter G., ed. *Gunnery Ferguson's Diary*. Hantsport, NS: Lancelot Press, 1985.

Roy, Reginald, ed. *The Journal of Private Fraser*. Victoria, BC: Sono Nis Press, 1985

Scott, Canon Frederick George. *The Great War As I Saw It*. Vancouver: The Clarke and Stuart Company, 1934.

Sheldon-Williams, Ralf Frederic Lardy. *The Canadian Front in France and Flanders*. London: A. and C. Black, 1920.

Steele, Harwood. *The Canadians in France, 1915-1918*. Toronto: The Copp Clark Company, 1920.

Wheeler, Victor. *The 50th Battalion in No Man's Land*. Calgary: Alberta Historical Resources, 1980.

Accounts of the Canadian Corps

Aitken, Sir Max. *Canada in Flanders*. Vol. 1. London: Hodder and Stoughton, 1916.

Canada. Report of the Ministry. *Overseas Military Forces of Canada, 1918*. London, 1918.

Dancocks, Daniel G. *Gallant Canadians*. Calgary: The Calgary Highlanders Regimental Funds Foundation, 1990.

—. *Legacy of Valour*. Edmonton: Hurtig, 1986.

—. *Spearhead to Victory*. Edmonton: Hurtig, 1987.

—. *Welcome to Flanders Fields*. Toronto: McClelland and Stewart, 1988.

Goodspeed, D.J. *The Road Past Vimy*. Toronto: Macmillan of Canada, 1969.

Hyatt, A.M.J. *General Sir Arthur Currie*. Toronto: University of Toronto Press in collaboration with Canadian War Museum, Canadian Museum of Civilization and National Museums of Canada, 1987.

MacArthur, D.C. *The History of the Fifty-Fifth Battery, C.F.A.* Hamilton: H.S. Longhurst, 1919.
MacDermont, T.W.L. *The Seventh.* Montreal: The Seventh Canadian Siege Battery Association, 1953.
MacDonald, J.A. *Gun-fire: An Historical Narrative of the 4th Bde. C.F.A. in the Great War (1914-18).* Compiled by 4th Brigade, C.F.A. Association, 1929.
McNaughton, A.G.L. "Counter-Battery Work." *Canadian Defence Quarterly* 3, 4 (1926).
—. "The Development of Artillery in the Great War." *Canadian Defence Quarterly* 6, 2 (1929).
McWilliams, James, and R. James Steel. *Gas! The Battle for Ypres, 1915.* St. Catharines, ON: Vanwell Publishing Limited, 1985.
—. *The Suicide Battalion.* Edmonton: Hurtig Publishers, 1978.
Morton, Desmond. *A Peculiar Kind of Politics.* Toronto: University of Toronto Press, 1982
—. *When Your Number's Up.* Toronto: Random House of Canada, 1993.
Nicholson, G.W.L. *Canadian Expeditionary Force 1914-1919.* Ottawa: Roger Duhamel, Queen's Printer and Controller of Stationary, 1962.
—. *The Gunners of Canada.* Vol. 1. Toronto: McClelland and Stewart, 1967.
Rawling, Bill. *Surviving Trench Warfare.* Toronto: University of Toronto Press, 1992.
—. "Communications in the Canadian Corps, 1915-1918: Wartime Technological Progress Revisited." *Canadian Military History* 3, 2 (1994).
Shriver, Shane. "Orchestra to Victory." Master of War Studies thesis, Royal Military College, 1995.
Swettenham, John. *McNaughton.* vol. 1. Toronto: The Ryerson Press, 1968.
—. *To Seize the Victory: The Canadian Corps in World War I.* Toronto: Ryerson, 1965.

Works on Gas Warfare

Auld, S.J.M. *Gas and Flame.* N.p.: George H. Doran, 1919.
Avery, Donald H. *The Science of War: Canadian Scientists and Allied Military Technology during the Second World War.* Toronto: University of Toronto Press, 1998.
Bailliu, Jacques J. "Canada and Chemical Warfare." Master of War Studies thesis, Royal Military College, 1989.
Brooksbank, Alan. *Gas, Alert!* Melbourne: Robertson and Mullens, 1938.
Brown, Fredric J. *Chemical Warfare: A Study in Restraints.* Princeton, NJ: Princeton University Press, 1968.
Bryden, John. *Deadly Allies.* Toronto: McClelland and Stewart, 1989.
Cameron, Donald A. *Chemical Warfare.* New York: International Pamphlets, 1930.
Farrow, Edward S. *Gas Warfare.* New York: E.P. Dutton and Company, 1920.
Foulkes, C.H. *Gas: The Story of the Special Brigade.* London: William B. Blackwood and Sons, 1936.
Fries, Amos A., and Clarence J. West. *Chemical Warfare.* New York: McGraw-Hill Book Company, 1921.
Gander, T.J. *Nuclear, Biological and Chemical Warfare.* London: Ian Allan, 1987.
Gilchrist, Harry, and Philip Matz. *The Residual Effects of Warfare Gases.* Government Printing Press, 1933.
Haber, Ludwig Fritz. *The Poisonous Cloud.* Oxford: Clarendon Press, 1986.
Haldane, J.B.S. *Callinicus. A Defence of Chemical Warfare.* New York: E.P. Dutton and Company, 1925.
—. "Chemistry & Peace." *The Atlantic Monthly* (January 1925).
Hanslian, Rudolph. "Gas Warfare: A German Apologia." *Canadian Defence Quarterly* 6, 1 (1928).
Harris, Robert, and Jeremy Paxman. *A Higher Form of Killing.* London: Chatto and Windus, 1982.
Hartley, Harold. "A General Comparison of British and German Methods of Gas Warfare." *Journal of the Royal Artillery* (February 1920).
Heller, Charles E. *Chemical Warfare in World War I: The American Experience, 1917-1918,* Leavenworth Papers no. 10. Fort Leavenworth, KS: Combat Studies Institute, 1984
—. "The Peril of Unpreparedness: The American Expeditionary Force and Chemical Warfare." *Military Review* 65, 1 (1985).
Hersh, Seymour. *Chemical and Biological Warfare: America's Hidden Arsenals.* Indianapolis: The Bobbs-Merrill Company, 1968.
Hessel, F.A. *Chemistry in Warfare.* New York: Hastings House, 1940.

Hogg, Ian. *Gas*. New York: Ballantine Books, 1975.

Holmes, Richard. *Firing Line*. London: Pimlico, 1985.

Jones, Simon. "Under a Green Sea: The British Responses to Gas Warfare, Part 1 & 2." *The Great War* 1, 4 (August 1989) and 2, 1 (November 1989).

Kendall, James. *Breathe Freely! The Truth about Poison Gas*. New York: D. Appleton-Century Company, 1938.

Krause, Joachim, and Charles K. Mallory. *Chemical Weapons in Soviet Military Doctrine*. Boulder, CO: Westview Press, 1992.

Langer, William. *Gas and Flame in World War I*. New York: Knopf, 1965.

Lefebure, Victor. *The Riddle of the Rhine*. London: W. Collins Sons, 1921.

M. *The Story of the Development Division Chemical Warfare Service*. N.p.: General Electric Company, 1920.

Moore, William. *Gas Attack*. London: Leo Cooper, 1987.

Palazzo, Albert. "Tradition, Innovation, and the Pursuit of the Decisive Battle: Poison Gas and the British Army on the Western Front, 1915-1918." Ph.D diss., Ohio State University, 1996.

Prentiss, Augustin M. *Chemicals in War*. New York: McGraw-Hill Book Company, 1937.

Price, Richard. *Chemical Weapons Taboo*. Ithaca, NY: Cornell University Press, 1997.

Richter, Donald. *Chemical Soldiers: British Gas Warfare in World War I*. KS: University Press of Kansas, 1992.

Sartori, Mario. *The War Gases*. London: J. & A. Churchill, 1940.

Slotten, Hugh. R. "Humane Chemistry or Scientific Barbarism? American Responses to World War I Poison Gas, 1915-1930." *Journal of American History* 77, 2 (September 1990).

Spiers, Edward. *Chemical Warfare*. Chicago: University of Illinois Press, 1986.

Stockholm International Peace Research Institute (SIPRI). *The Problem of Chemical and Biological Warfare*. Vol. 1, *The Rise of CB Weapons*. Stockholm: Almquist and Wiksell, 1971.

Thomas, Andy. *Effects of Chemical Warfare: A Selective Review and Bibliography of British State Papers*. London: Taylor and Francis, 1985.

Thuillier, Sir Henry F. *Gas in the Next War*. London: Geoffrey Bles, 1938.

Trumpener, Ulrich. "The Road to Ypres: The Beginnings of Gas Warfare in World War I." *Journal of Modern History* 47 (September 1975).

Utgoff, Victor A. *The Challenge of Chemical Weapons*. London: The Macmillan Press, 1990.

Van Courtland Moon, John Ellis. "U.S. Chemical Warfare Policy in World War II." *Journal of Military History* 60 (July 1996).

Wachtel, Curt. *Chemical Warfare*. New York: Chemical Publishing, 1941.

Waitt, Alden. *Gas Warfare*. New York: Duell, Sloan and Pearce, 1942

Medical Works and Studies of Morale

Baynes, J. *Morale: A Study of Men and Courage*. London: Cassell, 1967.

Gabriel, Richard A. *No More Heroes: Madness and Psychiatry in War*. New York: Hill and Wang, 1987.

Keirstead, Robin Glen. "The Canadian Military Medical Experience During the Great War, 1914-1918." Master's thesis, Queen's University, 1982.

Kellett, Anthony. *Combat Motivation: The Behaviour of Soldiers in Battle*. Boston: Kluwer-Nijhoff, 1982.

Macphail, Sir Andrew. *Official History of the Canadian Forces in the Great War: The Medical Services*. Ottawa: F.A. Acland, 1925.

Macpherson, Sir W.G., *Official History of the War: Medical Services Diseases of the War*. Vol. 2. London: HMSO, 1923.

Meakins, J.C. and J.G. Walker. "The After-Effects of Irritant Gas Poisoning." *Canadian Medical Association Journal* 9, 11 (1919).

Moran, Lord Charles. *The Anatomy of Courage*. London: Constable, 1945.

Morton, Desmond. "Military Medicine and State Medicine: Historical Notes on the Canadian Army Medical Corps in the first World War 1914-1919." In *Canadian Health Care,* edited by C. David Naylor. Montreal-Kingston: McGill-Queens University Press, 1992.

—. *Winning the Second Battle: Canadian Veterans and the Return to Civilian Life, 1915-1930*. Toronto: University of Toronto Press, 1987.

Nicolson, G.W.L. *Canada's Nursing Sisters*. Toronto: Samuel, Stevens and Hakkert, 1975.

—. *Seventy Years of Service: A History of the Royal Canadian Army Medical Corps*. Ottawa: Borealis Press, 1977.

Peat, G.B. "The Effects of Gassing As Seen at a Casualty Clearing Station." *Canadian Medical Association Journal* 8, 1 (1918).

Penhallow, Dunlap Pearce. *Military Surgery*. London: Oxford University Press, 1918.

Richardson, Frank. *Fighting Spirit: A Study of Psychological Factors in War*. London: Leo Cooper, 1978.

Snell, A.E. *The CAMC with the Canadian Corps during the Last Hundred Days of the Great War*. Ottawa: F.A. Acland, 1924.

Zdunich, Darlene J. "Tuberculosis and the Canadian Veterans of World War One." MA thesis, University of Calgary, 1984.

Index

Skey, Warren, 113
Small box respirator (SBR): fighting with, 196, 203-4, 236; introduction and instruction in use, 87-9, 93, 117; training with, 124, 165
Smith, T.B., 75
Smith-Dorrien, Horace, 12
Somme, Battle of, 76-86; Canadians on, 82-6; ineffective gas, 79
Special Companies: Beam attacks, 175; Canadian, 142-3; during March Offensive, 174; establishment of, 47-8; 1 March 1917, 98-100; first use of gas at Loos, 49-51; at Hill 70, 126-8; pre-Vimy, 108; 16 January 1917, 95-6; use of gas on Somme, 77-9; viewed with mistrust, 52-3, 77, 95, 231
Stevens, Lester, 25-6, 29
Stewart, H. Ronald, 26
Stewart, J.S., 140
Stokes mortar, 105-6
Strathy, G.S., 154
Stretcher bearers, 139, 146-7
Sulzbach, Herbert, 187

Tear gas. See Lachrymatory (tear) gas
Thompson, F.G., 168
Thuillier, H.F., 65
Treaty of Versailles, 227
Trench foot, 55
Tuberculosis, 75, 220-1
Tubman, Russell, 139
Turner, Sir Richard, 26, 69-70, 115
Twigg, G.S., 44

United States, failure to ratify 1925 Convention, 234
Urine, 25

Valenciennes, France, 208-9
Verdun, Battle of, 65-7; clearing shells at, 3; lethal gas shell introduced, 66-7

Veterans, postwar care of, 86-7, 218-21
Vimy Ridge, Battle of, 106-11
Vinson, Jocko, 34

Wadsworth, George, 75
Walker, Frank, 84
Walker, James, 28
Walkinshaw, William, 32, 142
Ward, Albert S., 233
Warden, J.W., 24
Waterloo, Battle of, 209
Watson, David, 97-8, 102
Wavell, Lord, 237
Weapon of mass destruction, 222, 237
Webber, Ox, 199
Wellington, Duke of, 215
Wells, H.G., 226
West, Albert, 94, 123, 171, 196, 207
Wheeler, Victor, 67, 78, 117, 134, 198
White Star, 99
Williams, Claude, 80
Winslow, W.G., 75
Woods, A.W., 26
Woods, William, 114
Wright, G., 156
Wright, W.J., 87

Ypres, 2nd Battle of: advance warning of gas, 19; Canadian stand at, 20-30; French rout at, 20-2; gas on 24 April, 24-9; mythology of, 5; Operation Disinfection 18; poor strategic ground, 13
Ypres, 3rd Battle. See Passchendaele

Zobel, Georg, 176
Zweig, Arnold, 67